the seventies

Also by Bruce J. Schulman

FROM COTTON BELT TO SUNBELT
Federal Policy, Economic Development, and the
Transformation of the South, 1938–1980

LYNDON B. JOHNSON AND AMERICAN LIBERALISM

the seventies

The Great Shift in American Culture, Society, and Politics

Bruce J. Schulman

DA CAPO PRESS

Designed by Lisa Chovnik

Cataloging-in-Publication data for this book is available from the Library of Congress.

First Da Capo Press edition 2002
Reprinted by arrangement with The Free Press/Simon & Schuster Inc.
ISBN-13 978-0-306-81126-5; ISBN-10 0-306-81126-X

Published by Da Capo Press
A Member of the Perseus Books Group
http://www.dacapopress.com

Da Capo Press books are available at special discounts for bulk purchases in the U.S. by corporations, institutions, and other organizations. For more information, please contact the Special Markets Department at the Perseus Books Group, 11 Cambridge Center, Cambridge, MA 02142, or call (800) 255-1514 or (617) 252-5298, or e-mail j.mccrary@perseusbooks.com.

20 19 18 17

For My Friends,

Fellow Children of the Seventies

contents

preface

A GENERATION AGO WILLIAM E. LEUCHTENBURG PUBLISHED HIS evocative, popular histories of the 1920s and the 1930s. Appearing just two decades after the events he chronicled, *The Perils of Prosperity* and *Franklin D. Roosevelt and the New Deal* mapped out what was then the very recent past. The author and his audience had lived through and vividly remembered the events that these books retold. Leuchtenburg cut a broad swath through American history, leavening the standard account of politics and policy with tales of mah-jongg tournaments and labor unrest, Broadway musicals and crackpot pension schemes. The books were also decidedly personal. Leuchtenburg never injected himself into the text, but readers could detect that he had grappled with his own, and his generation's, coming of age.[1]

This book follows, haltingly, in those footsteps. It attempts a rich, evocative portrait of the United States in the 1970s. It analyzes not only presidential politics and national policy but the broader social and cultural experiences of the recent past: the agonies of busing, the shake of disco, the new power and consciousness of the elderly, the rise of the Sunbelt, and the brie, chardonnay, and BMWs of yuppies. The narrative allows readers to relive familiar moments, stumble on forgotten, surprising incidents from their lifetimes, and rethink both from a broader, deeper, historical perspective. It dissects the meaning and analyzes the enduring influence of those not-so-bygone days.

Of course, when Leuchtenburg completed his history of the 1930s, he felt no need to justify his topic. Americans understood the Great Depression as a life-altering, world-shattering event. The New Deal remained vividly alive; every day millions of Americans cashed social security checks, deposited them in federally insured bank accounts, and used the proceeds to repay GI bill mortgages and guaranteed student loans. The Roosevelt coalition—the odd alliance of African Americans, labor, farmers, and urban white ethnics that FDR had assembled—still dominated American politics. The nation's leaders, Democrats and Republicans alike, measured themselves against FDR's achievements.[2]

The task of a historian writing about the 1970s seems much less clear. Most Americans regard the Seventies as an eminently forgettable decade—an era of bad clothes, bad hair, and bad music impossible to take seriously. Contemporaries dismissed it as a "Pinto of a decade," referring to Ford's mysteriously exploding compact car. "The perfect Seventies symbol," one critic complained, "was the Pet Rock, which just sat there doing nothing."[3]

"Of all the decades of the twentieth century," recalled another Seventies chronicler, "it would be hard to pick out one with a less distinctive, recognizable character."[4] The very term *the Sixties* conjures a whole set of political, social, and cultural associations. So does *the Eighties*. References to a "Sixties veteran" or an "Eighties outlook" evoke knowing nods and clear, if stereotyped, images. But the term *Seventies sensibility* elicits only laughter. It dredges up vague reminiscences of wild fashions and vapid dance music. It calls forth a "wasted generation," a rootless youth culture wavering between the political commitments of the 1960s and the career ambitions of the 1980s—a generation that spent much of its uncertain time "wasted."

To the extent that the Seventies recall more serious concerns, they form a dreary catalogue of depressing events: hostages in Iran and defeat in Vietnam, double-digit inflation and lines at the gas pumps. The era seems to have accomplished nothing worth remembering, and nothing remains except the stuff of harmless nostalgia—nostalgia nourished by the remoteness and apparent insignificance of those years.

This impression could hardly be more wrong. The Seventies transformed American economic and cultural life as much as, if not more than, the revolutions in manners and morals of the 1920s and the 1960s. The decade reshaped the political landscape more dramatically than the 1930s. In race relations, religion, family life, politics, and popular culture, the 1970s marked the most significant watershed of modern U.S. history, the beginning of our own time. One year alone, 1973, witnessed the end of American intervention in Vietnam, the U.S. Supreme Court decision in *Roe v. Wade,* the exposure of the Watergate conspiracies, the Indian occupation of Wounded Knee, and the first Arab oil shock. Billie Jean King won the Battle of the Sexes, *The Godfather* swept the Academy Awards, and a young evangelical preacher named Jim Bakker appeared on the airwaves, intent on creating "God's television."

Americans might have stopped talking about revolution, ceasing the utopian blather that filled the air and the airwaves during the late 1960s. But the era witnessed fundamental changes. Over the course of the long 1970s, the nation's center of gravity shifted south and west. Political power, economic dynamism, and cultural authority more and more emanated from the sprawling, entrepreneurial communities of America's southern rim. When Senator

Barry Goldwater galloped out of the Southwest in 1964, preaching a brash mixture of patriotism and militarism, libertarian disregard for big government and reactionary solicitude for states' rights, the northeastern establishment sniggered. Old-line Republicans, the scions of Wall Street and the captains of Rustbelt industry, like New York governor Nelson Rockefeller, were dumbfounded that the upstart Arizonan had captured their party's presidential nomination. The nation's political and cultural elites, and the vast majority of voters, thought Goldwater simply nuts. He had spent too much time out in the desert sun.

Only in the Deep South did Goldwater find support, where his opposition to the Civil Rights Act and hostility to federal intervention won him the votes of hard-line segregationists. Yet Dixie's embrace of Goldwater only deepened the dominant North's scorn and loathing. The South seemed even more benighted than the desert Southwest that had produced Goldwater. In the northern imagination, it remained a backward, brutal place, entirely out of step with modern life. Sometimes the South seemed quaintly bathed in moonlight and magnolias; more often it registered as a menacing landscape of ignorant Bible thumpers, redneck sheriffs, and reckless lynch mobs. Either way, the region exerted little real influence before the 1970s.

Southern politics was surely colorful, but it had little to teach the nation. Beset by demagogues and one-party rule, its racial obsessions, disdain for taxes and social programs, and virulent anticommunism seemed out of step with Sixties America. True, the region controlled a sizable bloc of votes on Capitol Hill and several key congressional committees. But it could merely obstruct, rather than create, national policy. Lyndon Johnson had long believed the country would never elect a southerner president. Even after he gained the White House, he complained about the condescending chauvinism of the "Harvards" who ran the American establishment.[5]

During the 1960s southern culture won even less respect than southern politics. Most Americans regarded the region as a land of moonshine and fiddle music, racism and possum stew—a place they passed through as quickly as possible on the way to Florida. Being a white Southerner in those days, journalist Blanche McCrary Boyd recalled, was "a bit like being Eichmann's daughter: people don't assume you're guilty, but they wonder how you've been affected."[6]

Then during the Seventies, the tides of American life turned. A booming economy and burgeoning population transformed the South and Southwest. Renamed the Sunbelt, this outcast region wrested control of national politics, sending the winning candidate to the White House in every election after 1964. The region's power centered no longer in the recalcitrant, segregationist Deep South but along its periphery—in the skyscrapers of Atlanta, the space centers and shopping malls of Houston, the sprawling subdivisions of suburban Charlotte and northern Virginia, the retirement centers of Florida. In 1972, a half million people swarmed President Richard Nixon's motorcade route along Peachtree Street in Atlanta. The South, Nixon confessed, had always formed a crucial element in his electoral game plan. But the president denied cynically exploiting the racial resentments of white southerners. He had pursued "an American strategy," he claimed, not a "Southern strategy." After all, the president explained, Michigan cared about busing and military strength as much as Alabama did. The Sunbelt South's issues and outlook, Nixon recognized, would soon define the contours of an emerging new majority in American politics.[7]

During the Seventies, this influence would extend far beyond the political arena. Shorn of the most overt forms of racial brutality, a domesticated white southern culture flourished. Country music and southern rock, cowboy boots and pork rinds, even Pentecostal churches and the Confederate flag appeared throughout the nation. In 1973, the Country Music Association held its annual convention in Manhattan, and Mayor John Lindsay declared Country Music Day in New York City. "There's a swing over to the simple, the clean, to the healthy," a Yankee convert to the Nashville sound enthused. "Country music celebrates the goodness in America, faith in America, patriotism."[8] The brash, freewheeling boosterism of the Sunbelt South gradually enveloped the nation; by the time of the Los Angeles Olympics and Ronald Reagan's 1984 reelection campaign, it had become the national style.

This southernization of American life also translated into new-found respect for religion—a broad, nationwide interest in the experience of spiritual rebirth. "Not too long ago," one southern minister explained in 1974, "the Gospel according to Billy Graham was strictly a southern product. Now, that gospel of individual salvation . . . appeals to persons throughout the land who struggle with the torment of littleness, trying to gain some sense of instant worth and welcome from an indifferent civilization that is too complex for their coping." As the old-line Protestant churches—the calm, rational, polite observances of the Northeast and Midwest—declined during the Seventies, an arc of ecstatic religious enthusiasm spread across the nation from the Baptist revivals of Virginia to the New Age retreats of California.[9]

These changes in latitude encouraged broader changes in attitudes.

Around the globe, the 1970s witnessed declining faith in government pro-grams—skepticism about large-scale public efforts to remake the world. Eco-nomic malaise and political crisis sent the welfare state into retreat and prompted new respect for capitalism throughout the industrialized world. But in the United States, these international trends played out in distinctive ways and followed unusual directions. Americans developed a deeper, more thor-ough suspicion of the instruments of public life and a more profound disillu-sionment with the corruption and inefficiency of public institutions. The ideal of social solidarity, the conception of a national community with duties and obligations to one's fellow citizens, elicited greater skepticism during the 1970s, while the private sphere commanded uncommon, and sometimes undeserved, respect.

Seventies Americans developed an unusual faith in the market. More and more, they turned to the private sphere, relying on business rather than government to provide essential services and even to construct the spaces where ordinary Americans would meet, shop, and socialize. Businessmen, management guru Peter Drucker rightly prophesied in 1973, would soon realize their fondest wish: "that the United States employ private enterprise, rather than government, to satisfy the country's social and economic needs."[10]

Increasingly, all sorts of Americans, even those with dreams of radical reform, looked to the entrepreneur and the marketplace as the agent of national progress and dynamic social change. Richard Nixon uncovered this sentiment in 1972, beginning his push for a new conservative American majority. Ronald Reagan completed it in 1984 amid the celebrations of the Los Angeles Olympics, the first staged entirely without public support.

But the transformations of the Seventies amounted to more than a con-servative, southern ascendancy. The era ushered in another sort of change in latitude. Hair was no longer an issue. Fashions became outrageous, sexual behavior less restrained. A new ethic of personal liberation trumped older notions of decency, civility, and restraint. Americans widely embraced this looser code of conduct. Even those who had never been hippies, or never even liked hippies, displayed a willingness to let it all hang loose.

In 1979, *New York Times* correspondent Robert Reinhold journeyed to middle America. Reporting from Des Moines, Iowa, Reinhold found evidence of a new informality everywhere he looked. Even the police force had let its hair down; Iowa police officers wore long hair, beards, and mustaches. Previously anyone who admitted ever using marijuana could not be considered for a job on the force. Now, Reinhold learned, the department had recently changed its regulations. If prospective officers just promised to obey the law after they donned the uniform—wink, wink—they remained eligible for the police academy.[11]

Americans enjoyed the freedom to reinvent themselves. "All sorts of people," one journalist noted, "suddenly appeared as other than they were: stockbrokers dressed up as for safari; English professors looked like stevedores; grandmothers in pant suits, young girls in granny dresses." Not just the government, but all sources of authority became targets for distrust and mockery. Academe, the legal and medical professions, and professional athletes all lost credibility and public trust. Even science, the triumphant force that had landed a man on the moon, seemed increasingly suspect.[12]

Seventies popular culture, from the iconoclastic cinema of Martin Scorcese and Roman Polanski, to the outrageous lyrics and ear-shattering screams of punk rock, to the irreverent comedy of *Saturday Night Live*, revealed a contempt for authority, a sense that the powers that be had rotted to the core. Even the era's partisans of decency, including the self-styled Moral Majority, eschewed the decorum, the formality, the courtesy of their forebears and adopted a defiant, in-your-face style. During the Seventies, the forces of God and the forces of Mammon refused to show deference to established leaders and institutions.

Instead Americans constructed, and relied on, alternatives to the public sphere and the national community. The decade unleashed a frenzy of new associations and affiliations: religious pilgrimages and secular communes, senior citizen centers and ethnic organizations, neighborhood associations and mall-walking societies. The "dominant thrust of American civilization, one contemporary critic concluded, was "a quest for personal fulfillment within a small community."[13] This implosion of American public life and attempt to reconstruct the nation as a congeries of separate private refuges revealed itself across the traditional political spectrum and among all demographic groups. It energized the political left as well as the right. It appeared in the suburbs and in cities, in religion and secular life. Politics aimed more and more to protect and nourish privatism.[14]

It is easy to mock the overwrought chronologies that lay such heavy weight on years that end with zero. But during the long 1970s, fifteen malaise- and mayhem-filled years, from 1969 to 1984, the United States experienced a remarkable makeover. Its economic outlook, political ideology, cultural assumptions, and fundamental social arrangements changed. This book describes and analyzes those transformations.

This book also hopes to find a voice for the children of the Seventies. The history of the contemporary United States, as little of it that has been considered, debated, and written, has borne the imprint of our older siblings. The taunt we heard as teenagers—that we had missed out on the Sixties, the real turning point of U.S. history—has become the standard interpretation of the recent past. Our image of the Sixties as an era of radicalism and revolution persists, even if the era's most potent political legacy has been conservative.

Of course, every generation invents its own traditions. As mine exchanged license plates to beat the system of odd-even gas rationing enforced during the Arab oil embargo, or campaigned on behalf of school budgets targeted by the tax revolt, we knew that much was happening, that American public life was being transformed. Our prospects appeared far different, not only from those of our parents but from those of our older brothers and sisters too. But we could not understand or characterize these changes, and as a generation we still have not. *The Seventies* seeks to begin that process of revision, to challenge the interpretation of the Sixties veterans and recover a history for the "wasted generation."

introduction

THE SIXTIES AND THE POSTWAR LEGACY

THE SEVENTIES BEGAN, OF COURSE, IN THE WAKE OF "THE SIXTIES" and have remained ever since in their shadow—the sickly, neglected, disappointing stepsister to that brash, bruising blockbuster of a decade. "The sober, gloomy seventies," as one journalist put it, "seemed like little more than just a prolonged anticlimax to the manic excitements of the sixties." Sure, pundits constantly debate the era's parameters, suggesting that the "real Sixties" did not begin until the escalation of the war in Vietnam, the riots in Watts, or the Summer of Love, or that they lasted until Nixon's resignation, the fall of Saigon, the breakup of the Beatles or release of "The Hustle." But they agree on a common portrait—the same mug shot of the Sixties as a time of radical protest and flower power, polarization, experimentation, and upheaval. Depending on one's point of view, they are the source of everything good or everything evil in contemporary life.[1]

If one date delineated the end of the Sixties and the beginning of the Seventies, it was the year 1968. It struck many observers, then and now, as a revolutionary moment. Nineteen sixty-eight marked simultaneously an *annus mirabilis* and an *annus horribilis*, a year of miracles and a year of horrors. For many it seemed to be the Year of the Barricades, to quote the title of one book on the tumultuous events of 1968. Certainly, violent confrontations between the generations erupted around the world. In France, left-wing students occupied the University of Paris. Led by a man known simply as Danny the Red, students seized parts of the Sorbonne and clashed with police on the streets of the Latin Quarter. On May 13, huge crowds marched in protest against the sitting government, against university regulations, against the distribution of wealth and power in French society. Prime Minister Georges Pompidou warned that "our civilization is being questioned—not the government, not the institutions, not even France, but the materialistic and soulless modern society." He compared the chaotic scene to the "hopeless days of the 15th century, where the structures of the Middle Ages were collapsing."[2]

1

Rebels manned a different sort of barricade a few hundred miles to the east. In Prague, the capital of communist-dominated Czechoslovakia, student protests in late 1967 had blossomed into the Prague Spring—a buoyant, defiant, just plain ballsy challenging of the Soviet-backed regime. The Prague Spring offered a small dose of political opening and a cultural renaissance, inspired by rock music and avant-garde poetry. And then, horribly, Soviet tanks trampled those hopes, rumbling into Czechoslovakia to re-install a hard-line communist dictatorship.

Across the Atlantic, the United States would not prove immune to violent confrontation. An explosion of racial outrage after the assassination of Martin Luther King, Jr., brought smashed windows and tense confrontations between police and protesters within a few blocks of the White House. A few weeks later, radical students at Columbia University in New York City brought the barricades into the ivory tower. The Columbia unrest unfolded at a time of growing student protest across the country—against the war in Vietnam, against restrictive campus policies, and against traditional curricula and courses. At Columbia, violent protests led to the cancellation of final exams and an early end to spring semester. The campus revolt also convinced many Americans that revolution was at hand—that young radicals had moved from mere protest toward power. They would seize control of "the machine," if it would not cease to pursue inhumane ends.[3]

The Sixties appeared as a historical divide, a decade of turmoil with the future hanging in the balance. But the era, and its climactic twelve months, have also been recalled, as "the Year the Dream Died"—the year, to quote one journalist, "when for so many, the dream of a nobler, optimistic America died, and the reality of a skeptical conservative America began to fill the void."[4]

In April, an assassin murdered Martin Luther King, Jr., the man most closely associated with such noble dreams. After King's death, his vision of racial harmony—even the modest hope of the races living side by side in peace—evaporated. 1968 marked the fourth consecutive year of massive racial violence in America's cities. The end was nowhere in sight, and indeed a race war on the nation's streets seemed a real possibility.

Certainly African Americans displayed growing frustration at the slow pace of reform. Militance bubbled through the nation's black neighborhoods, fueled by the radical black nationalism of organizations such as the Black Panther party and leaders like Stokely Carmichael. "When white America killed Dr. King," Carmichael warned after the shooting in Memphis, "she declared war on black America and there could be no alternative to retribution. . . .

Black people have to survive and the only way they will survive is by getting guns."[5]

At the same time, white backlash mounted in the nation's cities and suburbs, a seething resentment most powerfully revealed in the enthusiasm for the independent campaign of George C. Wallace. In 1968, the Alabama governor famous for his stand-off with Martin Luther King during the Selma marches launched a third-party campaign for president. Wallace combined his hostility to civil rights with a populist contempt for the high and mighty. Champion of the little guy, he denounced "briefcase totin' bureaucrats," pointy-headed intellectuals, and federal judges who wouldn't mind their own business. Crowds roared approval as the governor mocked "Yale Ph.D.s who can't tie their own shoelaces, hypocrites who if you opened their briefcases you'll find nothing in them but a peanut butter sandwich."[6]

In September 1968, national polls showed Wallace with the support of nearly 25 percent of American voters; the Alabama governor was running strong not only in the white South, where his defense of racial segregation had made him a hero, but also in the urban North. In Rustbelt cities, Wallace's advocacy of law and order, contempt for antiwar protesters, and opposition to further civil rights advances won him the admiration of many working-class white ethnics. The early Sixties vision of peaceful, nonviolent reform—of ending poverty and racism—evaporated.

In their distress, many Americans looked to a leader who could heal the nation's wounds. They found their man in Senator Robert F. Kennedy, out on the campaign trail for president. On the night of King's assassination, Bobby Kennedy rejected his wife's advice to cancel his scheduled appearance in Indianapolis and instead addressed the crowd. Kennedy paid tribute to King's life and work and then appealed directly to his audience. "For those of you who are black and are tempted to be filled with hatred and distrust at the injustice of such an act, against all white people, I can only say that I feel in my own heart the same kind of feeling. I had a member of my family killed." But, the candidate pleaded, "we have to make an effort to understand, to go beyond these rather difficult times. . . . What we need in the United States is not division," Bobby concluded. "What we need in the United States is not hatred; what we need in the United States is not violence or lawlessness, but love and wisdom and compassion toward one another, and a feeling of justice toward those who still suffer within our country, whether they be white or they be black."[7]

Kennedy resuscitated the hopes for peaceful, meaningful reform. His campaign, after tough fights across the country, faced its decisive test in the June California primary—the contest that would likely decide whether he could win his party's nomination for president. Kennedy won the primary, addressed the cheering crowd in his campaign hotel, and headed toward the press room for interviews. On the way, a young man fired a snub-nosed revolver at Bobby from point-blank range. He collapsed onto his back. Five others fell in the hail of bullets. All of them would survive. But the next day, after three hours of surgery and other heroic efforts to revive him, Robert Kennedy died.

If those assassinations did not extinguish the extravagant hopes of the era, one small, historically insignificant event in the fall of 1968 signaled the end of the optimistic, liberal 1960s. On October 20, thirty-nine-year-old Jacqueline Kennedy, widow of the martyred president, married a sixty-two-year-old Greek shipping magnate, Aristotle Socrates Onassis. The mystery of this event—why would she? how could she?—shocked the nation for weeks. Comedian Bob Hope made light of it. Referring to Spiro Agnew, the Greek-American governor of Maryland running for vice president on the Republican ticket, Hope jested, "Nixon has a Greek running mate and now everyone wants one."[8] For most, it was no laughing matter but the tawdry end of Camelot. The shining knight had died, and now the swarthy villain carried off his noble lady. The dream that was the 1960s, it seemed, had died. The stormy, uncertain Seventies had begun.

The End of "The Great American Ride"

Its drama aside, 1968 should not be torn from the fibers and wrappings of history; its real significance lay as a cultural divide. The last days of the Sixties signaled the end of the post-World War II era, with its baby boom and economic boom, its anticommunist hysteria and expansive government, and the beginning of another age, the long 1970s, which defined the terms of contemporary American life. After two decades of postwar prosperity, Seventies Americans took for granted a set of political assumptions, economic achievements, and cultural prejudices. But after 1969 Americans entered a disturbing new world. The experiences of the postwar generation would offer little guidance.

During the postwar era America enjoyed unchallenged international hegemony and unprecedented affluence.[9] The boom ushered ordinary working Americans into a comfortable middle-class lifestyle; millions of blue-collar workers owned their own homes, garaged late-model cars, and sent their children to college. The economy hummed so smoothly that the nation had enough left over to fund a massive war on poverty. A series of federal programs essentially eliminated want among previously hard-hit populations, like the elderly, and reduced the overall poverty rate from more than 20 percent in the late 1950s to 12 percent by the early 1970s.[10]

The postwar years also established a pattern of expansive government. The national government provided Americans with subsidized home mortgages and easy terms on student loans. Strong federal support for unions offered high wages and job security for industrial workers, not to mention lucrative employment in defense and aerospace plants. Washington built a system of interstate highways, opening previously isolated areas to travel and commerce. The federal government permeated nearly every aspect of American life in the 1950s and 1960s—guaranteeing civil rights and voting rights for African Americans, sending astronauts to the moon, subsidizing farmers, regulating air travel, and uncovering the dangers of smoking.

The continuous expansion of the federal establishment, even under Republican president Dwight D. Eisenhower, pointed to a key element of the postwar era: the liberal consensus that made big government possible. From the mid-1940s through the mid-1960s, little disagreement emerged over the fundamental principles for organizing American life. Most Americans accepted the activist state, with its commitments to the protection of individual rights, the promotion of economic prosperity, and the establishment of some rudimentary form of political equality and social justice for all Americans. Few real conservatives and only a handful of genuine radicals exerted influence in the 1950s and 1960s.[11]

The liberal coalition in turn relied on northern regional ascendancy. The national policy establishment, the party elites, and the most potent political machines resided in the Northeast and industrial Midwest. The old manufacturing centers, what would be called the Rustbelt, still dominated American economic life, supplying the nation's most prominent business leaders and labor chieftains. New York City remained the undisputed cultural capital; Hollywood was just a place of crass upstarts, who earned money hand over fist but looked "back East" for legitimacy. The South barely occasioned a thought in the corridors of power, except to elicit smug head shaking over its economic backwardness, gothic politics, and barbaric racial caste system. The cotton fields of Alabama seemed scarcely less foreign than the jungles of Vietnam or the steppes of Russia—and no less un-American.

By the end of the Sixties, all of these defining features of post-World War II America had broken down. The cold war had begun to thaw. True, tensions between the free world and the communist bloc remained high; the brutal crushing of the Prague Spring left no doubts in American policymaking circles about the ruthlessness of the Soviet Union. And a hot war still raged against communism in Vietnam. But the rigid, dangerous cold war—the scary state of all but war that had existed in the 1940s and 1950s, when many Americans truly feared nuclear annihilation—was giving way to a more stable form of co-existence.

In July 1968, U.S. president Lyndon Baines Johnson signed with the Soviets and more than fifty other nations the Treaty on Non-Proliferation of Nuclear Weapons, banning the spread of nuclear technology, materials, and knowledge. Such an agreement would have been unthinkable just ten years earlier, when it was widely accepted that Americans could never trust, could never negotiate with or even have normal contact with the reds. The treaty was but one of eight agreements LBJ signed with the Soviets, ranging from cut-backs in the production of nuclear materials to establishing commercial air service between the United States and the Soviet Union. The nation and the rest of the world were pointing toward what Richard Nixon would soon call the era of détente.

But if the relaxed international tensions offered some hope, the seeming loss of U.S. global hegemony remained deeply unsettling. The United States, the world's strongest nation with the most powerful, technologically sophisti-cated military, found itself locked in a confusing, bloody stalemate, half a world away in Vietnam. Victory was always around the corner the nation's leaders endlessly proclaimed, but the American people were growing restless.

Then, in the wee hours of January 30, 1968, during Tet, the celebration of the Vietnamese New Year, communist commandos blasted a hole in the pro-tective wall surrounding the U.S. embassy in Saigon, the most visible symbol of the American presence in South Vietnam. For six hours, nineteen guerrillas fired mortars into the building. The audacious raid, captured by television cameras, formed only a tiny part of a simultaneous assault on every major region in South Vietnam. Enemy forces took the Americans by surprise, seized the city of Hue, and struck at more than one hundred targets throughout Viet-nam. U.S. troops eventually beat back the offensive, recapturing the cities, inflicting horrific casualties on the Vietcong, and maintaining the South Viet-namese government's precarious hold on the country. Elated by the communists' breakout into open battle, U.S. commanding officer General William Westmoreland claimed a major victory.[12]

Tet turned out to be a decisive engagement—not on the battlefields of Vietnam as General Westmoreland hoped, but in the living rooms of America. The offensive made clear that there was plenty of fight left in the enemy, that it could attack at will; even the U.S. headquarters in Saigon were at risk. Support for the war drained away instantly; Tet vividly demonstrated that U.S. strategy had failed. Immediately before the offensive, despite years of antiwar protests, only 28 percent of Americans opposed the war effort. Twice as many, 56 percent, told Gallup pollsters that they supported it. One month later, hawks and doves each tallied 40 percent. Tet had changed millions of minds.[13]

Other setbacks around the world highlighted the nation's frustration in Vietnam. The United States sat helpless while Soviet tanks crushed the Prague Spring. Meanwhile, North Korea seized the U.S.S. *Pueblo*, claiming it had violated their territorial waters. The crisis, and the sailors' captivity, dragged on for months. Despite its vast power, the United States could do little.

Disturbing as that was, the loss of global economic hegemony and the bursting of the postwar boom might have been even harder to accept. Since World War II, the dollar had been the world's currency, the global economic stabilizer. But by 1970, the all-powerful greenback faced sustained attack as foreign investors dumped dollars, driving down its value and forcing the United States to take extraordinary steps to preserve the international monetary system. In 1968, the Federal Reserve Board raised interest rates to 5 1/2 percent, their highest level since 1929, the eve of the Great Depression. Inflation accelerated; prices rose at the then-alarming rate of 4 percent per year. Sixty percent of Americans warned the Gallup organization that the high cost of living was the most urgent problem facing them and their families.[14]

The shocking financial news hinted at the approaching end of that greatest of great rides, the long postwar boom. That phenomenal economic growth—the nation's vaulting advances in productivity, output, and wages—had allowed Americans to accomplish unprecedented achievements. The United States fought the cold war and rebuilt Europe and Japan. It incorporated millions of working Americans into a home-owning, college-educated middle class. And it still had enough left over to lift millions of Americans out of desperate poverty and to establish the social safety net for all citizens.

By 1970, all that was fading into memory. The economic struggles of the postwar decades had centered around the problems of an affluent society—

around the tensions spawned by vast economic growth and pockets of poverty amid plenty. The Seventies would grapple with the problems of stagflation— the crippling coupling of high rates of inflation and economic stagnation, the seemingly impossible combination of rising prices with high unemployment, slow growth, and declining increases in productivity. For the first time since the Great Depression, talk of limits and diminishing expectations filled presidential addresses and dinner table conversations.

This new economic regime drastically altered American attitudes about taxation. During the 1950s and 1960s, Americans not only experienced the most rapid advances in investment, productivity, income, and national wealth; they paid the highest taxes in U.S. history. The corporate income tax accounted for nearly double its current share of tax receipts. The steeply graduated personal income tax reached a top rate of more than 90 percent. The bite on wealthy taxpayers convinced some movie stars, like the young Ronald Reagan, that it was not worth making more than two movies a year. After 1969, Americans would resent these burdens and launch a sustained revolt against taxation.

Cracks in the Consensus

By 1970, the great American ride had stalled. Even more troubling, the dominant liberal consensus had started to crumble. White backlash against civil rights and taxes revealed mounting resentment among previously loyal members of the liberal Democratic party coalition. For years, urban white ethnics had expressed discontent with the changing faces of their neighborhoods—the seeming encroachment of minority communities, the construction of housing projects and garbage dumps, the rising crime rates and disrespect for police. Often they had punished liberal politicians in local elections, gravitating toward law-and-order candidates who combined a conservative social agenda with a working-class touch. Still, they had remained loyal soldiers of the liberal coalition in state and national elections, supporting the Democratic party's stance on civil rights in the South and social spending in northern cities. By the end of the Sixties, many such voters had grown disaffected with national liberalism. Ready to abandon their old champions, they drifted unmoored through the currents, unwilling to hitch themselves to a conservatism many still found elitist or extremist.[15]

In the wings a renascent conservative movement waited to make the most of that discontent. Still, conservatism remained weak, neither well organized nor well respected by ordinary voters.[16] In the Sixties, the most potent attacks on the liberal consensus came not from the right but from the political left—from radicals who assailed the liberal establishment. Young radicals, members of a self-described New Left, dismissed liberal reform and asserted the necessity of direct action. Liberals believed the political system gave voice to individuals; they just needed to vote, participate, stand up and make themselves heard. New Leftists bristled at the naiveté of that faith. Bureaucracy, corporate power, and the inhumane machine-like operations of American institutions, they asserted, stifled creativity and the expressive potential of individuals and groups. Liberals assisted the poor through paternalistic aid programs; radicals wanted to empower poor communities to reform themselves. While liberals had supported the war in Vietnam as a noble and necessary fight for freedom against tyranny, radicals increasingly saw it as an act of imperialist domination and repression.

In 1968, the radical challenge to liberalism crested around the world and across the United States, most pointedly at Columbia University in New York. Responding to the growing unrest, Grayson Kirk, the sixty-four-year-old president of Columbia, denounced the younger generation's disrespect for established authority. "Our young people," Kirk declared, "in disturbing numbers, appear to reject all forms of authority, from whatever source derived, and they have taken refuge in a turbulent and inchoate nihilism whose sole objectives are destructive. I know of no time in our history when the gap between the generations has been wider or more potentially dangerous."[17]

Kirk soon received his response from Mark Rudd, leader of the Columbia chapter of Students for a Democratic Society (SDS), the principal radical students' organization. Already known as a firebrand, Rudd had taken time off from school to visit Cuba, had denounced the national leadership of SDS as too moderate, and had briefly taken over President Kirk's office in a protest against the university's participation in cold war arms research. Rudd responded to Kirk's speech in an open letter that clearly sketched the differences between radicals and liberals: "While you call for order and respect for authority, we call for justice and freedom." Demonstrating that the New Left placed liberation above formality, order, and due process, Rudd deliberately adopted the shocking vernacular of the emerging counterculture. "There is only one thing left to say," he concluded. "It may sound nihilistic to you, since it is the opening shot in a war of liberation.... Up against the wall, motherfucker."[18]

The words would soon seem prophetic. Columbia announced plans to construct a new gymnasium on nearby parkland, in the heart of Harlem, an

African American neighborhood. Responding to what they perceived as a racist encroachment on traditionally black public space, Rudd and other student radicals occupied the administration building and seized the dean of the college. Eventually black students and neighborhood activists joined the protest, convincing the white students to leave the building and turn the demonstration over to them. But instead of disbanding, they marched into President Kirk's office. The protesters released the captured dean, but over the next few days students occupied several other campus buildings. As the crisis continued, the students broadened their focus. They demanded not only the cancellation of the gym project, but steps to combat racism and to terminate Columbia's ties to the military and the war in Vietnam. Finally, after lengthy negotiations failed, 1,000 New York City police officers poured onto the campus, bodily removing the protesters from five buildings. Some students resisted, sparking violent confrontations with the police. Columbia students launched a general strike; the administration canceled final exams and shut down the university.[19]

Columbia seemed to mark, in one New Leftist's words, "a new tactical stage in the resistance movement." As protests closed campuses around the nation, radicals appeared ready to confront the establishment directly. Student radicals, SDS leader Tom Hayden asserted, had escalated from "the overnight occupation of buildings to permanent occupations, from mill-ins to the creation of revolutionary communities, from symbolic civil disobedience to barricaded resistance." Hayden foresaw the possibility of actions "too massive for the police to handle." We "are moving toward power," he concluded, "the power to stop the machine if it cannot be made to serve humane ends."[20]

Writing in the *Washington Post*, Nicholas Von Hoffman concluded that "the condition of youth has changed in important ways. College is no longer a voluntary business. You go to college or you go to war; you get your degree or you resign yourself to a life of low-paying jobs." Students barely resembled "the rollicking adolescents of the old rah-rah collegiate culture." They might lack maturity, Von Hoffman conceded, "but they are serious people who take questions of war and peace, wealth and poverty, racism and emancipation personally and passionately. They do not agree with the way their universities deal with these questions. As a practical matter, they cannot leave the universities, so they are fighting for a part in the decision-making process."[21]

But while students fought for various reforms, they primarily struggled against something: the established order. And, this new way of thinking, this countercultural ethos, extended well beyond the relatively small number of self-conscious radicals on the nation's campuses. As even professional men discarded their fedoras and gray flannel suits, the entire culture opened up. Curse words ceased to shock; many moved into the accepted lexicon. Legal restrictions on personal behavior softened as states relaxed or repealed obscenity laws, abortion restrictions, and regulations prohibiting the sale of contraceptives.[22]

The new laws reflected broader, more informal shifts in sexual mores, living arrangements, dress, food, and social behavior. Young people shunned long-accepted routes to social and professional success. More and more young people chose to "live together without benefit of matrimony" or even just to share dwellings with groups of unrelated men and women on an entirely platonic basis. They challenged the parietal rules that governed the personal behavior of students on campuses—single-sex dorms, curfews, prohibitions against single women living off-campus. In 1970, University of Kansas students initiated a plan for coed dorms. "I believe that segregation of the sexes is unnatural," one sophomore wrote in support of the new system. "I would like to associate with women on a basis other than dating roles." Another student argued that coed housing would encourage men and women to "meet and interact in a situation relatively free of sexual overtones; that is, the participating individuals would be free to encounter one another as human beings, rather than having to play the traditional stereotyped male and female roles." The students admitted that such arrangements allowed freer and more common premarital sex, but they called for policies that would allow liberated individuals to form their own relationships, sexual and otherwise, on their own terms.[23]

The experiments in living arrangements pointed out broader changes in sex roles. Many women were demanding, as the newly formed National Organization for Women insisted, admittance to the rights and privileges of citizenship in truly equal partnership with men. Others sought an even more thoroughgoing reconstruction of American institutions along nonpatriarchal lines. These radical feminists burst onto the national scene in September 1968 with dramatic protests at the Miss America Pageant in Atlantic City. Demonstrators crowned a live sheep Miss America and paraded her down the boardwalk to protest the ways contestants—and all women—"were judged like animals at a county fair." Some chained themselves to a giant Miss America puppet, mocking women's submission to conventional standards of beauty. Others hurled "instruments of torture to women" into a "Freedom Trash Can":

high heels, girdles, bras, copies of *Ladies Home Journal* and *Cosmopolitan*, hair curlers, false eyelashes. (They had planned to burn the contents but never did.) Inside the convention hall protesters disrupted the pageant with cries of "Women's Liberation" and "Freedom for Women." These inspired acts of guerrilla theater won national attention for the emerging women's movement; they showed that even the nation's cherished assumptions about gender and the family might soon be up for reappraisal. The women also aroused considerable consternation in and hostility from the media because the demonstrators refused to speak with male reporters, forcing newspapers to reassign women reporters from the society pages and gossip columns.[24]

No single event, however, so vividly showcased the smashed remains of the old consensus—the sense that Americans, however much they might disagree on specifics, shared fundamental values and could solve disputes peaceably—than did the disruptions at the Democratic National Convention in Chicago. As thousands of demonstrators descended onto the streets and filled the parks of Chicago, the city's fabled boss, Mayor Richard Daley, girded for action. "As long as I am mayor of this city," Daley vowed, "there is going to be law and order in Chicago." To keep his promise, the Boss assembled a force of 12,000 Chicago police, 6,000 armed National Guardsmen, 6,000 U.S. Army troops, and 1,000 undercover intelligence agents from the Federal Bureau of Investigation (FBI), the CIA (which was, according to its charter, forbidden from surveillance within the United States), the army, and the navy.[25]

This imposing force determined to rein in a large phalanx of protesters. The motley crew of radicals included thousands of activists organized by the National Mobilization Committee to End the War in Vietnam. Led by SDS leaders such as Tom Hayden and Rennie Davis, the MOBE, as it was known, planned a series of demonstrations. These New Leftists tried to keep order among the protesters and, at least initially, to deploy them in effective demonstrations against the Democratic party and American intervention in Vietnam.

Then there were the Yippies. Led by Abbie Hoffman and Jerry Rubin, the Yippies planned not a protest but a Festival of Life—music, nakedness, drugs. They would not so much protest the war in Vietnam as dramatize a more fundamental internal conflict: the confrontation of a liberated, authentic culture with the phony, straitlaced, inhibited, greedy one that had brought on the war. The weekend before the convention started, the Yippies nominated their own presidential candidate—a huge sow they named Pigasus—and demanded that the porker receive Secret Service protection and a White House policy briefing.

They filled Chicago's Lincoln Park and clashed repeatedly with police determined to uphold the city's regulations against camping in the parks and organizing without permits.

For an entire week, the protesters and the Chicago police skirmished, on national television, with the whole world watching. Finally, on Wednesday—nomination day—15,000 people moved into Grant Park in the heart of downtown Chicago for a MOBE rally. During some speeches, a shirtless, long-haired man began to lower the American flag (planning, it was later reported, to turn it upside down in the international symbol of distress). But as he removed the flag, the police suddenly snapped. They charged into the crowd, swinging billy clubs indiscriminately, seizing demonstrators, clubbing them, and tossing them into paddy wagons.

Eventually the rally resumed, and demonstrators marched away from the park toward Michigan Avenue (Chicago's Main Street), specifically toward the Conrad Hilton Hotel, headquarters of many candidates and their supporters. What happened—later called the police riot—shocked bystanders. Television cameras broadcast the ugly scene directly into the convention hall and into living rooms around the country. For roughly half an hour, from 8:00 to 8:30 P.M., law and order disappeared entirely on Michigan Avenue. The police broke discipline and assaulted the marchers with clubs and tear gas; marchers fought back with rocks and insults. Someone hurled MOBE leader Tom Hayden through the picture window of the hotel bar. Tear gas drove Senator Eugene McCarthy, the leading antiwar candidate after the death of Bobby Kennedy, out of his hotel room. McCarthy rode the elevator to the fifteenth floor, where his staff had set up a rudimentary first aid station. McCarthy pitched in to help the injured and muttered, "It didn't have to be this way."[26]

Even Patrick Buchanan had to shake his head in amazement. Sent by Richard Nixon to observe the convention, the young conservative firebrand conceded that "the police had had enough, and deliberately went down that street to deliver some street justice."[27]

After Chicago, gloom descended onto the New Left. To be sure, opposition to the conflict in Vietnam did not flag after the battle of Michigan Avenue. Indeed, the antiwar movement mounted large protests in 1969 and 1970; many establishment figures, members of Congress, organizations of housewives, even veterans, joined a now-respectable opposition. But the New Left, the radical movement envisioning real change, fizzled after Chicago.[28] Many activists embraced new concerns—ecology, ethnicity, women's liberation.

Others literally headed for the hills, building new communities and alternative institutions undefiled by the corrupt mainstream with its napalm and aerosol spray. Even those who remained active lost the optimism and sense of revolutionary potential they had brought to Chicago. In those heady days, the pop-rock quartet Crosby, Stills, Nash, and Young had released a song about Chicago brimming with confidence about the possibilities for peaceful reform. But just two years later—after Richard Nixon had faced down protesters and expanded the war into Cambodia, after National Guardsmen had killed four student protesters at Kent State, after the war dragged on despite ever larger and more successful demonstrations—the prospects for remaking the world grew dim. Instead, Crosby, Stills, Nash, and Young sang about finding the "cost of freedom."

The Legacy of Woodstock

After the Chicago debacle, many young Americans, those politically active and those not, found both protest and going along with the system equally undesirable. The prospect of a genuine counterculture, a real alternative to the corrupt, violent, greedy, tactless mainstream, exerted powerful appeal. Only a small part of the Sixties generation had succumbed to the "hippie temptation"; during the fabled 1967 Summer of Love, the best estimates placed the number of hippies at roughly 100,000 young Americans. But that small, if rather boisterous, minority blossomed, in the words of one chronicler, into a "garden of millions of flower people by the early 1970s."[29]

During autumn 1968, a *Village Voice* reporter asked Country Joe McDonald, lead singer of Country Joe and the Fish, to "rap about the revolution." Country Joe's most famous song, "Feels Like I'm Fixin' to Die Rag," had directly attacked the war in Vietnam ("It's one, two, three, what are we fightin' for," the song demanded). But McDonald assured the interviewer that "there isn't going to be any revolution." To carry out a revolution, he explained, "you have to control things and most of the people I know aren't ready for that. They want a leaderless society."[30]

The *Voice* reporter remained dissatisfied. "What about the guerrillas?" he demanded. "I don't know any," Country Joe explained. "I know a lot of people wearing Che Guevara stuff . . . a bunch of tripped-out freaks." Then Barry Melton, Country Joe's guitarist, chimed in: "The revolution is just another word for working within the community." But the interviewer wasn't having it; he wanted to write about honest-to-goodness revolutionaries. "Hell," he protested, "you are the Revolution." No, concluded Country Joe, shaking his head. "I'm just living my lifestyle. That's what you should be doing."[31]

On the surface, Country Joe's renunciation of revolution and embrace of "lifestyle" sounded apolitical—even antipolitical, as if it rejected political action altogether. Certainly, looking back to the mid-1960s, it would not have been farfetched to demarcate a firm split between the student radicals—the New Left or antiwar movement—on the one hand and the counterculture or flower children on the other. A lack of understanding divided the Berkeley radicals intent on shutting down the draft induction center in Oakland and the Haight-Ashbury hippies staging the Human Be-In in Golden Gate Park. The same palpable tension separated the SDS radicals occupying the president's office at Columbia and the Yippies throwing dollar bills onto the floor of the New York Stock Exchange. There was even something of a difference in style; mid-1960s New Lefties looked well scrubbed, with crewcuts, ties, and serious, even earnest demeanors. Certainly, they looked different from the emerging counterculture with its long hair, beads, psychedelic fashions, and experiments with mind-altering drugs.

But the lines between the two always remained murky and amorphous, and after 1968, they vanished. Young radicals, even those most straightforwardly political—in the sense of trying to stop the war or directly influence government policy—had embraced the wider cultural critique of the counterculture. And the counterculture developed an essentially political edge—a rejection of the values, beliefs, and priorities of mainstream America. At Woodstock, Country Joe introduced "Fixin' to Die" by leading the assembled mass in an obscene chant: "Give me an F, Give me a U, Give me a C, Give me a K, What's that spell!" The F-U-C-K chant, with its deliberate attempt to shock sensibilities by rejecting established, repressive standards of propriety, asked why Americans could find such language profane, but not the war in Vietnam. It suggested an alternative, more liberated, and supposedly more honest and authentic way of being. The obscene chant was as much a political protest as the antiwar song that followed; political protest and countercultural sensibilities went hand in hand.[32]

In 1969, one SDS leader estimated that three-quarters of the organization's membership could be classified as hippies. "Now the talk has shifted to cultural revolution," pundits reflected. "Gentle grass is pushing up through the cement." Several broad forces fed into this widening of the counterculture after 1968. Frustration certainly contributed—the growing sense that straightforward, organized political protest had failed. The war dragged on, Nixon became president, GIs invaded Cambodia, and students died at Kent State. "It was not that we disagreed with the radical interpretation of America," one antiwar protester explained after he dropped out and moved to a commune in New Mexico. "It was that by the Nixon era that message was irrelevant." Young people concluded that protest had to evolve, somehow become more fundamental. If you could not convince the older generation to change its beliefs, to stop the war, you could refuse to participate.[33]

In fact, a general alienation from mainstream America, not just disillusionment with politics, fed the counterculture in the late 1960s and early 1970s. Many young people grew disgusted with the nation and its basic values. This discontent filled both veterans of Sixties radicalism and millions of young Americans who had never demonstrated interest in political protest. "I learned to despise my countrymen, my government and the entire English speaking world, with its history of genocide and international conquest," one disgruntled New Leftist wrote after decamping to the Vermont woods. "I was a normal kid." "America," another young man reflected in 1969. "Listen to it. I love the sound. I love what it could mean. I hate what it is."[34]

Polls revealed widespread disenchantment among American youth. In 1970–1971, one-third of America's college-age population felt that marriage had become obsolete and that having children was not very important. The number identifying religion, patriotism, and "living a clean, moral life" as "important values" plummeted. Fifty percent held no living American in high regard, and nearly half felt that America was "a sick society."[35] In this setting, many young Americans no longer saw any reason to heed established conventions about sex, drugs, authority, clothing, living arrangements, food—the fundamental ways of living their lives.

So what could you do if you found yourself in such a supposedly sick society? Country Joe had the answer: "You take drugs, you turn up the music very loud, you dance around, you build yourself a fantasy world where everything's beautiful." Frustration and alienation pushed Americans toward the counterculture, but also exerted a strong pull of its own: the conviction that it was possible to drop out of the polluted, corrupt mainstream and live according to one's values. Young Americans believed they could do it right, without the phoniness and hierarchy, the profit and power, the processed food and three-piece suits, the evening news and the suburban ranch house. They could build alternative institutions and create alternative families—a separate, authentic, parallel universe. "We were setting up a new world," Barry Melton, the Country Joe guitarist, recalled—"a new world that was going to run parallel to the old world but have as little to do with it as possible. We just weren't going to deal with straight people."[36]

Fed by these diverse streams, the counterculture burgeoned in the early 1970s. The senior portraits in any high school or college yearbook display its broad influence. A 1966 edition, or even 1967 or 1968, shows clean-cut faces, ties, and demure dresses; they resemble stereotyped images of the 1950s. But the 1972 or 1974 yearbook reveals shaggy hair, beads, granny glasses. Of course, no one could precisely measure the counterculture, or distinguish the dedicated freak or head from the fellow traveler or counter-consumer, who simply adopted a style without much content. As one tie-dyed anthropologist put it, "There were no hippie organizations, no membership cards, no meetings, no age limits. . . . One did not *have to* drop out to 'qualify' as a hippie, or *have to* take drugs, participate in sex orgies, live in a commune, listen to rock, grow long hair. No minimum requirements. No *have to*." The movement is "not a beard," a University of Utah student explained. "It is not a weird, colorful costume, it is not marijuana. The hippie movement is a philosophy, a way of life." It implied rejection of the dominant culture and a decision to practice alternate lifestyles.[37]

Certainly the counterculture embraced several salient features: dope, as an entry way to expanded or altered consciousness, heightened awareness, and communal experience; freer sexual mores and living arrangements; a new relationship to nature; distinctive dress and foodways; and a commitment to communal living. Freaks rejected capitalist materialism, especially the grind of workaday jobs and the emphasis on property and acquisition. They constructed alternative institutions—food co-ops, underground newspapers, free medical clinics. In most cities and university towns, hip neighborhoods emerged, with natural food restaurants, head shops, Zen bakeries, independent record stores.

The counterculture also relied on music as a means of communication, a communal ritual, a gathering of tribes. After the success of the Monterey Pop Festival in 1967 (featuring the first major performances of Jimi Hendrix and Janis Joplin), rock festivals spread around the country. They offered a potent mix of counterculture and capitalism, barefoot hippies and big-bucks event promoters. One hundred thousand people gathered for the Atlanta Pop Festival. In Seattle, helicopters dropped flowers on the assembled revelers.

But it was Woodstock that would transform the nature of the rock festival, create its mythology, raise its most extravagant hopes. Like all of the other festivals, Woodstock began as a commercial venture. Four producers offered farmer Max Yasgur $50,000 to use his farm near Bethel, New York. They hoped 50,000 rock fans would pay $18 each for three days of performances by more than twenty acts, including Jimi Hendrix, Janis Joplin, The Who, The Grateful Dead, Jefferson Airplane, John Sebastian, Sly and the Family Stone, Arlo Guthrie, Country Joe and the Fish, and Richie Havens.

Yet Woodstock became something much, much bigger. Before the first band came onstage, a massive pilgrimage of young people clogged the roads, forming the most massive traffic jam in U.S. history. They crashed the gates; eventually 400,000 people camped on the grounds, frolicking in the mud, listening to the music, cooking and eating together, even giving birth. The logistical problems were daunting: inadequate sanitation facilities, insufficient food and water, delivering medical supplies. But somehow it worked. Even the promoters, who took a financial bath, thought a new society had been born.

The real festival, organizers told one journalist, would not end with Woodstock. The concert marked "this generation and this culture's" departure from the old generation and the old culture. "You see how they function on their own—without cops, without guns, without clubs, without hassles. Everybody pulls together and everybody helps each other and it works." No matter "what happens when they go back to the city, this thing has happened and it proves that it can happen." Singer-songwriter John Sebastian agreed. Mounting the stage, he called the scene "the biggest mindfucker of all time." Sebastian had "never seen anything like this. There was Newport," he remembered, referring to the annual folk festival in Rhode Island, "but they owned it. It was something different."[38]

Woodstock fueled ecstatic hopes that a new generation had emerged, that an alternative to the corrupt mainstream could be, was being, constructed. A few months later, another massive outdoor concert opened at Altamont, California, with the Rolling Stones as featured act. Anxious for "Woodstock West," the audience of about 300,000 remained generally peaceful, the mood celebratory. But close to the stage, the scene grew ugly; brawls and bad acid trips led to a number of ugly scenes. In a particularly ill-advised move, the Stones offered the Hell's Angels $500 worth of beer to guard the stage. As the crowd pushed closer, the Angels began beating people, busting pool cues over their heads. Eventually, four people died at Altamont including a young black man, beaten and stabbed to death by the Angels as he danced too close to the stage.[39]

If Woodstock seemed idyllic, the birthplace of a new culture, Altamont swept into the open all the ugly features of the counterculture—"the greed, the hype, the hustle," to quote one observer. At Altamont, the Woodstock generation learned that its fondest hopes, its most ambitious objectives would not be easily met; it would have to confront the darker realities of the age.

Among those harsh truths was the concerted opposition of the establishment. The mainstream press attacked the hippies and the festivals as harbingers of dope, debauchery, and destruction.[40] And the opposition fired more than harsh words. Vandals bombed Trans-Love Energies Commune in Detroit; others shot out the windows at the offices of the *Street Journal,* an underground newspaper in San Diego. When Dennis Hopper and Peter Fonda made the cult classic *Easy Rider* (1969), they encountered violence while filming the movie in the South. They had expected the taunts: "Look at the Commies, the queers, is it a boy or a girl." But they were stunned by the stories they heard "of kids getting their heads broken with clubs or slashed with rusty razor blades." Patrons in one bar jumped the longhaired filmmakers themselves. "Don't be scared, go and try to change America," Hopper concluded, "but if you're going to wear a badge, whether it's long hair or, or black skin, learn to protect yourself."[41]

The film itself dramatized this resistance, tracing the motorcycle journey of two drug-dealing hippies across the South. Persecuted by rednecks and hounded by police, the sojourners cannot get service at a restaurant or a room at a motel. Their brand of freedom, the alcoholic lawyer played by Jack Nicholson explains, threatens the complacency of ordinary Americans. The bikers' very existence mocks their constrained lives, dramatizing the compromises they have made and the shackles they endure.[42]

Despite the resistance from outside and its own contradictions and difficulties, the counterculture expanded in the Seventies, spreading a less formal, more open and freewheeling way of life. But the real efforts at cultural revolution, at creating a sustainable alternative, collapsed or became diluted. Communes drifted apart; underground papers mainstreamed or failed; free clinics applied for government funding. Standing on a hill in the desert in 1971, gonzo journalist Hunter S. Thompson recalled the feelings of imminent change he had experienced a few years earlier—"that sense of inevitable victory over the forces of Old and Evil. Not in any mean or military sense; we didn't need that. Our energy would simply *prevail.*" But now, "with the right kind of eyes," he could almost see "the high-water mark—that place where the wave finally broke and rolled back."[43]

The wave seemed to crest at the end of the Sixties. The Democratic party left Chicago in turmoil. The broad liberal coalition that had been its foundation, forming the bedrock of American politics for a generation, lay in ruins. The nation was divided, confused, seemingly in uproar. In the winter of 1968–1969, the nation turned its longing eyes toward California. There, rested and ready, if never tanned like T-shirts and bumper stickers would one day proclaim, waited Richard Milhous Nixon. On Election Day, he promised to heal a wounded people. But he had other plans.

PART I

"WE'RE FINALLY ON OUR OWN"

1969–1976

1

"DOWN TO THE NUT-CUTTING"

The Nixon Presidency and American Public Life

AS THE 1968 CAMPAIGN REACHED ITS UNCERTAIN CONCLUSION, climaxing that year of miracles and of horrors, Richard Nixon noticed a placard at a rally in Deshler, Ohio. Speaking at New York City's Madison Square Garden, Nixon remembered the scene: "There were many signs like those I see here. But one sign held by a teenager said, 'Bring us together again.' My friends," the nation's next president concluded, "America needs to be brought together."[1]

Those generous words generated little attention from the national media. During the 1968 campaign, Nixon had repeatedly rejected his speechwriters' suggestions that he offer comfort to the nation. Even in a year marked by unprecedented strife, Nixon had voiced disdain for "uplift" and had thrived on hard-hitting, polarizing rhetoric. But a few days later, in his moment of triumph, Nixon returned briefly to the theme of national unity and the message of healing. "I saw many signs in this campaign," Nixon reflected on the morning after the election. "Some of them were not friendly and some were very friendly. But the one that touched me most was one that I saw in Deshler, Ohio, at the end of a long day of whistlestopping." A "teenager held up a sign, 'Bring Us Together.' And that will be the great objective of this Administration at the outset, to bring the American people together."[2]

But President Nixon would rarely repeat that message and never mean it. With the long-sought prize within his grasp, it was time, as Nixon put it on election eve, to "get down to the nut-cutting." As he celebrated with his staff the next day, Nixon recounted a story about eating lamb fries on the campaign trail in Missouri a few years earlier. They had tasted like breaded veal but turned out to be "sheep's nuts. When this is over," Nixon told his closest aides, "we'll go out and have a mess of them."[3]

Of course, such metaphors had long been the familiar lingo of backroom politics—the vernacular of the all-male, decidedly macho, authentically smoke-filled rooms of the campaign trail. But Nixon had more than usual relish for the language of revenge and castration.[4] Over the next six years, Nixon's ambitious and cunning policy agenda would poison American politics and fragment American society. His presidency, often deliberately, sometimes unintentionally, drilled a deep well of cynicism about national politics—about the possibilities for community and communication, about the capacity of government to address the nation's needs, about the dignity and necessity of public service itself. In the process, Nixon shifted the balance of power in American politics and the terms of debate in American culture.

Tricky Dick

Richard Nixon hated the establishment. He loathed the prep school and private club set, the opera-goers and intellectuals, the northeastern Ivy League elite. Born in what then formed part of southern California's agricultural "Inland Empire," Nixon grew up in the small Quaker community of Whittier. He attended Whittier College, ever resenting the Ivy Leaguers he felt lorded over him with their superior educations, before taking his law degree at Duke. Before World War II, Duke had yet to become an elite college; it remained a young upstart and very much a southern university. At Duke, Nixon learned contempt for both the social snobbery and the liberal racial outlook of the Northeast. In December 1937, during his final year of law school, Nixon made the rounds of New York's most prestigious law firms. The humiliating rejections he suffered only deepened his contempt for the northeastern elite.[5]

After military service in World War II, Nixon returned to California and climbed the greasy pole, reaching first the House of Representatives, then the U.S. Senate, eventually ascending to the vice presidency of the United States. From this exalted position, Nixon assailed the fortress of the establishment. Even as vice president, he remained ever the outsider—too crude, too naked in his ambitions. The elite never welcomed the driven young southern Californian, even as he entered its comfortable corridors of power.

Nixon's resentments persisted as well: his crude disregard for Jews, his contempt for African Americans, his hatred of the press. But most of all he hated the establishment, for its wealth and connections, its intellectual and cultural hauteur, its exclusiveness. "In this period of our history, the leaders and the educated class are decadent," President Nixon instructed his chief of staff, H. R. Haldeman. The educated become "brighter in the head, but weaker in the spine." The nation's elite, in Nixon's mind, no longer possessed any character.[6] Nixon would prove it to them, and prove it in the most cunning of ways.

Nixon's presidency presented more than just a fascinating, and baffling, psychological profile. It even accomplished more than the unprecedented abuse of power Americans have too narrowly labeled "Watergate." His administration also posed a crucial historical problem about the evolution of contemporary American politics and public policy. Was Nixon the last of the liberals, or the first of the conservatives? Did his domestic presidency mark the last gasp of postwar liberalism—of energetic, activist government? Or did it mark the onset of a new, more cautious era—of small government, fiscal conservatism, diverting resources and initiative from the public to the private sector?

In some ways, Nixon did seem like the last interventionist liberal. He doubled the budgets for the National Endowment for the Arts (NEA) and the National Endowment for the Humanities (NEH). He proposed a guaranteed income for all Americans, signed the nation's principal environmental protection laws, and expanded affirmative action for racial minorities. Under Nixon's watch, the regulatory state swelled; federal agencies began monitoring nearly every aspect of American life. The Nixon administration created the Occupational Health and Safety Administration and instituted the first peacetime wage and price controls in U.S. history.

Nixon even conceded that "I am now a Keynesian in economics." He embraced the idea that a humming economy was the responsibility of the federal government and that the White House should actively intervene in economic affairs, carefully calibrating the policy controls, to ensure robust growth and low unemployment. Nixon even dispensed with the gold standard, that most reassuring symbol of conservative fiscal orthodoxy.[7]

By the middle of his first term, Nixon's seeming unwillingness to crush liberalism and disband social programs angered many committed conservatives. Patrick Buchanan, the president's in-house right-wing fire-eater, warned that conservatives felt Nixon had betrayed them. "They are the niggers of the Nixon administration," Buchanan fumed in a scathing seven-page memo.[8]

On the other hand, the Nixon era seemed to initiate a new, more conservative era in American politics. Nixon intervened on behalf of southern school districts, supporting efforts to curtail busing and slow the pace of school desegregation. He attacked the Warren Court, replacing such liberal icons as Abe Fortas and Earl Warren with Warren Burger and William Rehnquist (and even unsuccessfully attempted to appoint two southern conservatives to the Supreme Court). He dismantled, or at least attempted to eliminate, the principal agencies of 1960s liberalism, such as the Office of Economic Opportunity (which ran Lyndon Johnson's war on poverty) and the legal services program. While he signed the popular legislation restricting air and water pollution, Nixon also established procedures for economic cost-benefit review of all environmental regulations. And he made it clear that officials should scrap or water down any pollution control that might slow the economy or antagonize business.

Nixon also pioneered what came to be called devolution—transferring authority from the federal government to state and local governments and from the public sector to the private sphere. Through a complicated series of initiatives—a combination of block grants, revenue sharing, and the like—Nixon consigned to the states policy areas that had been the responsibility of the federal government. He also took problems and programs that had been thought to require public attention and shifted them to business and the private sector. Indeed, when Nixon left office in August 1974, CBS Evening News commentator Rod MacLeish described devolution as Nixon's major achievement. "As president," MacLeish told a national television audience, "Mr. Nixon made serious policy efforts to disburse responsibility as well as money for the alleviation of our domestic problems."[9]

By the end of his first term, Nixon had embraced small government as his campaign theme. Concluding that cutting government could become a winning strategy, Nixon declared in his second inaugural address that "government must learn to take less from people so that people can do more for themselves." Reversing John F. Kennedy's famous call for collective sacrifice, Nixon instructed, "In our own lives, let each of us ask—not just what will government do for me, but what can I do for myself?"[10]

Faced with such a contradictory record, Nixon watchers have been tempted to split the difference. But Nixon the president did more than combine economic liberalism with social conservatism. He was no mere transitional president, a passage from one era to another that embraced elements of both, although many scholars have portrayed him as such. Others have dismissed Nixon as nothing more than opportunistic, swaying with the prevailing political winds. Primarily interested in foreign affairs, Nixon viewed domestic policy as a nuisance; he would do anything so long as it would not cost him votes.

Splitting the difference, however, mistakes not only Nixon's character, but his presidency's decisive influence on American political culture. Although Nixon was both a transitional president and an opportunist, those assessments miss his historical significance—the ways that the man (the psychological puzzle) and the policies (the historical problem) intertwined.

Not for nothing did Nixon earn the nickname Tricky Dick. Nixon was indeed the first of the conservatives. He fooled many observers, then and now, because he pursued this conservative agenda—this assault on public life—in a particularly devious sort of way. Unlike Barry Goldwater before him and Ronald Reagan after him, Nixon never took on big government directly. He rarely assailed the liberal establishment he so furiously hated and so openly resented. He did not attack liberal programs or the agencies and political networks that undergirded them. Rather, he subtly, cunningly undermined them. Nixon wanted to destroy the liberal establishment by stripping it of its bases of support and its sources of funds.

Federal support for the arts and humanities offered a vivid case in point. Of course, antipathy to federal arts support has become a basic tenet of contemporary American conservatism. Given Nixon's hostility toward artists and intellectuals and his own lack of personal charisma and glamour, many expected the worst from Nixon on cultural policy. After Kennedy's style—bringing talented musicians, writers, and artists into the White House—and Johnson's substance—creating the national arts and humanities endowments—observers wondered what the unfashionable, anti-intellectual Nixon would bring.[11]

"White House reporters," *Washingtonian* magazine reported in 1969, thought Nixon's social secretary was "deliberately planning dull parties. Cabinet members have been sneaking out of state dinners. . . . Gone are the scenes from Broadway shows, the performances by top ballet companies or appearances by musicians like Van Cliburn." Elegant desserts are out, the Washington establishment complained; "cottage cheese with ketchup is in."[12] These charges of philistinism stung so much that the Nixon White House hastily arranged a jazz evening to dispel its dour image and invited Duke Ellington to refute charges that Nixon disliked black entertainers.[13]

But what of the substance? What of Nixon's actual arts policies? In 1969, when Nixon took office, the National Endowment for the Arts received an annual budget appropriation of $7.7 million; it received $8.2 million in 1970. For the 1971 budget, Nixon asked Congress to double the appropriation for the arts: he requested $16.3 million. The next year he doubled it again. By the time Nixon left the White House, arts spending had reached $61 million (and Nixon had requested even more, $72 million, in that year's budget).[14]

Nixon's arts record astounded many observers, then and now. To be sure, arts spending offered a relatively cheap way to counter Nixon's reputation for philistinism—his image, to quote one ungenerous contemporary, as a "Square Elephant." But a budget-conscious conservative, even one so jealous of his political profile as Richard Nixon, would not have unthinkingly multiplied arts spending eightfold. On the surface, Nixon's generosity toward the NEA benefited the northeastern museum and opera crowd, the very people he denounced as decadent and spineless—the people who most despised Nixon for his vulgarity, ambition, and toughness.

In fact, Nixon wanted to strip the cultural elite of its power and perquisites, but he knew that dismantling or cutting the arts endowments would provoke opposition and allow critics to denounce him as an opponent of culture. Instead, he accomplished the same goal of defunding the liberal arts establishment, simultaneously insulating himself from criticism. While expanding the NEA and the NEH, he shifted arts funding in new directions.

During the 1960s, federal arts dollars had gone almost exclusively to established institutions of high culture in major cities—museums, symphony orchestras—and to leading avant-garde artists, or at least to up-and-coming artists working along similar lines. The panels awarding NEA grants for painting, for example, were made up almost entirely of famous, successful abstract artists and the museum curators who exhibited their work. They made grants that reinforced their notions of what was best and most deserving—overwhelmingly New York–based abstract art.[15]

Nixon redirected federal arts policy and reallocated federal arts dollars. First, he distributed more and more resources to regional and local arts authorities and cultural endeavors, shifting money and support from the northeastern elite to the nation's heartland. Second, he shifted the emphasis from elite, avant-garde forms of artistic expression to more popular and populist forms: representational painting, commemorative sculptures, folklore, folk art, folk music. Third, Nixon's arts policies focused spending on youth. The endowments underwrote local art centers designed to keep young Americans off the streets—to encourage "correct," productive use of leisure time (instead of protests or riots). Finally, Nixon used arts policy to advance his administration's ideological agenda, such as sending the pop-rock group Blood, Sweat and Tears on a concert tour through Eastern Europe to showcase American artistic freedom.[16]

Despite Nixon's massive injection of capital, the northeastern elite received a smaller share of arts funding, saw most resources go to projects it disliked, and, most important, lost control of arts spending to more heavily Republican, conservative local and regional interests. Yet the cultural community could hardly complain. No other president, after all, had supported the arts and humanities so generously. Dick Nixon had proved very tricky indeed.

A similar pattern emerged in federal housing policy. Nixon did not propose to get the government out of the business of providing housing for the poor, as outspoken conservatives like Arizona senator Barry Goldwater favored. Nor did Nixon drastically cut or shut down federal housing programs, as Ronald Reagan attempted in the 1980s. Instead the Nixon administration maintained and even expanded federal housing, while at the same time circumventing and eroding the liberal, Democratic network that had always supported, benefited from, and controlled public housing.[17]

Politics makes strange bedfellows, but there was perhaps no odder combination than the allies who supported public housing: developers who received government money to develop their properties, often in areas where they could never have secured private funds; construction companies that won lucrative government contracts to build the housing units; the building crafts trades, labor unions whose members enjoyed jobs at high union wage levels; and the social services establishment, the bureaucrats and social workers who administered public housing projects. All of these groups barely got along; most hated each other. But they all wanted to build public housing, and they all supported the politicians—the liberal Democrats—who favored it. They supported them with funds, campaign workers, information, and votes.

Nixon sought to sunder that alliance. Cutting housing aid would have united all those interests—all those uneasy bedfellows—against him. So instead he maintained, and even increased, spending on public housing. But he also rechanneled it. Wherever possible, the Nixon administration redirected funding from specific projects and contracts to block grants. The new system encouraged squabbling for shares of the allocated money. Nixon also shifted resources from building and maintaining public housing to handing out rent subsidies, so poor tenants could rent from private landlords.[18] This policy defunded the liberal network; the money would not flow freely to the builders, the unions, the housing administrator, and they no longer faithfully rewarded liberal Democrats with their support. But urban Democrats could hardly oppose a policy that put more aid directly in the hands of poor tenants. So liberals lost control of housing policy and lost the support of the housing network.

A similar calculus manifested itself in the Nixon administration's approach to environmental protection. Except for national parks, the president evinced little interest in natural resource or pollution issues. He delegated responsibility to domestic policy adviser John Ehrlichman and cabinet secretary John Whitaker, ordering them to "just keep me out of trouble on environmental issues." But with the Santa Barbara oil spill and Los Angeles smog reports alerting millions of Americans to the dangers of pollution and many young activists discovering ecology, the administration felt intense pressure to present a vigorous environmental agenda. According to Whitaker, "hysteria" defined the mood on environmental issues in Washington. "The press gave the issue extraordinary coverage. Congress responded by producing environment-related bills by the bushel, and the President was in danger of being left behind."[19]

Just keeping out of trouble required aggressive action. Despite strong reservations, Nixon signed a tough Clean Air Act in 1970. He preferred legislation friendlier to business but recognized the futility of a veto; the Congress would easily have overridden it. The president also reorganized the nation's pollution control programs, briefly considering a cabinet-level Department of Environmental Quality before establishing the Environmental Protection Agency (EPA). In February 1970, Nixon delivered a special message on environmental quality to the Congress. Drafted by Whitaker, the thirty-seven-point program detailed proposals for twenty-two separate pieces of legislation, including controls on strip mining, ocean dumping, pesticides, noise, automobile emissions, and water pollution. Nixon called it "the most far-reaching and comprehensive message on conservation and restoration of natural resources ever submitted to Congress by a President of the United States."[20]

But Nixon was no closet environmentalist, not even by default. He appointed strong leaders to head the EPA but drew a rigid distinction between sensible conservationists and irresponsible extremists. Environmentalists and consumer protection activists, Nixon told auto industry leaders, "aren't really one damn bit interested in safety or clean air. What they're interested in is destroying the system." They wanted the nation to "go back and live like a bunch of damned animals."[21] When it came down to "a flat choice between jobs and smoke," the president instructed John Ehrlichman on another occasion, he would not let nature lovers get in the way of a strong economy.[22]

When the entire nation paused to celebrate Earth Day in April 1970, President Nixon refused to notice. Although his cabinet officers appeared at events around the country and the White House staff participated in a televised clean-up of the Potomac River, the president kept his distance. During that same week the White House issued presidential proclamations for National Archery Week and National Boating Week, but none for Earth Day. The president had no wish to identify himself with the activist core of the conservation movement. In fact, he did the opposite, directing Secretary of the Interior Walter Hickel to endorse construction of the Alaska pipeline in his Earth Day address.[23]

Nixon tried to stake out a conservative version of environmentalism, sucking the wind out of his liberal opponents' sails. He endorsed elements of the ecological agenda while limiting the reach of environmental regulation and foreclosing more radical alternatives. Over and over again, Nixon ensured that environmental regulations would remain subordinate to economic growth and that they would rely much more heavily on market mechanisms and less on established bureaucratic and judicial controls. Nixon subjected all EPA decisions to cost-benefit review by the Office of Management and Budget. He developed an effluent fee proposal to control water and air emissions, relying on market incentives rather than regulation, standard setting, and judicial procedures. He established the EPA rather than the broad-based, more powerful agency that environmental groups favored.[24]

In 1972, Nixon openly revealed his reservations about environmentalism when he vetoed the Clean Water Act. The president denounced the bill, which tripled his own proposed spending on water pollution abatement, as a budget buster—the work of spendthrift, "charge-account congressmen." He also found it anticapitalist. Nixon believed its plans for zero emissions, secondary treatment of municipal water, and severe punishments for violations would cripple industry and punish taxpayers. But Nixon could not derail so popular a policy; his move out into the open met with overwhelming defeat and an immediate congressional override.[25]

The president mainly navigated a more subterranean channel. Nixon strove to restrict the federal role in solid waste management, preferring to devolve responsibilities to state and local governments.[26] When opportunities presented themselves, he exploited the popularity of conservation to deliver glancing blows to federal agencies and the liberal legislators who championed them.

Nixon's conservative environmentalism reached its crescendo with the president's "Legacy of Parks," the conservation issue closest to his heart. "As our cities and suburbs relentlessly expand, those priceless open spaces needed for recreation and accessible to people are swallowed up—often forever,"

Nixon declared. He proposed "new financing methods for purchasing open space and parklands now, before they are lost to us."[27]

This seemingly uncontroversial proposal stunned Nixon's own staff, since they had devised no such new financing methods. In fact, Nixon's own secretary of the interior referred to such promises of parks without the appropriations to establish them as "A Great Deception." But Nixon had a plan. Instead of spending new funds to purchase open spaces or build parks, Nixon decided to give away federally owned lands to state and local governments. Ultimately Nixon and his successor, Gerald Ford, would convert more than 80,000 acres of government property to recreational use. The policy created 642 parks, an achievement Nixon truly valued. But it also drained resources from federal bureaucrats. Once again, Nixon had socked it to the liberal establishment in a way they could not oppose.[28]

Toward a Guaranteed Income?

Of all Richard Nixon's domestic policies, the most celebrated and the most controversial proposal never actually materialized: the Family Assistance Plan (FAP). In August 1969, Nixon appeared before the nation with a radical scheme, a far-reaching program the federal government had never before even contemplated—a minimum guaranteed income for every American family. Nixon proposed to abolish the existing welfare system with its labyrinthine series of benefits: AFDC (Aid to Families with Dependent Children), food stamps, housing subsidies, furniture grants. Nixon also promised to eliminate the army of social workers who ran the system and the mountains of paperwork they produced—to get rid of all that and simply replace it with direct cash grants to the poor.[29]

"We face an urban crisis, a social crisis—and at the same time, a crisis of confidence in the capacity of government to do its job," Nixon explained when he announced the program. "Our states and cities find themselves sinking in a welfare quagmire, as case loads increase, as costs escalate, and as the welfare system stagnates enterprise and perpetuates dependency." The system, he complained, "created an incentive for fathers to desert their families," it spawned grossly unequal variations in benefit levels, it forced poor children to begin "life in an atmosphere of handout and dependency."[30]

An ominous "welfare crisis" loomed by the time Nixon took command of the war on poverty. Between 1960 and 1975 the number of relief recipients doubled, from 7 to 14 million people. Including in-kind assistance—food stamps, Medicaid, public housing—more than 24 million Americans received means-tested benefits by the end of the Nixon years.[31] By highlighting the problems of poverty, Lyndon Johnson's Great Society and the agencies it created had focused attention on the impoverished.[32] Daniel Patrick Moynihan, the former Kennedy-Johnson poverty warrior who ran Nixon's Urban Affairs Council, became especially concerned with the explosion of AFDC costs in New York City. Although the economy hummed and unemployment had actually decreased, New York's welfare caseload had tripled in only five years. Moynihan and Nixon became convinced (wrongly) that New York's troubles portended the imminent collapse of the national welfare system.[33]

Most observers, across the American political spectrum, agreed that something had to be done about welfare. On the far left, welfare radicals like the National Welfare Rights Organization (NWRO) sought to empower the poor. A group representing mostly single mothers, the NWRO encouraged poor people to apply for public assistance—to demand welfare as a right, not to accept it reluctantly and shamefully. And in fact, the vast expansion in caseloads during the 1960s stemmed not from growing numbers of people eligible for welfare but from a huge increase in the number of already eligible poor people who applied for welfare. In 1960, only about one-third of the Americans eligible for welfare actually received it; by the early 1970s, the figure had climbed to 90 percent, thanks in part to the agitation of advocates like the NWRO.[34]

At the other end of the spectrum, free market economist Milton Friedman, a leading conservative guru, promoted his plan for a negative income tax. The grab-bag of welfare programs, Friedman asserted, served only the interests of the legislators who enacted them and the bureaucrats who administered them. Poverty resulted not from failed institutions, broken homes, or the legacy of slavery, but from a pure and simple shortage of cash. Government could cure poverty by dispensing money directly to the needy through the tax system; Americans earning less than an established minimum would receive money from the Internal Revenue Service (IRS) just as those above the threshold paid in their taxes. The negative income tax would allow poor citizens to purchase the goods and services they needed rather than the ones their congressmen and social workers insisted they should have.[35]

Friedman was no great ally of public assistance, and he wanted to get government out of the welfare business. That sentiment appealed to Nixon. "Nixon didn't like welfare workers," his aide Martin Anderson recalled in a television documentary. A shift to cash grants would undermine the entire welfare establishment, circumventing the bureaucrats, the psychologists, and the social workers.

Nixon embraced the radical analyses of Friedman and the NWRO, rejecting the proposals for moderate, incremental welfare reform circulating on Capitol Hill and within the social service agencies. He would replace the entire AFDC system with a national minimum standard, available to the welfare poor and working poor alike. "What I am proposing," Nixon announced, "is that the Federal Government build a foundation under the income of every American family with dependent children that cannot care for itself—and wherever in America that family may live." A federal minimum would support all such families, intact or "broken," working or on welfare.[36] The program would include work incentives (to encourage earnings, benefits would be reduced by only fifty cents for every dollar earned) and work requirements (every recipient except mothers of preschool children would have to accept employment or job training). "A guaranteed income," Nixon explained, distinguishing his plan from rival proposals, "establishes a right without any responsibilities. Family assistance recognizes a need and establishes a responsibility."[37]

Nixon seemingly pressed for a liberal goal: one that would expand welfare and extend benefits to millions of working poor. A guaranteed income for all Americans truly aimed to unite the fractured nation, to make every citizen a member of a national community with national standards. Assistance for every family seemed to envision everyone as part of the same national family. But however extravagant the hopes of FAP supporters, Nixon's guaranteed income plan pursued an authentically conservative objective. Nixon sought to dismantle the welfare system and the agencies and programs that administered it, eliminate the social workers who ran them, and starve the liberal networks they nourished.[38]

Certainly Nixon cared more about undercutting his liberal opposition than about putting FAP into effect. While analysts disagreed then and today about Nixon's commitment to welfare reform, he certainly made little effort to secure its passage. Despite Moynihan's urging that he spend political capital to secure congressional approval, the president remained on the sidelines, allowing his most far-reaching policy proposal to wither and die.[39]

And expire it did. Congressional Democrats and their liberal allies denounced Nixon's guaranteed minimum as too low.[40] Demanding a much higher income floor—roughly four times the level Nixon offered—the NWRO urged supporters to "Zap FAP." The NWRO also encouraged Americans to "Live

Like a Dog" on the proposed budget, which they computed to just nineteen cents a meal per person. Mainstream liberal organizations like the National Association for the Advancement of Colored People, the American Friends Service Committee, and the Methodist church also denounced Nixon's plan.[41] Meanwhile, conservatives opposed FAP because it would extend public assistance to millions more Americans and add billions of dollars to the federal budget.

Representative Wilbur Mills (D, Arkansas), chairman of the Ways and Means Committee, steered FAP through the House, adding sweeteners for the states that offered low benefits. But the Senate Finance Committee, largely controlled by southern and rural legislators, buried the plan. Nixon resubmitted FAP three times but never worked to secure its passage. In 1972, when Democratic presidential candidate George McGovern announced his own proposed "demogrant" of a thousand dollars for every man, woman, and child in the United States, the FAP passed into oblivion. The very idea of replacing the welfare system with cash grants became the stuff of derisive jokes.[42]

Denounced by both left and right, FAP ended up on the ash heap of history, but it was no failure for Richard Nixon. By introducing the guaranteed income program, Nixon divided his opponents and torpedoed more generous proposals for welfare reform. His apparent boldness in meeting the welfare crisis insulated Nixon from criticism; no one could claim that he fiddled while New York and other cities burned (or at least went broke). At the same time, the president's solicitude for the working poor, antipathy to the welfare bureaucracy, and stringent work requirements appealed to blue-collar voters and appeased the Republican right wing. Even in defeat, Nixon had pulled off a remarkable tactical victory.

The Silent Majority

Nixon's indirect, underhanded strategy with regard to welfare, environmental protection, housing, and the arts represented more than a career politician's cunning or a pathological liar's need to be devious. Every one of these maneuvers advanced Nixon's larger political objective: his ambition to transform American politics by creating a new majority coalition in the United States.

Nixon had long envisioned such a realignment. His 1968 campaign had hinged on winning over two sets of voters that normally remained loyal Democrats but appeared ready to switch parties. First, Nixon targeted white southerners. By hinting he would slow the pace of desegregation, Nixon's "southern strategy" drew Dixie's yellow-dog Democrats and prosperous new migrants to the metropolitan South into the emerging Republican majority. Second, Nixon went after blue-collar northerners—white ethnics who for generations had voted their pocketbooks and supported liberal Democrats, but had recently become alarmed about the social issues—crime, drugs, loose morals, streets filled with antiwar protestors and black militants.

In 1968, white southerners seemed ripe for this strategy. Many had opposed the civil rights revolution and resented the northern liberals they felt had imposed on them an odious second Reconstruction. In 1964, many southerners had abandoned the Democrats—the "Party of the Fathers"—and cast votes for Senator Barry Goldwater, an outspoken opponent of the Civil Rights Act. Goldwater won five Deep South states.

Nixon certainly welcomed the votes of disgruntled segregationists. The campaign enlisted South Carolina senator Strom Thurmond, the former Dixiecrat leader and recent convert to the GOP, to rally white southerners. Thurmond promised that Nixon would support local control of public schools. Nixon even hired a Thurmond protégé to coordinate his campaign in the South and bombarded the region with advertisements warning against wasted votes for Alabama governor George Wallace, the hero of massive resistance running a third-party campaign for president.[43]

Still, in 1968 Nixon carefully chose not to tread in Thurmond or Goldwater's footsteps. The campaign recognized that Wallace had locked up the Deep South. Nixon understood that overt racial appeals for the Wallace vote would alienate moderates, and even many conservatives, in the burgeoning suburbs of the metropolitan South. So Nixon largely conceded the segregationist, rural Deep South that Goldwater had won and constructed a plurality connecting the Sunbelt with blue-collar Rustbelt neighborhoods.[44]

In a very close race, Nixon's strategists focused on middle-class white voters in the industrializing subdivisions of the peripheral South. The population of the South's major metropolises, Nixon recognized, had doubled or even tripled in the 1950s and 1960s. New suburbs were crowded with professionals and skilled workers from outside the South and young families who had come of age after the *Brown* decision and found massive resistance self-defeating.[45]

In September 1968, Nixon launched a campaign swing through Dixie in Charlotte, North Carolina. There, he addressed a polite, well-dressed, middle-class crowd. He made his familiar stump appeal to forgotten Americans, never even mentioning race. Pressed later by an interviewer, he staked out a middle ground, affirming support for *Brown* but criticizing the Democrats and the courts for pushing too hard, too fast. Nixon cleverly laid out a moderate approach, neither championing minority rights like Hubert Humphrey nor defending segregation and states' rights like Goldwater and Wallace. He simultaneously endorsed local desegregation efforts—the nominally color-blind freedom-of-choice plans that had enrolled a few black students in formerly all-black schools across the South and Southwest—and opposed openly race-conscious remedies like busing that threatened dramatic changes in the status quo.[46]

That strategy appealed to crucial swing voters in the 1968 election, helping the Republican standard-bearer win Virginia, the Carolinas, Florida, Tennessee, and Kentucky. Nixon's southern strategy offered more than a short-term political prize. It was premised on the fundamental demographic and political shifts that would continue throughout the Seventies and would give a new shape to American life.[47]

A young political consultant named Kevin Phillips diagnosed this power shift in a series of position papers for the Nixon campaign and in a 1969 book, *The Emerging Republican Majority.* Phillips identified a new locus of power in national politics, a region he called the Sunbelt that connected the booming subdivisions of the metropolitan South, the sun country of Florida and southern California, and the desert Southwest. Phillips described the Sunbelt's conservative leanings and its potential as the foundation for a political realignment. The "huge postwar white middle class push to the Florida-California sun country" seemed to be forging a new political era. "The persons most drawn to the new sun culture are the pleasure-seekers, the bored, the ambitious, the space-age technicians and the retired—a super-slice of the rootless, socially mobile group known as the American middle class." The region's politics, he concluded, "is bound to cast a lengthening national shadow."[48]

Nixon and his top advisers recognized the growing influence of the Sunbelt South in national politics. Shortly after becoming president, Nixon changed his voting residence from New York to Florida. "The time has come," he declared in 1970, "to "stop kicking the South around." He detected not only the rise of the Sunbelt but the growing influence of a Sunbelt mind-set in American life generally. The South and Southwest seemed to embody a new set of cultural attitudes about race, taxation, defense, government spending, and social mores—Sunbelt attitudes that might eventually spread into the suburbs and working-class neighborhoods of the old North.[49]

In August 1970, while vacationing in San Clemente, Pat Buchanan alerted Nixon to *The Real Majority,* a political manual for the coming decade by

Richard M. Scammon and Ben J. Wattenberg. Hoping to revive their own party, these two disaffected Democrats mapped the political landscape in Nixonian terms. The voter in the center, they asserted, the key to assembling a winning coalition, was a "47 year old Catholic housewife in Dayton, Ohio whose husband is a machinist." Since the 1930s, she and her blue-collar husband had always voted Democratic. According to Scammon and Wattenberg, they had voted their pocketbooks, looking to liberal Democrats for strong unions, high wages, cheap mortgages, and college loans for their children. But now, at the end of the 1960s, they might defect to the Republicans and vote conservative on social issues. "To know that the lady in Dayton is afraid to walk the streets alone at night," Scammon and Wattenberg explained, "to know that she has a mixed view about blacks and civil rights because before moving to the suburbs she lived in a neighborhood that became all black, to know that her brother-in-law is a policeman, to know that she does not have the money to move if her new neighborhood deteriorates, to know that she is deeply distressed that her son is going to a community junior college where LSD was found on campus—to know all this is the beginning of contemporary political wisdom."[50]

The book thrilled Nixon. If he did nothing to deny blue-collar workers their fat pay envelopes and hit hard on rioters, protesters, and drugs, he could forge a new conservative majority. "P [the president] talked about Real Majority and need to get that thinking over to all our people," Haldeman reported. "Wants to hit pornography, dope, bad kids." Nixon himself asserted that the Republicans needed to "preempt the Social Issue in order to get the Democrats on the defensive. We should aim our strategy primarily at disaffected Democrats, at blue-collar workers, and at working-class white ethnics. We should," the president concluded, "set out to capture the vote of the forty-seven-year-old Dayton housewife."[51]

Nixon made wooing these voters—Americans he famously named the Silent Majority in a 1969 speech—the subject of concerted effort. Indeed for several years, Nixon envisioned creating a new political party—he usually called it the Independent Conservative party—to foster a wholesale realignment of American politics. This new party would unite white southerners, the Silent Majority, and traditionally Republican rural and suburban conservatives around social issues. It would ostracize the socially liberal, economically conservative eastern establishment—Wall Street and business Republicans like Nelson Rockefeller who had long dominated Republican party affairs—and attack liberal Democrats for playing so heavily to "the fashionable, but unrepresentative constituencies of the young, the poor, the racial minorities, and the students."[52]

Nixon envisioned a new party that would appeal to the "Okie from Muskogee," the hero of Merle Haggard's 1969 country and western hit. "I'm proud to be an Okie from Muskogee," Haggard declared, "a place where even squares can have a ball." Nixon admired Haggard's anthem as the authentic voice of the Silent Majority; Haggard's Oklahoma town honored the values of millions of worried, disgruntled Americans. "We don't smoke marijuana in Muskogee," the singer explained. "We don't take our trips on LSD. We don't burn our draft cards down on Main Street. We like livin' right and bein' free." The song so impressed the president that Nixon invited Haggard to perform at the White House.[53]

To build this new political agenda, Nixon not only inflamed the Silent Majority about social issues and appealed to the national pride of working Americans. He also took a number of concrete steps. First, he reached out to organized labor. Recognizing the social conservatism and deep-rooted patriotism of union Democrats, Nixon believed he could pry their votes away from the party of FDR. After National Guardsmen shot and killed antiwar marchers at Kent State University, 150,000 hard hats paraded for flag and country down New York's Broadway. Outraged that New York's liberal mayor had dropped the flag on city hall to half-staff in honor of the slain antiwar protesters, the construction workers denounced (and even beat up a handful of) hippies and student radicals, defended the war in Vietnam, and supported their president in the White House. Nixon deeply appreciated the construction workers' show of support, and the march reinforced his determination to incorporate labor into his New American Majority. The president offered generous loopholes for organized labor in his wage and price controls, horrifying Wall Street and business interests.[54]

Second, Nixon named Texas governor John Connally, a former protégé of Lyndon Johnson, as his secretary of the treasury. By naming Connally to his cabinet and grooming him as his successor, Nixon hoped to entice conservative southern Democrats into his new majority. The president also understood that Connally would happily dispense with Republican economic orthodoxy and keep working people happy about their paychecks while Nixon stung the Democrats on social issues.

Nixon also valued Connally's Lone Star state charisma. Henry Kissinger thought that "there was no American public figure Nixon held in such awe. Connally's swaggering self-assurance," Kissinger reflected, "fulfilled Nixon's image of how a leader should act; he found it possible to emulate this conduct only in marginal comments on memoranda, never face to face." And Nixon never denigrated Connally behind his back, "a boon not granted to many."[55]

In August 1971, under Connally's leadership, Nixon reversed field on economic policies. He adopted wage and price controls to cool inflation, a series of tax cuts to stimulate the economy in time for the 1972 elections, and he closed the gold window and allowed the dollar to float against other currencies, ending the Bretton Woods monetary system that had stabilized the international currency markets since World War II.

His mission accomplished, Connally returned to his native Texas in 1972 and took control of "Democrats for Nixon." The president imagined Connally as his natural successor. "By structuring it right," Haldeman recalled Nixon's ruminations in his diary, "we could develop a new majority party. Under a new name. Get control of the Congress without an election, simply by realignment, and make a truly historic change in the entire American political structure." From this coalition, with Nixon and Connally as "the strong men," Connally "clearly would emerge as the candidate for the new party in '76, and the P would strongly back him in that."[56]

As the 1972 election approached, Nixon made little use of traditional party labels, touting his connections to Democrats like Connally and downplaying his own Republican affiliation. "Use the new American Majority," he told Haldeman, "not Republican majority." Nixon would seek the "election of Congressman and Senators who will support the P[resident], not who are Republicans."[57]

Nixon even trumpeted his frequent escapes to La Casa Pacifica, his seaside retreat in San Clemente, California, as an assault on the establishment. Appealing to his new conservative majority, Nixon instructed his staff to tout his San Clemente home as the "Western White House." White House communications director Herb Klein informed reporters that the "San Clemente operation gives Westerners a symbolic share in the business of government. . . ." It proved that "Government is not an exclusively Eastern institution."[58]

Nixon recognized by 1971 that the center of the American political spectrum had shifted toward the right. The archetypal Dayton housewife and her machinist husband were becoming fed up with liberals, bureaucracy, and big government. Many of them had moved to southern California, the outskirts of

Houston, the suburbs of Charlotte and Atlanta. Increasingly these one-time loyal Democrats and millions of others like them believed that government programs helped only other people, not themselves. "We've had enough social programs: forced integration, education, housing," Nixon told his chief of staff as the 1972 election approached. "People don't want more on welfare. They don't want to help the working poor, and our mood has to be harder on this, not softer."[59]

Nixon instructed his staff to adopt a tougher, more openly conservative stance. Attorney General John Mitchell launched a furious attack against black militants and student protesters in *Women's Wear Daily*. Mitchell tore into "these stupid kids" on college campuses and "the professors are just as bad if not worse. They don't know anything. Nor do these stupid bastards who are ruining our educational institutions." This country, Mitchell warned, "is going so far right you are not even going to recognize it." Nixon applauded his attorney general's hard line. "John—Good Job," he wrote. "Don't back off."[60]

Nixon's strategy paid rich dividends in November 1972. He won reelection by a landslide over Democratic challenger George McGovern, in the process assembling the new majority of his fondest political dreams. Both organized labor and the white South went heavily for Nixon in 1972.

After winning reelection, Nixon decided to promote what he called a conservative revolution. "Now I planned to give expression to the more conservative values and beliefs of the New Majority throughout the country," Nixon recalled in his memoirs, "and use my power to put some teeth in my new American Revolution."[61] Sounding his new conservative theme, Nixon declared in his second inaugural address, "Let us remember that America was not built by government but by people; not by welfare, but by work."[62]

Still, the president understood that although Americans opposed expansive government in principle, in practice they demanded many specific public programs. Nixon understood, as he put it in a cabinet meeting, that "government spending is a lousy issue. People are for spending." The only way to slash popular programs was to portray cuts as "the only way to avoid inflation and higher taxes. . . . You never win," the president explained, "on the question of screwing up rich kids. You have to hit on higher taxes. You never debate the programs. By cutting the budget back, we are avoiding more taxes, and that's the line we have to use."[63]

The budget thus became the instrument of Nixon's conservative revolution. The president set stringent targets for the fiscal year ending June 1973; to reach them, he refused to spend more than $12 billion that the Congress had already appropriated. This infuriated the Congress, which soon would debate whether these "impoundments" merited impeachment.[64]

The impoundments were just the beginning. Having sundered the liberal policy networks and collapsed the liberal electoral coalition, Nixon next aimed to slash domestic spending. In February 1973, he proposed a shocking budget for the 1974 fiscal year, featuring deep cuts in government programs. Nixon proposed to eliminate urban renewal, impacted-area aid for school districts near military bases, hospital construction grants, soil management payments to farmers, and the Rural Electrification Administration. He slashed spending on milk for schoolchildren, mental health facilities, compensatory education for poor students. He meant to reverse the Great Society, calling for the abolition of the Office of Economic Opportunity, the vanguard of Lyndon Johnson's war on poverty.[65]

Nixon would see neither his new American revolution nor his new majority politics through to completion. By the time he unveiled his rightward shift and his harsh budgets, the nation had become obsessed with the unfolding story of scandal in the White House. But, oddly, Nixon's personal failures—a scandal so large that he would become the first (and thus far only) president driven from office—would only aid his larger agenda. In trusting too much in government," Nixon intoned, "we have asked more of it than we can deliver." The time has come to turn away from activist government and replace it with "a new feeling of self-discipline.[66]

In retrospect, most observers have read Nixon's declaration ironically; Watergate certainly proved that Americans had trusted too much in Nixon's government. But although the scandals brought down a Republican conservative and helped to elect the only Democratic president of the era, their principal effect was to discredit government itself. Watergate only intensified Americans' alienation from public life: their contempt for the secrecy, inefficiency, and failures of "big government."

Watergate

Richard Nixon admired John Connally and envied the Texan's charismatic style—his confidence, his swagger, his broad smile as he ground opponents into the dust. But as Henry Kissinger understood, Nixon emulated Connally only in the comments he wrote in the margins of memos, never face-to-face. "For Connally," Kissinger recalled, "a victory was meaningless unless his opponent knew he had been defeated; for Nixon the most exquisite triumphs were those in which the victim did not know who had done him in, or maybe even immediately that he had been done in." Nixon's policies, his cunning attempts to shrink liberal government, employed this insidious modus operandi.[67]

"Watergate"—the covert agencies Nixon established in the White House and the wide range of illegal and subversive activities they conducted—was but the most obvious of Nixon's efforts to narrow the space for political organizing and public action in American life. When Nixon ordered his aides to harass Democratic National Committee chairman Lawrence O'Brien or to "blow the safe" at the Brookings Institution to remove files that might embarrass his political enemies, he pursued the same agenda as he had with public housing or affirmative action. Nixon was trying to undermine the liberal establishment and to build a new conservative majority by foul means and fouler ones.

Watergate would leave a tangled legacy. Most obviously, it triggered the "gating" of American life. Every subsequent scandal—no matter how petty—has received the suffix "-gate." In the quarter-century after Richard Nixon left office, Americans would endure "Contragate," "Koreagate," "Debategate," "Travelgate," "Whitewatergate," "Filegate," even "Fornigate." (The practice would even spread overseas. During the 1980s, "Inkatha-gate" would appear in South Africa and "SIDEgate" in Argentina.)[68] From this misleading practice, millions drew the unfortunate conclusion that these scandals somehow resembled each other—that they all revealed the same corrupt, sleazy political underworld.

But the "-gate" suffix confused old-fashioned graft with true constitutional crises. Worst of all, the practice led Americans to conflate Watergate with all the other "-gates" it seemed to generate. Watergate was unique; it forever altered the way Americans understood politics and the presidency, the way they reported and discussed national politics, the way they conceived, investigated, and understood wrongdoing by government officials.[69]

Watergate was much more than a bungled attempt to break into the Democratic National Committee Headquarters in the Watergate apartment and office complex and bug the telephones of Democratic National chairman Lawrence O'Brien. Nixon's abuse of power preceded the burglary and extended far beyond it. In the course of unraveling the Watergate story, investigators uncovered a wide range of sordid and illegal activities—a rogue government. Ever since Nixon's secret bombing and invasion of Cambodia in

1969–1970 and the furor when those missions leaked to the press, the Nixon White House had mounted a campaign of extralegal and illegal activities. What Attorney General John Mitchell called the "White House horrors" was not an occasional lapse, an exceptional event, but a routine, everyday occurrence—embracing both the ordinary, small abuses of office common in U.S. history and the extraordinary.[70]

In June 1971, a year before the Watergate break-in, Nixon's newly installed hidden tape system recorded a conversation in the Oval Office between the president and his two top aides, chief of staff H. R. (Bob) Haldeman and national security adviser Henry Kissinger. Haldeman suggested that the Brookings Institution, a Washington think tank, possessed classified files on Vietnam that would prove embarrassing to the Johnson administration. Nixon reminded Haldeman of a plan he had approved for White House–sponsored break-ins as part of a domestic surveillance operation aimed at his opponents. "Bob? Bob? Now do you remember Huston's plan? Implement it." Haldeman tried to fob Nixon off, but the president remained adamant: "I want it implemented. . . . Goddamnit, get in and get those files. Blow the safe and get it."[71]

The conversation seems almost comic to contemporary listeners—the most powerful man in the country, maybe even the world, talking with top aides about burglarizing the Brookings Institution to retrieve a file that might help them blackmail the retired ex-president. What was this guy thinking? But it revealed the administration's characteristic habit of mind—the standard mode of operations at the Nixon White House. A few days later, in an equally banal conversation, Nixon discussed infiltrating radical protest groups with undercover agents and selling ambassadorships in the same meeting.[72]

Nixon's defenders have noted that the president lacked advance knowledge of the specific plans for the Watergate break-in, but Nixon had ordered his aides to wiretap his opponents, including Larry O'Brien, and to get the names of campaign contributors to the Democratic National Committee so that he could punish them. He also had approved the so-called Gemstone plan under whose aegis the Watergate burglars were operating. "What in the name of God are we doing on this?" Nixon demanded of Haldeman. "Are we looking over the financial contributors to the Democratic National Committee? Are we running their tax returns? Is the Justice Department checking to see if there is [sic] any anti-trust suits? Do we have anything going on any of these things?" After Haldeman reported no progress, Nixon exploded: "We better forget the

Goddamn campaign right now, this minute, not tomorrow, no. . . . We have all this power and we aren't using it. . . . I'm just thinking about, for example, if there's information on Larry O'Brien. If there is, I wouldn't wait."[73] The burglars hardly needed Nixon's explicit authorization.

The cover-up began immediately after the burglary. Nixon ordered the CIA to halt the FBI investigation, authorized the payment of hush money to the burglars, had aides lie under oath, and fired the special prosecutor (prompting the resignations of the attorney general and the associate attorney general) when the investigation grew too close.

The Watergate probes exposed a whole range of criminal activities (and new ones continue to emerge as Nixon materials are opened to the public). Assembled to plug leaks to the press, the "White House Plumbers" burglarized the California offices of the psychologist treating Daniel Ellsberg, the former Pentagon employee who had leaked the Pentagon Papers to the *New York Times,* in search of damaging material on Ellsberg in the psychologist's records.

Meanwhile, the Campaign to Re-Elect the President, best known by its apt acronym CREEP, employed Donald Segretti and his dirty tricks squad. Devoted to a pastime Segretti called "ratfucking," Nixon campaign operatives sabotaged their opponents. They arranged fake rallies in their rivals' names and left behind irate vendors and caterers, demanding to be paid for events that the opponents had never scheduled. During the 1972 New Hampshire primary, the dirty tricksters embarrassed Democratic front-runner Edmund Muskie by fabricating the "Canuck letter," a document purportedly penned by Muskie that insulted the state's large French Canadian population.

The president's men tried to plant a spy in the secret service detail assigned to Senator George McGovern, and they actually placed one on his press plane with a fabricated press credential. Nixon used the IRS and the Justice Department to harass enemies and reward friends, ordered surveillance on Ted Kennedy in an attempt to unearth dirt on the Massachusett senator, and conducted illegal wiretaps of political enemies and even of officials in his own government. The list of charges was so long, complex, and well documented that President Nixon felt it necessary to go on national television and assure Americans that he was not a crook.

During the fall of 1972, the cover-up worked pretty well. Only a few persistent journalists, principally *Washington Post* reporters Carl Bernstein and Bob Woodward, disturbed the administration's sleep. By following the money trail (the money on the burglars, much of it in consecutive serial numbers),

Woodward and Bernstein tied the burglary to CREEP; they also exposed the campaign committee's money-laundering operation—the way the campaign evaded reporting regulations by funneling money through Mexican banks.

By the spring of 1973, the story had started to unravel. The White House particularly worried that the men arrested for the burglary would soon break their silence. On April 15, 1973, White House counsel John Dean, who had assumed principal responsibility for running the cover-up, reported to Nixon that the scheme was collapsing. "There's a cancer on the Presidency," Dean warned Nixon. The two men then discussed raising $1 million in hush money to keep the burglars quiet.

The trail grew hotter, and in the spring of 1973, Nixon bowed to public pressure and appointed Archibald Cox as a special prosecutor. He also fired his loyal lieutenants, chief of staff Bob Haldeman and domestic policy adviser John Ehrlichman. Eventually they would serve jail sentences, along with John Mitchell, the one-time attorney general and director of CREEP, his deputy Jeb Magruder, and numerous other minor villains.

Meanwhile, the Senate Select Committee to investigate the affair opened nationally televised hearings that riveted the nation. Dean admitted his role in the affair and implicated Nixon's closest aides—Haldeman, Ehrlichman, Mitchell. But the ambitious young lawyer had received partial immunity in return for his testimony, so his credibility remained suspect. Most stunning, a minor witness, presidential assistant Alexander Butterfield, let slip the existence of the secret Oval Office tapes.

In the fall of 1973, the scandal inched ever closer to the Oval Office. In what became known as the Saturday Night Massacre, Nixon fired special prosecutor Archibald Cox. Refusing to carry out the order, Attorney General Elliott Richardson resigned. So did his assistant, Associate Attorney General William Ruckleshaus. The number three man at the Justice Department, Solicitor General Robert Bork, finally complied.

By this time, Watergate had become a national obsession. The novelist and essayist Mary McCarthy toured the nation in April 1973 and discovered that "in every city I arrived at, the local papers were full of Watergate; regardless of their politics and of pressure, if any, from their advertisers, they were keeping their readers in touch with the most minor episodes in this fantastic crime serial." Almost "more amazing than the daily disclosures themselves," McCarthy concluded, "was the evidence that the story was being told, democratically, to the entire population, which was discussing it democratically, as if at a town meeting."[74]

Among other developments, Watergate fever helped launch the career of a young cartoonist named Garry Trudeau, just a few years out of Yale College. Largely because of his Watergate satires, Trudeau successfully transformed a strip he began drawing for his college newspaper into a nationally syndicated cartoon. "It would be a disservice to Mr. Mitchell [Nixon's stand-in] and his character to prejudge the man," Doonesbury's college radio disc jockey, Megaphone Mark Slackmeyer, opined in a famous strip. "But everything known to date could lead one to conclude he's guilty. That's GUILTY! GUILTY, GUILTY, GUILTY!"[75]

In July 1974, the House Judiciary Committee agreed and voted articles of impeachment against the president. Before the full House could act, Nixon resigned. "I have never been a quitter," he told the nation. "To leave office before my term is completed is abhorrent to every instinct in my body." Without remorse, Nixon explained simply that "because of the Watergate matter I might not have the support of the Congress that I would consider necessary."[76] As he bade farewell to his staff the next day, emotion crept into the disgraced president's voice: "Always remember others may hate you, but those who hate you don't win unless you hate them, and then you destroy yourself." No pundit could have written a more appropriate epitaph.[77]

A month later, the new president, Gerald R. Ford, issued a blanket pardon of Nixon. Ford's unprecedented action—usually presidents award executive clemency after a criminal has been tried and convicted—ended the affair without even a statement of contrition from the unindicted co-conspirator.

Separately, Nixon's abuses of power and financial wrongdoings might have amounted to little more than dirty politics. Together, as North Carolina senator Sam Ervin put it, they became an attempt to subvert American democracy. "One shudders to think," Ervin declared at the end of the affair, "that the Watergate conspiracies might have been effectively concealed had it not been for the courage of Judge Sirica, the investigative reporting of Carl Bernstein, Bob Woodward, and other representatives of free press, the labors of the Senate Committee and the dedication of the Special Prosecutors." In reality, few Americans shivered at the idea. "They all did it, Nixon just got caught," is what many Americans believed. Watergate's impact remained ambiguous, uncertain, contested.[78]

At the time, observers like Thomas Cronin and Arthur M. Schlesinger, Jr., blamed a "swollen," even "imperial" presidency as the motive force behind Watergate. Presidents had become too strong, they said, and had acquired too much autonomy and authority. Executive power had steadily mounted since

World War II; misusing it had become an almost irresistible temptation. To be sure, Cronin and Schlesinger conceded, Nixon possessed unusual criminal tendencies. But the problem lay in the office rather than the man—in its potential for unchecked abuses of power. After all, LBJ had recklessly expanded the Vietnam War without consulting the Congress or informing the nation.[79]

Many shared that analysis. In the immediate aftermath of Watergate, the United States placed new controls on presidential power: the War Powers Resolution, limiting executive authority to mount sustained military operations without explicit congressional approval; campaign finance reform for national elections; the 1978 Ethics in Government Act with its provision for independent counsel to investigate wrongdoing in the executive branch. Both a presidential commission and a Senate committee investigated the illegal activities of the CIA and the FBI, and the Congress established new intelligence committees to oversee their operations at home and abroad.

After Nixon's resignation, the new president, Gerald Ford, asserted that the experience of Watergate had vindicated the American political process. "Our Constitutional system works," Ford declared. But that declaration was met with knowing nods. Few observers shared Ford's confidence; instead most Americans decided that the political system was corrupt, the politicians all crooks.

Watergate added fuel to a widespread cynicism about politics, politicians, government itself as an instrument of the collective good. Already weakened by Nixon's divisive politics, Watergate piled the last straw on the political system. It confirmed the man on the street's—or the Dayton housewife's—growing distrust of American institutions and American leaders. A few years later, President Jimmy Carter would refer to this cynicism as a national "crisis of confidence."

Intimations of Decline

Watergate marked a low point in American public life—not the deepest point in a steep valley but a dark hole in a widening crater. Only eight months after Richard Nixon left the White House in disgrace, the capital of South Vietnam, Saigon, fell to the communists. Like their humiliated president, the last U.S. personnel and thousands of Vietnamese refugees fled by helicopter, some of them desperately clinging to the aircraft's landing struts as they whirled away.

Many Americans sensed that the nation had entered a period of decline. No longer able to lead the world, the United States could no longer even find its own way at home. These intimations of decline were everywhere to be heard and seen in the early 1970s—as the war ground toward defeat, as the Watergate cover-up unraveled, as the Arab oil embargo humiliated a seemingly impotent nation, as the economy worsened. Even those who could not point to specific political events like the war or the scandal felt that something had passed—that the American Century, however abbreviated, had ended.

To be sure, Watergate hardly initiated these fears of decline. In 1970, Andrew Hacker, then professor of government at Cornell University, published *The End of the American Era,* a widely hailed jeremiad that captured the nation's sinking mood. Analyzing an "ungovernable nation" of "two hundred million egos," Hacker concluded that "the United States is now about to join other nations of the world which were once prepossessing and are now little more than plots of bounded terrain. Like them," Hacker explained ruefully, "the United States will continue to be inhabited by human life; however, Americans will no longer possess that spirit which transforms a people into a citizenry and turns territory into a nation." *Newsweek* reiterated the professor's mournful message: "We have arrived at a plateau in our history, the years of middle age and decline."[80]

Early in 1972, "American Pie," a rambling, eight-and-a-half-minute ballad by obscure singer-songwriter Don McLean, reached number one on the pop charts and sparked something of a sensation. Humming the catchy melody, the nation stopped short. Americans painstakingly attempted to decipher McLean's vague references to the "King," the "Jester," and the "Day the Music Died."[81] While "American Pie" turned out to be a rather simplistic allegory of recent musical history, Americans nonetheless wrestled with its seemingly pregnant lyrics for weeks. "The suggestive vagueness of *American Pie* [italics in original]," *Time* explained, "may be one of its greatest strengths. Trying to identify its various references has become something of a parlor game."[82] Whatever its specific meaning, the song evoked intense feelings of collective loss, of ruined innocence and diminished potency, that gripped the nation in the Nixon years.

The talk of decline became so widespread that in the summer of 1973, as the Senate Select Committee ferreted out Nixon's misdeeds on national television, a Canadian journalist named Gordon Sinclair delivered a kind of pep talk on the Canadian Broadcasting Service. Cataloguing the achievements and the generosity of the United States, Sinclair castigated those who gloated about the nation's troubles. "I can name you five thousand times," he concluded, "when the Americans raced to the help of other people in trouble.

Can you name me even one time when someone else raced to the Americans in trouble?"[83]

Sinclair's tribute, "Americans (A Canadian's View)," struck a patriotic nerve among Americans tired of and resistant to the rhetoric of decline. The *Chicago Tribune,* the *Washington Post,* and *U.S. News and World Report* reprinted Sinclair's homily. The first of three 45 rpm singles by recording artist Byron MacGregor recited the editorial to the accompaniment of "America the Beautiful" and reached number four on *Billboard's* Top 100. Sinclair recorded his own version to the strains of "The Battle Hymn of the Republic" and shortly before his death in 1974, country singer Tex Ritter scored a hit with his mournful rendition. "Our neighbors have faced it alone," Sinclair complained, as an orchestra brought "America" to a rising crescendo, "and I'm one Canadian who's damn tired of hearing them kicked around. They will come out of this thing with their flag high, and when they do, they're entitled to thumb their noses at the lands that are gloating over their present troubles."[84]

But Sinclair's pep talk could not assuage a pervasive sense of things gone wrong. A crisis of confidence had indeed taken hold in the wake of national events.

In 1976, playwright-screenwriter Paddy Chayefsky, director Sidney Lumet, and actors Peter Finch, William Holden, and Faye Dunaway offered an acid report on the state of the nation and the prospects for the future. In the feature film *Network,* Chayefsky, one of early television's pioneers from the days of live TV dramas, turned against the medium and the gullible couch potatoes that watched it. In this film, a long-time TV news anchor loses his job because the show is no longer generating sufficiently robust ratings. The network brass now want less journalism and more entertainment.

In what was supposed to be his final broadcast, the distraught anchor lashes out at the corruption of American institutions and the powerlessness and apathy of ordinary citizens. Climaxing his desperate screed, he asks Americans to vent their discontent: open your windows and scream, "I'm mad as hell and I'm not going to take it anymore." Cynical executives exploit the phenomenon this broadcast creates, making the anchor the star of a new, thoroughly manipulative prime-time program, until the forces unleashed by his lunatic ravings threaten the corporate power structure and require his elimination.

Network meant to excoriate the media and the credulous folk manipulated by it, but the film's most memorable scene took on a life of its own. For the next several years, across the United States, in cities, schools, and shopping centers, there would be outbreaks of people shouting, "I'm mad as hell and I'm not going to take it anymore!" On college campuses, mysterious signs appeared, fliers announcing, "IMAHAINGTTIAM Midnight." And at the witching hour, hundreds of students would stick their heads out the window and scream, "I'm mad as hell and I'm not going to take it anymore!"

Obviously Watergate could not account for the production of *Network* or for these unexpected and extraordinary responses to it. Nor did Nixon's White House horrors alone sustain the national malaise. In fact, Watergate impressed many contemporary observers as a bizarre series of events presided over by a singular villain; it had been "historic but irrelevant." A year after Nixon left office, CBS News correspondent Bruce Morton concluded that "the fact is Watergate didn't change much." A decade later, many pundits echoed Morton's assessment. "Most experts," the *Los Angeles Times* reported on the tenth anniversary of Nixon's ouster, "find no evidence that the traumatic ousting of a U.S. President has caused any basic change in public attitudes about either the American system of government or the persons who occupy public positions." Sure, public confidence in government waned after Watergate, but it had been declining since the race riots and antiwar protests of the mid-1960s.[85]

Still, Nixon's presidency, and its dramatic end, nourished a profound unease with a direction that American life had taken. And the scandal's most conspicuous and enduring effect ironically realized some of Richard Nixon's most grandiose objectives. Watergate gave a boost to conservatism and conservative Republican politicians. That effect did not immediately appear; in the first blip after Nixon's ruin, the Republicans took a bath as the Democrats won big in the 1974 midterm elections. In 1976, enough resentment persisted that Gerald Ford, Nixon's pardoner, narrowly lost the presidency to an unknown whose platform consisted of a fairly convincing promise that he would never lie to the American people.

But the general trends bolstered conservatives. The ultimate lesson of Watergate remained "you can't trust the government." The scandal reinforced a generalized antigovernment passion whose main effect worked against Democrats and liberals and for Republicans and conservatives. Even President Jimmy Carter represented a more conservative faction of the Democratic party: southern, fiscally responsible, suspicious of labor unions and government regulation.[86]

When convicted felon and former attorney general John Mitchell left Washington, reporters mocked his earlier prediction. "In the next ten years," Mitchell had prophesied, "this country will go so far to the right you won't recognize it." Reporters shook their heads, but John Mitchell would have the last laugh.

And perhaps his chief would enjoy it. In retirement, Nixon would witness his enemies in disarray, their conception of government as the instrument of national purpose discredited, their vision of an inclusive national community debased. The nut-cutting accomplished, Nixon and everyone else forgot that distant promise to bring us together.

2

E PLURIBUS PLURES

From Racial Integration to "Diversity"

IN JANUARY 1975 A NEW SITUATION COMEDY DEBUTED ON CBS. The latest in a series of spin-offs from *All in the Family*, Norman Lear's comedy about the lovable bigot Archie Bunker and his working-class family in Queens, *The Jeffersons* focused on the adventures of Archie's black neighbors, George and Louise Jefferson. Unlike the Bunkers, who remained resolutely shabby and blue collar, the Jeffersons enjoyed social mobility. They had "moved on up to a deluxe apartment in the sky."

The new series prompted viewers and reviewers to take stock of the civil rights revolution. On the one hand, *The Jeffersons* signaled real racial progress: the nation accepted a television series about a middle-class black family in a mostly white neighborhood. At a time when few black characters appeared regularly on television, and most of those lived in stereotypically dire straits, that was quite an achievement. The series even featured an interracial couple, the Willises, who kissed passionately on the screen.[1]

Naming its principals "Jefferson," after the founding father most closely associated with the notion of human equality, the series touted the fundamental equality of all Americans; it envisioned a place where individuals were judged by the content of their characters, not the color of their skin. Some critics wondered whether the show was not too optimistic. The interracial Willis family encountered hostility from no one but the insufferable George Jefferson. And George's frequent troubles owed more to his own boorishness than to the trials of institutional discrimination. *Washington Post* reporter Joel Dreyfuss worried about the "dangerous political message" in a program "that never seems to show George challenged by racism."[2]

But if *The Jeffersons* offered a world without overt racial hostility, it still depicted the clash of irreconcilably conflicting white and black cultures. It seemed to concede the ultimate futility of integration in American life. Most of the series' humor—George Jefferson's disdain for and inability to understand "honkies," the liberal white characters' amusing and patronizing efforts to talk jive—derived from the juxtaposition of utterly foreign manners and morals. The Jeffersons were foreigners in upper-class New York society; it was as if the series had placed a Frenchman on the Upper East Side or, as *The Jeffersons* actually did for comic effect, an Englishman.

The Jeffersons marked the crest of the civil rights movement, the summit of its material achievements, and the beginning of the end of the integrationist ideal. The public purpose of the Sixties—the shared commitment of minority activists, liberal intellectuals, and northern white voters to removing explicit racial barriers—gave way in the Seventies. "Separate but equal," the mantra of southern segregationists, had become anathema as a concept and as public policy. But the idea of distinct groups, with their own culture and politics, their own objectives and destinies, would prove more enticing and more enduring than Sixties Americans might have imagined. George Jefferson, and the new ideal of diversity, would take Americans far from Thomas Jefferson's vision of equality.

The Civil Rights Revolution: A Scorecard

The civil rights revolution breached the previously insurmountable wall of racism in American law, politics, education, and economic life. Black students flooded into the nation's colleges and universities; by the mid-1970s, black enrollments in institutions of higher learning equaled the representation of African Americans in the nation at large, and as many black high school graduates (in percentage terms) went on to college as did their white counterparts. In 1974, 600 black students matriculated at the University of Alabama. Once a symbol of the white South's massive resistance to the struggle for racial justice, the university's famous football squad fielded an integrated roster, and segregationist governor George Wallace was on hand to crown a black woman as the school's 1973 homecoming queen.[3]

African Americans also moved into politics and public life. In the decade after the passage of the Voting Rights Act, the polls opened to millions of previously disfranchised and dispossessed voters. In the southern states, where blacks had never exercised the fundamental rights of democracy, registration rates doubled and the number of black public officials multiplied. In 1967, Cleveland voters elected Carl Stokes the first African American mayor of a major American city. Stokes and new black mayors in Detroit and Atlanta launched a wave of "firsts" during the early 1970s: the first African American admiral in the U.S. Navy, the first black southerners elected to Congress since Reconstruction, the first black secretary of the army, the first black bishop in the Episcopal church, the first black member of the New York Stock Exchange.[4]

Desegregation opened hotels, restaurants, and other public accommodations to people of all races and helped narrow the economic gap between whites and minorities. As the federal government moved aggressively to end legal segregation, the budget of the Equal Employment Opportunity Commission exploded, from a token $3 million in 1966 to more than $111 million by the end of the Seventies. By 1972, every department of the federal government possessed its own equal opportunity office. Meanwhile, the poverty rate for black households declined. Although black families remained far more likely to suffer deprivation than whites, the racial gap closed steadily between 1959 and 1974.[5]

Even some of the most encrusted attitudes about race seemed to be falling by the wayside. In 1963, half of white survey respondents said they would object if a member of their family "wanted to bring a black friend home for dinner"; by 1982, only 22 percent demurred. In 1958, nearly two-thirds of white voters told pollsters that they would refuse to vote for a "generally well-qualified" black candidate for president, even if nominated by their own party. A quarter-century later, 80 percent of white voters claimed they would support such a candidate.[6]

But the rise of the black middle class offered the most dramatic evidence of racial progress. Over the past thirty years, the number of black families officially labeled as "affluent" by the Census Bureau—with household incomes exceeding $50,000—mushroomed by more than 400 percent. A "church-going, home-owning, child rearing, back-yard barbecuing, traffic jam-cursing black middle class" flourished, notable only, according to one analyst, "for the very ordinariness with which its members go about their classically American suburban affairs." Nowhere else was this more apparent than in the sprawling subdivisions of Prince Georges County, Maryland, on the outskirts of Washington, D.C. Prince Georges had evolved from virtually all-white to a majority-black county, while the average income and educational levels increased and property values soared. Historically, the term *black bourgeoisie* had applied to African Americans at the top of a segregated and degraded community—Pullman porters, barbers, head waiters, ministers, undertakers. By the end of the 1970s, "black middle class" denoted simply "that segment of the nation's middle class that happen to be black," one no longer dependent on the patronage of a segregated black economy. The civil rights revolution had won a great triumph.[7]

But it had also been a horrible failure. Stagnation settled onto the United States in the mid-1970s, slowing the economic progress of black Americans. Economic malaise particularly injured working-class blacks, many of whom fell into poverty and despair. At the same time, a disproportionately large number of middle-class blacks drew their sustenance from government jobs. Many private employers remained unwilling to hire, and especially to promote, racial minorities. It was no accident that Prince Georges County bordered the nation's capital.[8]

"The desegregation of public facilities cost nothing," Martin Luther King, Jr., noted just before his death, "neither did the election and appointment of a few black public officials." True racial justice could not be had at such bargain prices. The failure of true racial integration, the principal goal of early civil rights activists, highlighted this somber fact. Segregation disappeared in arenas of casual contact between Americans—restaurants, airports and train stations, hotel lobbies. But schools and neighborhoods remained rigidly separated. Even thriving middle-class blacks continued to face residential segregation. When a subdivision acquired a visible black presence, it usually "tipped," shifting from overwhelmingly white to nearly all black practically overnight.

In this respect, the experience of African Americans contrasted sharply with that of other racial minorities. Prospering Latinos and Asian Americans moved into integrated suburbs without substantial white flight. One leading study of race relations concluded that white Americans simply did not wish to live among black neighbors.[9]

In the aftermath of the civil rights revolution and urban racial disturbances of the 1960s, whites fled the triple-decker row houses and high-rise apartments of urban America. In Boston, blacks had accounted for less than 10 percent of the Hub's population in 1960; by 1980, they made up 22 percent. Whites emptied out of Detroit, Cleveland, Baltimore, St. Louis, Milwaukee, Brooklyn, and Buffalo. It was not the allure of greener suburban pastures but discontent over school desegregation, welfare, and rising black militance that drove city dwellers to the lily-white suburbs. Cities with small black populations continued to grow. It was once "one big happy Flatbush family," a nostalgic Brooklynite explained to an inquiring sociologist, referring to the borough's main thoroughfare. "But now? Ninety-five percent of them have been mugged and moved away."[10]

Nothing else so promoted white flight or exacerbated racial hostility as court-ordered busing. In a series of decisions during the early 1970s, the Supreme Court addressed the persistent problem of school segregation, still lingering fifteen years after the court's landmark *Brown* decision. In *Swann v. Charlotte-Mecklenburg Board of Education* (1971), a unanimous Court ruled that preservation of neighborhood schools could no longer justify racial imbalance. *Swann* authorized drastic measures, "awkward, inconvenient and even bizarre in some situations," to maximize desegregation and specifically recommended busing as a remedy. Two years later, the Court applied this doctrine outside the South for the first time. In *Keyes v. Denver School District #1* (1973), the Court found northern communities responsible for school board decisions and public policies that had isolated black students just as effectively as any Jim Crow law. Federal courts around the country began issuing desegregation plans.

A third ruling, however, *Milliken v. Bradley* (1974), established the limits for forced busing. In a contentious five-to-four decision, the Supreme Court struck down a lower court's plan to bus students between overwhelmingly black Detroit and neighboring white suburbs. Outlying communities, Chief Justice Burger asserted, must not be held responsible for the problems of the cities they surrounded. *Millikin* spared the suburbs the agonies of busing, hastened white flight beyond the city limits, and made it possible for those with means to abandon any commitment to city schools or to education for their less advantaged neighbors.[11]

The nation's struggling city dwellers, black and white, Latino and Asian American, would bear the brunt of the struggle for integration and the agonies of busing. Boston dramatized the nation's anguish. In 1974, a federal judge ordered mandatory busing to desegregate the city's schools, sparking bitter protests and violent outbursts in classrooms and schoolyards. Armed riot police patrolled South Boston and Charlestown, white neighborhoods that greeted black children with derisive signs taunting, "We don't want any niggers in our school" and "Monkeys get out of our neighborhood." The nation's cradle of liberty, the city that begot the abolitionists and helped educate Martin Luther King, became the home of "the bean, the cod, and the bigot." In April 1976, as Boston prepared to celebrate the nation's bicentennial, antibusing protesters attacked Ted Landsmark, a Yale-educated black lawyer and architect, as he rushed across City Hall Plaza to a meeting. A stunning *Boston Herald* photograph broadcast the grisly scene to a horrified world: white boys trying to impale a black man with the American flag.[12]

Frustration, disappointment, and feelings of betrayal increasingly gripped black America. Early in the decade, an overwhelming majority of African Americans told pollsters that they wanted to live in integrated neighborhoods and send their children to racially mixed schools. By the end of the Seventies, alienation had prevailed. By more than a two-to-one majority, surveyed African Americans declared that they felt closer to black people in Africa than to white people in America. African Americans had lost faith in the responsiveness of American institutions, in the possibility of redressing grievances through the normal channels in American society. It appeared that the civil rights movement had reached the limits of its achievements. A profound disillusionment developed, and withdrawal from frustrating, seemingly useless public discourse quickly followed.[13]

The Collapse of the Integrationist Ideal

From World War II until the early 1970s, liberal universalism—a belief in the fundamental unity and sameness of all humanity—had undergirded social activism and political reform in the United States. Nazism in Europe and segregation in the Jim Crow South had made liberal Americans suspicious of any claims of racial and ethnic difference. Beliefs that blacks or Latinos or women possessed distinctive natures or cultures were dismissed as prejudiced. Remaining differences were but an unfortunate legacy of discrimination and oppression.

Until about 1970, Americans had largely shared a core belief that all human beings were essentially the same, that differences among people did not—or at least should not—matter. In the words of Lyndon Johnson, "They cry the same tears, they feel hungry the same, they bleed the same."[14] This universalism reflected the public purpose of the postwar generation, especially northern liberals and intellectuals. Southern segregation—with its active, overt separation of the races, its colored and white drinking fountains and bathrooms—became the scourge of the northeastern establishment. Union leaders, big city mayors, and university professors condemned southern Jim Crow. Even blue-collar white voters, the hard hats and schoolteachers uneasy about crime in their streets and new faces in their neighborhoods, admired Dr. King and supported the southern civil rights movement.

Integration remained their principal objective in the 1950s and early 1960s. Civil rights protesters demanded acknowledgment of blacks' essential human dignity and their fundamental rights as American citizens. "There will be nobody among us who will stand up and defy the Constitution of this nation," the Rev. Martin Luther King, Jr., asserted in Montgomery. King and his fellow protesters wanted to fulfill the Constitution, to purify American democracy, to take their rightful place at the national table.[15]

At the same time, scholarly writing stressed the essential Americanness of the black community and deemphasized cultural and racial distinctions. African Americans, according to one academic, were no more than "white men in black skins."[16] Popular culture celebrated this same universalism. The 1950s opened what critic Gerald Early has dubbed the "age of cultural crossover for the American Negro." Poet Gwendolyn Brooks won the Pulitzer Prize and novelist Ralph Ellison the National Book Award. Sidney Poitier emerged as a major film star. Harry Belafonte broke through as a popular singer. Jackie Robinson and Bill Russell won their respective sports' Most Valuable Player Awards. In Detroit, Berry Gordy, Jr., built the most successful company in the history of popular music. Unlike earlier black recording labels, Gordy's Motown aimed for the mainstream. In the midst of the integrationist age, Gordy could imagine a black company not restricted to the black market.[17]

The fabulous success of Sly and the Family Stone marked the apex of integrationism in American popular culture. Born Sylvester Stewart in Texas, Sly Stone came of age in Vallejo, California, a grim northern California port city beset with gang fights and youth riots during Sly's adolescence. Stone eventually attended radio school and landed a job as a disc jockey on KSOL, a San Francisco Bay Area station. He soon departed from the station's restrictive format; he played all types of music, even seasoning the station's soul specialties with Bob Dylan and the Beatles. At the same time, he formed a band—and what an unusual band it was. "The Family" included blacks and whites, women—not just as vocalists but as principal instrumentalists—and men. Sly donned outrageous clothes: one critic compared him to a "Fillmore district pimp gone stone crazy." His performances were even more outrageous and dynamic; he and the Family produced a startling fusion of white San Francisco rock, soul, British pop, jazz, and dance tunes—a music they called "a whole new thing."[18]

Sly and the Family's music evinced an incredible freedom—freedom of form, with band members trading lead vocals and instrumental solos, and freedom of content. And this integrated family sang of "different strokes for different folks," of an America with room for everyone. "Makes no difference what group I'm in," the Family declared in "Everyday People." "We got to live together." The Family's early hits, a smash with white and black kids alike, possessed, according to rock critic Greil Marcus, "all the good feeling of the March on Washington."[19]

In 1969, Sly and the Family Stone hit their peak at Woodstock, breaking the color line at the legendary countercultural festival. The band's essential optimism was not untempered—"there's cost for you to bear, they will try to make you crawl," as one hit put it—but the songs remained hopeful about the possibilities for individual achievement and racial concord in American life.[20]

By 1970, however, black America betrayed a mounting suspicion about the loving, unified American family that Sly Stone envisioned, of the integrationist ideal itself. Who is being integrated into what? critics asked. Civil rights activists, frustrated with the slow pace of racial progress and anxious to develop black power, denounced integration as a sell-out, the equivalent of assimilation. Integration meant merging into white society and adopting white culture, and newly race-conscious minorities rejected such "whitening." Black activists felt that even their liberal allies had thought of them as "white men with black skins"—had not granted them a heritage worthy of preservation and respect.[21]

In 1967, Harold Cruse sharpened the emerging critique of integration in *The Crisis of the Negro Intellectual.* Albert Murray, the African American cultural critic, praised the book as "the most imaginatively documented and politically sophisticated working prospectus on the built-in contradictions and disjunctions of the Negro Revolution." The *New York Times* called it a "mind-blowing experience of the first order." Mincing no words, Cruse mocked "those Negroes, and there are very many of them, who have accepted the full essence of the Great American Ideal of individualism" and "want to be full-fledged Americans, without regard to race, creed, or color." These naive, deluded universalists never stopped "to realize that this social animal is a figment of the American imagination. . . . They cite the American Constitution as the legal and moral authority in their quest for fully integrated status . . . and shy away from Negro ethnic group consciousness." Integration, Cruse asserted, was neither possible nor desirable: "The Negro Integrationist runs afoul of reality in pursuit of an illusion."[22]

By 1970, millions of black Americans were arriving at similar conclusions. To be sure, the most extreme forms of separatism never caught on with rank-and-file African Americans (polls showed that more whites than blacks favored the establishment of a separate black nation). But widespread approval of black cultural nationalism accompanied that suspicion of the most militant enunciations of black power. A 1970 *Time* magazine survey found the black mood more militant, more hopeful, more determined, and noted overwhelming support in the black community for Afro-American studies programs and other efforts to promote black pride. The new natural Afro hairstyles (which rejected the previously popular straightened look as assimilationist), the study of African languages, the celebration of distinctive clothing, food, and music all won mounting support.[23]

With the abandonment of the integrationist ideal, American conceptions of race shifted, in Harold Cruse's terms, from a "politics of civil rights" to a "politics of black ethnicity." The critique of integration reverberated throughout American cultural and intellectual life in the 1970s. Academic critics scoured the American past for alternative communitarian and republican traditions, and even defended a tolerant form of "ethnocentrism" as the proper way of conceiving of the self and the world.[24]

In this indictment of integration, ivory tower intellectuals harmonized with popular entertainers. Funk impresario George Clinton celebrated "Chocolate City," the all-black enclaves of urban America, imagining an administration with Ali as President, Richard Pryor Minister of Education, Stevie Wonder Secretary of Fine Arts, and Aretha Franklin the First Lady. Clinton neither lamented white flight nor ignored the hardscrabble realities of the black ghettoes; he simply accepted—and liked—what he found. "It's my piece of the rock and I dig you, CC," Clinton's group Parliament sang in 1975. "God bless Chocolate City and the vanilla suburbs."[25]

Sly and the Family Stone abandoned the integrationist ideal with less humor and more pain. In 1971, Sly and the Family released *There's a Riot Goin' On*, an album that issued a grim new report on the state of the nation. The album seemed to reconsider all of the earlier, optimistic tunes, to recall them to the factory. *Riot*'s lyrics focused on betrayal, failure, oppression, on being trapped; the music, lacking the raucous, celebratory quality of Sly's earlier records, offered just as much a reversal as the lyrics. The title track, "There's a riot goin' on," was blank. An old hit, "Thank You fallentinme be mice elf Agin," reappeared transmogrified. No longer an expression of gratitude for an American freedom, it became "Thank You for talkin' to me Africa," a thanksgiving prayer for the strength to stop running from the pistol-packin' devil, stand your ground, and wrestle him to the ground.[26]

Riot offered a black musician's anguished rejection of a nation that limited his freedom in palpable and disturbing ways. *There's a Riot Goin' On* was an album that Sly and the Family's audience, particularly its white listeners, did not want to hear. To a large extent, African Americans were rejecting the integrationist ideal, abandoning the hope of joining a single American community and actively shaping its destiny. Instead they increasingly saw themselves as a separate nation within a nation, with distinct needs and values. Nor were blacks the only Americans to reject integration as an assimilationist nightmare. Chicanos, Indians, Asian Americans, even white ethnics and the elderly would follow suit.[27]

From "Power" to Cultural Nationalism

The critique of integration began with the emergence of the black power movement in the mid-1960s. Militant black nationalism received its most potent enunciation from Malcolm X, a former street hustler and convict who in prison converted to the Nation of Islam and became the minister of the Nation's New York City mosque. Born Malcolm Little, the militant leader scorned integration, rejected nonviolence in favor of self-defense "by any means necessary," and urged pride in blackness.[28] His message appealed most strongly to northern urban blacks who had not participated in the early civil rights struggles. They admired Malcolm's radicalism, his background, his audacious willingness to stand up to whites. But his teachings also caught on among younger civil rights activists in the Student Non-Violent Coordinating Committee (SNCC), who became disillusioned with King's strategy of nonviolence. "The lie-down-before-your-oppressor philosophy," one young militant declared, "is now a treadmill upon which the Negro is running but getting nowhere fast."[29]

Black power, of course, meant different things to different people, but its central message was an assertion of political power.[30] Defining black power in 1967, James Boggs insisted that the movement must "concentrate on the issue of political power, refusing to redefine and explain away Black Power as *Black Everything except black political power.*" In October 1966, Bobby Seale and Huey P. Newton formed the Black Panther party in Oakland, California. Merging black nationalism with Marxist-Leninist doctrine, the party described black ghettoes as exploited colonies of the United States trapped within its borders. The party called itself a revolutionary vanguard that would lead the urban masses against their oppressors, first targeting "the military arm of our oppressors"—the police and the criminal justice system. It recruited heavily among ex-convicts and prison inmates and engaged in several bloody confrontations with police, including a 1967 fray that left one officer dead and a wounded Huey Newton in custody.[31]

Even the black arts movement, a self-consciously aesthetic endeavor, stressed political power. The movement's leader, poet and dramatist Amiri Baraka, called for a socially powerful, politically functional form of black expression. "We want 'poems that kill,'" Baraka wrote in his 1968 poem "Black Art." We want "Assassin poems, poems that shoot guns. Poems that wrestle cops into alleys and take their weapons leaving them dead with tongues pulled out and sent to Ireland." What distinguished these lethal stories, poems, and plays? They exploded in the mind of the reader or audience, shocking the oppressors, but most important, shocking the oppressed so that they would acquiesce no longer in their own oppression, cease to misunderstand and even to participate in their own degradation. Art was a vehicle to concrete economic and political power.[32]

Over the course of a decade, the cultural element of black power gradually supplanted the political as the movement's basic thrust. In the 1970s, many activists concluded that "black culture *was* Black Power"—that an assertion of power lay inherent in maintaining and expressing a distinctive culture through clothing, music, hairstyle, literature, cuisine, and the arts.[33] For the dispossessed, denied access to wealth and political institutions, cultural nationalism enhanced group autonomy and diminished black dependence on white society. Black culture staked out a sphere of activity relatively free from white influence and domination; it also advanced a positive, black-defined black identity that rejected white stereotypes.[34]

Even the Black Panther party gradually stressed cultural development and community control over armed revolution. The Panthers ran free breakfast and health care programs in black neighborhoods, passed out shoes and clothing to the needy, and offered screening for sickle cell anemia. It distributed groceries and opened liberation schools offering courses in Afro-American history and culture. While many of the programs originated as efforts to win the support of the black masses in preparation for the inevitable revolution, developing community pride and institutions soon became an end in itself. By the mid-1970s, this militant, exclusionary form of black power would occupy an influential place in American public discourse, and the same brand of cultural nationalism began to develop among other racial minorities.[35]

Just as Stokely Carmichael and the Black Panther party represented a younger, angrier generation than that of Martin Luther King, Jr., and Whitney Young and other established civil rights leaders, so a new cohort arose within other minority communities. These young activists also rejected integration and despised assimilation. In *Chicano Manifesto,* Armando Rendon renounced the success he had acquired in the white man's world and denounced the older generation—the Mexican American businessmen, politicians, and civic leaders who disclaimed their heritage "and will have nothing to do with *la causa.*" Unlike African Americans, who had vainly sought integration into and equality within an "Anglo dominated world" and "only recently sought anew a black identity and cultural separateness," the Chicano movement and those of American Indians and Asian Americans almost immediately advanced an anti-assimilationist, cultural nationalist agenda.[36]

In 1972, Rodolfo Acuna, founding chairman of the pioneering Chicano Studies Program at California State University at Northridge, published *Occupied America: The Chicano's Struggle Toward Liberation.* Acuna's book, one of the earliest academic studies of Mexican Americans, also offered the manifesto of a self-described activist-academic—one who captured a wider mood by titling his final two chapters "Goodbye America." The 1960s, Acuna wrote, "represented a decade of both awareness and disillusionment. Many Chicanos participated actively in the political life of the nation, during which they took a hard look at their assigned role in the United States, evaluated it and then decided that they had had enough, and so they bid good-bye to America." "Good-bye America" meant not leaving the soil, but denying the legitimacy of the name—recognizing that *America* was a "European term of occupation and colonization." "Good-bye America" signaled resistance against integration, oppression, "captivity."[37]

The cry of "Goodbye America" also represented an assertion of political power for Chicanos, akin to the cry of black power. The careers of the era's two best-known Mexican American leaders, Cesar Chávez and Corky Gonzales, revealed this basic drive toward cultural nationalism.[38] Chávez first arrived on the national scene in 1965, when thirteen hundred Filipino immigrant grape pickers, members of Larry Itilong's Agricultural Workers Organizing Committee, walked out of California vineyards, demanding recognition for their union, fairer wages, and improved working conditions. As they had in the past, the growers sought replacements, this time attempting to hire local Mexican Americans to break the strike. Itilong asked Chávez to persuade the members of his own fledgling farmworkers' union, the United Farm Workers Organizing Committee (UFWOC), to honor his picket lines. They did, and the great Delano grape strike began.

Born near Yuma, Arizona, in 1927, Chávez grew up as a migrant farmworker. He attended more than thirty different schools, eventually reaching the seventh grade, as his family followed the crops across the Southwest. After service in the U.S. Navy, Chávez landed in Delano in 1962 and concentrated on forming the farm labor organization that eventually became known as the UFWOC.

Chávez skillfully exploited the grape strike, transforming it from a mundane struggle for better wages and working conditions into a vehicle for dramatizing the plight of migrant farmworkers in general and rural Mexicans and Mexican Americans in particular. Borrowing techniques from the civil rights movement, Chávez mounted a series of direct action protests, including the famous grape boycott. Drawing on Mexican American traditions, he ran the UFWOC more like a *mutualista,* a nineteenth-century Mexican cooperative association, than a simple union. The UFWOC established a death benefit plan, a cooperative grocery, a theater group, and a Spanish-language newspaper. Chávez also invoked religious traditions, particularly the symbol of the Virgin of Guadeloupe, ingeniously deflecting accusations that his union was somehow communist. In 1970, the Delano grape strike was settled, and the UFWOC embraced a broader cultural nationalist program, an example of community building and Chicano activism in rural areas.

But by the 1970s, the Mexican American experience had become mostly urban, and it was in the cities that Chicano nationalism would flourish. The founding figure was Rodolfo "Corky" Gonzales, a one-time boxer and Democratic party operative who became disillusioned with conventional reform politics. In 1966, Gonzales formed the Crusade for Justice in Denver, an organization devoted to reform of the police and courts, better housing, more economic opportunity, and, significantly, "relevant education" for Chicanos. The Crusade became strongly nationalistic; at one point Gonzales considered appealing to the United Nations for a plebiscite in the Southwest to determine whether the people—*la raza*—might desire independence from the United States. Gradually Gonzales came to stress culture. During a Denver teachers' strike, Crusade volunteers stepped in to teach basic subjects, like science and math, but also offered courses in Chicano history, Spanish, and Mexican culture. A similar program continued after the strike ended. Crusade for Justice promulgated a "Plan of the Barrio," demanding housing that would meet Chicano cultural needs, education in Spanish, and *barrio*-owned businesses. Gonzales also founded the annual Chicano Youth Liberation Conferences, energizing young activists on college campuses.

The 1970s and 1980s witnessed a broad acceptance of this cultural nationalist agenda throughout Mexican American politics—in the drive for ethnic studies programs on college campuses, for bilingual education in the public schools, for community control. Critiques of integration and assimilation became *de rigeur;* dissenting voices portraying Mexican Americans as the latest in a series of immigrant success stories met scorn and derision.[39]

The same trend asserted itself among American Indians and Asian Americans. During the late 1960s and early 1970s, Indian activists invoked "red power" and launched militant protests against conditions on reservations, treaty violations by the U.S. government, and corrupt and abusive practices by the federal Bureau of Indian Affairs (BIA). Young activists increasingly allied with traditionalists, resisting both white society and the moderate, assimilationist leadership of many tribal governments. In 1969, three hundred Indians from fifty different tribes occupied Alcatraz Island in San Francisco Bay. They claimed a treaty right to take over surplus federal property and demanded conversion of the island into an Indian cultural center. The institution would revive "old Indian ways" and operate an Indian college, museum, and ecology center. The occupation lasted nineteen months before federal marshals peacefully removed the remaining protesters from the island. In 1973, two hundred armed Indians took over the South Dakota hamlet of Wounded Knee. In the end, two Indians lay dead and one federal marshal was severely wounded. The conflict revolved around demands for Indian sovereignty, treaty rights, and preservation of Native American cultural traditions. Throughout the country, Indians made clear that conventional methods of political participation and protest were no longer consistent with their unique history and cultural goals.[40]

Asian Americans reached similar conclusions, only more slowly, with cultural nationalism not really emerging until the late 1970s. It manifested itself in the campaign for ethnic studies programs on campus and for cultural institutions—museum exhibitions, theater works, newspapers, literary journals. It also appeared in efforts to take seriously their status as an ethnic minority in a society that continued to view issues of race in black and white terms. Indeed, until 1980, the U.S. Census Bureau listed Asians as "Other" on the census forms. "You're not accepted in minority circles," one Asian American complained, "but you're not part of the majority either. Where do you stand?"[41]

One violent incident—the murder of Vincent Chin in Detroit in 1982—added urgency to the Asian American quest for cultural identity. Two white autoworkers accosted the young Chinese American in a bar, denounced him as a "Jap," and blamed him for the loss of their jobs. A fistfight started; the autoworkers chased Chin with a baseball bat and beat him to death. The assailants were convicted of manslaughter, and the judge released them on probation, demanding that they pay only a small fine. The murder and lenient sentencing aroused widespread protest. Eventually the U.S. Department of Justice interceded and the principal assailant was sentenced to prison on federal civil rights charges. The Chin case aroused a determination to break silence, to speak out, to organize. At the same time, many young Asian Americans felt the need to seek out their roots—to reassert cultural identity in the arts, literature, and education and to reestablish community control of local institutions.[42]

This renewed search for memory received its most prominent expression among Japanese Americans in the redress movement. The Nisei, the children of Japanese immigrants born in the United States, had generally kept silent about their experiences in World War II internment camps and embraced the American dream. Until the late 1960s, the community had almost never investigated or commemorated the internment: there were no pilgrimages to the camps, no education campaigns about the forced relocation, no museum exhibitions. Organizations like the Japanese Americans Citizens League instead offered evidence of their true-blue Americanism, emphasizing the heroic military contributions of Japanese American soldiers in the U.S. armed services.[43]

Imbibing the cultural nationalist atmosphere of the 1970s, the children of the Nisei, the third-generation Sansei, recovered this lost past and encouraged their parents and grandparents to speak out. Eventually many came forward, and pressure for redress mounted. In 1980, President Carter formed a national commission to investigate the internment. The commission convened hearings around the country where people spoke out, many for the first time, about the painful experience of removal and incarceration. The commission finally issued its report during the Reagan administration, and Congress approved small reparation payments to surviving camp veterans.[44]

By the mid-1970s, cultural nationalism had become the dominant force in minority activism. The old drive toward integration had been thoroughly discredited. But the emphasis on preserving and expressing distinctive racial and ethnic cultures posed an obvious problem. Could America successfully combine several different types of cultural nationalism? Could Americans acknowledge difference and still share the same city, the same university, the same polity?

Inventing "Diversity"

During the 1970s Americans hit on an answer to those thorny questions: the idea of diversity. For policymakers, the prospect of unlike, unassimilable groups appeared as a good to be valued—not a problem but a promise. This emerging ideal of "diversity" reflected a variety of social, legal, and ideological developments in the 1970s and early 1980s.

The new thinking built on a demographic foundation—a massive new wave of immigration that literally changed the face, and the faces, of the nation's population. A torrent of new arrivals, both illegal and legal, streamed in from Asia and Latin America. It included the refugees from Vietnam after the fall of Saigon and the 1979–1980 *Mariel* boatlift from Cuba, but owed mainly to the reform of the immigration laws in 1965. Eliminating the odious quota system, which since 1921 had pretty much closed the gates to all but Western Europeans, LBJ's immigration reforms ushered in a flood of new arrivals from the Third World. In 1965, only 5 percent of new arrivals had embarked from Asia; by 1980, nearly half the immigrants had journeyed across the Pacific. Latin Americans also entered in droves. Unlike earlier waves of mass immigration, most of these sojourners arrived with families intact, not as single men, and they quickly established their own businesses and communities. By the 1980s, Koreans owned and operated more than 500 businesses in Chicago, "minorities" made up a majority of the city of Los Angeles, and West Indian blacks outnumbered native-born African Americans in the outer boroughs of New York City.[45]

But demographics alone did not reshape America's understanding of racial differences; law and public policy actively encouraged the shift from integration to diversity. Over the course of the 1970s, the rationale for affirmative action and the contours of civil rights programs slowly metamorphosed. The practical goal of such policies—increasing the representation of certain minority groups in universities, occupations, institutions—remained the same. But the justification for them shifted from integration—including disadvantaged minorities so they could become like everybody else—to diversity—welcoming racial and cultural differences into institutions so that they would reflect the multicultural nature of American society. Affirmative action was now supposed to promote and celebrate differences rather than eliminate distinctions.

While high-profile fights over busing captured the nation's attention, the federal government quietly expanded the reach of affirmative action. In 1969, the Office of Federal Contract Compliance (OFCC) promulgated the so-called Philadelphia Plan, requiring proportional representation of minorities in construction employment. The OFCC subsequently extended the rule to all federal contracts (1970) and added employment requirements for women (1971). At the same time, the Office of Civil Rights in the Department of Health, Education and Welfare issued requirements for bilingual education for students whose native language was not English. In 1977, Representative Parren Mitchell (D, Maryland), chairman of the Congressional Black Caucus, attached an amendment to the Public Works Employment Act, requiring that at least 10 percent of $4 billion appropriated for public works contracts be set aside for minority business enterprises. This widely emulated bill established the principle of minority set-asides; within a few years, more than three hundred such programs had emerged.[46]

The U.S. Supreme Court accelerated the drift toward diversity with its 1978 decision in *Regents of the University of California v. Bakke.* In 1973, Allan Paul Bakke, a balding, blond, blue-eyed thirty-two-year-old engineer applied for admission to the Medical School at the University of California, Davis. By all accounts, Bakke was a strong candidate; his academic record and standardized test scores placed him well above the average for students admitted to the medical school. The faculty interviewer who evaluated Bakke personally concluded that he was "a well-qualified candidate for admission whose main hardship is the unavoidable fact that he is now 33. . . . On the grounds of motivation, academic records, potential promise, endorsement by persons capable of reasonable judgments, personal appearance and decorum, maturity, and probable contribution to balance in the class, I believe Mr. Bakke must be considered as a very desirable applicant and I shall so recommend him." Nonetheless, the medical school did not admit Bakke. The school reserved 16 percent of the slots in the entering class for minority students, many of whom were recruited by a special minority admissions task force. Task force admittees presented substantially lower undergraduate grade point averages and dramatically lower test scores than did Bakke and other regular admittees to the medical school. After unsuccessfully petitioning the university and the Department of Health, Education and Welfare for redress, Bakke filed a suit in Yolo County Superior Court, maintaining that by reserving places for minority students "judged apart from and permitted to meet lower standards of admission than

Bakke," the institution's affirmative action program denied him equal protection of the law.[47]

Bakke's suit eventually reached the U.S. Supreme Court. While the case was pending, the dispute filled the pages and airwaves of the national press, sparking protest marches on college campuses, vigorous debate within the White House, and frenzied lobbying in Washington corridors.[48] The Court heard oral arguments in the fall of 1977 but did not hand down a decision until the following June. By a five-to-four margin, a bitterly divided court upheld Allan Bakke's claim that the University of California had wrongfully denied him admission to its medical school. Four justices ruling in Bakke's favor held all race-based programs illegal, arguing that the "plain language" of the 1964 Civil Rights Act forbade excluding any individual from a public benefit on racial grounds. The four dissenters affirmed the legality of race-based affirmative action programs to relieve the debilitating effects of discrimination. Justice Lewis Powell's swing vote in favor of Bakke split the difference on the fundamental question; institutions could not exclude individuals solely on the basis of race, but race and ethnicity could be considered in a broader assessment of admission qualifications. "It was a landmark occasion," one distinguished law professor conceded, "but the court failed to produce a landmark decision."[49]

Although the Court had struck down so-called reverse discrimination in admissions and hiring, it did not outlaw all race-conscious affirmative action. Justice Powell's decisive opinion held that "a diverse student body" remained "a constitutionally permissible goal for an institution of higher education," even where remedying past discrimination or promoting racial integration would not pass judicial muster. To comply with the law, universities, businesses, and other institutions began to stress diversity rather than eliminating discrimination or promoting integration.

Inadvertently, *Bakke* encouraged the triumph of diversity. Universities actually stepped up affirmative action in the wake of the decision, using the Court-approved need to achieve cultural diversity as their rationale. In many cases, such as at UCLA, earlier efforts to recruit students gave way to hard-target proportional representation schemes.[50]

Meanwhile, law and public policy also reinforced the celebration of diversity in regard to bilingual education. In *Lau v. Nichols* (1974), the Supreme Court required that school districts take affirmative steps to identify and teach students with limited English proficiency (LEP). The resulting guidelines, known as the Lau remedies, forbade immersion courses, English as a second language, and other methods designed to teach English language skills and rapidly integrate LEP students into the standard curriculum. Instead, the federal government required native-language instruction in math, science, and social studies for elementary and intermediate-level students whose primary language was not English. The prevailing idea was not integration, but to respect and preserve the cultural integrity of non-English speakers, primarily of Hispanics, who made up 80 percent of LEP students in the late 1970s. In fact, the Lau remedies encouraged schools to staff the new courses with representatives of the appropriate minority groups. If districts could not find appropriately trained teachers, they should employ "paraprofessional persons with the necessary languages and cultural background."[51]

In 1979 the newly created U.S. Department of Education moved to expand and formalize bilingual education. The proposed regulations would have forced districts to hire 50,000 new certified bilingual teachers and to establish hundreds of new programs. An uproar ensued; Chicago school officials, for instance, complained that they were expected to find native-language instructors for 90,000 students in 139 separate languages. The new regulations were never imposed.[52]

Still, the rollback never challenged the fundamental legal and ideological rationale for bilingual, bicultural education in the nation's schools. Many school districts, especially in areas with large Latino populations, maintained booming programs in service of the now-triumphant ideal of diversity. In fact, in 1979, black parents in Michigan sued to have their children taught in black English. A federal judge ordered the school district in Ann Arbor, Michigan, to offer special language programs for African American students. These policies revised the basic notions of citizenship, challenging the very idea of a national community.[53]

The ideological shift to diversity led to a reconception of the very nature of America—to see the nation not as a melting pot where many different peoples and cultures contributed to one common stew, but as discrete peoples and cultures sharing the same places—a tapestry, salad bowl, or rainbow. "The American flag," the Reverend Jesse Jackson declared at the 1988 Democratic National Convention, "is red, white and blue. But America is red, white, black, brown, and yellow—all the colors of a rainbow."[54]

In this view, which became the dominant way of conceiving of race relations in the 1970s and 1980s, there was no such thing as American culture. Instead, there were many American cultures. The "discriminatory separate-but-equal doctrine of the past," Harold Cruse asserted, would give way to a democratic "plural-but-equal" future. Indeed, the emphasis on diversity, on cultural autonomy and difference, echoed throughout 1970s America. White ethnics picked it up, as did feminists and gay rights advocates and even the elderly. A new conception of the public arena emerged: Americans based their claims on the commonweal (and, increasingly, their demands for exemption from its responsibilities) less on their common rights and privileges as citizens than on their specific cultural identities.[55]

The idea of diversity won such broad (if only shallow) acceptance that during the 1980s, diversity management became a multimillion-dollar industry. Thousands of American businesses hired diversity consultants to relieve racial tensions and train employees to "value difference." By 1990, almost half of the Fortune 500 companies employed full-time staff responsible for managing diversity. Textbooks, university curricula, and museum exhibitions reflected the new emphasis on multiculturalism, and government bureaucrats routinely received sensitivity training.[56]

This shift from integration to diversity was neither unchallenged nor complete.[57] But the center of gravity had drifted toward multiculturalism. If Americans remained suspicious of minority cultural nationalism, assimilation and integration had few champions. The prominent Catholic intellectual Michael Novak encapsulated the era's prevailing mood when he called the 1970s the "decade of the Ethnics." Pausing on his intellectual odyssey from Sixties radical to Eighties conservative at the waystation of cultural diversity, Novak celebrated the new ethnic politics. "It asserts that *groups* can structure the rules and goals and procedures of American life," Novak declared in *The Rise of the Unmeltable Ethnics*. "It asserts that individuals, if they do not wish to, do not have to 'melt.'" For better or worse, the nation's diverse subcultures would no longer submit to a single dominant, universalizing, WASP "Superculture."[58]

Disco Nites, Rapper's Delites

American popular culture reenacted the debate between integration and diversity in the 1970s. The nation's moviehouses, record stores, and dance clubs witnessed an extended, if not always conscious and articulate, dispute between the fading integrationist ideal and the emerging nationalist sensibility.

The silliest pop fashion of the Seventies, the most mocked cultural event of that much maligned decade, most clearly invoked and straddled the ideological debate between universalism and diversity. Disco, according to *Rolling*

Stone, "was the most self-contained genre in the history of pop, the most clearly defined, and the most despised. No other pop musical form has ever attracted such rabid partisans and fanatical foes, dividing audiences along racial and sexual lines, even as its function . . . was to turn the pop audience into one big happy family."[59]

The musical form took its name from the reemergence of dance clubs in the early 1970s. These discotheques featured technologically empowered disc jockeys as masters of ceremony. Equipped with two turntables, the skillful DJ would shift seamlessly from song to song, maintaining the fevered excitement of the sweaty revelers on the dance floor, occasionally delighting the audience with surprising, unexpected segues. "Pulsing and stroboscopic lights, set to the rhythm of the dance music, completed the Dionysian scene."[60]

Both sociologically and musically, disco offered an outlet for disenfranchised groups. As popular music, especially youth-oriented rock and roll, became increasingly white, male, and macho in the early 1970s, alternative cultural streams fed the disco phenomenon: black pride, female sexual assertion, gay liberation. Disco signaled more than the revival of dancing; like Woodstock, it fostered the gathering of a community. "Only this community was urban, democratic, and stylish," disco's most impassioned defender maintained, held together not by muddy self-importance and countercultural esprit, but by dancing. In the words of self-described polyester sociologist Jefferson Morley, "The sense of belonging only increased as disco dancing grew more group-oriented. . . . The shared ceremony of the dance formed a communal affirmation outside the church, the family, and other institutions."[61]

Most important, disco acknowledged dancers' solidarity across racial and cultural lines. It held out the allure of integration. Synthesizing (sometimes literally synthesizing with the aid of new electronic instruments) distinct musical styles and cultural expressions, disco artists fused black, gay, and Latin strands and found a huge, mass audience. Critics denounced disco as gimmicky, commercialized, inauthentic—but their horror concealed a deeper uneasiness. At a time when policymakers, artists, and intellectuals all backed away from integration, a cosmopolitan, cross-cultural musical fad raised hackles.

And for those reasons, disco was hated with more intensity than any other form of popular music before or since. Throughout the nation's vanilla suburbs, the white noose surrounding the increasingly black and Latino central cities, white youth rallied behind the slogan, "Disco sucks." Clubs and concert halls sponsored "disco sucks nights," occasionally resulting in ugly racial incidents. The antidisco frenzy reached its peak in Chicago on a hot July night in 1979. Desperate to revive sagging attendance at home games, the White Sox sponsored Disco Demolition Nite at Comiskey Park. Before a game with the Detroit Tigers, the master of ceremonies detonated a mountain of disco records piled up on the stadium floor. Thousands of white teenagers flooded onto the field; the resulting riot lasted for two hours, causing much damage, many injuries, and isolated incidents of mayhem in the surrounding black community. The White Sox forfeited the game.

How could mindless dance music evoke such fear and loathing? Disco, in its naive togetherness, its sexy, "stoopid" intermingling of musical and cultural styles, challenged racism and pluralism, discrimination and diversity. It obviously threatened suburban white boys who found it too feminine, too gay, too black. But its hybrid form also mocked ethnic nationalists dedicated to preserving distinct black and Latino cultural identities. The black musical establishment hated disco just as fervently as white rock-and-rollers did. African American critics labeled disco assimilationist: they dismissed it as bleached and blue-eyed funk. When disco crossed over from the club scene to the mass market, English and Australian megastars like the Rolling Stones, Rod Stewart, and the Bee Gees embraced the form. Foreign producers like Georgio Moroder recorded unknown black performers like Donna Summer. But America's leading recording artists, black and white, shied away.[62]

And why not? Disco featured impresarios like Miami's Harry Wayne Casey, a white record retailer who wrote songs and produced records for black artists and fronted KC and the Sunshine Band, a multiracial band that landed a dozen songs on the *Billboard* Hot 100 between 1973 and 1978. "A white boy in a sequined jumpsuit who sounded utterly black," Casey was something of a poster boy for the discredited, receding integrationist ideal in Seventies America.

Disco, finally, represented a kind of cultural lag. It celebrated the last gasp of an idealistic, unrealistic innocence in race relations that American politics and most popular cultural expression had cast aside. Godfather of Soul James Brown lent his image and name to Black and Brown Trading stamps, a nationalist program to concentrate black purchasing power in ghetto communities. On movie screens, a wave of black-dominated films appeared, mostly cheap potboilers depicting the struggles of heroically bad and "bad" African Americans against a hopelessly corrupt, depraved white America. Most of these "blaxploitation" films featured hypersoulful protagonists—"Super Blacks" who outpunched and outwitted whites. To be sure, blaxploitation flicks—with their heroes' promises to "stick it to whitey"—invoked more of the style than the substance of black power. But they betrayed a broader desire to highlight and celebrate racial and cultural differences.[63]

If disco marked the receding past, rap, which also owed its origins to dance club DJs modifying records with their turntables, represented the future. In 1979, this underground music surfaced on the national scene when "Rapper's Delight" hit the charts. By the mid-1980s, it would become dominant in the black community and cross over to white audiences.[64]

Like disco, rap originated in a mostly black underground milieu and crossed over, winning mainstream appeal with mostly white, middle-class audiences. But the racial politics of rap, and the source of its appeal, could hardly have been more different. Disco appealed to mature audiences interested in dancing and to young white women. It rejected the heroic, and somewhat macho, rituals of Seventies rock with stadium crowds watching distant performers perched on elaborate scaffolding. Disco stressed commonalities between performers and audience, and among audience members, even if it celebrated only the mindless universal pleasure of shaking your booty. When the film *Saturday Night Fever* catapulted white performers like John Travolta and the Bee Gees into international stardom, critics derided disco as assimilationist or complained about the whitening of disco.[65]

Rap reached its mass audience by a very different process—not by blunting its distinctive African American origins or its black nationalism but by highlighting those very elements. Rap promoters and producers soon realized that the music's main audience, young white suburban males, enthusiastically embraced the most outrageously militant black rappers, hungering for the underground world of violence, sex, and the devil-may-care outrageousness of militant anthems like NWA's "Fuck tha Police." Rap's hallmark celebration of the mean streets trumpeted in uncompromising language the unbreachable gulf between black, Latino, and white worlds. Rap mocked the melting pot. It pronounced integration dead before arrival.[66]

In fact, rappers were only throwing dirt on an already cold grave. By the end of the Seventies, most American intellectuals, minority politicians, and popular performers had tossed aside the dream of integration and undermined the assumptions of liberal universalism. In 1975, *Newsweek* columnist Meg Greenfield surveyed the American cultural landscape and found it "an ethnic bath, an affirmative-action program gone mad." Considering a fall television lineup featuring *The Jeffersons*, Freddie Prinze's *Chico and the Man*, and assorted white ethnics, Greenfield wondered, "What are the networks trying to tell us?"

Greenfield recognized the superficiality of prime-time ethnicity. "Give or take a little spaghetti sauce, they are variations on the same family," she explained, "a warmhearted mama, an irascible and comic papa, a couple of facetious adolescents and an elder female relative who is both a social drag and religious nut." Still, the networks, and for that matter Hollywood, the record companies, and the nation's radio stations, had not embraced ethnic diversity for nothing. The new TV lineup reflected a broader "retribalization" of American life, a breakdown of social ties and faith in a common national destiny. "The sense of identity and common purpose each was able to supply," Greenfield perceived, "being a worker, being an American—is now more readily supplied for many people by an ethnic or racial or cultural bond."[67]

Of course, much was gained from this new awareness. Beyond network TV, in music clubs, art museums, classrooms, theaters, and streets, Americans encountered a new cultural vibrancy and developed new respect for previously ignored works of scholarship and imagination. But the demise of liberal universalism and the celebration of diversity exaserbated the political crisis of the 1970s. Politics always revolves around citizenship—around defining the "we," marking out an "us" against a "them." Everyone desires good schools, good housing, roads, and health care for "us"; few wish to spend their hard-earned dollars on "them."

Hubert Humphrey, last of the great liberal universalists, understood this principle well. Humphrey devoted the final years of his life to the Humphrey-Hawkins Full Employment Act, a proposal to guarantee employment as a basic right of citizenship for all adult Americans. Humphrey fought for enactment of the measure that he envisioned not just as a jobs program, but as an antidote to the divisive racial politics of the early 1970s, a way to rally divided and divisive ethnic constituencies around "common denominators." Blacks and minorities' only hopes, he asserted, lay in a universalist politics built around "mutual needs, mutual wants, common hopes, the same fears."[68]

For the entire postwar era, from the 1940s to the 1970s, reformers had heeded Humphrey's advice. American politics pushed toward widening the circle of the "we," downplaying difference and including more in "us." That strategy might have been assimilationist, but it allowed liberals like Humphrey to provide economic security and political power to millions of disenfranchised Americans. It made activist government possible and popular. But during the early 1970s, Americans retreated from that expansive, universalist vision. Instead of widening the "we," the nation reconstructed itself as a congeries of many narrower units. Not only racial minorities but large sections of the white majority turned toward a politics of identity. Humphrey's way of seeing passed even before his death in 1978. When President Jimmy Carter attempted to honor the Minnesotan's memory at the 1980 convention, he perpetrated the ultimate Freudian slip, dismissing him as "Hubert Horatio Hornblower."

In January 1977, ABC broadcast *Roots*, an adaptation of Alex Haley's bestselling family history that drew the largest audience in television history. More than half the population of the United States, 130 million Americans, watched at least some part of the eight-night miniseries. Haley's efforts to recover his family's heritage, his tale of rebellious slaves in the Old South and proud noblemen in West Africa, transfixed the entire nation.

The phenomenal success of *Roots*, however, did not betoken a new respect for African American history or a new ability to empathize with the sufferings and essential human dignity of black Americans and Africans. Haley himself understood that the appeal lay in the quest—that family, lineage, and ancestry aroused the imaginations of Americans—that everyone wanted to celebrate roots, explore identities, cut themselves off from the run-of-the-mill main and emphasize a distinctive heritage. Americans rediscovered their families, their ethnicity, their spirituality. They looked back—but almost exclusively at themselves.

3

"PLUGGING IN"

Seeking and Finding in the Seventies

"MOST GULLS DON'T BOTHER TO LEARN MORE THAN THE SIMPLE facts of flight—how to get from shore to food and back again," explained *Jonathan Livingston Seagull,* the most surprising bestseller of the 1970s. "For most gulls it's not flying that matters, but eating. For this gull, though, it was not eating that mattered but flight. More than anything else, Jonathan Livingston Seagull loved to fly."[1]

Rejected by numerous publishers and dismissed by critics, Richard Bach's illustrated parable became a cultural phenomenon in the early 1970s. Millions of seekers found wisdom and inspiration in this saga of an extraordinary individual, one who renounced the grim routine of the workaday world, the years of soulless "scrabbling after fish heads." Instead he soared, dove, looped, and sped through the air. Jonathan Livingston Seagull could not content himself with the lot of ordinary seagulls—the low, slow flying, the screeching, the pursuit of crumbs from fishing boats. Summoned before the Council Flock, Jonathan defended his unorthodox conduct. "'Irresponsibility? My brothers!' he cried. 'Who is more responsible than a gull who finds and follows a higher meaning, a higher purpose for life?'"[2]

Without guile or self-consciousness, *Jonathan Livingston Seagull* distilled the myriad spiritual journeys of the Seventies into a simple allegory. It marked an extension and transformation of the Sixties search for wholeness and authenticity. Civil rights activists and antiwar radicals of the 1960s had struggled against alienation as much as against injustice, poverty, and imperialism. They had found in radical political commitments not only vehicles for political protest but the foundations for more meaningful lives: a beloved community and a participatory democracy. But Sixties radicals found it easier to build new homes for themselves than to rebuild American political culture. In the

1970s, they bequeathed their crusade for self-liberation to the nation; the phenomenon of personal transformation became broader but also more inwardly focused.[3]

Richard Bach understood that the search for authenticity had become detached from the radical politics of the 1960s. Still, numerous publishers turned down the former aviator's slight parable of a seagull that learns to soar like an eagle and becomes a guru for his fellows. Eventually Macmillan published *Jonathan Livingston Seagull* on the cheap with no advertising or marketing campaign. *Publisher's Weekly* dismissed *Seagull* as "a wispy little fable," with prose that "gets a mite too icky poo for comfort." Bookstores did not know where to shelve it—with picture books (there were dozens of photos of seagulls in flight), nature books, children's literature, or philosophy.[4]

Booksellers need not have worried; copies of *Seagull* flew out of their stores before they could nest on the shelves. In August 1972 Avon Books paid over $1 million for the paperback rights, then the largest such sale in publishing history. The book sold well among evangelical Protestants and New Age seekers, Christians, Jews, and devotees of Eastern spirituality. *Time* wondered how "an illustrated parable concerning a seagull who learns aerobatics" could become "the decade's pop publishing miracle."[5]

The slender book laid out an appealing doctrine for the spiritual awakening of the 1970s. It emphasized the personal experience of the transcendent, encouraged self-exploration and self-discovery, and preached resistance against established institutions. Bach's best-seller preached an essentially personal goal of perfection. It described a corrupt, unworkable society that needlessly constrained its true soarers and seekers. National politics, a sense of national identity and community, strove to bottle up the centrifugal forces that tore at American society, to hold together its diverse, competing elements. Bach and millions of other Americans—newly proud Italians and Poles, newly organized senior citizens and Christian youth, children of Jesus and the new consciousness—wanted to puncture that container, to spill out and disburse its contents.

In his famous essay on the "Me Decade," Tom Wolfe observed Americans' obsession with self-exploration—the millions seeking new identities and new sources of spiritual awareness.[6] In particular Wolfe discerned two related phenomena. The first of these he called "plugging in"—the strange sight of ordinary people in America "breaking off from conventional society, from family, neighborhood and community and creating worlds of their own." Young people founded communes, old folks gathered in retirement centers and roamed the countryside in recreational vehicles, spiritual seekers sold off the family possessions and moved to ashrams and New Age institutes. They escaped the established communities of the old industrial and cultural centers, filling the churches and hot tubs of the South and Southwest.

Wolfe's essay identified this process of fragmentation and separation—people discovering and cultivating distinct identities, going off by themselves, literally or figuratively. But he also noted a second, related phenomenon: a widespread, eclectic religious revival. Wolfe detected a wave of intense religious enthusiasm and exaltation, a successor to the Great Awakening of the mid-eighteenth century and the Second Great Awakening with its mass revivals in the early nineteenth century. "We are now," Wolfe concluded, "seeing the upward roll of the third great religious wave in American history." Like the others, "it began in a flood of ecstasy"—a torrent of new births. But this Third Great Awakening, while embracing established religious traditions (especially a revival of evangelical Protestantism), was "built up from more diverse and exotic sources than the first two, from therapeutic movements as well as overtly religious ones," Eastern religions, encounter sessions, est, yoga, the New Age.[7]

In the ferment of the 1970s, Wolfe and many others detected a change in the nation's basic chemistry. For generations, American politics and culture had acted like a universal solvent: dissolving ethnic and regional loyalties, diluting sectarian strife and religious enthusiasm, concealing unbridgeable generation gaps behind a forever young facade. But in the seventies, this melting pot gave way, in one astute observer's words, "to a centrifuge" that spun the nation's communities around "and distributed them across the landscape according to new principles." Americans chased new pasts, new futures, new Gods—and they chased them by and for themselves.[8]

Honor Thy Godfathers: The Revival of White Ethnicity

The clamor of cultural nationalism echoed throughout the United States in the late 1960s and 1970s, spreading from the black power movement to other racial minorities, and eventually manifesting itself in an ethnic revival among white Americans. For decades, the dominant trend among American ethnics—Irish and Italians, Eastern European Jews and Eastern Orthodox Slavs, Poles, Greeks, and French Canadians—had been toward integration into the nation's economic, cultural, and political mainstream. Immigrants and their descendants had strived—some grudgingly, most enthusiastically—to assimilate. The huddled masses quickly became "American," which meant, as journalist Peter Schrag fumed in *The Decline of the WASP*, "to become WASP."[9]

"Our Man, his country," Schrag concluded. "Not some sheeny-chink-dago-wop, not some yellowbellied Jap Polack hunky. . . . not some guy with sauerkraut and Limburger cheese on his breath, but an American. White Anglo-Saxon Protestant." But no more. By the early 1970s, white ethnics were not only ascending to dominant positions in American letters, politics, and business, they were ceasing to emulate WASP models and repudiate their ethnic heritages. Increasingly they rejected their previous assimilationist tendencies and affirmed ethnic pride—their right to a separate identity within the larger framework of a pluralist, multicultural nation.10 A flood of books and articles celebrated this supposed triumph of ethnicity over the corrosive forces of assimilation: *The Decline of the WASP, Blood of My Blood, That Most Distressful Nation, The Rise of the Unmeltable Ethnics*. A cover story in the *New York Times Magazine* captured this wave. "America," its title asserted, "is NOT a Melting Pot."11

Ethnic organizations and demands for rights flourished. In June 1971, thousands of proud Italian Americans, waving miniature red, white, and green Italian flags, thronged New York's Columbus Circle for the second annual Italian Unity Day sponsored by the Italian American Civil Rights League. Columbus Circle made a fitting setting for the rally; the *Circolo di Columbo* shared its name with the league's founder, reputed Mafia capo Joseph Colombo, Sr. Colombo had organized the league in 1970 to protest alleged FBI harassment of Italian Americans, and it soon expanded into a formidable organization with more than twenty-five chapters and some 50,000 members. Believing, in Colombo's words, that "there is a conspiracy against all Italian people in this country," the league convinced the producers of the television series *The FBI* to delete references to the Mafia and successfully lobbied New York governor Nelson Rockefeller and U.S. attorney general John Mitchell to mute their references to the mob. At the league's request, Alka Seltzer discontinued a popular television commercial that featured what the league considered a slogan demeaning to Italians: "Mamma mia, thatsa some spicy meatball." Colombo also announced an alliance with Rabbi Meir Kahane, head of the militant Jewish Defense League, to fight what they called harassment by the federal government.12

The Italian American Civil Rights League joined a rising crescendo of angry ethnic voices. "We called ourselves Americans," remembered Barbara Mikulski, then an ambitious young member of Baltimore's Southeast Community Organization. "We were called 'wop,' 'polack' and 'hunky,'" stereotyped as "gangsters or dumb clods in dirty sweat shirts." In the Seventies, ethnics would stand up for themselves, offering a new "Agenda for America" as groups "organized in their own communities" and developed "creative structures for community control."[13]

A few months after the Columbus Circle rally, in the autumn of 1971, dozens of American Jewish communities welcomed the long-awaited Freedom Bus as it traveled across the United States. Staging rallies and collecting signatures along the route, these freedom riders focused national attention on repeated human rights violations by an unsympathetic government. They took their model from the fight against racial segregation in the Jim Crow South. But this new generation of freedom riders locked onto another struggle—one particular to the Jewish community. They sought the rescue of Russian Jewry from the anti-Semitic policies of the Soviet Union.[14]

These latter-day freedom riders—two Soviet émigrés escorted by a contingent of American Jewish activists—resembled the original freedom riders of the civil rights era in name only. In fact, their efforts to relieve Soviet Jewry represented a major turning point for American Jews—what one scholar called a "turning inward."[15] Following the era's cultural nationalist trend, Jewish activists turned insular in the 1970s. Soviet Jews, for example, had suffered discrimination for decades, but it was not until the late 1960s that the movement acquired a mass base and pursued attention-getting tactics.[16]

At the same time, American Zionism gained unprecedented strength. In the wake of the 1967 Six Day War, which pitted Israel against neighboring Arab states, an effusive outpouring of American Jewish support for Israel astonished and pleasantly surprised Jewish leaders. This identification with the Jewish state intensified during the 1970s. In large numbers, young American Jews traveled to Israel as kibbutz volunteers, students, and visitors. "Just another foreigner," sang the pop group Safam in 1983, about an American Jew in the northern Galilee town of Kiryat Schmona. "But these strangers are my brothers and they take me by the hand."[17]

The ethnic awakening stirred even long-settled immigrant communities. Surveying the success of his own ethnic group, Father Andrew Greeley lamented what he termed the "taming of the American Irish." The Irish, Greeley feared, had exchanged their "explicit sense of distinction as a group and their consciousness of a heritage" for the fruits of American prosperity. Still, Greeley hoped to revive the lost heritage among "that most distressful nation." He concluded on a note of ethnic renaissance: "Maybe the Irish haven't been tamed at all."[18]

Signs of ethnic revival were everywhere to be seen in the early 1970s.[19] In 1972, a Polish Catholic ex-radical intellectual named Michael Novak surveyed the new ethnicity in a landmark book, *The Rise of the Unmeltable Ethnics.* According to Novak, a WASP conception of American culture had long dominated American life. Individuals could become assimilated—by adopting WASP manners, values, customs, and beliefs—but groups could not assimilate. Against this WASP conception of America, Novak argued, a new ethnic politics had emerged: "It asserts that groups can structure the rules and goals and procedures of American life. It asserts that individuals, if they do not wish to, do not have to 'melt.'" During the 1970s—what Novak termed the Decade of the Ethnics—subcultures were "refusing to concede the legitimacy of one (modernized WASP) 'Superculture.'"[20]

This upsurge of white ethnicity also manifested itself in some of the era's most influential and enduring cultural products. In art, in fiction, especially in film, a new model appeared—a revised narrative. For centuries, stories of the melting pot—tales of the arrival of immigrants on these shores and their rapid assimilation into American society—had dominated American letters. Often these stories celebrated the efficacy of the melting pot and the opportunities available in a golden land. Sometimes they struck an elegiac note, mourning all that was lost as the children of immigrants turned their backs on the old country and its traditions. But they were always tales of assimilation. Like it or not, immigrants melted into the American mainstream.

Fueled by the ethnic revival and the cultural nationalist turn of the late Sixties and early Seventies, a new type of immigrant saga emerged—tales of failed assimilation, of deassimilation, of the lingering, inescapable imprint of the ethnic heritage. In 1972, Francis Ford Coppola directed an adaptation of Mario Puzo's best-selling novel about a Mafia don and his family. *The Godfather,* among its many cinematic achievements, embraced the new immigrant counternarrative of the ethnic revival.

At the center of the film lay the story of Michael Corleone, son of the Godfather, played by the then unknown actor Al Pacino. The studio had wanted to cast Robert Redford in the role, but Coppola insisted on Pacino, seeking an actor "who wore the mark of Sicily on his face."[21] As the film begins, Michael is estranged from his heritage; he repudiates his family and its ways. He even courts a non-Italian and will marry outside the group. Michael is educated and has served in the U.S. armed forces; he rejects his past.

In the opening scene, Michael, attired in his military uniform, has returned for a family wedding. Talking with his date, the outsider Kay, he recounts a horror story—how Michael's father had launched the career of a Sinatra-like crooner by making his bandleader, who would not free him from an unfavorable contract, "an offer he couldn't refuse." The brazen brutality shocks Kay, but Michael reassures her: "That's my family, Kay, that's not me."[22]

By the end of the movie, however, Michael has deassimilated. He has decided to carry on his family's legacy, to embrace his heritage. In one of the most famous sequences in American film, Michael Corleone emerges, literally and figuratively, as the new Godfather—becoming Godfather at the baptism of a child as his men carry out the ruthless shooting spree that establishes him as mob capo. Ethnicity is destiny. No solvent, not even the bubbling American melting pot, can dissolve the bonds between father and son, ethnic and old country.[23]

In film, politics, and letters, white ethnics honored their godfathers in the early 1970s; they plugged into distinct, special, separate identities. "The ethnic American feels unappreciated for the contribution he makes to society," Barbara Mikulski warned the Urban Task Force of the U.S. Catholic Conference. "In many ways he is treated like the machine he operates or the pencil he pushes." American institutions had made no effort to assist "kids named Colstiani, Slukowski or Klima." But now white ethnics had discovered themselves and rediscovered their pasts. No longer would they mask their "warmth, charm, and zesty communal spirit"; no longer would they kowtow to "Yankee patricians" or "phoney white liberals."[24]

Honor Thy Grandparents: The Elderly Mobilize

A similar sense of cultural identity and a comparable political mobilization developed among the elderly in the early 1970s. Older Americans began to organize themselves separately as senior citizens to agitate for their rights, to see themselves as a distinct group with distinctive interests. At the same time, America's elderly increasingly removed themselves from their families and communities, setting off for retirement colonies and leisure developments.

The graying of the nation's population underlay the startling growth of "gray power." Between 1900 and 1980, average life expectancy increased by more than twenty-five years. In 1776, at the founding of the republic, only 2 percent of the nation's population—every fiftieth American—reached age sixty-five. In 1900, the elderly still made up just 4 percent of the overwhelmingly young nation. But by 1980, senior citizens tallied 11 percent of the nation's total; every ninth American had reached the golden years.[25]

The elderly also enjoyed improved economic prospects. Throughout the nation's history, poverty had been a familiar visitor at the bedside of America's aged. As late as 1950, more than a third of the nation's elderly survived on poverty rations. But the generation that retired in the late 1960s and 1970s had profited handsomely from postwar prosperity. Many older Americans enjoyed generous company pensions, maintained secure sources of income, and owned their own homes. They were also the beneficiaries of 1960s liberalism. Medicare and expanded social security guaranteed basic economic security for most older Americans. Other federal laws, such as the Employee Retirement Income Security Act of 1974, tightened pension plan protections. These heroic interventions erased most economic deprivation among the elderly. The poverty rate for senior citizens, a disheartening 33 percent in 1950, had plummeted to 14 percent in 1978.[26]

In the early 1970s, national attention began to focus on an increasingly well-organized, increasingly militant elderly population. In September 1970, senior activists convened ten forums for older Americans across New York State as part of a campaign to mobilize "senior power." In June 1971, the National Council of Senior Citizens staged a major rally in Washington, D.C. A few months later, bowing to pressure from elderly interest groups, President Nixon convened the White House Conference on Aging.

In May 1972, sixty-seven-year-old Maggie Kuhn of Philadelphia, one of the most outspoken senior citizens advocates, announced the formation of the Gray Panthers. For Kuhn, the echo was deliberate and serious. "Liberation movements are everywhere today," Kuhn asserted in her manifesto, "New Life for the Elderly." Into "this new age comes the budding revolution of old people. Like blacks and Mexican-Americans, Puerto Ricans, and Indians who have revolted against racism, the liberation of older adults seeks the end of ageism."[27]

The Gray Panthers advanced an ambitious agenda. New York leader Hope Bagger challenged mandatory retirement rules. Other self-described "agitators on the ageist front" lambasted the "social service approach to the problems of the elderly," seeing existing social programs as insensitive and chastising social workers for insufficiently respecting the dignity of the elderly. At the same time, Gray Panthers Media Watch campaigned against popular images of the elderly that made older people "look sick or bothersome or boring."[28]

Older persons, Maggie Kuhn insisted, "constitute a great national resource, which has been largely unrecognized, undervalued, and unused. The experience, wisdom and competence of older persons are greatly needed in every sector of society." Not only did American society need to change, but so did the elderly themselves. "We oldsters," Kuhn demanded, "have to make basic changes in our thinking about ourselves and our peers. We will have to 'reprogram' ourselves and adopt new personal and group life styles."[29]

The Gray Panthers and their allies mobilized around a number of grassroots causes: better health care, life cycle education, sexuality for the elderly, and so-called geriatric communes—places where the elderly could live together, in facilities suited to their needs, with a wide range of social and community activities. Their efforts bore fruit. President Nixon signed off on a massive, budget-busting increase in social security payments. The first payments, along with a letter claiming credit for the fattened checks, arrived shortly before the 1972 elections. In subsequent years, entitlements for senior citizens became sacrosanct. In the words of House Speaker Tip O'Neill, they were "the third rail of American politics. Touch it and you die."[30]

The American Association of Retired Persons (AARP), one of the nation's most formidable lobbying groups, generated much of the current. Founded in 1958 as an outgrowth of the National Retired Teachers Association, the AARP claimed just 1.5 million members in 1969. By 1980, after a decade of gray power, it enlisted more than 12 million members and wielded considerable influence in the nation's corridors of power. For nominal annual dues, members received publications like *Modern Maturity,* the country's largest-circulation magazine, membership discounts, access to group insurance plans, and the AARP's lobbying might.[31]

Meanwhile, corporate sponsors and media outlets recognized the elderly's mounting economic power and cultural authority. Lydia Bragger, one-time head of the Gray Panthers Media Watch, became much in demand as a consultant to broadcasters and advertisers. By the early 1980s, a new marketing niche had emerged, with an array of goods and services designed for and specifically targeted toward the elderly.[32]

Far more than previous generations of senior citizens, the new elderly retired early, their working lives and their old homes just reflections in the rear-view mirror. While most aged Americans continued to stay put, growing numbers set off for warmer climates and greener pastures—or perhaps greener fairways. The interstate mobility rate for the elderly—the likelihood that an older American would move across state lines—doubled from the 1950s to the 1980s. In winter, nearly a million "snowbirds," seasonal migrants, shared the golf courses, retirement developments, and recreational vehicle parks of the Sunbelt with the permanent retirees. By the early 1980s, Florida boasted a concentration of senior citizens nearly double that of the rest of the nation. Retirement villages so overwhelmed some counties on the Sunshine State's west coast that the median age approached sixty.[33]

Seniors flocked to retirement communities in the booming Sunbelt states. Senior citizen towns—age-segregated, amenity-rich developments—began to take shape in the 1960s when the Del Webb Corporation opened Sun City and Sun City West in the Phoenix area and Sun City Center in Florida. These minicities contained their own golf courses, swimming pools, recreation centers, security patrols, supermarkets, churches, medical clinics—and no residents under retirement age. Even more elderly Americans migrated to age-segregated retirement villages within ordinary cities and suburbs: luxury condos, retirement hotels, life-care facilities, congregate housing. By the mid-1970s, more mobile, less wealthy senior citizens parked their trailers in more than seven hundred senior citizens' mobile home parks.[34]

Some elderly activists worried about the popularity of retirement communities. Maggie Kuhn denounced them as "playpens and warehouses."[35] When journalist Frances FitzGerald visited Florida's Sun City West, she found a vibrant hamlet of active, healthy people, many of whom had retired well before age sixty-five. Few of them missed their jobs, their families, or their old homes. They had looked forward to "all the things they could do when they were no longer tied down by children and jobs," and Sun City had not disappointed them. The retirement community substituted for the extended family they had once known. It offered dozens of clubs and activities, but as the head of the Republican Club and leader of the local Cancer Drive put it, demanded (and received) little active involvement from "people who have participated so much they feel they don't have to anymore."[36]

Within those leisure centers, older Americans saw themselves as a distinct community with a separate identity. So during the Seventies, "oldsters," in Maggie Kuhn's words, "reprogrammed themselves." They broke off from the main, they found themselves; they plugged in. In Florida and the Arizona desert, the Rio Grande Valley and the Carolina piedmont, a new, more liberated elderly made their way far from the communities and commitments of their Rustbelt homes.[37]

Back to the Land

In 1971 Tom Wolfe made a lecture tour of Italy, shocking his audiences with reports on contemporary American life. "That ordinary workers could go off to suburbs and buy homes and create dream houses" amazed the Italians. The "new life of old people in America," with its retirement villages and snowbirds, "was still more astounding." But nothing so animated Wolfe's listeners as his tales of America's communes. "Everywhere I went, from Turin to Palermo," Wolfe reflected, "Italian students were interested in just one question: Was it really true that young people in America, no older than themselves, actually left home and lived communally according to their own rules?" The students understood that hippies practiced free sex and smoked dope and created their own fashions, but nothing so fascinated and appalled the Europeans as the thought of young people leaving home and building their own communities.[38]

During the late 1960s and early 1970s, these communal homes germinated around the country. Young Americans built communes, cooperatives, and collectives, ashrams, organic farms, and hip apartment buildings. "They left," one chronicler of the phenomenon explained, "not in a mass organized way or because some dark figure came to town and told them to." Spurred simply by an "awful awareness that wherever they had come from was no longer the place to stay," they set out on a collective exodus. But unlike the first wave of flower children who had swelled Haight-Ashbury and the East Village in the mid-Sixties, this band of migrants "was a little less noisy, a little more sophisticated, and a damned sight more serious about why they were leaving and what they were headed for." They lacked both the extravagant ambitions of the Summer of Love—the sense that it was possible to upend and replace the straight world—and its guileless innocence. They set off to build communities in the wilderness—"outposts, testing grounds, self-experimental laboratories"—and they succeeded. The *New York Times* estimated that 2,000 rural communes and 5,000 collectives had sprung up by the early 1970s.[39]

Rural communes formed a kind of back-to-the-land movement. "We're retribalizing," one communard explained. "We're learning self-sufficiency and rediscovering old technologies that are not destructive to themselves and the land. . . . And we're doing this, as much as possible, outside the existing structures, saying a fond farewell to the system, to Harvard, Selective Service, General Motors, IBM, A&P, IRS, CBS, DDT, USA."[40] Some hippies reinhabited abandoned towns, such as Georgeville Trading Post in Minnesota. Others constructed new villages of their own—Morning Star Ranch and Wheeler's Free in California, Pandanarum in Indiana, New Buffalo in New Mexico, The Farm in rural Tennessee.[41]

Most communes were small—a few buildings, a dozen or two dozen people. At Red Rocks, in southern Colorado, about twenty-five people lived in a large geodesic dome. There they cooked, worked, slept, healed the sick, gave birth; all the children born in the dome received the surname "Red Rocker." In southern Oregon, numerous cooperative farms cleared small holdings; many aimed at complete self-sufficiency, growing their own food, making their own clothing, and building their own shelter.[42]

Many of those heading toward rural communes had no experience with farming or life in the country. To serve their needs, Stewart Brand published *The Whole Earth Catalog* in 1968. It contained descriptions of supplies that could be ordered by mail—wood stoves, wind generators, Earth Shoes. It also offered advice: how to farm organically, give a massage, construct a teepee, perform a burial, meditate, raise chickens, practice Zen Buddhism. *The Whole Earth Catalog* announced three fundamental laws: "Everything's connected to everything; Everything's got to go somewhere; There's no such thing as a free lunch." Eventually the book went through numerous editions and inspired dozens of other guides. The *Mother Earth News* followed in the catalogue's footsteps and by 1978 reached a circulation of 400,000.[43]

The communes advanced a new way of thinking about the relationship between nature and society, about humanity's place in the environment. At the same time, events like the 1969 Santa Barbara oil spill alerted middle-class Americans to the dangers of environmental disaster, and many mainstream organizations worried about pollution, toxic waste, and development of wilderness lands; a new way of thinking about the natural world gained influence. Young people became concerned not just about pollution and human welfare, but with understanding and preserving ecosystems. Increasingly, they advanced an ecological perspective—a tuning in to the relationships among all organisms in natural systems. At one 1969 event, ex-Beat poet and countercultural guru Gary Snyder voiced the "non-negotiable demands of the earth," linking trees with blacks and the Vietnamese as "exploited minorities."[44]

After the disappointments of 1968, ecology emerged as a "fresh oppositional alternative." Unlike electoral politics or "waiting for the Revolution," environmentalism demanded immediate action within one's own home. Like the other great quests of the Seventies, it stressed immediate, local affiliations and personal transformation as the path to a new age.[45] For most counterculturalists, living in concert with nature implied simpler, less technological modes of life, often inspired by non-Western cultures. Hippies traded in the Day-Glo colors, groovy plastics, and mod fashions that had defined the

Haight-Ashbury Summer of Love for muted earth tones, Apache headbands, and Indian shawls. "They paved paradise and put up a parking lot," Joni Mitchell famously complained in her 1970 hit "Big Yellow Taxi." But Mitchell blamed hippies as well as squares; that nefarious development included a "pink hotel, a boutique, and a swingin' hot spot."[46]

"Brown rice," according to one historian, "became the icon of anti-modernity." Mid-Sixties hippies had been willing to eat anything in their search for intense experience. (As late as 1968, one alternative newspaper included a recipe for "bologna knish enchiladas," which consisted of bologna, white bread, and canned soup.) After 1970, the counterculture entirely banished processed foods. New foodways appeared, with an emphasis on natural, organic, largely vegetarian cuisine; whole grains and raw or home-cooked foods replaced bland, bleached, white bread and processed products. Brown rice and tofu, organically raised carrots, and home-made yogurt formed the building blocks; they were but the most obvious manifestations of a new way of life. By opting out of the mainstream even in the production of the most basic necessities of life, communards were constructing an alternative, do-it-yourself America.[47]

The new environmentalism grew out of this search for alternative institutions and spiritual renewal. Young people planted organic gardens, experimented with food production and communal living, and emulated romantic versions of Native American tribal culture.[48]

On April 22, 1970, the new environmentalism took root. Earth Day began as a political maneuver, an attempt to build a bridge between congressional advocates of environmental regulation and the emerging activism on the ground. In 1969, Senator Gaylord Nelson (D, Wisconsin), a leading voice for conservation during the Nixon years, proposed a "National Teach-in on the Crisis of the Environment." Nelson hoped both to strengthen the pressure for environmental legislation on Capitol Hill and to separate the ecology movement from its more radical, countercultural elements. The senator envisioned a relatively small commemoration of the day.[49] But, as he reflected, "once I announced the teach-in, it began to be carried by its own momentum. If we had actually been responsible for making the event happen, it might have taken several years and millions of dollars to pull it off. In the end, Earth Day became its own event." Earth Day became a huge, nationwide festival. In New York City, "thousands crowded into a block-long polyethylene bubble on 17th Street to breathe pure, filtered air. Before the enclosure had been open to the public half an hour the pure air carried unmistakable whiffs of marijuana." Across the

Hudson River in Hoboken, New Jersey, revelers dumped into the water a coffin containing the names of the nation's polluted waterways. In Boston, protesters marched against noise pollution and the supersonic transport. At Indiana University, population control activists threw birth control pills into the crowd.[50]

Still, the old-line conservation groups remained suspicious and kept their distance. Mainstream organizations like the Audubon Society, the National Wildlife Federation, and the Sierra Club bridled at the media coverage lavished on the new environmentalism; they worried also that countercultural, grass-roots activism would divert attention from their efforts. "We cannot afford to let up on the battles for old-fashioned Wilderness Areas, for more National Parks, for preservation of forests and streams and meadows and the earth's beautiful wild places," the Sierra Club's vice president warned.[51]

During the Seventies, new ecology action groups burgeoned in communes, college towns, hip neighborhoods, and minority communities. These long-haired greens advocated and popularized a radical view of the relationship between nature and humanity. "Deep Ecology" challenged the anthropocentric outlook of most mainstream environmentalists, with their stress on human welfare and aesthetic appreciation of natural beauty. Instead, the alternative organizations immersed humans within ecosystems, asserting the rights and interests of other species and the need to bring people into harmony with natural systems. Groups like Earth First! emerging from mid-1970s debates within the Wilderness Society, expressed hostility to industrial society and Western notions of the human conquest of nature.[52]

These organizations cross-fertilized and vitalized the traditional conservation establishment. The new greens legitimated the mainstream groups, granting them the status of moderate voices and honest brokers within the political system. But the new environmentalism also upped the ante for reform, making possible legislation like the Endangered Species Act of 1973. The act set up powerful mechanisms to protect endangered species—even obscure, rare plants and animals—and it applied unprecedented brakes on development to preserve the critical habitats of threatened life forms. The law reflected the biocentric, almost religious ideals of alternative environmentalism.[53]

In all its forms, the return to the land in the early Seventies served spiritual ends. It offered a weapon against alienation, a tool for self-realization. Young ecologists and communards sought not so much to remake the nation as to create "islands of decency" within it. They built "intentional communities," shelters from the storm of modern consumer society.

These efforts, as one of their number understood, involved a "mystical sort

of faith that through work and their anarchical mode of life they can redis-
cover their own functionalism as human beings." They shared, William
Hedgepath wrote, "a common bond with the early Christians." Across America, many others sought spiritual sustenance, but their conceptions of decency
pointed in a different direction.[54]

The Third Great Awakening

Journeys of discovery became commonplace in the Seventies. The personal
odysseys of white ethnics, the elderly, racial minorities, and ecologists also fed
into a widespread religious revival—an outpouring of enthusiasm and spiritual experimentation that ran the gamut of American religious life, from New
Right Christians to New Age seekers, students of the Book of Revelation and
the Torah, the Bhagavad Gita and the I Ching.

Among all branches of American Jewry, for example, the process of turning inward had profound effects on religious practice. Reform Jews began
advocating greater respect for ritual; in many Reform synagogues, yarmulkes
and prayer shawls reappeared. Leaders of Conservative Jewry pressed for
stricter religious interpretations, while more and more Orthodox children
remained within the traditional fold. Assailing the impersonal, worldly qualities of some synagogues, the *Havurah* movement established fellowships where
"small groups could meet, unburden their hearts and minds and build a Jewish
world of their own."[55] While climbing intermarriage rates and creeping secularism threatened the American Jewish community, active Jews revitalized religious practice and intensified religious instruction. Jewish summer camps and
day schools proliferated. By the 1980s, nearly five hundred Jewish day schools
operated around the United States, and Jewish camps burst at the seams.[56]

American Christianity also experienced a fever of religious energy in the
1970s. The tally of affiliated Christians—the percentage of Americans who
regularly attended worship services—rose little, but that slow growth masked
dramatic shifts among the competing denominations. Catholicism experienced little upheaval. The mainstream, moderate and liberal Protestant
churches suffered heavy losses; membership in the Presbyterian church plummeted 15 percent from 1973 to 1983, and the United Methodist church lost 8
percent of its parishioners.[57] Meanwhile, membership in evangelical Protestant churches exploded. A 1978 study classified nearly a quarter of the nation
as evangelical. In a 1986 Gallup poll, 32 percent of Americans described themselves as "born again" or evangelical Christians. The Pentecostal and charis-

matic denominations, with their strict morality, fundamentalist theology, and spirit-filled worship services (often including speaking in tongues), particularly flourished. The Assemblies of God, a leading charismatic denomination, grew by 95 percent in the decade and a half after 1973.[58]

Everywhere across the United States in the 1970s and 1980s, signs appeared—signs often taken for wonders—of the mounting influence of evangelical Christianity. In 1976, Jimmy Carter, a born-again Baptist, became president of the United States. In 1980, revivalist Billy Graham's newspaper, *Decision*, reached a circulation of 24 million. Religious radio stations numbered over a thousand, broadcasting the good news along with more than one hundred Christian television stations.[59] The so-called televangelists—Jim Bakker, Pat Robertson, Jimmy Swaggart, Oral Roberts—became national figures, and later figures of national scandal. Polls revealed that nearly half of Americans regarded the Bible as the actual word of God. A sizable majority claimed they had "no doubts" Jesus would return to earth, and 80 percent expressed the belief that they would appear before God on Judgment Day.[60]

The single best-selling nonfiction book of the 1970s was not *The Joy of Sex* or even *The Joy of Cooking*, but Hal Lindsey's apocalyptic pronouncement, *The Late Great Planet Earth*. Published in 1970, 9 million copies of Lindsey's narration of the coming apocalypse and interpretation of the Book of Revelation circulated in print by 1978. By 1990, Lindsey's book, which explained revelation in terms of the nuclear age, had sold 28 million copies and become a movie featuring narration by Orson Welles. Lindsey's best-seller topped a long list of popular prophecy books. In 1978, the *New York Times Book Review* noted the shockingly large sales of evangelical booksellers, and the publishing world quickly took note; ABC purchased Waco, Texas–based Word Books, and Harper and Row absorbed Zondervan, a leading publisher of prophecy texts.[61]

To be sure, this evangelical revival represented no simple, straightforward upsurge in religious enthusiasm. American evangelicalism remained a large, complicated, multifaceted community.[62] Still, a series of core beliefs united the broad, diverse phalanx of American evangelicalism as it boomed in the 1970s. First, evangelicals emphasized the sanctity of Scripture, the importance of the Bible as portal to the will and word of God. One religious bumper sticker captured this precept: "Begin Your Day with Nutrition: Read the Bible."[63]

Second, the evangelical revival was nourished by the expectation of an apocalypse—the conviction that the end of days would soon arrive. During the Seventies, American evangelicals found abundant and manifest omens of the end in the workings of nature, the tangles of the cold war and Middle Eastern politics, the hedonism of the sexual revolution. Although they differed on its imminence, nearly all evangelicals agreed on the need to prepare for Judgment Day. So widely did apocalyptic belief spread that canny entrepreneurs sold Rapture wristwatches: "one hour nearer the Lord's return," they claimed.[64]

Third, and most important, evangelical Christians stressed personal conversion—the process of being touched by the Holy Spirit, of being reborn in Christ. They emphasized the individual's experience of grace, the personal discovery of one's own salvation. "Jesus on Board," fittingly declared one religious bumper sticker in the early 1980s. "Beam Me Up, Jesus." "God Already Made My Day."

The evangelical revival echoed throughout American culture in the 1970s and early 1980s. Religious music filled the airwaves. In the early 1970s, vaguely Christian hits like Norman Greenbaum's "Spirit in the Sky" and Ray Stevens's "Everything Is Beautiful" climbed the charts. By the end of the decade an entirely new musical category emerged: Christian contemporary music (CCM). Musically, Christian contemporary recordings lacked inspiration. "Whether it's rap, heavy metal or pop," one CCM critic explained, "the music is indistinguishable from its secular counterpart." What defined the genre was "confessional lyrics"—explicit references to Jesus or being born again. CCM formed part of "a parallel Christian culture, enabling kids to be normal, blue-jean-wearing, music-loving American teenagers without abandoning their faith, . . . to be devout without being nerdy."[65]

This parallel universe proved surprisingly vast. Indeed, the recording industry long underreported sales of CCM because it sold mainly in evangelical record stores, which *Billboard* and other mainstream surveys did not poll. When Soundscan began compiling actual sales by computer bar codes in the 1990s, many CCM records suddenly ascended the pop charts. And Columbia House, the nation's leading music club service, enrolled as many members in its Christian music club as in its long-established classical music club.[66]

CCM's biggest success story, vocalist Amy Grant, burst onto the CCM stage as a teenager in the late 1970s. Over the next two decades, Grant won five Grammy awards and sold more than 20 million records. The *New York Times* called her the "Michael Jackson of Gospel music"; *Life* dubbed her "the Madonna of Gospel rock."[67]

Amy Grant turned out to be the visible tip of the enormous iceberg of Christian contemporary music. Led Zeppelin soundalikes quoted from Paul's Epistle to the Ephesians. Churches sponsored Christian rock festivals, complete with hard-rock bands and kids frolicking in the mud. But unlike Woodstock, organizers advertised these "weekends that last a lifetime" as "ministry events," designed so that everyone who attends will "have a lifechanging experience with Jesus Christ."[68]

Meanwhile, Christian bookstores (almost all of them evangelical) proliferated around the country. These religious entrepreneurs, like the Amazing Grace Christian Superstore in California and the Shepherd's Shoppe in Illinois, vended not only Bibles in all shapes and sizes, but religious tracts, the writings of C. S. Lewis, music, and gift items. They featured posters, T-shirts, key chains, and the ubiquitous "Footprints" poem, a cloyingly sweet inspirational message superimposed on a photo of people walking on a beach in the twilight, on posters and greeting cards.[69]

They also sold Christian romances, a wildly successful new genre of popular fiction. These were romance novels, in the words of one publisher, "rated G . . . for godly, gratifying, and of course great." Bodices usually stayed unripped in these popular paperbacks; instead, budding love led to conversion and always concluded in Christian marriage.[70] In the guidelines to authors of Heartsongs Presents, a leading series of Christian romances, the editors explained that "the underlying theme in all of our romances is the belief that a true and honest faith in God is the foundation for any romantic relationship. Although we are not looking for 'sermons in novel form,' the importance and need for a personal relationship with Jesus Christ should be apparent."[71]

Sex remained largely absent from inspirational romances, but the church rarely appeared either. Christian institutions and formalized religion figured surprisingly little in Christian romance. To some extent, religious publishers left out churches and preachers to protect market share. Their books needed to remain safely nondenominational and not alienate potential readers. But relegating churches to the background also stressed the personal relationship with God at the heart of evangelical Christianity and the broader religious revival of the 1970s. The protagonists of Christian romances often chat directly with their God.[72]

The evangelical awakening permeated American life, giving rise to a flourishing evangelical subculture with booming churches, schools, and service organizations. After 1970, fundamentalist Christians shed their image as ignorant rural hicks, unable and unwilling to make their way in the modern world. By the early 1970s, for example, the Reverent Jerry Falwell had built his Thomas Road Baptist Church in Lynchburg, Virginia, into one of the largest, most successful churches in the country. Like many of his comrades, Falwell's ministry filled the pews with middle-class professionals and educated suburbanites, attracted to the recipe for wholesome living, biblical devotion, and worldly success that Falwell preached from the pulpit. Around the country, similar evangelical Christian communities emerged, havens from the immoral, liberal, secular humanist nation that in their mind encircled them.[73]

The rise of conservative evangelicalism (and the corresponding collapse of mainline liberal Protestantism) contributed to what historians have called the loss of religion's integrative force. Religion, scholars concluded in the 1980s, "may be no less visible in American life today, but it is far more likely to divide than to integrate."[74]

On the face of it, the New Age or personal awareness movement of the 1970s and 1980s appeared to share little in common with the evangelical revival. *New Age* remained a somewhat amorphous term, encompassing a broad range of beliefs and activities. It included non-Western spiritual traditions (Zen Buddhism, yoga, the I Ching, Sufism, Shamanism, Native American spirituality) and a variety of supernatural phenomena and belief systems (channeling, Wicca, neopaganism, harmonic convergence, crystals). The New Age also claimed certain spiritualistic branches of environmentalism like Gaia worship and featured a variety of therapeutic disciplines (meditation, herbalism, holistic medicine, est, transactional psychology, and Arica). The movement "synthesized Western psychology, the occult, and Eastern spirituality."[75]

Although it possessed earlier antecedents, the New Age emerged circa 1971. "By that year," concluded the editors of the *New Age Encyclopedia*, "Eastern religion and transpersonal psychology (the key elements needed to create the distinctive New Age synthesis) had achieved a level of popularity, and metaphysical leaders could begin to articulate the New Age vision." *The East West Journal*, the first national periodical to serve the emerging movement, began publication in 1971, and Werner Erhard established est, the first and most influential self-motivation training seminar. In 1972, Baba Ram Dass, a "transformed refugee from the psychedelic age," appeared as the movement's first major prophet and published *Be Here Now*, the first of a series of influential treatises. That same year, the first national directories of New Age networks appeared: *The Year One Catalog* and the *Spiritual Community Guide*.[76]

By the late 1970s, the "consciousness revolution" had spread across the United States, reaching far beyond the remnants of the Sixties counterculture. From inexpensive yoga classes at the neighborhood YMCA to "luxurious awareness cruises" in the Caribbean, a vast network of therapeutic and spiritual outlets emerged, serving millions of Americans "dissatisfied with their lives, looking for a direct experience with God, or just plain bored." In 1973, even Star Trek actor Leonard Nimoy got in on the act, publishing *You and I*, his own collection of ponderous spiritual poems and kitsch poster photographs. One cynic claimed that the movement promised "a new you to anyone who can pay for it."[77]

The New Age spawned its own theologians: David Spangler, author of *Emergence: The Rebirth of the Sacred;* Marilyn Ferguson, whose bestselling *The Aquarian Conspiracy* became the movement's bible; and dissident Roman Catholic priest Matthew Fox. Fox's courses at Holy Name College in California included massage, yoga, tai chi, and guest lectures by Starhawk, a self-described witch. His book *Original Blessing* challenged Catholic doctrine's "overemphasis" on original sin. Father Fox also favored the ordination of women, gay rights, and rigorous environmentalism. Eventually the Vatican's Congregation for the Doctrine of Faith disciplined Fox for his unorthodox teachings.[78]

The awareness movement also had a spiritual center—the Esalen Institute, a place to soak up spirituality from the most respected gurus of the new consciousness while soaking in the clothing-optional hot tubs overlooking the Big Sur coast. Roughly ten thousand people a year journeyed to the institute's central California campus, attending seminars and bunking with roommates in rustic accommodations. Buckminster Fuller, Paul Tillich, Fritz Perls, and Spalding Gray all led seminars at Esalen. Ida P. Rolf founded her Guild for Structural Integration there and perfected the deep massage technique known as "Rolfing." Arica therapy and transactional psychology developed at Esalen. The institute became "a mecca for an entire generation, building ladders to higher consciousness faster than the pilgrims who flocked there could climb them."[79]

Esalen cofounder Michael Murphy functioned as something of the conscience of the human potential movement, policing some of the charlatans and fast-buck operators who threatened its serious spiritual mission. Esalen thus remained in tense relations with est, perhaps the movement's most notorious creation. Est—Erhard Seminars Training—was an awareness training program that offered a new life after a marathon $250 seminar. In founder Werner Erhard's words, est would force you to "throw away your belief system, tear yourself down, and put yourself back together again." Est led trainees to an experience "of the world as it is without the intercession of human understanding," and the seminars became phenomenally successful in the late 1970s. Country pop singer John Denver "got it." Sitcom actress Valerie Harper got it and testified on television that est had changed her life. "I got it!" confessed *Mademoiselle* correspondent Lisa Schwarzbaum, "arranged an equitable rent agreement with my landlord, handwashed eight blouses, swept my floor and now arrive for all appointments ten minutes early. If you have $250 and sixty hours to spare, there is an excellent chance you too will get it if you take est."[80]

Still, est's founder and guru, Werner Erhard, never could shed the stench of the all-American huckster. Born Jack Rosenberg, near Philadelphia, Erhard left his wife and children and ran off to St. Louis with a young woman named June Bryde (she became Werner's second wife, Ellen Erhard). After dabbling in scientology, Zen Buddhism, and encyclopedia sales, Erhard acquired a reputation as a motivational speaker and landed in the San Francisco Bay area.[81]

There, according to est legend, Erhard "got it." He navigated through a life-transforming experience on a California freeway into a higher spiritual plane. "To relate what I experienced to time is a true lie," Erhard told the *New York Times Magazine* in 1976. "It did not happen in time. . . . It didn't happen in some place. I wasn't on the freeway in my wife's car on the way to the city." Conceding that "to put it in the language I must locate it for you," Erhard asserted, "that does damage to it. There were no words attached to it. No feelings, no attitudes, no body sensations."[82]

Erhard transmitted his epiphany, what he and est adherents called "getting it," through intensive group training. The seminars permitted few bathroom, food, and sleep breaks, sometimes locking trainees in one room for eight hours. Spartan seating arrangements mortified the body, senseless repetition bored the mind, and blunt abuse formed an integral part of the training. "Don't give me your goddamn belief system, you dumb motherfucker," trainers castigated. "That's why your whole life doesn't work. Get rid of that shit." One San Francisco State professor described the training as "de-hypnosis"—an attempt "to release the individual from the cultural trance, the systematic self-delusion, to which most of us surrender our aliveness." At the end of the seminar, he "felt a surge of life."[83]

Est, Esalen, Rolfing, Zen, yoga, Arica, channeling, transactional psychology—the diverse strands of New Age spirituality—shared common features. First, many New Agers had abandoned the religious traditions of their birth, finding their inherited faiths unfulfilling. One scholar surmised that the baby boom generation, coming of age in the 1950s and early 1960s when organized religion had lost much of its spiritual dimension, became a "generation of seekers," restoring spirituality to its rightful place in religious life as they reached maturity. At the same time, many resented what they saw as the failed, bankrupt religious traditions of Western culture.[84]

Second, the New Age movement lacked any precise dogma or doctrine. On the contrary, individuals freely selected among multiple options in the "spiritual supermarket." Shoppers chose among "name brands of multifarious spiritual undertakings" but sought one kind of nutrition: self-discovery. Individual choice mattered so much because self-realization remained the seeker's objective.[85]

Third, New Age spirituality revolved around the ideal of transformation. "New Agers," the editors of the *New Age Encyclopedia* explained, "have either experienced or are diligently seeking a profound personal transformation from an old, unacceptable life to a new, exciting future." Spiritual rebirth, which like the evangelicals' experience of divine grace almost instantly transformed their lives, ensured that New Agers left behind "a life dominated by a set of negative aspects—oppressive 'orthodox' modes of thought, dysfunctional exploitative relationships, poverty, illness, boredom, purposelessness and/or hopelessness." Everyday life for New Agers "becomes one of openness and new equalitarian relationships with a sense of abundance, regained vitality and health, excitement, intensity, new meaning, and a new future."[86]

Critics, however, derided the personal awareness movement as solipsistic, a selfish shirking of social responsibility. One historian even called Werner Erhard "a kind of John the Baptist of Reaganism," purveyor of a "brutally individualistic message" that glorified the self at the expense of all social connection.[87] But New Agers rejected the charge, seeing personal transformation as the prerequisite for and the key to social revolution. A person's chief responsibility remained "working on one's self," but when enough people had attained New Age consciousness, a sort of critical mass would be reached, and new ways of thinking and being would prevail. "The essence of the New Age," according to its principal chronicler, "is the imposition of that vision of personal rebirth onto society and the world. Thus the New Age is ultimately a social vision of a world transformed, a heaven on earth."[88]

A handful of New Agers followed the lead of the writer David Spangler, who hoped to build the New Age immediately. Spangler sought to reorganize American business and politics around New Age principles. But while some New Agers were also social activists, the movement continued to emphasize personal growth. Most New Agers eschewed working through established political or institutional channels, relying instead on the imminent revolution in consciousness to foment social and political reform.[89]

On the face of it, the spiritual ferment of the New Age seemed to share little in common with the evangelical revival. In fact, one conservative Christian devoted an entire book to a denunciation: *The New Age Movement in Prophecy*. The book portrayed New Age seekers as "part of a cosmic conspiracy to install the Antichrist." Prominent Christian preachers denounced various New Age outlets as dangerous cults and threats to received religion.[90]

Yet the New Age did form part of a broad evangelical awakening in the sense of a faith based on a personal relationship with the divinity. Religious pilgrims of the 1970s, from New Age to New Right, shared the conviction that individuals needed to experience the divine directly—to feel God, not just hear about or study his commandments. They viewed themselves as dissenters, outsiders locked in struggle against unredeemed or unevolved America.

Even many American Roman Catholics turned toward this more personal God. Writing in *Christian Century,* editor-at-large Sally Cunneen reflected "On Being Roman Catholic in '72." Her own and her fellow communicants' disillusionment with "the one, true church" had produced an unexpected "move toward renewal" in American Catholicism, leaving her "free to seek Christ and the Father he obeyed through the changing Roman tradition as I relate my faith to my own life experience." Another lay Catholic, a participant in a 1980s study of religion among the baby boom generation, described a quiet sort of evangelical reformation within the church. "I can't live by what the church says, y'know," she told an interviewer. "I have to check my own self out with God."[91]

"Privatized spirituality" and the loss of the religious middle alarmed many observers, among them the authors of the 1985 sociological survey *Habits of the Heart.* One subject of that study, Sheila Larson, told interviewers, "I believe in God. I'm not a religious fanatic. I can't remember the last time I went to church." But Sheila nonetheless believed religion played a central role in her life. "My faith has carried me a long way. It's Sheilaism. Just my own little voice."[92]

"Sheilaism" took root in the 1970s. After 1970, the great American centrifuge spun freely, distributing visionary communities, new subcultures with newly discovered identities, across the American continent. Oddly, these new outposts concentrated in one half of the United States. From Jerry Falwell's church to the Esalen Institute, from the retirement villages of Florida and Arizona to the snowbirds in the Texas Rio Grande Valley, from the Christian recording studios of Nashville to the evangelical bookstores of Orange County, the nation's religious and communal pioneers plugged in across the southern tier of the nation. From Virginia down to Florida, across the Old Confederacy and through the Southwest to southern California, intrepid Americans settled in the Sunbelt. There they would wage a second war between the states—not with arms but with votes, dollars, and songs.

4

THE RISE OF THE SUNBELT AND THE "REDDENING" OF AMERICA

"SOUTHERN MAN, BETTER KEEP YOUR HEAD." With those words, singer-songwriter Neil Young handed down his indictment of southern life, his twangy rock 'n' roll ridicule of the ignorance, the brutality, the emptiness of poor white southern culture. "Southern change gonna come at last," Young promised in 1971, opening a decade-long debate through the pop charts on the fate of the redneck and the future of Dixie.

Seldom does sustained political debate appear explicitly on the FM radio band, but Young received an answer in 1974 from a group of north Florida good ol' boys. Calling themselves Lynyrd Skynyrd in mocking tribute to their high school gym teacher, Skynyrd wrapped themselves in the Confederate flag and adamantly defended the lifestyle and worldview of their fellow white southerners. "We heard Neil Young sing about her, we heard ol' Neil put her down," the band rejoined in its 1974 hit single "Sweet Home Alabama." "We hope Neil Young will remember/Southern Man don't need him around anyhow."

Young accepted this rebuke graciously (he repeatedly maintained that he thought "Sweet Home Alabama" a better song than "Southern Man"). But Young recognized, as did so many Americans north and south, that southern change had come at last. A quarter-century-long economic revolution had blown its way through the region. Bulldozers had ploughed under farms and forests; new factories and highways carved up hunting grounds; dams, power plants, and pollution had ruined rustic streams and ponds where many a man had spent many an afternoon fishing and drinking. Electric-powered air-conditioning cut through the unbearable heat and humidity of the long southern summer, increasing productivity, attracting businesses and skilled workers from the frostbitten, fast-paced North, and making the traditional southern lifestyle a thing of the past, the stuff of nostalgia.[1]

As the newest new South arose, with its North Carolinian Research Triangle, its NASA Space Centers, and its air-cooled glass office towers, the barbarism of southern life, the viciousness of segregation and racism, also withered. The heroic struggles of the civil rights movement had eliminated Jim Crow, the region's system of racial separation and degradation. Black southerners had broken down the most egregious barriers to their political participation and economic advancement. "I believe the South is gonna rise again," country singer Tanya Tucker crooned in 1974, "but not the way they thought it would back then. I see everybody hand-in-hand."

Of course, racism did not disappear even if the law forbade its worst public manifestations. Alabama governor George Wallace, famous for his uncompromising devotion to "Segregation now, Segregation forever," had won the loyalty of most white southerners with his recalcitrant defense of their embattled way of life. Wallace had won the South in the 1968 presidential election; only a would-be assassin's bullet prevented him from making another strong race four years later. Lynyrd Skynyrd honored Wallace in song, making it clear that they too "still loved the governor."

Still, by 1970, many white southerners, particularly those leading the economic upsurge, realized that such recalcitrance could not last. A rising South, in need of investment dollars and executive talent, could not afford a reputation for intolerance and backwardness. A herd of racial moderates, including Georgia's Jimmy Carter, stampeded the statehouses of the South, promising to bring the region into the national mainstream. As one official report put it, the fabled new South finally seemed to have arrived in the 1970s. "After 100 years as a prodigal region," the South was "coming home to the national family."[2] Change really would come at last.

In fact, "Southern Man" soon seemed even more prophetic. Three years after the release of "Sweet Home Alabama," a single-engine Convair 240 airplane carrying Lynyrd Skynyrd crashed into a swamp in Gillsburg, Mississippi. The accident claimed the lives of four people, including bandleader Ronnie Van Zandt, ending the career of Lynyrd Skynyrd and silencing its neo-Confederate message.[3]

Indeed, in September 1974, a few years before the Skynyrd plane crash, one event seemed to dramatize the last gasp of the hard-drinking, intolerant, violent way of life the band celebrated and the maturation of a new, suburban southern culture. As the nation bade farewell, for the first and only time in its history, to a sitting president of the United States, it simultaneously said good-bye, not once, but fifty-seven times in fifteen days, to a devil-may-care man on a motorcycle named Robert Evel Knievel.

Barnstorming across the country on his "Evel Knievel Says Goodbye" tour, the daredevil motorcyclist never failed to remind his audiences that no president had ever made a tour like this, no man had ever accomplished the feat he was about to attempt. Brandishing a gold-encrusted, diamond-studded hollow cane filled with vials of bourbon, Knievel tirelessly promoted his "farewell"— a jump across Idaho's Snake River Canyon aboard his "sky cycle," a red, white, and blue cross between a missile and a motorcycle. The rock-walled canyon reached nearly a mile across a 540-feet-deep chasm; Knievel's engineer, one of the leading designers of the Polaris missile and the Saturn rocket, gave him only a fifty-fifty chance of surviving the jump.

Millions of dollars awaited Knievel if he landed safely; television rights fees alone guaranteed $6 million (with expectations of earning twice that much from closed-circuit viewing sales); royalties from Evel Knievel toy cycles and Snake River Canyon jump apparel promised even more. But with several million dollars already in his bank accounts, Knievel insisted that cussedness and a sense of honor, not cash, had induced him to lay his life on the line. "I got drunk one night in Moose's Place in Kalispell, Montana," Knievel told an assembly of reporters in Los Angeles. "They had a picture of the Grand Canyon on the Wall. The more I drank the smaller it looked. I said I could do it and a man can't do anything better in this life than keep his word."[4]

The federal government had forbidden him from catapulting across the Grand Canyon, so Knievel leased land on the Snake River in Idaho instead. As he said goodbye to his almost all-white fans, Knievel made no attempt to disguise his loyalties: his contempt for liberals in Washington, for "women's libbers," for the speed limit and a full night's rest. Knievel was a tobacco-chewing, beer-guzzling good old boy; he was not sophisticated, not cosmopolitan, not a sober, besuited technocrat, certainly not black or Latino or ethnic.

Not surprisingly, the national press—the columnists and commentators of urban America—mocked Knievel. *The Nation* magazine denounced Snake River Canyon as "The Great Rip-Off."[5] Conservative commentator George Will described it as a "foul enterprise."[6] The press assigned to cover the attempt joked about holding a pep rally for the canyon. So palpable was their disdain for the bikers, the rebel yellers, the mobile home denizens and bourbon drinkers who descended on Twin Falls, Idaho, to watch the jump that one reporter wrote, "Even though the canyon is the underdog, it is rapidly becoming our sentimental favorite."[7]

Knievel appeared to many observers as a relic of a dying way of life, the "last of the white boys." His bravado bespoke a man with nothing left to lose. His farewell tour sounded the death knell for a stereotyped redneck way of life that much of the South was putting behind it—sexist, racist, free drinking, irresponsible, poor. Knievel represented a vanishing breed, increasingly isolated in an urbanizing (and suburbanizing) region, a land becoming more moon shot than moonshine, more entrepreneurial than agricultural. *Redneck*—a word that in the 1960s aroused dread, fear, and contempt—was becoming a romantic term for a lost world. Middle-class people used it, the novelist V. S. Naipaul observed, to describe a disappearing breed of virile, unintellectual man, "someone who wouldn't mind saying 'shit' in company."[8] Someone like Evel Knievel.

Thirty thousand people lined the canyon on September 8, a hot, windy day, with gritty white dust blowing everywhere. Knievel had promised the "coldest beer in the world" to everyone if his jump succeeded, and most of the audience craved just that by the time an afternoon of preliminaries ended and Knievel climbed into his sky cycle.

The attempt proved a major disappointment for both Knievel's fans and his enemies. A parachute opened before take-off, so the sleek rocket-cycle limped awkwardly off the launching pad, never reached full speed, and immediately began fluttering down into the canyon. Knievel remained aboard as the rocket slammed into rock, then perched on a ledge above the Snake River. Just sixteen minutes after the launch, a helicopter returned Knievel to the top of the canyon. The daredevil met the press, smiled for the cameras, and headed for the hired car that would bring him to the airport. As Knievel's limo left the launch site, it quickly screeched to a halt. Someone had let the air out of his tires.[9] The last of the white boys faded from the national scene.

But southern white culture did not crash with Lynyrd Skynyrd and Evel Knievel. It survived and flourished, promoting a mainstream, modernized version of itself. A transformed, commercialized southern white spread across the country, finding new resonance and influence in central Alabama and the Central Valley of California, in West Virginia and western Kansas, Nevada and Arizona.

"Bubba," the archetypal poor white working man, might have gone the way of the dinosaur, but his descendant—what cartoonist Doug Marlette (the creator of the comic strip *Kudzu*) called "faux Bubba"—was on the rise. Hundreds of thousands of white Americans, most of them residing in the states spanning the southern rim of the nation from the Carolinas to Florida and across to southern California, considered themselves "half a redneck," to quote a Mississippian interviewed by V. S. Naipaul. They were bankers and engineers, suburbanites and retirees, but they proudly displayed the badges of a domesticated, commercialized redneck outlook: driving pickup trucks, listening to country music, watching stock car races, and flying Confederate flags. They were not the plantation overseers or the ignorant hillbillies of the past, but they rejected the political and social outlook of the Frostbelt and the New Deal. The Evel Knievels all but vanished from the landscape and in their place stood respectable citizens, albeit ones who looked toward fishing holes and country scenes as their ideals rather than college campuses and urban brownstones. The commercialization, export, and political awakening of the faux Bubba had begun.[10]

The Sunbelt Boom and the "Second War Between the States"

A century after the last shot of the Civil War was fired, the South had at long last accepted defeat. In the wake of the civil rights revolution and the economic boom, the region no longer clung to a "southern way of life." But a hundred years later, after World War II, this "loser" reaped the spoils of victory. The Sunbelt South boomed in the 1970s while the old industrial heartland faced almost catastrophic decline. The *New York Times* devoted a four-part series to Dixie's resurgence: "All day and through the lonely night, the moving vans push southward, the 14-wheeled boxcars of the highway, changing the demographic face of America." As the United States approached its bicentennial, "a restless and historic movement" shifted people and power away from the northern states that had dominated American life since the nation's birth. Regional conflict once again captured national attention. *Business Week* even ran a cover story on "The Second War Between the States."[11]

This battle was fought not over race but over government largesse. It specifically revolved around an arcane statistic, the federal balance of payments. Leaders of the Frostbelt, the industrial belt of the Northeast and Midwest, complained that their states paid the lion's share of federal taxes even though most of the money was spent in the South and Southwest. While the Frostbelt contributed more dollars in taxes than it received in federal spending, the Sunbelt won a favorable balance of payments. Northern leaders blamed the imbalance for the decline of the Rustbelt—for the southwesterly migration of people, jobs, and money in the 1960s and 1970s. During that period, Alabama, the slowest-growing Sunbelt state, had expanded its job rolls at twice the rate of New England and four times as fast as New York and Pennsylvania.

New York governor Hugh Carey led the Frostbelt offensive. If federal spending was not redirected northward and the decline of the Frostbelt reversed, it would become, in Carey's words, "a great national museum" where tourists would "see industrial plants as artifacts" and visit "the great railroad stations where the trains used to run." The Arab oil embargoes of 1973 and 1979 intensified this emergency. Skyrocketing oil prices brought hardship to the Northeast and Midwest, while in the Oil Patch—the energy-rich southwestern states of Texas, Louisiana, and Oklahoma—prosperous new migrants pasted bumper stickers on their cars in response to Carey's anguished call for redress that read, "Let 'Em Shiver in the Dark."[12]

The Frostbelt's grievance peaked in 1976. Carey and his colleagues in northern statehouses formed the Coalition of Northeast Governors to lobby Washington for more generous aid. At the same time Massachusetts congressman Michael Harrington organized the Midwest-Northeast Economic Advancement Coalition, a caucus of about 200 congressmen dedicated to redirecting federal dollars north of the Mason-Dixon line. "Like blacks, Hispanics, women and homosexuals," one New Yorker complained, "Northeasterners are an oppressed minority. We are only beginning to realize how badly the federal government discriminates against us."[13]

Sunbelt leaders responded vehemently. Newspapers blamed the Frostbelt's malaise on its own inept and misguided policies. Southern politicians organized their own counterlobbies. "We are going to be eaten alive," Georgia governor George Busbee warned, "if we don't wake up and react." The battle became so heated that prominent national officials, like Texas senator Lloyd Bentsen and President-elect Jimmy Carter, tried to salve the regional wounds. Carter promised to deliver funds to the areas that needed them most "on a community-by-community basis" rather than "North versus South."[14]

This battle over the federal balance of payments highlighted a broader regional division—a deeper cultural and political conflict that was emerging in the early 1970s. In 1969, Kevin Phillips first diagnosed this sectional cleavage. Coining the term *Sunbelt,* Phillips identified a booming region stretching across the continental underbelly of the United States from Virginia and Florida to southern California. In *The Emerging Republican Majority,* Phillips portrayed the emerging South and West as the seedbed of a conservative majority in the United States, the foundation for a generation of Republican dominance in national politics.

Phillips's analysis spawned considerable ballyhoo when it appeared as *The Emerging Republican Majority* in 1969. *Newsweek* called the book "the Political

Bible of the Nixon Era," and although Phillips repeatedly denied it, many pundits considered Phillips's compilation of graphs and charts to have been the blueprint for Nixon's "southern strategy," his successful effort to win the White House by bringing white southerners into the Republican electoral coalition. Writing in *Esquire*, liberal commentator Garry Wills was impressed, and depressed, by Phillips's designation of the Sunbelt as "a new geographic and demographic phenomenon of great importance." Wills looked fearfully at this growing region, seeing "a particularly bilious compound of the new and the old, of space programs and retirement villas, honky-tonks and superconservatism."[15]

A second controversial book, published in 1975, ratified and reiterated Phillips's argument concerning regional conflict. In *Power Shift*, Kirkpatrick Sale, a veteran of the 1960s radical left, reached similar conclusions. Sale, too, noted a "power shift" from the Northeast to the "southern rim," but he dreaded the new power of the Sunbelt as much as Phillips had anticipated it. According to Sale, the pillars of the southern rim, the bases for its spectacular growth and its waxing cultural power, were a handful of large industries: corporate agribusiness, defense, aerospace, oil, and leisure. Atop this economic foundation rested a conservative, reactionary, racist cowboy culture. From Orange County, North Carolina, to Orange County, California, the "3 Rs" defined the southern rim; not reading, 'riting, and 'rithmetic, but "racism, rightism, and repression."

So whether you cheered it like Kevin Phillips or feared it like Kirkpatrick Sale, few doubted in 1970s America that a resurgent conservative and potentially Republican Sunbelt was a force to be reckoned with. People of all sorts flocked South. The Sunbelt, after all, had hosted the religious revival of the 1970s. Into the region white Americans had fled the heterogeneity and the racial conflict of northeastern cities. There the elderly had built their own separate communities, and suburban shopping centers sprang up.

Sunbelt cities, the fastest-growing areas in the nation, reflected the privatism, the insularity, that was coming to dominate American life. These were cities without downtowns—vast sprawls where no one walked the streets and suburban malls served as the principal public meeting spaces. "Atlanta is the apotheosis of suburban malldom," William S. Kowinski declared in his study, *The Malling of America*. As for Houston, the other great Sunbelt city of the Seventies, its downtown had become a forest of skyscrapers, office buildings, and hotels with little connection to the streets around them. The city's real center—the Galleria shopping mall—rose up a few miles to west. "All of these environments are internal," Kowinski noted, controlled, private spaces "fed by the air-conditioned, rolling environments of automobiles."[16]

The *San Diego Union* saw in the rise of the Sunbelt not just a new regional balance of power, but "America II emerging from the diminished promise of America I." The citizens of America II, the new majority of Americans living in the South and West, were innovators—sick of intrusive government and inhospitable communities. They were "building new kinds of cities less centralized and more livable than the congested urban centers of the North and East."[17]

Commentators could see in the Sunbelt the dawning of a new America because the power shift manifested itself in every aspect of American life, including the popularity of football as a spectator sport. During the 1970s, NFL football supplanted baseball as America's premier professional sport (the old national pastime would regain some ground a decade later). Baseball, despite its pastoral nature, remained closely associated with urban America, with the old industrial heartland. Before 1958, Missouri marked both the southern and western extreme of major league baseball in the United States. Even in the 1980s, only three of twenty-six major league baseball teams competed in the South. Meanwhile, the National Football League had placed twice as many teams in the Old Confederacy. It opened up the Florida market, one of the anchors of Sunbelt growth, twenty years before baseball would place a team in the Sunshine State.

During the 1970s, the Dallas Cowboys football club, under the computerized direction of their Christian technocrat coach Tom Landry, earned the moniker "America's Team." Coach Landry emerged as the quintessential Sunbelt man—half committed conservative and defender of traditional lifestyles, half entrepreneurial innovator.

The prominence of football was but a single, visible symptom of the region's continuing transformation since World War II. The dimensions of change alone proved staggering. A swarm of people headed South in the 1950s, 1960s, and 1970s. Retirees purchased condos in Florida or drove shiny new mobile homes across the southern rim. The armed forces ordered millions south for boot camp and active service, and eventually many decided to spend their retirements and pursue new careers in the Sunbelt. The defense and aerospace industries filled the suburbs surrounding Los Angeles, Houston, Dallas, Las Vegas, Atlanta, and North Carolina's Research Triangle Park. Between 1970 and 1990, the South's population exploded by 40 percent, twice the national rate.

Meanwhile, many laid-off industrial workers fled the Rustbelt for opportunities in the Oil Patch or Florida. Although black southerners and quite a few poor whites continued to migrate northward through the 1950s and 1960s, the southern states experienced rapid population and employment growth, far outstripping the rival Frostbelt.

These gains in people and jobs reflected industrial diversification—a shift from the rural, farm-based economy of the plantation South to the high-tech, service, and industrial labor force of today. Before World War II, more than a third of the southern workforce remained on the land, and the lion's share of its industrial workers toiled in low-paying, labor-intensive mills—making cotton textiles or hosiery, sawing lumber, distilling turpentine and tar for ships. The economy of plantation and cotton mill barely fed and clothed the region's people, poorly housed them, did not even shelter them from disease. One 1938 report described the South as a belt of "sickness, misery, and unnecessary death."[18] The region offered few profit opportunities that might lure investment capital or managerial expertise, and even fewer fat pay envelopes to stimulate consumption and finance economic expansion.

By the 1970s, that had all changed. The South had shed its rural, agricultural heritage. Certainly many southerners continued to rely on the product of field, forest, and mine for their livelihoods, but no more so than in other sections of the country. Much of the rural culture disappeared: mechanical cotton-pickers staggered across the fields, replacing departed sharecroppers. The tradition of the "furnish," allowing tenant farmers hunting, wood gathering, and fishing rights on neighboring lands, disappeared as bulldozers ploughed under those acres. New crops, especially soybeans and livestock, covered ground that had once been dedicated almost exclusively to cotton or tobacco. Meanwhile, modern industries—electronics, defense, transport equipment, and government—grew rapidly.

Sunbelt boosters credited their region's boom to its favorable business climate. The Fantus Service, a consulting group, confirmed the South's reputation for hospitality to industry in 1975 when it placed Texas at the top of its list of business climate rankings. Alabama placed second, Virginia third, and South Carolina, North Carolina, and Arkansas helped round out the top ten. "Northerners are missing the key point about the Sunbelt's boom," *Fortune* reported in 1977. "It's booming in great part because it's pro-business—and Northern cities, by and large, aren't."[19]

But just what accounted for the Sunbelt's attractiveness to industry, skilled workers, and educated managers? Which factors really drove the region's development? First, there was the South and Southwest's warm weather and abundant resources. A tropical climate and beautiful beaches lured millions of people, with billions of dollars in their pockets, to Florida. Mild winters and recreational opportunities throughout the region appealed to retirees and their families, to the many educated northerners who worried increasingly about their "quality of life."

These "citizens of America II" were many things, but they were not union members. And low labor costs for industry, especially low levels of union membership, was another major ingredient in the Sunbelt's favorable business climate. In 1976, one-quarter of the nation's nonagricultural workers carried union cards; these men and women had pulled themselves up from the assembly line into a solid middle-class existence. Working people built homes and communities with the help of the United Auto Workers in Flint, Michigan, the United Steelworkers in Pittsburgh, the Brewery Workers in Milwaukee, or the Longshoremen in Brooklyn. These unions and these communities had risen with the great industrial revolution in the heartland, and they were falling with it too. Union halls, once centers of social life, emptied as membership declined and factories closed down.

In the South, however, only 14 percent of nonfarmworkers belonged to unions in 1976. And as time passed, the nation more and more resembled the South. By the late 1980s, only 16 percent of American workers remained in unions; a big reason for the steady drop was the continuing movement of jobs from the union shop Frostbelt to the nonunion Sunbelt, from heavy manufacturing like steel and autos to Sunbelt industries like electronics and aerospace.

For their part, southern and western state governments spared no effort to maintain union-free environments. In the 1950s, most Sunbelt states enacted so-called right-to-work laws—antiunion regulations that restricted labor organizers and limited fund raising by unions. Most telling, they outlawed the closed shop (where all employees must be union members) and often banned the so-called union shop (the arrangement whereby all workers in a union factory paid mandatory union dues even if they chose not to join the union). Right-to-work laws cut the legs right out from under labor organizers in the Sunbelt, who already faced a difficult struggle in the historically antiunion South and West.

State governments also lured jobs and factories through aggressive promotion and special inducements. They offered generous subsidies to relocating businesses—free land and facilities, publicly financed training programs, and long-term tax abatements. Southern governors became famous for their "fishing expeditions"—ceaseless efforts to reel in businesses from other regions and from foreign nations. In 1970, half of annual foreign investment into the United States went below the Mason-Dixon line.[20]

Still, as Hugh Carey's complaints and the broader Sunbelt-Frostbelt battle dramatized, the decisive factor in the rise of the Sunbelt was government action. Kirkpatrick Sale highlighted this irony—an antigovernment region so dependent on that which it claimed most to despise. The southern rim, Sale declared in *Power Shift*, was "an economy built on money from Washington."[21] Sale might have exaggerated the impact of direct federal handouts in the region, but along with other, more indirect federal programs, government money did reverse the regional balance of power.[22]

Large-scale agribusiness owed its existence and its success to federal agricultural programs. No wonder southern novelist William Faulkner lamented the passing of the rural South by declaring, "We no longer farm in Mississippi cottonfields. We farm now in Washington corridors and Congressional committeerooms." The oil industry drew succor from tax breaks, including the famed depletion allowance, and from subsidized pipeline construction. Meanwhile, the federal highway network kept up a nearly insatiable demand for gasoline. Social security helped to build the region's retirement villas and golf courses. Defense and technology firms depended on military spending. "Our economy is no longer agricultural," Faulkner said. "Our economy is the Federal Government."[23]

Certainly the South and Southwest displayed remarkable prowess at securing federal largesse. Links between Sunbelt politicians and Pentagon brass turned the region into the world's largest and richest fortress and armory. Such efforts made South Carolina congressman L. Mendel Rivers legendary. Into his Charleston district, Rivers, the chairman of the House Armed Services Committee, poured an air force base, a naval base, a Polaris missile maintenance center, a naval shipyard, a submarine training station, a naval hospital, a mine warfare center, and the Sixth Naval District Headquarters. As if that was not enough, defense contractors like McDonnell-Douglas, Avco, GE, and Lockheed established factories in the area. One of the congressman's colleagues joked, "You put anything else down there in your district, Mendel, it's going to sink."[24]

The space program proved yet another bonanza for the South, the clearest example of government action as a tool for regional development. NASA ran Project Apollo, its glamorous, multibillion-dollar moon program, from five separate facilities stretching in a crescent along the Southeast from Florida to Texas. The space program even concentrated its research funds in southern labs and universities.

By the mid-1970s, then, a number of northern leaders awoke to this alliance between government action and Sunbelt boosterism and began worrying about increasing southern power in national affairs. Their fears were well founded.

First, economic growth brought people, and with population came more congressional seats, more electoral votes, more political power. As Kevin Phillips prophesied, the electoral map outlined the decisive significance of Sunbelt votes in national politics. Every president elected since John Kennedy has hailed from the southern rim: Johnson and the two Bushes from Texas, Nixon and Reagan from southern California, Carter from Georgia, and Clinton from Arkansas. (Michigander Gerald Ford, an appointed president, never won a national election.)

Second, the solid Democratic South passed into oblivion. For more than a century, the white South had belonged to the Democrats, the "Party of the Fathers," which had resisted Lincoln and "Black Reconstruction." The South had long remained a one-party culture; its voters were called yellow-dog Democrats because they would vote the straight party line even if the Democrats put a mangy yellow dog on the ballot. After World War II, as the national Democratic party endorsed the civil rights cause, the solid South cracked. A number of southern states cast their electoral votes for General Eisenhower in the 1950s, and the Deep South voiced its resentment against Lyndon Johnson and his civil rights program by supporting Barry Goldwater in 1964. This racial backlash attracted long-time southerners to the GOP; it also helped win Republican votes from some of the new migrants to the southern rim.

The Republican party also harvested the fruits of southern economic development. The businessmen and professionals, managers and engineers who flooded the burgeoning cities and endless suburbs of the Sunbelt were a natural constituency for the GOP. Not only did Republican presidential candidates come to rely on southern votes, but for the first time since Reconstruction, the region began sending Republicans to the House and Senate and to the governors' mansions.

Third, the Sunbelt boom signaled the emergence of a new political force, a new kind of conservatism. For generations, American conservatism had been associated with the moneyed patricians of the Northeast, with Wall Street,

Brooks Brothers, exclusive country clubs, and the "better sort" of prep school. Prudence, fiscal restraint, and noblesse oblige were its hallmarks. By 1970, however, American conservatism was emerging from a slow, painful transformation. As the geographic locus of conservative politics had moved south and west, its nature had changed; it became more populist, more middle class, more antiestablishment.[25]

Along with the bonfire of political power, the Sunbelt boom ignited a cultural revival—the strongest reassertion of southern cultural identity and regional pride since the Civil War. By the early 1970s, embarrassment over segregation had faded away, and the South rejoined the national mainstream on questions of race relations. On the one hand, the worst excesses of southern racism had been outlawed, and African Americans began voting in southern elections. Atlanta sent black representatives to the mayor's office (Maynard Jackson), the state legislature (Julian Bond), and the U.S. House of Representatives (Andrew Young). A new generation of white politicians, led by Governors Rubin Askew of Florida and Jimmy Carter of Georgia, proved that a combination of racial moderation and economic boosterism could win elections in the South. The region no longer remained captive to the extremist politics of overt racial demagoguery.

On the other hand, as southern racial politics became tamer, the rest of the nation became more and more racially polarized. The civil rights struggle had moved northward. As Denver, Boston, and New York exploded in violent disputes over court-ordered busing and affirmative action, the South's new, more genteel version of racial politics became acceptable, even fashionable across the nation. Legal segregation and denying blacks the vote—these were repugnant. But few white Americans approved of busing and other forms of mandatory integration. Even more acceptable—and effective in winning votes—was opposition to government social programs perceived as benefiting blacks: welfare, job training, and urban renewal. In its rejection of the welfare state, the Sunbelt now defined the national mainstream on race relations and political economy. Southerners no longer felt ashamed of their region, no longer were blackballed as bigoted, retrograde, out of step. On the contrary, their culture—at least the Seventies version of it—became increasingly popular in the very places where it had been most disdained.

Redneck Chic

This revival of white southern culture reared up most forcefully in the region's most popular medium: country music. According to country music scholar

Melton McLaurin, lyrical themes in country music passed through three stages after the end of World War II—three eras reflecting the region's economic and social development. Between V-J Day and the mid-1950s, Nashville musicians picked, strummed, and sang about a quaint and peaceful South, full of happy, down-home, plain folk. Attempting to build a national market for their records, this generation of country crooners ironed out their southern accents and twangy guitar solos; they tried to tame and domesticate the South for national consumption.[26]

The Montgomery bus boycott of 1955 and the racial strife that followed it, particularly the dramatic images of white southerners unleashing police dogs or taking aim at black protesters, quickly derailed Nashville's efforts to market a quaint South full of hospitable, down-to-earth people. Rosy portraits of contemporary life all but dropped out of country lyrics in the late 1950s and early 1960s, replaced with a nostalgia for older days, tempered with the acknowledgment of the region's social problems and its people's continuing poverty and hard luck.

But with the Seventies, the tempering of civil rights protest in the South and the first fruits of the Sunbelt boom, a new, defiant, resurgent South found its way into country music. Merle Haggard's "Okie from Muskogee" heralded this trend, but it was Loretta Lynn's 1970 hit "Coal Miner's Daughter" that truly reasserted southern chauvinism. Lynn's unabashed pride in her humble origins and her region's culture unleashed a torrent of more militant southern nationalism from Nashville. The Charlie Daniels Band released "The South's Gonna Do It Again" in 1974. John Denver won the 1975 Country Music Entertainer of the Year Award for "Thank God I'm a Country Boy." Three years later Hank Williams, Jr., recorded "The South's Gonna Rattle Again" and "If Heaven Ain't a Lot like Dixie," and Alabama climbed the charts in 1982 with "Dixieland Delight." These songs mocked the Frostbelt and trumpeted the good life, the relaxed pace, even the prosperity and peace of the new South.[27]

More than that, they boasted a populist, conservative political philosophy. Without overt racial messages, they expressed subtle antiblack or anticity sentiments, usually directed against welfare and government programs. "There's folks who never work and they got plenty," Merle Haggard complained in "Big City." In another song, a slow, mournful ballad, Haggard asked over and over again, "Are the Good Times Really Over?" He longed for former and better days before welfare when "a man could still work and still would," before "microwave ovens, when a girl could still cook and still would." Is "the best of the free life behind us now, are the good times really over for good?" Haggard, of course, promised that they were not. Opposition to liberals, to bureaucrats, to trendy northerners became familiar motifs; in Muskogee, for instance, leather boots were "still in style for manly footwear."

The message and the music of country won increasing popularity throughout the 1970s and 1980s. Country radio outlets opened across the nation, record sales soared, and crossover hits—country songs that shot up the national pop music charts—became commonplace. It appears now that country's audience was broader and wider throughout this period than industry analysts had imagined. *Billboard* magazine long underrated the sales and appeal of country music with its unscientific method of telephone polling.[28]

But even then, keen observers noted the broad national appeal of country and engaged in considerable debate about the boundaries of the genre. Just which musicians should be counted as country performers? Just how southern was the form? On the one hand, southern places and themes dominated the lyrics of country music, and white southerners dominated the industry as writers, performers, and producers. Many commentators portrayed country as the principal treasury of white southern experience, a cultural map of the reemergent Sunbelt South of the Seventies and Eighties.

On the other hand, a number of experts pointed to the national audience for the Nashville sound, the entry of nonsoutherners into the business, and the appeal of the country lifestyle across rural America—in the mountain West, the inland valleys of the Pacific Coast states, the desert Southwest, the Great Plains. Confederate flags flew prominently in all of those places, pickup trucks with gun racks roared down the highways, and stock car races drew hundreds of thousands of devoted spectators.

Country music mapped out a southern cultural politics, cultural geographer Ben Marsh conceded in *Harper's* magazine in 1977, but country flourished not so much in the real South as in a symbolic South. Country lyrics continued to champion poor whites, frequently plotting the working stiff's revenge against welfare chiselers, taxes, and the boss man, taking pride in a hardscrabble, marginal, rural way of life. A cascade of songs explicitly celebrated the virtues of "rednecks" and "hillbillies," transforming these terms of derogation into badges of honor. Johnny Russell's "Red Necks, White Sox, and Blue Ribbon Beer" led the wave in the 1973, followed by Jerry Jeff Walker's "Redneck Mother" and Vernon Oxford's "Redneck! (The Redneck National Anthem)." The paradox these songs presented was that genuine rednecks could not account for the sales of these records. There were too few of them to make up the country audience.[29]

Some of the southern anthems tried to deal with this incongruity. Tanya Tucker's "The South Is Gonna Rise Again," recorded in 1974, showed just how much the rise of the Sunbelt had contributed to the rebirth of southern chauvinism: "I see wooded parks and big skyscrapers/Where dirty rundown shacks stood once before/I see sons and daughters of sharecroppers but they're not pickin' cotton anymore." Tucker's ballad was unusually magnanimous, seeing in the Sunbelt South "human kindness as we forget the bad and keep the good." But she acknowledged that the folks once denounced as rednecks were now drinking scotch and making business deals.[30]

Still, most country songs remained true to the conventions of the genre. They continued telling tales of the poor man, even if the music and the populist conservatism it espoused were embraced by more prosperous people—by millions of migrants to the South's cities and suburbs, refugees from the rural South and the urban North. Most were not rednecks by birth, fewer still rednecks by social position. But they adopted the term *redneck* as a badge of honor, a fashion statement, a gesture of resistance against high taxes, liberals, racial integration, women's liberation, and hippies. Instead of "the Greening of America," the new consciousness predicted by the Sixties counterculture, the Seventies Sunbelt began a redneck revival. One wry observer termed it the "Reddening of America."[31]

The old South had died, and few Americans—southerners included—would have wanted it back if they could only remember it as it truly was. Yet "redneck" culture, in a commercialized form, thrived and spread in the 1970s and 1980s. Country music, cowboy boots, pickup trucks, and even the Confederate flag became familiar badges of an influential American subculture. Millions of middle-class and upper-class Americans became "half a redneck." Along with boots and trucks, these demi-rednecks also brandished a set of shared political attitudes: they resented government interference, although they excluded military procurement from their hit list of despised government programs. They disliked bureaucrats, pointy-headed intellectuals, and "welfare Cadillacs."

Their beliefs and resentments created a potent political force. Sunbelt conservatives accomplished what Sixties radicals had only dreamed of: they captured a political party and won control of the White House. Demi-rednecks formed the foundation for conservative populism, the tax revolt, and the Reaganite assault on the welfare state. The ascendant Sunbelt, a new political force, was primed to accelerate the erosion of American public life.

"RUNNIN' ON EMPTY"

1976–1979

5

JIMMY CARTER AND THE CRISIS OF CONFIDENCE

AMERICA WAITED IN A DEEP FREEZE. BETWEEN THE ELECTION OF Jimmy Carter in November 1976 and his inauguration as president two months later, record cold temperatures gripped the frigid nation. Snow fell on Miami Beach and solid ice stalled barge traffic on the Mississippi, while oil and gas shortages shut down assembly lines and closed schools. In Detroit, the once-proud symbol of American industrial might, the electric company reduced voltage, dimming lights and darkening moods across the state of Michigan. "The great American ride," as novelist John Updike called it—thirty years of unchallenged power, uninterrupted progress, and unbroken prosperity—had run out of gas.[1]

Just then, James Earl Carter, Jr., arrived, prepared to nurse an ailing nation's wounds. "Our people were sick at heart," the new president reflected, and "wanted new leadership that could heal us, and give us once again a government of which we could feel proud." Jimmy Carter's narrow victory in the 1976 election reflected the nation's mood ("hopeful, sort of," as *Time* Magazine phrased it). Carter himself embodied the yearnings and preoccupations of his people; he was truly a man of his times, a man for his times.

Carter emerged from the renascent Sunbelt South. To be sure, in 1976 many Americans continued to treat the South as a suspect nation. They thought, according to Carter, "that since I am a southern governor, I must be a secret racist." But the shoe did not fit; Carter was very much a product of the newest new South. Peanut farmer and nuclear engineer, practical-minded naval officer and deeply spiritual Sunday school teacher, Carter's life recounted the South's odyssey from Cotton Belt to Sunbelt. As governor of Georgia, Carter had built wooded parks and big skyscrapers where dirty run-down shacks stood once before.[2]

Carter also tapped into the upsurge of religious enthusiasm sweeping across the nation. At the time of his inauguration, the Gallup organization observed "the beginning of a religious revival." Since 1970, the number of

Americans reporting a growing role for religion in their lives had tripled. A lot of Americans, the pollsters concluded, had returned to religion for "guidance on how to live in these crowded and affluent times."[3] Carter's sincere and generous faith appealed to his countrymen. Opponents' attempts to portray Carter as an intolerant fundamentalist backfired; even a hostile journalist concluded that he was not a "rigid proselytizer who wants to convert the country to his own vision of small-town, Sunday school values."[4]

In his notorious *Playboy* interview, the one in which he made the famous remark about "feeling lust in his heart," candidate Carter sparred with interviewer Robert Scheer. Scheer tried to make a fool out of Carter. He attempted first to expose Carter's heart-felt religious convictions as a fraud and then to portray him as a fanatic itching to impose religious dogma on an unwilling population. Carter held Scheer off, doggedly demanding respect for his religious beliefs while affirming tolerance for other traditions and compassion for sinners. Carter out-pointed his interviewer, reminding him that Baptist teachings warned against judging one's fellow man and insisting it was "ridiculous" to think he would "run around breaking down people's doors to see if they were fornicating." Scheer himself concluded that Carter was "a guy who believes in his personal God and will let the rest of us believe whatever the hell we want."[5]

His religious beliefs, Carter asserted, made it impossible that he would ever lie or cheat like Richard Nixon. In this respect, Carter tapped into another legacy of the Nixon era; he rode the wave of post-Watergate fears of the imperial presidency. Carter promised to dismantle the White House palace guard: he would have no Haldeman or Ehrlichman standing between him and his staff; he would not centralize power in the White House and undercut his cabinet officers. In a decision his close advisers would later regret, Carter did not even appoint a chief of staff to run the executive office in the first two years of his administration.[6]

At the same time, Carter moved to make the presidency less overbearing, less secret, less regal. He de-pomped the White House, doing away with government cars for his staff (a gesture that saved very little and caused real inefficiency and inconvenience). He got rid of the Prussian-style uniforms Nixon had used to dress the White House guards and ended the practice of playing "Hail to the Chief" upon his arrival. *Doonesbury* cartoonist Garry Trudeau mocked these symbolic acts; Trudeau furnished the Carter administration with a "Secretary of Symbolism." But the gestures appealed to a nation weary from Watergate; they tapped into the widespread revulsion against government that the Nixon years had spawned.[7]

Carter pledged not only to be open and honest. He promised a thoroughly different leadership style than either Nixon or Lyndon Johnson before him. Carter boasted about his lack of ideology, his dearth of fixed political positions. But even before he took office, candidate Carter developed a reputation for "fuzziness," which he defended as a virtue—a tendency to analyze each question individually, a willingness to offer complicated answers to complex questions.[8]

In 1976, in a nation fed up with the old politics and the old politicians, a nation suffering through economic decline and deeply divided over race and ethnicity, Carter's engineering mind-set appealed. Voters appreciated his nonpartisan, problem-solving approach. "The complexity of national policy," one commentator insisted, needed "someone who doesn't see everything the same way, who recognizes most of the very close calls and the complexity of them." Carter "was quite good at that," chief economic adviser Charles Schulze believed, even if, as it eventually turned out, that made for "lousy leadership."[9]

It certainly made for uninspiring oratory. Endlessly frustrating his own speechwriters, Carter distrusted rhetoric altogether. Having cut his political teeth in races against Georgia firebrands Herman Talmadge and Lester Maddox, Carter saw emotional oratory as demagoguery, relics of an irrational politics that had no place in modern America. Carter believed in filling his speeches with hard facts. His favorite word, as candidate and as president, was *comprehensive;* the nation, he believed, needed a comprehensive energy policy, a comprehensive urban policy, a comprehensive approach to health care and the economy. His national energy program contained 113 separate proposals. His staff assembled decision memos with dozens of presidential actions to approve or veto. For welfare reform, the "monster memo" laying out his proposal ran 62 single-spaced pages; for Carter's comprehensive urban policy, a 178-page memorandum included 43 different policy initiatives.[10]

At the outset, voters found Carter's bland style and lack of ideological vigor reassuring—an antidote to the wrongheaded sureties that had landed the nation in Vietnam and Watergate. "Comprehensiveness" appealed too, because Carter portrayed it as the only protection against parochialism. Small and incremental change, Carter asserted, inevitably fell victim to narrow special interests, each inveigling a juicy piece of the pie. Only by wiping the slate clean could Americans protect the national interest and serve the common good.[11]

Texas congresswoman Barbara Jordan had struck this note in her nominating speech for Carter during the 1976 Democratic convention: "This is the great danger America faces, that we will cease to be one nation and become instead a collection of interest groups; city against suburb, region against region, individual against individual. Each seeking to satisfy private wants." Jimmy Carter, she promised, would speak for America. "What we've been trying to do in this Administration," a White House official explained in 1977, "through actions and words, is to restore and recreate our sense of community and of the common good."[12]

Still, Carter's ambitions for rekindling national unity and enacting comprehensive policy could not be confused with profligacy. He shared little in common with 1960s liberal Democrats like Hubert Humphrey, George McGovern, or Ted Kennedy. Carter pledged to balance the federal budget by the end of his first term, a shocking promise at the time. Neither Nixon nor Ford had called for a balanced budget, and for a Democrat, such an appeal amounted to heresy. Carter anticipated, and indeed inaugurated, the fiscal conservatism that would dominate American public policy in the 1980s. "We have learned that *more* is not necessarily *better*," he warned in his inaugural address, "that even our great Nation has its recognized limits, and that we can neither answer all problems nor solve all problems. We can not afford to do everything. . . . We must simply do our best."[13]

In all these ways, Jimmy Carter seemed to feed into and feed off the national psyche in 1976. In that dismal year, when the forced grandeur of the bicentennial barely masked widespread fears of national decline, Carter's modesty and wholesomeness spoke to a national yearning for simpler, quieter times. Even his lack of eloquence seemed reassuring; this straightforward, uninspiring man really would not lie to the American people. But well meaning as Carter was, he would not be able to pull the nation out of its developing malaise. A product of the Seventies, the president could not escape its grip. In the end, the forces that doomed his presidency would also give rise to one of the lasting cultural legacies of the decade. Americans would not seek solace from their government even during a national economic crisis. Looking more to Wall Street than to Pennsylvania Avenue, they took matters into their own hands and upended the financial and political order.

False Starts

Carter's first days in office met with considerable success. He took immediate steps toward reorganizing the executive branch, at once reducing government paperwork and slowing the issue of new regulations. "It is a major goal of my administration," the president declared soon after taking office, "to free the

American people from the burden of over-regulation." Carter made cost-ben-efit analysis a mandatory prerequisite for any new government action, created a regulatory review council to minimize the costs of new regulations, and pro-mulgated a "regulatory calendar" that gave industry notice of proposed regu-lations and the opportunity to oppose them.[14]

Carter also moved to deregulate American business, particularly in the air-line, trucking, banking, and communications industries. In June 1977, Carter appointed Cornell University economist and deregulation guru Alfred Kahn as chairman of the Civil Aeronautics Board. Kahn immediately opened the air-line industry to competition, completing the process after Carter signed the Airline Deregulation Act in 1978. "We effected a really revolutionary change in the relationship of government to business," Kahn asserted. "We overturned the law which had been in existence for years."[15]

Carter's overnight achievements did not end with arcane reforms in regu-latory law and government organization. Just one day after becoming presi-dent, Carter redeemed one of his most controversial campaign promises: his pledge to put the Vietnam War behind the nation by granting a limited pardon to Vietnam draft resisters. He also initiated new jobs programs for unem-ployed veterans.[16]

Still, the major domestic initiatives of Carter's early presidency—the three E's of energy, environment, and economy—proved more difficult nuts to crack. Two weeks after his inauguration, as the United States continued to suffer through an unusually cold winter and a crippling shortage of natural gas, President Carter delivered his first nationally televised address. Wearing an unbuttoned cardigan (and no formal suit coat), Carter announced that within ninety days, by April 20, 1977, he would present a "comprehensive [there's that word again] long-range energy policy."[17]

The "cardigan speech" addressed the long-festering "energy crisis." The nation's dwindling supplies of fuel and reliance on foreign exports had first received national attention in 1973 when the Organization of Petroleum Exporting Countries (OPEC) had punished the United States for its support of Israel by slapping an embargo on oil sales. The Arab oil embargo created des-perate fuel shortages, drove up the prices of gasoline and heating oil, caused long lines at the gas pumps, and humiliated the nation on the international stage. The world's great superpower seemed suddenly toothless, helpless, liter-ally and metaphorically out of gas.

Nixon and Ford had both attempted to resolve the energy crisis, but they found consensus impossible to forge. Only ending price controls could stimulate production of new energy supplies, but unregulated prices would boost inflation and irritate consumers. Nixon and Ford had judiciously avoided the inevitable clash of competing interests. After all, energy policy, according to House Speaker Tip O'Neill, represented "perhaps the most parochial issue that could have ever hit the floor."[18]

In the mid-1970s, although the nation's energy problems remained acute, memories of the embargo were fading, and Americans gleefully returned to their gas-guzzling ways. By the summer of 1976, consumption of gas and electricity had returned to pre-embargo levels and the nation actually imported a greater share of its oil than in 1972.[19] In January, C. W. McCall's novelty record, "Convoy," hit number one on both the country and pop music charts. Capitalizing on the CB (citizens band radio) craze, "Convoy" made popular terms like "Breaker 1-9" and "10-4." The song romanticized an eighty-five-truck convoy that rolled across the country, defying authority and breaking through police barricades. Along with "eleven long-haired friends of Jesus and a chartreuse microbus," McCoy's glorious eighteen-wheelers crashed through toll barriers and police helicopters. (The song even spawned an unsuccessful movie, starring Ali McGraw.) Americans would not easily accommodate to an age of limits.[20]

But Jimmy Carter determined to assault the energy crisis head on. Sporadic fuel shortages, he believed, made the United States vulnerable to foreign blackmail and domestic economic havoc. The Baptist moralist in Carter found the irresponsible waste of precious resources morally repugnant, while the nuclear engineer in him believed that careful study and, yes, comprehensive action could solve the problem. Moreover, an attack on the energy crisis fit Carter's conception of presidential leadership. Only the president, Carter insisted, could be counted on to make policy for the nation as a whole—to consider freezing tenants in Boston as well as oil barons in Austin. Carter set out to formulate a national energy policy, soon known by the acronym NEP (despite its unfortunate echoes of V. I. Lenin's New Economic Policy).

To devise the program, Carter named James R. Schlesinger his special adviser on energy. The appointment of Schlesinger, the secretary of defense under Nixon and Ford, signaled Carter's determination to forge a plan with bipartisan national appeal. The president gave his new energy czar stringent guidelines: to devise the program within ninety days; to make it comprehensive—an all-or-nothing proposal that rival interests could not pick apart; and to maintain total secrecy, so that constituencies in the Congress, the lobbying community, and the nation at large would be unable to influence the plan.[21]

Three months later, Schlesinger prepared to unveil the NEP. The plan envisaged an orderly transition from a long period of "cheap and abundant energy used wastefully and without regard to international and environmental imperatives to an era of more expensive energy with concomitant regard for efficiency, conservation, international and environmental concerns." But the program's details hardly promised order; it included a bewildering array of proposals. Schlesinger proposed conservation measures such as a "gas guzzler tax" on low-mileage cars, tax credits for solar power and home insulation, and new fuel efficiency standards for buildings, cars, and refrigerators. The plan also suggested efforts to "value energy now at its true value"—complicated schemes that would gradually remove price controls on oil and gas. In all, the NEP featured 113 separate proposals.[22]

Carter appeared on national television and presented the highlights of the plan. "Tonight I want to have an unpleasant talk with you about a problem unprecedented in our history. With the exception of war, this is the greatest challenge our country will face during our lifetimes. The energy crisis has not yet overwhelmed us, but it will if we do not act quickly." The fight for a national energy policy, he boldly announced, would become "the moral equivalent of war."[23]

Newsweek reported the speech favorably: "Some of the time he was Jimmy the evangelist, preaching to a nation living in energy sin. Then he was Jimmy the engineer, rattling off statistics and throwing around terms like retrofitting and cogeneration. And then he was Jimmy the leader, summoning the nation to fight the 'moral equivalent of war' and calling on everyone to sacrifice for the commonweal." A Gallup poll showed widespread support for the energy plan and for Carter himself.[24]

Carter sent the NEP up Capitol Hill, where it landed practically dead on arrival. The Senate ignored Carter's plea for an all-or-nothing program; the leadership split up the proposal into six separate bills, each reported to a different congressional committee. That breakup created just the feeding frenzy Carter had feared; lobbyists easily buried much of the plan.[25]

Carter's comprehensive approach—devising a program in secret and presenting it as a finished product—alienated his allies and energized his opponents. Schlesinger not only froze out Congress; he even kept Carter's senior advisers in the dark. The force-fed package infuriated Carter's supporters both inside and outside the White House. Energy policy, the president reflected in his memoirs, was like "chewing on a rock that lasted the whole four years."26

Carter made another frustrating false start in environmental policy. While his predecessors had signed key environmental legislation, Carter was the first successful presidential candidate to campaign on environmental issues, and his administration established an ambitious environmentalist agenda. Early on, Carter focused on reform of the nation's water policy, targeting the massive and massively expensive dams, locks, and canals constructed by the Army Corps of Engineers, the Bureau of Reclamation, and the Tennessee Valley Authority. These projects had long been the scourge of environmentalists, who blamed them for locking up wild rivers, destroying natural habitats, endangering fish and wildlife, and spewing out pollution. The projects also infuriated economy-minded officials, who rightly viewed as wasteful the prized pork barrel spending that pumped federal dollars into the districts of influential members of Congress.27

Carter hoped to dry up the dams' reservoirs of water and cash. Two weeks after his inauguration, he identified twenty-two projects as "prime candidates for termination of funding on both environmental and economic grounds."28 But he was unable—or unwilling—to grasp the political challenges involved in goring so sacred a cow on Capitol Hill. Despite his objections, Congress forced him to accept most of the wasteful, expensive water projects. The president and his administration appeared feeble and blundering.29

Carter's handling of the Tellico dam, the most important environmental controversy of his administration, alienated all parties. The Tellico fight dramatized the rise of a new environmentalist ethos in the United States, a burgeoning movement to preserve the nation's wild places, flora, and fauna. The new environmentalism repudiated the older conservationist ideal, associated with turn-of-the-century reformers like Theodore Roosevelt, who stressed managed, efficient use of natural resources and had dismissed preservationists as sentimental tree huggers. As Tellico dam went up on the Little Tennessee River, a University of Tennessee zoologist established that a tiny fish, the snail darter, would face extinction if its habitat behind the dam was flooded. The Department of Interior placed the fish on the endangered species list, and construction on the dam halted.

Eventually dam supporters in Congress sneaked onto an important appropriations bill a rider ordering the completion of Tellico and exempting the project from the Endangered Species Act and other relevant federal laws.

Carter reluctantly swallowed the poison pill and approved the law. Still, Tellico backers were so unsure this provision would stand up in court that only a few hours after Carter signed the bill, bulldozers were at work, completing the destruction of the snail darter habitat. The Tellico fight radicalized many environmentalists. It revealed Jimmy Carter as an untrustworthy ally and an ineffective president.[30]

Still, nothing else frustrated and confused the administration so much as the nation's stubborn economic maladies. Jimmy Carter entered the White House during a major crisis in American economic life, amid the disintegration of the long, sweet summer of postwar prosperity. Unprecedented in its size, scope, and duration, that boom had touched nearly every American; it lifted blue-collar workers and their families into comfortable middle-class homes, stimulated laggard regions, made possible the liberalism of John F. Kennedy's New Frontier and Lyndon Johnson's Great Society. But during the early 1970s, that bubble burst. Economic growth and productivity advances slowed. A new term, *stagflation,* entered the lexicon, signifying a virtually inconceivable combination of galloping inflation with anemic growth and tenacious unemployment.[31]

This lifeless economy left many policy intellectuals, including Charles Schulze, the future chairman of Carter's Council of Economic Advisers, scrambling to explain what conventional orthodoxy had held impossible. At the same time, OPEC oil shocks, wild international currency fluctuations, and the first serious peacetime shortages in the nation's history made it seem that Americans no longer could control their own economic destiny.[32]

At the same time, Carter had entered the White House with additional commitments to a wide range of other policies—deregulation, energy conservation, minimum wage increases, national health insurance—that cross-cut his basic objectives to restrain inflation and prevent recession. In the short run, for example, decontrolling energy would raise gas prices and threaten layoffs in the automobile industry. Civil service reform required the support of public employees' unions, thus tempering the Carter administration's efforts to cap federal workers' pay raises in the fight against inflation. "One always knew that he wanted to spend as little money as possible," domestic policy adviser Stuart Eizenstat recalled, "and yet at the same time he wanted welfare reform, he wanted national health insurance, he wanted job training programs."[33]

Carter and his key economic advisers attempted to balance these commitments by keeping a quick trigger finger on the policy controls—a tendency to zigzag between stimulus and contraction as economic conditions changed. So often did the administration submit austere March revisions to more expansive January budget proposals that one wag discerned a pattern of holiday cheer followed by Lenten repentance.[34]

Despite the apparent confusion, Carter's economic record formed a clear pattern. The economy boomed, experiencing three years of rapid growth. Real per capita income rose, and unemployment, while remaining high, was lower than in the earlier Ford or later Reagan years. Still, the rapid growth proved unhealthy. Like a cancer, the boom carried with it staggering inflation, a deteriorating dollar, and, finally, a severe election year recession.[35]

At the beginning of the Carter presidency, fiscal stimulus topped the administration's economic priorities. During the campaign, unemployment had been the nation's most pressing concern. A November 1976 Gallup poll reported that 31 percent of Americans ranked joblessness as the most important problem facing the nation; five months later, 39 percent listed unemployment as their chief concern. During the transition, Carter's advisers raced to develop a program, which the president sent up Capitol Hill immediately after he took office. The package included small permanent tax reductions, a public service jobs program, stepped-up spending for public works, and, as its centerpiece, a one-time-only fifty-dollar rebate to every taxpayer.[36]

Despite these generous spending programs, the president tried to hold spending for public works and public service employment well below the levels desired by congressional Democrats. He tried to devise automatic triggers that would shut off program funding as soon as unemployment fell. He fought organized labor and congressional Democrats to moderate increases in the minimum wage. Most important, in April 1977, Carter withdrew the proposed fifty-dollar rebate. Intended as a single, concentrated dose of economic stimulation, the president had harbored doubts about the proposal from the beginning, and as the economy improved and the need for such medicine diminished, he decided to change course. Budget cutters in the Office of Management and Budget thought it a "wise and courageous decision," but the withdrawal unleashed a "firestorm of criticism from Capitol Hill," angering congressional leaders who had shepherded the proposal through the House of Representatives despite their own reservations. The rebate cancellation also made Carter appear a waffler on economic policy, creating an image that he never would shake.[37]

Nonetheless, the thrust of economic policy during Carter's first year pointed mainly in a traditional Democratic direction. Carter signed a minimum wage bill in November 1977. Public works programs created about 200,000 jobs, 425,000 new slots in public service employment and training programs, and a major youth program. "As a result, in part, of the stimulus package," the first-year summary concluded, "the economy *has* improved." These "accomplishments" would soon come to haunt Carter's economic team. The emphasis on unemployment and recovery pursued a combination of policies that heated up the inflationary spiral. More important, first-year policies stoked appetites for more budgetary goodies; they did not teach the constituencies the need for restraint and made sacrifices a tougher sell in years ahead.[38]

So in domestic affairs, Carter made false starts on all three E's. Forced to back off ambitious proposals, he appeared ineffective, impotent. He could neither slake the thirst of congressional leaders for spending in their districts nor tame the demands of influential constituencies. In December 1977, a chastened Carter appeared at a dinner honoring Hubert Humphrey. The president wondered how Senator Humphrey "gets younger and younger" while he grew grayer and older. Senator Humphrey, Carter explained, answering his own question, "has been here in Washington long enough to know how to handle the political scene and I haven't learned yet."[39]

The Great Inflation and the Money Revolution

Nothing so exacerbated this national malaise as the unchecked, out-of-control rage of inflation. The cost of living leaped up at double-digit rates: interest rates reached 20 percent; the value of savings eroded; the prices of meat, milk, and heating oil rose out of sight. "It required no public opinion surveys," journalist Theodore H. White reflected, "to recognize that Americans had begun to shiver at the way prices were rising."[40]

The Great Depression of the 1930s had left an indelible impression on an entire generation of Americans. Memories of Hoovervilles and bread lines had dominated American politics for half a century. The great inflation of the 1970s was such a transformative event. Although few Americans jumped out of windows or rode the rails in search of work, their hard-earned savings accounts became worthless as the insidious wage-and-price spiral ate away the value of their hard-won dollars.

The experience of the Carter years turned many Americans, previously conservative in their financial dealings, into speculators and investors. To let savings sit in a bank in the age of inflation was to lose everything. Alfred Kahn concluded that "the ten years of inflation that we have experienced have given rise to a permanent change in our attitudes toward savings." Americans spent more, borrowed more, and when they saved, demanded higher returns than regulated bank deposits would allow. Financial institutions gradually slipped through the regulatory net, offering a whole new range of products: credit cards arriving in the mail from anonymous institutions far from home, cash management accounts and money market funds, discount stock brokerages and direct-marketed mutual funds. A brave new world of personal finance opened, with all its attendant opportunities and dangers.[41]

A new policy regime emerged as well. From the 1930s through the 1960s, American voters refused to countenance rising unemployment or inaction in the face of an economic downturn. Herbert Hoover remained the bogeyman of American politics. Even Republican presidents Dwight Eisenhower and Richard Nixon aggressively spent and inflated their way out of recessions.

Jimmy Carter exorcised the ghost of Hoover and depression. Inflation became as ominous and as unacceptable as unemployment had once been. In the decades after Carter left the White House, Americans would tolerate draconian policies—tight money, recession, slashed social spending, anemic growth—in order to tame the inflationary spiral. And Jimmy Carter's hapless preaching about a national malaise would rival Hoover's misplaced confidence in rugged individualism after the 1929 crash. Dubbing him "Jimmy Hoover," contemporary commentators suggested that Carter had made "his own name a synonym for economic mismanagement," compiling so bleak a record as to rival "Herbert Hoover's dawdling at the onset of the Great Depression."[42]

The failed battle against inflation was not simply a matter of misjudging the threat. From the start, Carter and his top officials understood the intractability and political dangers that inflation posed. In fact, Carter himself, given his native fiscal conservatism and desire to balance the budget, seemed more alert to inflation dangers than were his principal economic and domestic policy advisers. Even before he took office, the president's confidant, fellow Georgian Bert Lance, warned that Carter could not win reelection if he failed to bring down inflation.[43]

After some token efforts in Carter's first year in office, the administration stepped up its efforts in 1978. Carter announced firm voluntary guidelines on wages and prices and appointed Robert Strauss as special counselor on inflation. Calling on his formidable skills as a lobbyist and wheeler-dealer, Strauss set up an impressive "jawboning" operation, imploring business, labor, and consumers to show restraint. At the same time, President Carter spurned more serious proposals, such as a plan for draconian budget cuts, because

1978 was an election year and congressmen needed to bring home the bacon to their constituents.[44]

Carter's tepid policies could not hold back inflation. In August 1978, chaos in international currency markets dropped the dollar to new lows against the German mark and the Japanese yen. The inflation rate hurtled upward. AFL-CIO president George Meany denounced an agreement with the postal workers that kept pay increases within the administration guidelines, ensuring that the rank and file would reject the contract and infuriating President Carter. In that atmosphere of crisis, Jerry Rafshoon, Carter's image maker and communications adviser, sent the president an impassioned alarm. "It is impossible to overestimate the importance of the inflation issue to your presidency," Rafshoon warned. "It affects every American in a very palpable way. It causes insecurity and anxiety. It affects the American Dream." Rafshoon insisted that the nation remained favorably disposed toward Carter but wanted a "President who is 'in control.'" Failure to "demonstrate some control over inflation will make it very difficult for most Americans to be enthusiastic about your Presidency." Rafshoon recommended the toughest possible anti-inflation program: "it would be difficult to err on the side of too tough a program." Such staunchness, however, would cast down "the gauntlet with George Meany—if not the whole labor leadership. The business community won't be happy either." Carter returned the memo with a handwritten note—"Jerry OK."[45]

But it was not to be. Other advisers convinced the president to delay aggressive action, leaving time for his staff to devise a program and prepare the ground for an announcement.[46] Months of tortuous, internal White House debate culminated in Carter's October 24, 1978, address from the Oval Office. The speech was characteristically modest. Carter confessed to not having all the answers to the inflation problem and called on the American people to join together in the fight, challenging those who say "that we have lost our ability to act as a nation rather than as a collection of special interests." Carter also announced a series of new initiatives. He promised to cut the federal budget deficit for fiscal year 1980 to $33 billion, a hard-and-fast commitment that cheered budget hawks in his administration. He promised to fill only one of every two vacancies in the national service, established new wage and price guidelines, and limited federal procurement to contractors who obeyed those standards.[47]

The speech represented a genuine turning point in administration policy. Until then, most of Carter's advisers had believed that they could control inflation while still fighting unemployment and pursuing other goals. After October 1978, nearly everyone in the White House agreed that real restraint was necessary. Carter signaled this new discipline in the weeks after his speech by vetoing four pieces of legislation, a dramatic change for a president who eschewed the veto during his first years in office.[48]

Carter also appointed Alfred Kahn as his special adviser on inflation and chairman of the Council on Wage and Price Stability. The outspoken former professor and expert on the economics of regulation had won wide acclaim as the architect of airline deregulation and brought instant credibility to the president's battle against inflation. Kahn accepted the job despite serious reservations about the potential effectiveness of the president's program. Inflation, Kahn believed, "was not just an economic problem but a profoundly social problem—a sign of a society in some degree in dissolution, in which individuals and groups seek their self-interest and demand money compensation and government programs that simply add up to more than the economy is capable of supplying."[49]

One journalist described the new inflation czar as "the rumpled professor with the thick stack of briefing papers seemingly sewn to his arm, the man whose combination of self-deprecating wit and breathtaking, almost pathological, candor caused him to say (it sometimes seemed) whatever unedited phrase happened to pop into his head." He is "the kind of guy," *New York Times* reporter James Reston wrote, "who can make failure seem attractive."[50]

And a failure it was. The old tools of economic policy no longer worked. "Everybody's desperate tryin to make ends meet," pop parodist Warren Zevon crooned in a live version of his song "Mohammed's Radio," with lyrics altered to capture the times. "Work all day, they still can't pay the price of gasoline and meat.... Even Jimmy Carter," the verse concluded, "has got the highway blues."[51]

Still, the administration hesitated. The White House refused to tangle with milk and sugar producers; it abandoned a federal pay cap because it riled "important and friendly unions."[52] Then OPEC launched a new round of price increases, prompting even more horrendous inflation. The inflation rate, 6.5 percent in 1977 and 7.7 percent for 1978 despite Carter's best efforts, careened out of control. For 1979, the annual rate hit 11.3 percent, and the administration appeared powerless to deal with it.[53] Not until the final months of his presidency did Carter firmly move to stop inflation. In the fall of 1979, he named Paul Volcker to chair the Federal Reserve Board. Dramatically contracting the money supply, Volcker slowed inflation by strangling the economy and produced a recession that complicated the administration's woes.[54]

By that time, it would be too late to save Jimmy Carter. The president sank to record lows in the approval ratings; the mark of 33 percent approval he amassed in a June 1979 *New York Times*–CBS poll scored lower than even the troughs for Ford and LBJ.[55]

But Jimmy Carter was not the principal casualty of the Great Inflation. Depression babies—people who grew up during the 1930s—possessed a certain approach to life, a certain suspicion about good times, a thriftiness, a tendency to reuse tea bags and never throw anything away. The Great Inflation produced its own generation, altering Americans' relationship to money, government, and each other.[56]

First, Americans developed dramatically new attitudes toward credit and credit cards. In 1973, when Dee Hock, creator of the Visa card, installed his computerized authorization system, credit card spending totaled nearly $14 billion and was growing at a brisk but not outlandish clip of about $3.5 billion a year. But over the next decade it roared ahead, reaching $66 billion by 1982, almost a fivefold increase.[57]

Credit cards made it easier for Americans to borrow, but plastic was not the only reason, or even the main reason, for the broad cultural shifts in attitudes toward spending and debt. Credit cards just provided an easy way to borrow more. In 1975, for instance, credit card debt hovered around $15 billion, but total consumer borrowing reached an astounding $167 billion. By 1979 it had almost doubled again, to $315 billion. Credit cards did not turn thrifty Americans into frenetic borrowers. The Great Inflation did.[58]

Until the 1970s, there had been a generalized resistance to credit and debt. Borrowing remained tainted, a sign of moral weakness. Thrift had long been the great American virtue: remember Benjamin Franklin's admonitions against waste and excess in his *Autobiography*. But with double-digit inflation, thriftiness became just plain dumb. Saving money meant paying for tomorrow's higher-priced goods with yesterday's diminished dollars. Borrowing, on the other hand, made sense. You could purchase something today, before the price went up, and pay for it later with inflated dollars that were worth less.[59]

Writing in the *New York Times*, a young Paine Webber economist named Christopher Rupkey argued that his cohort, the inflation generation, had left behind their Depression baby parents. With baldness and boldness that must have made his elders blanch, Rupkey told his generation to buy now and worry later. "'Never buy what you can't afford' was the admonition of our parents," Rupkey wrote. "Today the statement has been changed to, 'You can't afford not to buy it." More young couples "live in the same comfortable homes and sit in the same sumptuous sofas that are equal or better than those of their parents, many of whom worked for years to obtain what their children get with a simple flash of a credit card. . . . Get your money out of the bank and spend it!" Rupkey concluded, "Inflation gives the most it has to give to those with the largest pile of debts."[60]

A new zest for credit was one major consequence of the Great Inflation. And then there were money market funds. The Great Inflation changed Americans from savers to investors. To do so required a series of major reforms in the world of money and finance. But before any of that could happen, someone had to breach what financial journalist Joseph Nocera called "the Great Wall of Q." The Great Wall of Q, alas, turned out to be far less exciting than it sounded (neither the latest construction of Mao Tse-tung, nor an exotic character on *Star Trek*). It referred to a federal banking regulation that capped the interest rates that banks could pay to depositors—the interest on regular passbook savings accounts. The Federal Reserve, the agency that manned the wall, kept that number very low. As market interest rates rose to 10, 12, 15 percent, the passbook savings rate remained at just 5 percent; it hovered there from 1973 to 1979, when the Fed grudgingly raised it to 5 and 1/4 percent.[61]

Regulation Q had taken effect in 1933, in the midst of the Great Depression, while thousands of banks were collapsing. Many of those banks failed because in the competition for business, they had overpaid depositors, offering high interest rates on savings accounts. Regulation Q prevented banks from spending themselves to death. It helped stabilize the tottering American banking industry of the 1930s.

It also made many a happy life for American bankers, allowing them to live by the sacred 8-4-2 rule: lend money at 8 percent, pay 4 percent for deposits, and be on the golf course by 2. Before the 1970s, hardly anyone complained. But the Great Inflation changed all that. If you put your money in a savings account at 5 percent in a year when inflation reached 8 percent, your money actually lost value. If you kept your savings in a bank at 5 percent when treasury bills (restricted to the wealthy since they began at denominations of $10,000) were paying 9 percent, you were losing the chance to earn greater returns in the open market.

Something had to give. A handful of enterprising businessmen drilled a hole through the regulatory barrier and created the money market mutual fund (MMMF). Like a traditional equity mutual fund, many small investors sent their money to a fund manager who oversaw a large, diverse portfolio. But instead of buying stocks, MMMFs invested in short-term debt instruments. They purchased mainly treasury bills and jumbo certificates of deposit (CDs) of $100,000, which were exempt from Regulation Q. That meant that investors in the fund—small savers—would gain access to market interest at rates high above passbook savings accounts. And because the funds invested in short-term, mainly government securities, risk to the investors' principal remained very small.

As inflation and interest rates climbed, many Americans clambered through the gap in the regulatory wall. In the first couple of years after the government approved the opening of money market funds in 1972, Americans joined hesitantly. Money market funds seemed too different from bank accounts. Deposits were not insured. Patrons could not find fund companies just around the corner. Money market funds remained inconvenient. To get money out, a customer had to send a letter and wait a few days before receiving a check in the mail and cashing it at a bank.[62]

To make money accounts work—to induce Americans to cross the Rubicon from savers to investors—fund managers had to make money market funds look and feel more like ordinary bank accounts. That task fell to a quiet, reserved Boston brahmin, the son of the boss at Fidelity Investments, a Boston-based equity mutual fund company. In 1972 Edward C. Johnson III took over Fidelity Investments in his own right, after the retirement of his father. No one would have guessed at Ned Johnson's financial and managerial genius. Brahmin that he was, he played his cards close to the vest, but he turned out to be one of the principal architects of the money revolution.[63]

Johnson added check writing privileges to the money market fund. This innovation stunned the industry—not so much because of the technical obstacles Fidelity had to overcome to make it work (which were formidable), but because it went against one of the industry's most cherished notions. "Make it easy to put money into a fund," proclaimed an old mutual fund saw, "but hard to take money out." Check writing turned this inherited wisdom on its head; Fidelity made it simpler to take money out of a fund than to put it in. "The philosophy in the mutual fund business has always been, 'Get the money in and hope they [the customers] stay in forever.' Our attitude," Johnson explained, "was that if they could come and go easily, you would end up with a lot more people."[64]

In just a few months Johnson's money market fund, the Fidelity Daily Income Trust (FDIT), pulled in more than $500 million, much of it from people who had never before invested a dollar in a mutual fund company.

But Ned Johnson did not just succeed in making the money market fund a viable alternative to a bank account. His real genius lay in turning financial services into a business that sold goods like any other consumer product industry. "We took ideas from Procter & Gamble," one Fidelity executive told a reporter from *Institutional Investor*. "If one company can sell fifteen different brands of soap flakes," he concluded, "why can't another peddle as many bond funds?"[65]

Johnson and Fidelity broke ground in other ways. At a time when it seemed déclassé, they advertised directly and reached millions of Americans who did not have brokers—people who were not the country club sort likely to have brokers. Fidelity targeted middle-class victims of the Great Inflation—people seeking alternatives to their money-losing passbook savings accounts. As FDIT boomed, Johnson installed a new computerized telephone system so that Fidelity could have direct ties to its customers.[66]

As inflation roared and other companies mimicked Fidelity, the money market fund became king. In 1974, Americans invested only $1.7 billion in money funds; by 1982, the funds held more than $200 billion. The Great Inflation had changed the fundamental calculus. Americans no longer wondered whether to risk their savings in a money market fund. Leaving money in the bank posed the greater danger.[67]

Once Americans were willing to let their savings ride on an investment and once brokers, dealers, and fund companies were willing to sell financial products like hamburgers, the process would not stop with money market funds. After all, money market funds were investments dressed up to look as much as possible like secure, boring, conservative bank accounts. Fidelity soon used its advertising, telephone, and marketing innovations to sell stock mutual funds directly to ordinary Americans. It did so with fabulous success, especially after Ned Johnson handed the reins of Fidelity's Magellan Fund to a Boston Irish kid named Peter Lynch in 1977. Under Lynch, Magellan became a legendary success, drawing billions of dollars and millions of Americans into the stock market for the first time.

Then there was Charles Schwab. On May 1, 1975, the New York Stock Exchange initiated sweeping changes that would help bring Wall Street to Main Street. After 183 years of enforcing fixed brokerage commissions, ensuring there would be no price competition among stock brokers, the exchange, under pressure from the federal government to deregulate, loosened its grip on commission prices. For decades, the exchange had kept commission prices high—so high that small stock purchases were not worthwhile. When the May

Day deregulation arrived, Chuck Schwab was poised to take advantage of it. His company, Charles Schwab and Co., became the first discount brokerage, offering bare-bones services at rock-bottom prices. Schwab caught the big Wall Street firms off-guard. After decontrol, they actually raised their prices. They just had not considered serving the great American middle class, a mass that had never before displayed any interest in the stock market.[68]

In just four years, Schwab's business blossomed. On May Day, there had been just one office processing 2,000 accounts. By the end of 1979, Schwab's brokerage claimed 70,000 customer accounts, seventeen offices, and revenues of $18 million. Schwab's discount brokerage proved so successful that many blueblood firms reluctantly copied his approach.[69]

No firm adapted better to the new environment than Merrill Lynch Pierce Fenner & Smith. Merrill had missed the boat on May Day, raising its commissions along with the established brokerage houses. But by the end of the 1970s, under the leadership of future Reagan administration insider Donald Regan, the Merrill Lynch bull was back on the rampage. In 1977 Regan introduced the cash management account (CMA), an innovation that, according to *Fortune*, dazzled customers and scared the competition.[70]

The CMA united in one account a stock and bond portfolio, a money market fund, a checking account, and a new sort of credit card. As long as the customer retained a large enough balance, Merrill's laminated plastic functioned as a debit card, automatically withdrawing funds from the account to cover charge purchases. If card purchases exceeded the balance, the CMA immediately opened a margin account, allowing customers to borrow against the value of their securities portfolios. That allowed investors to enjoy the rising value of their stocks and bonds—to liquefy their portfolios—without having to sell their securities. At one stroke, Merrill's CMA offered services traditionally provided by mutual fund companies, brokerages, and banks.[71]

The CMA showed off Don Regan's brilliance and daring at the helm of Merrill Lynch, particularly the clever ways Merrill flouted financial regulations through a partnership with Columbus, Ohio–based Banc One. But, as *Fortune* concluded, the CMA was as much "a creature of circumstances as of cleverness." An inflationary spiral always prompted innovations in finance—devices designed to make investments more liquid. "Both the theory and the law of money and credit" were "left far behind, and gasping."[72]

Charles Schwab, Donald Regan, and Ned Johnson merely helped to complete the financial revolution that the Great Inflation had initiated. But if these developments displayed the American people's easy capacity for adaptation, they also suggested darker, more sinister forces. Journalist and social critic Theodore H. White detected in the reactions to inflation a "contagion of fear." Conversation was "stained and drenched in money talk, by what it cost to live or what it cost to enjoy life." White recalled restaurant meals "with the host sneaking a glance at the tab and stunned, surreptitiously adding up the figures to verify the total." Working people suffered most. "They winced and ached. Some mysterious power was hollowing their hopes and dreams, their plans for a house or their children's college education.... Promises had been made to all of them over the two decades; but now the promises were being redeemed in money which might become as worthless as Confederate dollars." Americans, White concluded, felt that government must protect them from inflation, must check the ever-rising tide.[73]

The Crisis of Confidence

In 1977, 1978, 1979, Jimmy Carter had produced no cure for the national disease. Inflation roared through the double-digit barrier. Cities sank into disrepair; the South Bronx, which Carter visited in 1977, became, in one commentator's words, "the legendary symbol of the despair of the 1970s." Across the nation, rising prices swelled property taxes, and angry homeowners rebelled against taxation and government in general.[74]

Meanwhile, energy supplies dwindled, lines reappeared at service stations, and many states ordered gasoline rationing. Carter summoned his advisers to Camp David in March 1979 to develop responses to the crisis. "We've got to do what is in the best interests of the country," one aide concluded, "but it's damned hard to see how anything we do will be in the best interests of Jimmy Carter." They dawdled. By the end of June, 60 percent of the nation's gas stations had closed because of fuel shortages.[75]

Jimmy Carter tracked his abysmal poll numbers as his popularity descended to new depths. Carter also recognized a broader discontent across the angry land—a revulsion against established institutions. In the summer of 1979, Carter cancelled a scheduled address on the energy crisis and retreated to the presidential compound at Camp David. He reflected on the deeper causes of the gas crisis—the shortages of political and spiritual energy, which he decided posed far greater dangers than the shortfall of oil. At Camp David Carter met with more than one hundred visitors—politicians, business and labor leaders, clergymen. He made a series of unannounced helicopter visits to speak with average families in their homes.

On July 15, he delivered what became known as the "malaise speech," although he never used that term. Carter began by reporting on what he had learned during his sojourn in the Maryland woods. "First of all, I got a lot of personal advice. Let me quote a few of the typical comments that I wrote down." A southern governor warned, "Mr. President, you are not leading this Nation—you're just managing the government." A young woman in Pennsylvania told him, "I feel so far from the government. I feel like ordinary people are excluded from political power." This "kind of summarized a lot of other statements: 'Mr. President, we are confronted with a moral and a spiritual crisis.'"[76]

His ten days in the wilderness, Carter concluded, had confirmed his "belief in the decency and the strength and the wisdom of the American people, but it also bore out some of my longstanding concerns about our Nation's underlying problems." The president admitted that government action remained important and that he had achieved only mixed success. "But after listening to the American people I have been reminded that all the legislation in the world can't fix what's wrong with America." The nation faced a menace more dangerous than energy or inflation, a "fundamental threat to American democracy." The "threat is nearly invisible in ordinary ways. It is a crisis of confidence. It is a crisis that strikes at the very heart and soul and spirit of our national will. We see this crisis in the growing doubt about the meaning of our own lives and in the loss of unity of purpose for our Nation."[77]

Carter concluded with a message of hope: "We know the strength of America. We are strong. We can regain our unity. We can regain our confidence." The president carefully painted a way out. He accepted much of the blame himself but made it clear that there was something wrong with American public life—a kind of self-indulgence, a kind of narrowness and parochialism.[78]

The speech initially reassured the nation, but its glow soon wore off. A few days later, Carter reshuffled his administration, asking his entire cabinet to submit letters of resignation and asking five cabinet secretaries to step down. The purge angered many Washington insiders; fear of further dismissals gripped the White House staff. Worse yet, Americans interpreted the mass request for resignations as a sign of panic. Carter had not erased his image of weakness.

Finally, weeks after diagnosing the crisis of confidence, Carter took his first genuinely forceful step to contain inflation. He appointed Paul Volcker chairman of the Federal Reserve Board. Volcker quickly and brutally ironed inflation out of the economy. He immediately prescribed bitter medicine. Rather than manipulating interest rates, the indirect method the Fed normally used, Volcker decided to contract the money supply directly—to reduce the money in circulation by controlling bank reserves. Top White House officials opposed the move. They feared the inevitable recession Volcker's extreme approach would bring during an election year. In the end, Carter acquiesced. He had no choice. Interest rates immediately skyrocketed to 15 percent, the dollar stabilized, and the economy stalled. Carter also announced temporary controls on consumer credit and asked Americans to stop buying goods and services with borrowed money.[79]

The new program prescribed the right medicine at the wrong time. The credit controls worked all too well. In fact, Americans responded far beyond expectations to the president's call for discipline. Like a child, the country seemed eager to please, and consumer spending plummeted. The second quarter of 1980 showed the steepest drop in GNP in American history.[80]

The ensuing "quickie recession" dragged into the election season, and Carter trailed badly as long as the economy remained the principal issue. The Carter campaign focused instead on Reagan's fitness for office, a strategy that gained ground until Reagan and Carter met for their one and only televised debate a week before the election. On the one hand, Americans harbored serious doubts about candidate Reagan. He seemed too bellicose, too extreme, too unskilled, just too plain sleepy to be president. On the other hand, the horrors of inflation, gas rationing, the new, uncertain money revolution, had left the nation desperate for change, ready for rescue by that man on a horse come to save America at the last moment. Ronald Reagan was symbolically, ideologically, and literally (at least while visiting his Santa Barbara ranch) that man on horseback.

The debate had set the stage. Reagan stared at the camera and asked the American people what turned out to be the campaign's crucial question: "Are you better off than you were four years ago? Is it easier for you to go and buy things in stores than it was four years ago? Is there more or less unemployment?" America answered those questions—and sent Jimmy Carter packing.[81]

President Reagan disparaged Carter's sermons about a national crisis of spirit and pointedly tried to banish any lingering malaise. During Reagan's presidency, a new confidence emerged. But the financial revolution that gave birth to the individual middle-class investor would remain in place. Even during a national economic emergency, Americans had learned to rely on themselves more than on their government, and the new president would encourage this wide-open, individualist spirit.

Poor Jimmy Carter. He arrived as the redeemer, restoring "our sense of community and of the common good." He left Washington as the terminator, a potent symbol for the futility of government and naiveté of reformist zeal. During the Reagan years, Jimmy Carter became a joke. He seemed for a time as much a relic of the despised, disparaged Seventies as yellow smiley faces, disco records, and leisure suits.

6

"THIS AIN'T NO FOOLIN' AROUND"
Rebellion and Authority in Seventies Popular Culture

SATURDAY NIGHT FEVER CARVED OUT FOR ITSELF A MEMORABLE, if slightly ridiculous, place in the history of American popular culture. The 1977 film catapulted little-known television actor John Travolta into big-screen stardom. Its soundtrack, featuring recordings by the Bee Gees, became briefly the biggest-selling album of all time and inaugurated a new (and newly profitable) series of collaborations between film studios and record companies. Together the movie and the soundtrack represented the apotheosis of disco. A white-suited Travolta, right hand awkwardly pointed over head in disco dance, became the archetypal image of 1970s America—a graphic depiction of its polyester fakery, its senseless hedonism, its supposed cultural bankruptcy.

But the film itself essayed a far more serious, and darker, portrait of American life in the era of malaise. In *Saturday Night Fever*, disco dancing emerged as an escape, an ultimately unreachable exit from a bleak world of stifling families, pinched circumstances, and decaying neighborhoods. *Saturday Night Fever* simmered in the era's pervasive ethnic conflict. Travolta's Tony Manero, a working-class outer-borough Italian, aspired to the affluence, the glamour, and the polish of WASP Manhattan.

The economic downturn of the Carter years also loomed large in Manero's Brooklyn. Tony works a dead-end job in a paint store. On Saturday night, he begs his boss for an advance to buy a "beautiful shirt" before returning home for a painful supper with his unemployed and thus unmanned father. Tony's mother has defiantly bought pork chops even though the family cannot keep up with the rising price of meat. "Life goin' nowhere," moaned the Bee Gees in "Stayin' Alive," the film's signature song. "Somebody help me."

Still, *Saturday Night Fever*'s ludicrous features—the Bee Gees' falsetto vocals, Travolta's white leisure suit, the melodramatic dance contests—proved more enduring mementos of Seventies America than the film's dark subject matter. Americans still find it difficult to take the Seventies seriously. As novelist Mark Salzman put it in his memoir about growing up in suburbia in the Seventies, "It seemed that everybody had been stoned since the ninth grade except me. I was the only guy in my industrial-arts class who wasn't making a water pipe out of plumbing fixtures."[1]

The prevailing concept of the Seventies remains the idea of the "Me Decade"—an era of narcissism, selfishness, personal rather than political awareness. "The '70s was the decade in which people put emphasis on the skin, on the surface, rather than on the root of things," novelist Norman Mailer complained in 1979. "It was the decade in which image became preeminent because nothing deeper was going on."[2]

Pundits and historians portrayed the Me Decade as the antidote to or repudiation of the activist, altruistic 1960s. When Apple Computer cofounder Steven Wozniak attempted to revive the Woodstock spirit in the early 1980s, he called his venture the "Us Festival." Wozniak billed the three-day celebration of rock music and computer technology as a deliberate effort to usher in an "Us Generation" of social action and communal engagement that would supplant the so-called Me Generation of the 1970s.[3]

Cultural arbiters bemoaned the decade "as a betrayal of sixties passion and idealism, a trashy postscript that found the broad torrents of pop culture siphoned off into tinkling displays of dandyism, self-parody, and androgyny. Instead of Pete Townshend and Jimi Hendrix sacrificing their guitars on pagan altars, we had David Bowie all aglitter, the New York Dolls in downtown drag, midnight showings of 'The Rocky Horror Picture Show.'"[4]

But film and TV critic James Wolcott denounced that dismissive view. "How," he asked, "could a decade that gave us the Rolling Stones' strung-out masterpiece *Exile on Main Street*, the epic scrotum hollers of Led Zeppelin, the booty-shake of disco and funk and the rash of punk rock be dismissed as dull and enervated?" And such energy and experimentation was not confined to popular music. "The seventies were the last time when movies seemed signed with the sweat of a director's brow rather than packaged by a committee of cellular phones. Martin Scorcese, Brian De Palma, Francis Ford Coppola, and Robert Altman invested each film with an integral vision. Looking back on the music and the movies," Wolcott concluded, "one is impressed by their personal stake, their quick incision."[5]

Americans remember the insipid antics of the Brady Bunch; theatrical rock performers from Kiss and Alice Cooper to Pink Floyd and David Bowie with their costumes, makeup, and laser shows; the bleached, tamed movie disco of the Bee Gees and John Travolta; the escapist, high-tech disaster films *Jaws, Earthquake,* and *The Towering Inferno*. But there was also something deeper going on. The same distrust of the powers that be that undermined traditional sources of authority and fractured public life also spurred creative, personal, highly charged art that addressed just that discontent. The decade's most potent and memorable cultural products raised an upturned middle finger at conventional sources of authority—be they the White House, the record companies, or the Hollywood studios. But this rebellious streak remained knowing, jaded, circumspect. It lacked the utopian naiveté of the Sixties, the optimism that David might do more than rouse and anger Goliath. Seventies Americans recognized that a freer, more meaningful life and an authentic, more personal art was "no longer just a matter of running away from Mommy, as it were, but a tough-minded confrontation with the dark powers of a new age." They reshaped the cultural landscape with a blend of outrage and resignation, passion and black humor, and forged a new sensibility, a distinctively skeptical style. The rebels would lose their lopsided battle against a softened mass culture, but in the process they would create important, enduring popular culture.

"You Talkin' to Me?": The Noble Outlaw in Seventies Culture

The 1970s career of Bob Dylan encapsulated the era's contempt for authority and produced some of its memorable surprises. Despite a long and various career spanning almost four decades, his name still conjures icons from the Sixties: the fresh-faced protest singer who strummed "Blowin' in the Wind"; the motorcycle-crashing, acid-tongued rebel who shocked the Newport Folk Festival by going electric and penned angry anthems like "Positively 4th Street" and "Like a Rolling Stone"; or the countercultural hero who experimented with drugs and retreated to Big Pink, a communal house in upstate New York, before resurfacing with his backup band.

But Bob Dylan produced his best and most influential work during the Seventies. In one particularly frenetic and fertile two-year period, Dylan released four albums and conducted a memorable major tour with the Band. Two of those albums—*Blood on the Tracks* (1974) and *Desire* (1975)—particularly expressed the era's fears and experience, capturing and defining its zeitgeist.

For example, Dylan's work from the Seventies focused on renegotiating relationships in an age of divorce, after feminism, with marriage seemingly irrelevant. Women always left men on *Blood on the Tracks*, not the other way around. " In "Simple Twist of Fate," Dylan's narrator woke in a lonely room, the woman long gone. And although "he told himself he did not care," he felt an "emptiness inside."

Evoking the myriad spiritual quests of the Third Great Awakening, the records also conducted explorations of religion, mysticism, and spirituality, culminating with Dylan's vaguely Christian records of the early 1980s. *Desire* brimmed over with references to Isis, Buddha, and Magdalena, to salvation and resurrection, to soothsayers and Fathers (with a capital F). *Blood on the Tracks*, noted Paul Cowan in the *Village Voice*, "was filled with religious imagery, with hints that the wounded, weary Dylan seeks 'shelter,' not as a woman's warm home, but as the peace of God."6

But most important, Dylan's recordings emphasized distrust of authority—a suspicion of established institutions. The singer voiced this distrust of constituted authority in a celebration of noble outlaws: the shadowy Jack of Hearts in "Lily, Rosemary and the Jack of Hearts"; the nameless adventurer-voyeur in "Black Diamond Bay"; the romantic portrait of assassinated mafioso Joey Gallo in "Joey." Dylan's Gallo, like all of his other heroes, "remained always on the outside of whatever side there was."7

Championing the cause of yet another outlaw underdog, "Hurricane" most powerfully evoked this antipathy to American institutions. By 1975, Rubin "Hurricane" Carter, former number one contender for the middleweight boxing championship, had languished for nine years in a New Jersey prison, serving hard time for a triple murder that he claimed he never committed. Carter's conviction had rested largely on the evidence of two police informants, who subsequently recanted much of their testimony. Dylan helped launch a national defense fund for the boxer and wrote a song to advance the cause.

Dylan's angry anthem allowed no doubt about the ex-boxer's innocence. Carter was "the man the authorities came to blame for somethin' that he never done, put in a prison cell, but one time he could-a been the champion of the world." The song portrayed Carter as a gentle man who plied his violent trade only for pay and preferred quiet pleasures. Racism—"If you're black you might as well not show up on the street"—and police corruption had stolen Hurricane's one shot at glory, his good name, his manhood.

But the song did more than merely trumpet the innocence and virtue of the outlaw—the Buddha-like boxer in a ten-foot cell. It exposed the corruption, the rotting core of the nation's public life. While Carter wallowed in prison, the real criminals, "in their coats and their ties, are free to drink martinis and watch the sun rise." To see Carter "obviously framed," Dylan concluded, "couldn't help but make me fell ashamed to live in a land where justice is a game."[8]

Dylan's suspicion of established institutions proved particularly revealing and resonant. The underlying theme in Seventies popular culture—the subterranean current running under both product (the films and songs and novels being made) and process (the way they were being made, marketed, and distributed)—was the battle between large, constituted authority and its opponents. The films, music, and literature of the era pitted a self-styled outlaw band of rebels against the massive global conglomerates that were coming to dominate the culture industries and were, in their relentless search for the largest possible mass markets, blunting the edges of artistic expression.

The film world graphically illustrated this conflict. The late Sixties and Seventies witnessed the birth of the so-called new Hollywood—a rejection of the film industry's time-tested methods "in favor of freelance, catch-as-catch-can, location-oriented, director-controlled projects."[9] The old studios finally crumbled, along with the system in which a few major film companies controlled all the talent, the filmmaking process, and the content. Freed from these controls, a cinematic renaissance took place. *New Yorker* film critic Pauline Kael looked back on the 1970s two decades later as Hollywood's single authentic golden age.[10] The decade produced such artists and films as Francis Ford Coppola's *The Conversation* and *The Godfather* Parts 1 and 2, Martin Scorcese's *Mean Streets* and *Taxi Driver*, Robert Altman's *Nashville* and *McCabe and Mrs. Miller*, John Cassavetes' *A Woman Under the Influence*, and Roman Polanski's *Chinatown*, to name just a few.

These films resisted the major authorities and megacorporations of the film industry; they remained examples of strong directorial autonomy in the selection of locations, the casting, the filmmaking itself. More important, these movies explored dark subjects and advanced iconoclastic arguments. They assailed, mocked, undercut, and exposed the established sources of authority in American life. They echoed Bob Dylan's pronouncement that "the dream is over, the Great American Dream is over."[11]

In Roman Polanski's *Chinatown* (1974), Jake Gittes, the down-on-his-luck private detective played by Jack Nicholson, slowly unpeels the corruption infesting every layer of southern California society. Set in 1930s Los Angeles,

Chinatown dramatized 1970s reservations about political power and the public sector. The film's high-minded liberal, Water Department chief engineer Hollis Mulwray, first appears under a gigantic portrait of Franklin Delano Roosevelt, that ultimate symbol of benevolent government. But Mulwray is naive, and he dies a violent death. Investigating that murder, Gittes ultimately glimpses in the region's most powerful man—its behind-the-scenes powerbroker depicted with uncanny vividness by John Huston—a view of pure, unmitigated, unalloyed evil. The audience looks into society's core in *Chinatown* and finds it rotten.

Martin Scorcese's 1976 film *Taxi Driver* tapped this same vein of discontent. Prowling the nighttime world of New York City, Robert De Niro plays Travis Bickle, a Vietnam-era veteran—despairing, confused, seething with rage. "All the animals come out at night," Bickle confides in the audience through voiceover narration—"whores, skunk pussies, buggers, queens, fairies, dopers, junkies, sick, venal. Someday a real rain will come and wash all this scum off the streets." Bickle's signature expression, accosting his reflection in a mirror at a gunpoint, is an ironic growl: "You talkin' to me?"

Rejected by an attractive political campaign aide, Bickle even contemplates assassinating the candidate. Instead he arms himself and rages against the city: "Listen you fuckers, you screwheads. Here is a man who would not take it anymore. A man who stood up against the scum, the cunts, the dogs, the filth, the shit. Here is someone who stood up." As Bickle's invective subsides into incoherent, inarticulate fury, a shot of his scribbled diary closes in on the words "Here is" followed by three menacing dots. Ultimately Bickle does stand up, freeing a twelve-year-old child prostitute in a bloodbath of incredible violence. The film ends with Bickle—the deranged, enraged taxi driver—celebrated as a hero. But Bickle is far scarier than the filth he excoriates, and the film discloses something very wrong about American society. If Travis Bickle is a savior, then what kind of nation has America become?

This critical perspective, this hostility to mainstream America and its values, appeared widely in the cinema of the Seventies; it was not confined to searing dramas by maverick directors. The 1977 comedy *Fun with Dick and Jane,* directed by Hollywood journeyman Ted Kotcheff (best known for the first Rambo movie), starred Jane Fonda and George Segal as a well-to-do suburban couple living the high life until Segal, a successful aerospace executive, loses his job. With prices soaring out of control and the economy going South, the company ruthlessly casts off its loyal employees. The couple slowly loses its purchase on middle-class respectability. Repo men seize everything—the car, the furniture, even the shrubs. So how does a hard-pressed young couple get by in the age of malaise? They steal. They rob banks. They flip an upturned finger at the authorities, the police, the company.

Not surprisingly, as American cinema enjoyed this outpouring of caustic, critical attacks on traditional sources of authority, the film empire struck back. If half of the story of Seventies cinema concerned the independent directors and their dark, personal visions, the other half featured a new Hollywood corporate order struggling to assert itself amid the ruin of the studio system. International megaconglomerates absorbed the film companies: Trans-America Corporation took over United Artists; MCA engulfed Universal Pictures; Gulf & Western absorbed Paramount; and the Kinney Corporation, known as the King of Parking Lots, bought Warner Brothers.[12]

The new corporate regime struggled to find blockbusters, formula pictures, sequel makers, franchises that would reach mass audiences. They could not afford movies like *Taxi Driver, Fun with Dick and Jane, Shaft,* or *Hester Street*—films with edgy messages that found specialized audiences. The new order concocted the winning recipe in 1975 with *Jaws*—the shark-on-a-beach thriller directed by the young Steven Spielberg. *Jaws* set the pattern for corporate Hollywood blockbusters, pioneering the techniques of saturation openings, extensive television advertising, and side-business deals in souvenirs, T-shirts, and toys. *Jaws* proved, according to film historian Robert Sklar, that Hollywood was unwilling "to sustain itself on dissidence."[13]

By contrast, *Jaws* and subsequent movies like it—films with broad enough appeal to reap the benefits of prime-time television advertising and wide simultaneous release—revealed a potential new mass market. *Jaws* offered a carefully crafted (and completely unthreatening) escapist nightmare, and it broke records at the box office. Among "the victims of a monster shark," in Sklar's words, lay the "dream of a personal, participatory cinema"—an idea that thrived in "a time of public turmoil, when Hollywood along with other powerful American institutions seemed in helpless disarray."[14]

Gimme Gimme Shock Treatment!

Popular music clearly illustrated this prevailing tension between iconoclasm and authority, between David and Goliath. By the mid-1970s, multinational corporations like Gulf & Western and CBS controlled most of the music industry. Like President Carter, these businesses faced a nation increasingly riven by race, ethnicity, age, region, ideology, and style. The pop music world and the institutions that had served it—Top 40 radio, chain stores and record clubs, *American Bandstand*—no longer commanded a broad musical common ground. The market had fragmented into many niches.[15]

The new conglomerates were not content with small, specialized markets. They bought out black record companies and produced bleached disco for the suburbs. They created and promoted a handful of megastars, with stadium tours and massive advertising campaigns. The industry sought out big theatrical acts and foisted on the public artificial creations like the Bay City Rollers, a foursome of derivative English moptops hailed as the second coming of the Beatles.[16]

Marketing-inspired excess ruled as the record companies spawned theatrical stars in elaborate costumes. Kiss painted their faces and dressed in platform shoes and shiny spandex pants; the group's "concerts" featured snow machines, rockets, smoke bombs, and levitating drum sets. Encouraged by his agent and record company, Alice Cooper's shows featured even more bizarre displays: live chickens tossed into the audience, mock executions in fake electric chairs, decapitations of dolls. Cooper freely admitted the commercial instincts that inspired his antics. "I am the most American rock act," Cooper declared. "I love money." A parody of the time, *Rolling Stone* critic Greil Marcus recalled, "had a rock star demanding that his label fund the recording of his next album in outer space." It hardly sounded like satire. Rock music, Marcus lamented, had become "an ordinary social fact, like a commute or a highway construction project. It became a habit, a structure, an invisible oppression." Surveying the Seventies music scene, *Billboard* magazine reporter Nelson George called the era the "age of corporations."[17]

The release of *Frampton Comes Alive* in 1976 marked the signal event in the emergence of corporate rock. A&M Records discovered a mediocre, undistinguished British rocker named Peter Frampton and packaged him as something for everyone—part guitar hero, part punk, part heavy metal, part Deadhead, part bluesman. *Frampton Comes Alive*, like most other Seventies corporate rock, offered music with no soul, no message, no recognizable quality to distinguish it from what came before. Yet it became the biggest-selling album of all time—the first multiplatinum record.

The ascendance of corporate rock prompted a response. In 1978, Marcus's friend Lester Bangs, an outspoken champion of the alternative music scene, harshly criticized the recording industry. The "music business today," Bangs declared in the *Village Voice,* "still must be recognized as by definition an enemy, if not the most crucial enemy, of music and the people who try to perform it honestly."[18] Resistance emerged not just from the poisoned pens of critics; it arose out of grungy clubs and dusty garages, from college campuses and independent record stores. America discovered punk.

Like earlier efforts to revive popular music from periods of lethargy and staleness, American punk imported ideas and inspiration from England and eventually domesticated them. American punk grew out of and mimicked, but significantly altered, a politico-musical movement that originally flourished in Great Britain.[19] English punk reflected a concrete political agenda; British punkers voiced the discontent of white working-class youth—yobbos facing nothing but dead-end jobs. The Sex Pistols' irreverent, controversial version of "God Save the Queen" ended with the chorus "no future, no future, no future for you" repeated over and over again.

English punk thus remained class music, yet another chapter in the long, self-conscious British class struggle. It represented resistance against the privileges of a clear upper class—complaints in a culture where class was clearly acknowledged.

In the mid-1970s a bunch of London "rude boys" called the Clash burst onto the scene. Their lead singer had busied himself reading radical tracts, and their first album included "Career Opportunities," a hit single about economic dead ends. "They offered me the office, offered me the shop. They said I'd better take anything they'd got," the band growled at breakneck pace. "Every job they offer you is to keep you out the dock. Career opportunities—the ones that never knock."

The Clash's most successful album, *London Calling* (1979), sharpened this indictment of modern society and its oppressive institutions. In "Clampdown," the band depicted contemporary English institutions in the harshest terms, even linking them to the horrors of fascism. The song concluded with a passionate declaration of independence and resistance: "No man born with a living soul can be working for the clampdown."

But the Clash did not merely complain about oppression; they openly advocated revolution, "Kick over the wall, cause governments to fall," the band demanded," urging listeners to fight in the streets and topple governments. "Let fury have the hour, anger can be power," the band insisted. "Do you know that you can use it?" When race riots broke out in London, the Clash suggested that its white, working-class followers stage their own white riot. The band self-consciously allied itself with Marxist revolutionary movements around the globe, such as the Red Brigade in Italy and the Sandinistas in Nicaragua.

Despite common roots, American punk lacked that political edge, that overt class consciousness. Still, it borrowed much from the Brits and domesticated it for American consumption. First, American punk retained the outrageousness—the raw, unproduced sound, the brazen lyrics, the edgy and even offensive style. Punk rockers never hesitated to offend. They adopted a rebellious, in-your-face stance. A group calling itself Dead Kennedys obviously enjoyed flouting established notions of good taste.

Second, they played similar music—loud, fast, hard driving, coarse. Punk records were essentially unproduced: few backing tracks, little mixing and remixing, often recorded live in the studio without multiple takes or overdubs. While some critics felt performers like the Ramones sounded sloppy and unprofessional, the band deliberately shunned the polished sounds of mainstream rock.[20] The raw sound reaffirmed a kind of rock 'n' roll democracy—anyone could pick up a guitar and make music—and it emphasized simplicity, experience, and emotion over heavily produced, highly stylized compositions. "The punks who made records in 1977," one writer insisted, "didn't know which chords came next." They just hurled themselves against the musical and political establishment. But their songs carried wallop because the music stayed as tough as the words.[21]

This reflected a third trait that English and American punk bands shared—a kind of rock purity or asceticism. At a time when mainstream popular musicians emphasized costume and makeup, punk rockers sported jeans, T-shirts, and leather jackets. "The whole thing was a reaction to the hippie stadium music," punk rocker Richard Hell declared. "The ripped T-shirts meant that I don't give a fuck about stardom and all that or glamour and going to rock shows to see someone pretend to be perfect."[22] Rock concerts had become elaborate spectacles with lasers, live animals, and exploding walls; punkers like the Ramones simply walked on stage, barked "1-2-3-4," and played the songs. Punk rejected the technical wizardry that had come to dominate rock music—from the new instruments used to produce music to the carefully calculated ways that promoters mounted concert tours.[23]

That asceticism signaled a fourth element that American bands derived from the English, but really made their own. For if American punk possessed a political message, it was anticorporatism, an attack on the domination of the business by a few big record companies and all that implied: the emphasis on megahits, superstars, and big-ticket acts; the neglect of new groups, new music, and new messages; the slick production values and massive theatrical shows. Corporate rock also meant mainstream distribution: airplay on AM Top 40 radio, chain store record sales, advertisements in national press.

American punk rejected all that. College radio stations played the music; alternative and independent record stores sold it. The performers played in small clubs, close to their audiences. In suburban Connecticut, where *Punk Magazine* writer Legs McNeil spent his youth before making the Lower Manhattan scene in the mid-Seventies, "rock was this big thing that came to a stadium. The concept of people playing their own rock and roll in a hole in the Bowery, to maybe 30 people, was amazing."[24]

Most important, punk artists recorded on independent labels—small record companies that signed the acts and made the records that the megadealing big corporations rejected. Late Seventies punk recreated the ferment of rock 'n' roll's birth in the 1950s, when thousands of new groups made records and genuine surprises came off the radio.[25]

Punk shared this anticorporatism with another contemporaneous, related movement known as New Wave. For although American punk never became class music, in the sense of explicitly expressing the grievances of a social class as did English punk, it was associated with a certain demographic type: high school dropouts in a Queens garage, not-very-good surfers drifting around southern California beach towns. American punk reflected a working-class aesthetic.

New Wave amounted to punk's cognate among educated, upper-middle-class college kids. It shared much with American punk—the anticorporate agenda and the asceticism; New Wave performers preferred thin ties and suit jackets to jeans and leather jackets, but still eschewed the glittery rock star model. "When we started," Talking Heads drummer Chris Frantz recalled, audiences "seemed to think that you had to wear platform shoes and tight leather pants and you had to lead a decadent lifestyle. We came on stage looking like a bunch of Jesuits."[26] New Wave also preserved the raw, unpolished music and the links to clubs and independent labels.

Indeed, both movements shared a birthplace and a headquarters—a Lower Manhattan club called CBGB at the corner of Bleecker Street and the Bowery. The club opened in 1973 with that seemingly ill-fitting name. CBGB stood for Country, Blue Grass and the Blues, but the club's full name, CBGB & OMFUG, also promised "other music for uplifting gourmandizers" for a cheap one-dollar admission fee. "Just going to the bathroom" in that long, dark, and narrow club, one music critic recalled, "was an invitation to encounter every sort of downtown denizen and substance consumption known to man (and woman) at the time. Musicians mingled with groupies and fans and one another; writers schmoozed with each other and with musicians." In its heyday, from 1975 to 1978, CBGB became the home turf and launching pad of such performers as the Ramones, the Dictators, Television, Patti Smith, Blondie, Tuff Darts, and Richard Hall and the Voidoids.[27]

That dingy, sweaty, dark place also launched a trio of refugees from the Rhode Island School of Design—a group that combined minimalistically spare instrumentals with its lead singer's characteristic bug-eyed, chicken-squawk vocals. Originally a trio, Talking Heads later added a renegade from Jonathan Richman's Modern Lovers to form a four-person band. Thus fortified, Talking Heads burst onto the pop scene with a debut album, *Talking Heads '77*, and its follow-up, *More Songs About Buildings and Food*. The songs bathed in alienation and disappointment—the stultifying dreariness of the workaday world, the detached isolation of outsiders who cannot connect with other people. In one song, a bland civil servant stuttered about his building "with every convenience." In another, brutal vocals mocked the very idea of compassion and connection: "So many people have so many problems, I'm not interested in their problems." Yet the music, in bassist Tina Weymouth's words, seemed "to raise the banal to the sublime." Spare, uncluttered, rhythmic, funky, it provoked laughter amid the gloom.

On their next album, *Fear of Music* (1979), Talking Heads spun off "Life During Wartime," a postapocalyptic nightmare at once horrifying and hilarious. "This ain't no party, this ain't no disco," the chorus declared. "It ain't the Mudd Club, or CBGB's. I ain't got time for that now." But the lyrics lied. The song itself and the world it evoked were nothing but a big party. The performers and their audience joked about (and danced through) a nightmare landscape. Without the tedious zealotry of much Sixties protest music, Talking Heads marked a clear alternative to the mainstream in the era's signature style.

Toward a New Sensibility

Talking Heads, the Ramones, and the other representatives of the 1970s alternative rock scene embodied one final attribute in addition to outrageousness, asceticism, and anticorporatism: irony. They were not painfully earnest or deadly serious. Rock music and rock heroes from the first British invasion of the mid-1960s through the acid groups of the late Sixties, to the synths and crunching guitar heroes of the Seventies, right up to British punk acts like the Clash had been very, very serious. The Seventies produced a new kind of rocker and, with them, a new attitude that pervaded American society.

This irony betrayed a wider transformation in sensibility. As *Spy* magazine, the insouciant New York monthly of the 1980s, noted, the nation's preferred hand signals encapsulated a shift in attitude. The late Sixties had favored the peace sign—index and middle fingers in a V—which proclaimed a world of possibilities, the emphatic conviction that young Americans could build a new and better world. During the mid-1970s, the peace sign gave way to "the finger," the single upturned middle digit. That obscene gesture lacked the hopefulness of the Sixties but still expressed a clear point of view. As the decade ended, however, a new gesture appeared: two bent fingers in the shape of inverted commas, signaling everything within quotation marks—everything ironic, nothing serious.[28]

It became a characteristic mode of thought and expression, a Seventies sensibility. It implied a certain kind of knowingness—an ability to see things for what they were, without romantic illusions. Pop troubadour Jonathan Richman captured this sensibility when he interrupted one of his own songs for a "Monologue About Bermuda." Richman had begun his career as leader of the Modern Lovers, a protopunk, proto–New Wave band on the Boston rock scene in the early 1970s. The Lovers included future Talking Head Jerry Harrison and future Cars drummer David Robinson, and their performances had achieved something like legendary status long before their first album was released in 1975.[29]

The Modern Lovers made serious, loud music. They played their own songs, expressed their own experiences. Their music was raw, rebellious, and irreverent; Richman even described it as "snotty." Then the band traveled to Bermuda. "We were playing kind of like triphammers," Richman recalled. "We were kind of serious. We had a fair amount of equipment for a group back then." The band's stance proclaimed, "You know this is pretty important." But the act just bored their audiences.[30]

The Lovers could not compete with the Bermuda strollers—the street musicians in windbreakers and dark sunglasses. The strollers' big, fat guitar sound, playful lyrics, and off-color rhymes intoxicated the college students on spring break and they opened Richman's eyes. "Ohhh! We really are stiff," he thought. "These guys really are looser than us."[31]

The band did not last—not after Jonathan started listening to bongos, buying calypso records, and writing whimsical, personal, idiosyncratic music that defied both the prevailing image of a serious rock star and his own earlier persona as an earnest, tortured young artist. Richman recorded songs in the character of a two-year-old child, a jilted lover of Cleopatra, even from the point of view of a misunderstood, underappreciated mosquito. In many ways, Richman's post-Bermuda music evoked and defined the sensibility of the Seventies.

Sometimes the sentiment remained simple and direct, easily discerned in the lyrics. One song made fun of stolid, unflashy midwesterners but nonetheless conveyed a genuine respect for them. "They're not trying on the dance floor," Richman joked. "Like Sheboygan or Eau Claire, they're just there." But heartland taciturnity obscured sincerity and power. "They're not tryin' much there on the floor," the song concludes, "and they're moving me more."

But mostly, it remained subtler and more profound. The most obvious marker of the Seventies sensibility—its signature in literature, film, music, politics, advertising—was a kind of double identity. Seventies performers produced works that were a parody of something—a biting, knowing satire—and simultaneously the very thing itself. Consider Nick Lowe's paean to the down-on-her-luck silent screen star Marie Provost. Provost had been dead two or three weeks when the cops "bust into her lonely nest" and discover her corpse. The humor, the parody is savage—a drippy, sing-songy three-minute pop song that describes a sordid and disgusting scene: Marie's decaying remains devoured by her starving dog. "She was a winner," Lowe croons, "who became a doggie's dinner." And the song disclaims any sympathy for the victim; it refuses even the slightest gesture of generosity in retelling her story: "She never meant that much to me, poor Marie." But those lyrics do not accompany raw, hard instrumentals with grinding guitars and tough, gravelly vocals; it is a happy, formulaic pop tune. "Marie Provost" subverted the form while still enjoying it.[32]

Jonathan's Richman's records reveled in this kind of fond satire. "Abdul and Cleopatra" updated the smarmy love song, with Egyptian-style guitar solos and absurd lyrics about the ancient queen of the Nile and her imaginary suitor. The tune skewered the silly love songs then still clinging to the top of the pop charts, but loved them nonetheless. Richman obviously enjoyed the hokey rhymes and silly guitar riffs, even while making fun of them. Richman and his band, one rock critic understood, "sang about hating hippies, because they wore attitudes like shades, so complete in their smugness, so complete that they never noticed *anything*, because they cut themselves off from everything that was good and alive and wonderful about the modern world." With the world in disarray, the nation in decay, the culture passionless and clichéd, some Seventies artists found relief, hope, humor, and joy in the unlikeliest of places. "You weren't supposed to like these things and we did," one chronicler of Seventies pop culture remembered.[33]

Seventies sensibility, then, offered a kind of antidote to the melodrama of the Sixties sensibility, an antidote devised by a generation of youth just plain sick and tired of being told how they missed out on the glory days. Americans who came of age during the 1970s, in the words of disco enthusiast Jefferson Morley, "were less idealistic but more realistic. Less wild and less authentic and less sincere but also less melodramatic and less violent. Less courageous but also less foolish. Less moralistic but more ethical." They "were a sweeter, sadder, sexier, funnier bunch than the kids of the 60s and they've never forgiven us for it."[34]

Still, there was much in life, as in art, that made Seventies Americans grimace. The collective wince of the late 1960s and early 1970s—the profound anguish over Vietnam, race riots, Watergate—gave way to the national smirk of the Carter years—the malaise that President Carter diagnosed in his crisis-of-confidence speech. But this omnipresent skepticism—this sense that nothing is serious, nothing can be trusted—undermined a campaign for national renewal, one that would have to be based on ardent conviction. Punk rockers and maverick directors forged new paths; ironically, they helped clear the way for a more wide-open, southwestern libertarianism that would share little with them but a defiant style and a set of common enemies.

7

BATTLES OF THE SEXES
Women, Men, and the Family

IN THE EARLY SEVENTIES, BEFORE DISCO AND PUNK, WATERGATE and Jimmy Carter, a sporting event captured the nation's imagination. On September 20, 1973, a capacity crowd thronged the Houston Astrodome for the "Battle of the Sexes." In living rooms and bars, a television audience of more than 45 million Americans, the largest ever for a tennis match, tuned in to watch fifty-five-year-old ex-Wimbledon champion Bobby Riggs challenge the world's top-ranked women's player, Billie Jean King.

An acknowledged advocate of women's liberation, King had struggled for several years to bring gender equality to women's tennis. "At first, when I was becoming aware," King recalled just before the match, "I blamed the system but when I began to analyze it I realized the 'system' is men." The movement, King told *Boston Globe* columnist Bud Collins, was "showing the gains women can make in a male-dominated area," and "sports is a place where everybody can see those gains."[1]

Initially King had ignored Riggs's repeated challenges—his taunts that women players were inferior, that women athletes did not deserve equal prize money, that even an old man could beat the best female player. But another of the world's top players, Australian champion Margaret Court, had agreed to play Riggs on Mother's Day 1973. Psyched out by Riggs's jibes and unprepared for a major match just weeks after the birth of her first child, Court lost badly. Worse, she lost her cool and seemed to confirm Riggs's charges that women players could not handle pressure without bursting into tears. Although the Riggs-Court match mustered only a tiny crowd, it generated sufficiently high Nielsen ratings to attract the attention of ABC sports chief Roone Arledge. Arledge, the great impresario of television sports, sensed a ratings and advertising bonanza, and set the stage for Riggs's next match on ABC's *Wide World of Sports*.

After Court's defeat, King felt she could no longer ignore Riggs. "I knew that it would make a huge impression for the future of girls' and women's athletics," she later recalled. She also believed the match would mean a lot for American women in general, "their self-esteem, and for men to understand that we both should be trying to work together and really appreciate each other's skills and learn to be good to each other no matter what our gender."[2]

The match quickly became a media circus. ABC paid the event's promoters more than $700,000 for broadcast rights, and the network collected over $1 million in advertising fees from sponsors, both records for an event of this kind. The Astrodome milked the event for all it was worth—selling souvenir program advertising, designating an official sponsor, even charging admission to practice sessions in a temporary bubble erected in the stadium's parking lot. Each player was guaranteed $100,000 dollars, with another $100,000 in prize money for the victor. If King won, she would almost double her yearly earnings as the world's top player.

Las Vegas made Riggs a five-to-two favorite, but most Americans laid down their bets in offices and private homes. Riggs captured the national mood when he characterized the match as the "battle of the sexes. Man against woman; sex against sex. Husbands argue with wives, bosses with secretaries. Everybody wants to bet."[3] But the circus atmosphere obscured something more momentous. On the day of the match, the *Boston Globe* reported that "apparently an awful lot of people, both men and women, are taking this match seriously."[4]

ABC Sports assigned Howard Cosell, its controversial and famously pompous commentator, to report the match along with Virginia Slims tour pro Rosie Casals. King arrived first, carried out onto the court like a gladiator by four muscular track stars. Cosell, focusing on King's appearance rather than her skills, commented, "Billie Jean is an attractive young woman. Sometimes you get the feeling that if she would only let her hair grow down to her shoulders and take her glasses off we would have a star vying for a Hollywood screenplay."[5] Ever the huckster, Riggs entered in a golden rickshaw drawn by "Bobby's Bosom Buddies," a team of models in tight-fitting red and gold outfits.

Riggs began the match in his bright yellow warm-up jacket, but King's superior play quickly forced him to shed his sweats. King clearly outclassed the aging ex-champ; Riggs never even came close as most of King's winners whizzed by untouched. "Funny," Cosell commented, "I suppose we all expected this match to have some high humor in it. Instead it seems to have become a very, very serious thing because the comedy has gone out of Bobby Riggs."

When King easily captured the first two sets, Cosell dispensed with beauty tips for the champion and began noting King's supposedly masculine style of play. "As King walks back," Cosell said, "she looks more like a man than a lady."[6]

During the third and final set, the overwhelmed Riggs asked for a ten-minute break to massage his cramped legs. The self-proclaimed male chauvinist pig heard boos for the first time. "He'd been the crowd's darling when he came on," Bud Collins reported, "but now he was going down—and they were turning thumbs down like Romans in the Coliseum."[7] King won the Battle of the Sexes in straight sets: 6-4, 6-3, 6-3. In the words of feminist media critic Susan Douglas, she "beat the living crap out of Bobby Riggs." As "women like me screamed with delight in our living rooms, she not only vindicated female athletes and feminism but also inspired many of us to get in shape—not because it would make us beautiful but because it would make us strong and healthy."[8] Even Howard Cosell dropped the insouciance. As Riggs's final volley dribbled into the net, he announced, "Equality for women!"

The bombastic commentator exaggerated less than he knew. King's victory marked a watershed in the expansion of women's athletics in the United States. In 1971, girls remained primarily on the sidelines. Limited to cheers and pom-poms, they accounted for just 7 percent of high school athletes. By 1978, girls made up 32 percent of the athletes in high school locker rooms. College sports followed a similar trend.[9]

Title IX of the 1972 Education Act amendments played a crucial role in this process. Although the law did not take effect until 1978, it prohibited sex discrimination in any educational program receiving federal aid, threatening to withdraw federal funding from institutions that failed to devote resources to women's athletics. Initially many schools balked, but King's victory swept away resistance to Title IX. After the match, institutions dropped planned court challenges; they no longer felt comfortable claiming that women lacked the desire and the ability to compete in interscholastic athletics.[10]

But the Battle of the Sexes dramatized far more than women's achievement in sport. It also signaled the arrival of the women's movement as a broad cultural force. For the first time in U.S. history, the majority of American women worked outside the home. Married women, even mothers of small children, had flooded the workplace. In 1970, the labor force included only 30 percent of women with children under six years old; by 1985, more than half the mothers of small children held paying jobs. Many American women had always worked, of course, especially the poor and minority women. But a new trend developed; women not only had jobs, they pursued careers. During the

Seventies, hospitals, law offices, architecture firms, and faculty lounges opened to aspiring women.[11]

Not just on the tennis court, but in business, politics, and personal relationships, American women gained a new sense of who they were. Even fashions reflected the new awareness. "In recent years," the Boston Women's Health Book Collective reflected, "many women have become as concerned with comfort and practicality as with style and appearance. Increasingly women wear pants; they're easier to move in, warmer in cold weather, and offer greater protection against the eyes of men on the street."[12]

Change even filtered into the language. "What's a Ms.?" a new feminist magazine asked in its spring 1972 preview issue. "For more than twenty years, Ms. has appeared in secretarial handbooks as the suggested form of address when a woman's marital status is unknown." But now, "Ms. is being adopted as a standard form of address by women who want to be recognized as individuals, rather than being identified by their relationship with a man. After all, if *Mr.* is enough to indicate 'male,' then *Ms.* should be enough to indicate 'female.'"[13]

Women also gained a clearer sense of what they were fighting against, for not every opponent was as coarse as Bobby Riggs. Recalling her days as a graduate student at Columbia, novelist Cynthia Ozick remembered that she and one other student—a combative, noisy "Crazy Lady"—had been the only women in Lionel Trilling's famous graduate seminar. After a difficult semester, a "singular revelation crept coldly" through the young student. Because they formed "a connected blur of Woman, Lionel Trilling, master of ultimate distinctions, couldn't tell us apart." To the great critic, "it didn't matter that the Crazy Lady was crazy! He couldn't tell us apart!"[14]

These voyages of discovery were no accident; they grew out of the women's movement's signature feature: its reliance on small consciousness-raising groups. In the late 1960s, radical feminists recognized the importance of what the San Francisco group Sudsofloppen called "Free Space"—a place for women to "think about our lives, our society, and our potential for being creative individuals and for building a women's movement." Feminism's chief task, the Redstockings Collective's 1969 Manifesto affirmed, "is to develop female class consciousness through sharing experience and publicly exposing the sexist foundation of all our institutions. Consciousness-raising," Redstockings explained, "is not 'therapy,' which implies the existence of individual solutions and falsely assumes that the male-female relationship is purely personal, but the only method by which we can ensure that our program for liberation is based on the concrete realities of our lives."15

The gospel of consciousness raising originated among radical feminists, but small discussion groups soon spread around the country. Professional women, students, and suburban housewives discovered shared experiences and rethought their relationships with men, with institutions, with each other. For a dozen Boston-area women, "feelings of frustration and anger toward specific doctors and the medical maze in general" prompted them to "do something about those doctors who were condescending, paternalistic, judgmental, and non-informative." They undertook a summer project, which ultimately resulted in the publication of *Our Bodies, Ourselves: A Book by and for Women,* which became the bible of the women's health movement and the inspiration for feminist clinics and reforms in gynecology and obstetrics across the United States.16

But while the movement brought together millions of American women and made clear to them that the challenges they faced were not theirs alone, it also further fractured a coalition that had long struggled for unity and effectiveness. Women might share similar problems, but they possessed different ways of understanding and combating them. The movement itself divided into different groups with competing aims, and a potent opposition movement emerged. Many women—individuals and small groups—quite understandably became more concerned with their own private battles of the sexes than with the political struggles of women as a whole. The initial impact of feminism, essayist Vivian Gornick wrote, "came as a kind of explosion." For the nation as for millions of individual women, it was "shattering, scattering, everything tumbling about, the old world within splintering even as the new one was collecting." By decade's end, when the debris settled, women and men would find themselves in surprising new places, with transformed experiences and expectations. But despite its substantial achievements, feminism and the men's movement it spawned would ultimately succumb to the prevailing political culture of the Seventies and fail in their most ambitious attempts to reconstruct public life.17

Into the Mainstream

As the Seventies opened, the women's liberation movement commanded the attention of the nation for the first time. Nearly every major news outlet ran stories on women's lib in the first months of 1970. Most of these reports mocked the movement and the women within it. ABC News approvingly quoted Senator Jennings Randolph's description of women's libbers as "bra-less bubbleheads," and CBS News commentator Eric Sevareid dismissed feminist claims of oppression as unfounded and hysterical.[18]

But commentators like Sevareid, Randolph, and ABC's Cosell, who implied that feminists like Billie Jean King strived toward manliness, missed the target. "In no way do we want to become men," the authors of *Our Bodies, Ourselves* explained in the dominant idiom of the late 1960s and early 1970s. "We are women and we are proud of being women. What we do want is to reclaim the human qualities culturally labeled 'male' and integrate them with the human qualities that have been labeled 'female' so that we can all be fuller human people." Feminists routinely criticized the whole idea of fundamental differences, dismissing rhetoric about separate male and female natures, traits, or abilities as parts of the "tool-kit of oppression practiced by the patriarchy." In the early 1970s few women's libbers questioned that view.[19]

Despite that unanimity, the movement was divided in the early 1970s and would grow more so as the decade proceeded. One faction, a generally older cohort of liberal feminists, organized around the National Organization for Women (NOW). NOW had formed in 1966 under the leadership of Betty Friedan, author of the landmark 1963 book *The Feminine Mystique*. The organization included men as well as women and sought to "bring women into full participation in the mainstream of American society now . . . in truly equal partnership with men." NOW agitated for the equal rights amendment, legalized abortion, government-subsidized child care, and enforcement of laws against sex discrimination in employment and housing.[20]

The rival camp, a younger cohort of radical feminists, had come to women's liberation out of their experiences in the civil rights and anti–Vietnam War movements. The new left's ideology of liberation and the reality of sex discrimination within those movements led many young activists to see sexism as the root oppression and to move into the battle for women's liberation. Radical feminism possessed no national association like NOW; indeed, its adherents rejected such bureaucratic, hierarchical structures. Instead they formed hundreds of small cells or collectives—groups like Redstockings, WITCH (Women's International Terrorist Conspiracy from Hell), and the New York Radical Women.

While NOW liberals sought inclusion into established American institutions on equal terms with men, radical feminists scorned that "naive" objective. They wanted to eliminate the patriarchal sex caste system. "Marriage and the family must be abolished as institutions," Ti-Grace Atkinson asserted in 1967, "and 'love' as an ideology to justify them must also go."[21] The 1969 Redstockings Manifesto reiterated this rebellious spirit. "Women are an oppressed class," the New York radical feminist collective declared. "Our oppression is total, affecting every facet of our lives. We are exploited as sex objects, breeders, domestic servants, and cheap labor."[22]

Liberal feminists respected and occasionally emulated these dramatic tactics but found the ideology of radical feminism frightening and counterproductive. In 1970, Friedan warned against the diversionary radicalism that emphasized sexuality and threatened the abolition of marriage and the family. The movement, Friedan warned, needed to "overcome the wallowing, navelgazing rap sessions, the orgasm talk that leaves things unchanged, the rage that will produce a backlash—down with sex, down with love, down with childbearing." She worried that feminism's brightest and most committed young women might turn away from "serious political action."[23]

Still, both sides agreed that the existing system, whether they wished to reform or replace it, perpetuated artificial and invidious gender distinctions that should be eliminated. Only antifeminists like Phyllis Schlafly defended the differences between men and women as natural, ordained, and valuable. In 1970, no women's libber would abide Schlafly's claim that "where man is discursive, logical, abstract, or philosophical, woman tends to be emotional, personal, practical or mystical." Instead, they stressed the essential humanity of women and men, the need for women to reclaim traits and behaviors long denied them as unladylike.[24]

Such was the situation in the late 1960s. But the experiences of American women, the priorities of feminists, and the strategies of their opponents would shift dramatically over the next decade. The Sixties had left political women with crumbs from John F. Kennedy's table, the Presidential Commission on the Status of Women (PCSW) established in December 1961. Like most other commissions, it dawdled and delayed and finally issued a little-noticed report, affirming that women's roles should remain primarily maternal, but denouncing sex discrimination outside the home. The commission never even considered whether the very notions of traditional womanhood it celebrated themselves contributed to sexism. The PCSW demonstrated that even at a time when blacks, the poor, and rural America received concentrated attention from the national government, women remained on the political margins.[25]

In the Seventies, feminism changed all that. In 1971, another official women's policy board was established, this time by women themselves. The National Women's Political Caucus (NWPC) included movement leaders Betty Friedan and Gloria Steinem, members of Congress like Shirley Chisholm and Bella Abzug, civil rights champion Fannie Lou Hamer, United Auto Workers organizer Olga Madur, and even Elly Peterson of the Republican National Committee. The caucus sought to elect more women to public office, strengthen the influence of women in party affairs, and raise money for female candidates, especially after the creation of the Women's Campaign Fund in 1974.[26]

These organizations bankrolled female candidates, but not just any woman received their backing. Eligibility depended on support for "women's issues," broadly construed as opposition to sexism and the desire to move women into the political mainstream. "It can be done," Representative Patricia Schroeder (D, Colorado) reassured the NWPC. "Women can run. And win. You can do it!"[27]

Schroeder was right. During the 1970s women politicos moved into prominent roles in the affairs of the two major political parties, winning substantial numbers of delegate seats at the national conventions and influencing the party platforms. In 1968, women had occupied just 13 percent of the seats at the Democratic Convention; under pressure from the NWPC, the party adopted new guidelines favoring gender equality. Four years later women made up 40 percent of the delegates, and a woman, Jean Westwood, became the chair of the Democratic National Committee. The Republican party followed suit. Women's share of convention seats shot up from 17 percent in 1968 to 30 percent in 1972.[28]

Elective office also beckoned. Women's share of local offices more than doubled, as did the number of female state legislators. Shirley Chisholm mounted a presidential campaign. Ella Grasso won the governorship in Connecticut, becoming the "first lady Governor who was not a Governor's lady." Dixie Lee Ray soon followed suit in Washington State. In New York, Mary Anne Krupsak won the lieutenant governorship with the slogan, "She's Not One of the Boys," and Bella Abzug won a congressional seat, declaring, "This Woman Belongs in the House—The House of Representatives."[29]

Meanwhile, women fared well in the hurly-burly of big city politics. Democrat Jane Byrne won the mayoralty of Chicago, and Republican Kathy Whitmire took over city hall in Houston. Only a few more women won seats on Capitol Hill during the 1970s, but they represented a new breed of feminist congresswomen. They had won office in their own right rather than succeeded to their husbands' seats; they were younger and often had families.[30] Patricia Schroeder emerged as the leader of this new generation. Women, the newly elected Schroeder declared in 1972, "can no longer be mere spectators of the political process, critics on the sidelines; but active participants, playing an important and vital role out on the field."[31]

Women's entry into the political mainstream precipitated substantial policy changes during the 1970s. New laws prohibited sex discrimination in the armed services and educational institutions, and employment discrimination against pregnant women. The Women's Educational Equity Act Program, enacted in 1974, provided federal funds to public schools that actively countered sex role stereotypes and promoted equality of women's educational opportunities.[32]

These advances occasioned little controversy, but other feminist issues proved more contentious. First, activist women successfully fought to reform the law of rape. Inspired by feminist challenges, especially the 1970 Rape Speak-Out of radical feminists and the lobbying of the NOW Rape Task Force, many states revised rape statutes that had long made sexual violence nearly impossible to prosecute. "Rape is only a slightly forbidden fruit," feminists charged in 1971. "In New York State, for instance, the law stipulates that the woman must prove she was raped by force, that 'penetration' occurred, *and* that someone witnessed the rapist in the area of the attack."[33]

New laws barred the cross-examination of victims about their previous sexual history, a favored technique for intimidating women and undermining their testimony. Reformed statutes also dropped requirements for third-party witness testimony. Feminists fought to improve hospital services for rape victims. By mid-decade, 1,500 antirape task forces and study groups had emerged around the country, including 400 autonomous rape crisis centers. These feminist institutions offered self-defense training, hot lines, and shelters and support groups for victims. The Feminist Alliance Against Rape disseminated educational materials, published a national newsletter, and coordinated demands for reforms in courtroom procedures, the rules of evidence, and hospital policies. In 1977, women's groups sponsored "Take Back the Night" marches across the United States. Activists launched similar efforts to confront domestic violence.[34]

Second, feminists fought for safe and legal abortion. In the late 1960s and early 1970s, efforts to liberalize abortion laws won some success at the state level. In 1973, the U.S. Supreme Court legalized abortion across the nation in *Roe v. Wade.* But *Roe* did not end the political battle over reproductive rights. In many states, right-to-lifers attempted to restrict access to abortions. Feminists challenged these requirements in the courts and the state legislatures. Meanwhile, on Capitol Hill, Congressman Henry Hyde (R, Illinois) introduced a series of appropriation bill amendments to bar federal funds for abortion, except when the mother's life was threatened. A series of similar Hyde amendments made sure that reproductive rights remained at the forefront of feminist politics.

Third, activist women inaugurated the campaign for "comparable worth." During the late 1970s and early 1980s, women's incomes continued to lag far behind men's. The problem no longer simply required equal pay for equal work, a requirement already enshrined in law. Rather, the income gap reflected persistent occupational segregation and the undervaluing of women's work. Many typically female jobs, activist women argued, demanded similar or greater skill, effort, and talent than male occupations that received far greater compensation. For example, on average, licensed nurses earned less than truck drivers, child care providers less than unskilled construction workers.[35]

Fourth, feminists paid increasing attention to the feminization of poverty. Activists noted not only that women and children made up the majority of the poor, but that the nation's impoverished were increasingly young and female Feminists campaigned for subsidized child care for working mothers and stricter sanctions against deadbeat dads—those who did not meet their financial obligations to their children. This concern reflected the diversification of feminism by the late 1970s—broadening attention within the movement to the specific struggles of poor women, African American and Latina women, and single mothers.

The Equal Rights Amendment

By the early 1970s, feminism had won many substantial battles. Its most important struggles, however, still lay ahead. No other issue so concentrated the battle of the sexes in the Seventies as the Equal Rights Amendment (ERA), displaying at once the far-reaching consequences and the agonizing limits of women's liberation. Feminist agitation for an ERA dated back to the 1920s, to the immediate aftermath of the suffrage battle. In March 1972, Congress finally passed the ERA and sent it to the states for ratification. The amendment's text, disarmingly short and simple, hardly suggested the monumental changes in attitude and political latitude the ratification struggle would involve. The first of its three short paragraphs declared, "Equality of rights under the law shall not be denied or abridged by the United States or by any State on account of sex." Paragraphs two and three, the enabling clauses, authorized the Congress to "enforce, by appropriate legislation, the provisions of this article" and specified that "this amendment shall take effect two years after the date of ratification."

In the beginning, the ERA seemed certain to pass. On the very day Congress sent the amendment to the states, Hawaii ratified. Over the next two days, Delaware, Nebraska, New Hampshire, Idaho, and Iowa followed suit. "Ratification by mid-1973 looks probable, but not easy," *Ms.* magazine predicted. By 1977, thirty-five of the required thirty-eight states had ratified.[36]

But no more ever would; finally, in 1982, the amendment died. A thorough postmortem revealed a number of intertwined causes for its death. Certainly ERA suffered from its close association with the bitter struggle over abortion. Of the thirty-five states that ratified, thirty did so before the Supreme Court handed down *Roe v. Wade*. Although the ERA had no direct bearing on the abortion issue, both received the sponsorship and vocal backing of the women's movement, and both threatened to remove authority from state legislatures and concentrate that power in the federal courts.[37]

The ERA also had to contend with the emergence of a strong, well-organized antifeminist opposition, led by Phyllis Schlafly. Superficially, Schlafly seemed an odd candidate to lead women against feminism. A master organizer and brilliant speaker, she had run for public office, published several books, and lectured around the nation. In 1970s terms, she appeared as the model of a liberated woman.

Schlafly testified frequently before congressional committees, always urging more defense spending and fewer resources for social programs. She opposed the ERA as much for its impact on the political system (she thought it a scheme to enlarge government) as its effects on the traditional family. The amendment, she warned in 1977, "is a big grab for vast new federal power. It will take out of the hands of the state legislatures and transfer to Washington the last remaining piece of jurisdiction that the national politicians and bureaucrats haven't yet put their meddling fingers into."[38]

For these views, Schlafly became a darling of conservatives and won the nickname "Sweetheart of the Silent Majority." Antifeminism formed part of the emerging New Right in the 1970s, but it became a significant force in its own right, a movement of older, married women and younger religious women disturbed by the achievements and the cultural style of women's liberation. Schlafly and company came into prominence during the ERA fight, asserting that the amendment would harm women by destroying traditional family and sex roles. "The Positive Woman opposes ERA," Schlafly asserted, "because it would be hurtful to women, to men, to children, to the family, to local self-government, and to society as a whole."[39]

It was not just the prospect of shared bathrooms and homosexual marriages that frightened antifeminists, although Schlafly famously warned against both. Rather, ERA opponents worried that the amendment would eliminate all legal and traditional protections for married women. A woman's right to conjugal support would erode, weakening the legal requirement in many states that a husband provide his wife with a home. Men would be free to abandon their wives without the obligations of alimony or child support. Divorced mothers might lose their children to more affluent ex-husbands in custody suits.[40]

Antifeminists depicted housewifery as a bargain—a privilege to be protected—not as the trap Betty Friedan had identified in *The Feminine Mystique*. At anti-ERA rallies, women passed out home-baked goods, bearing labels with the motto: "My heart and my hand went into this dough/For the sake of the family please vote no." The defense of traditional gender roles often reflected powerful religious sentiments. Sexual equality, in many minds, violated biblical authority over women's proper roles and Christian teaching on wifely subservience. But Schlafly made the case in typically blunt language. "If you think diapers and dishes are a never-ending, repetitive routine," she noted, "just remember that most of the jobs outside the home are just as repetitious, tiresome, and boring."[41]

But there was another factor more crucial to the defeat of ERA than antifeminism: geography. By 1977, with the exception of Illinois, all of the states that failed to ratify the ERA lay in either the South or the mountain states with large Mormon populations—places where feminist groups lacked organization and influence. Although strong majorities of Americans across the nation, male and female, favored the ERA, ratification required action in Sunbelt states, where the amendment generated little support. In the South, the conservative movement linked the amendment to distant, out-of-touch elites. Sunbelt politicians associated the ERA with both an overweening Washington bureaucracy, intent on controlling life even within the home, and New York sexual permissiveness and perversion.[42]

Thus, the amendment failed—a defeat that proved more significant than the loss of the amendment's rather modest reforms. By the late 1970s, frustration over the amendment's failure and disenchantment with the potential for achieving thoroughgoing change in American society turned many of the most committed feminists away from protests and litigation, away from legal and constitutional reform. At the same time, these women's very experiences in the movement suggested a new strategy. They could focus on nurturing distinct and distinctive women's communities, establishing a female counterculture running parallel to the male-dominated, patriarchal mainstream and affirming values antithetical to it. Their efforts betokened a revival of cultural feminism.

Cultural Feminism and the Reassertion of Difference

"After years of trying to explain things to men and to change the outside world," movement experiences at last "gave birth to sisterhood." Exhausted "from dredging up facts and arguments for men whom we had previously thought advanced and intelligent," Gloria Steinem explained, "we make another simple discovery. Women understand. We may share experiences, make jokes, paint pictures, and describe humiliations that mean nothing to men, but women *understand.*" These "deep and personal connections of women," Steinem reflected in the pages of *Ms.*, "often ignore barriers of age, economics, worldly experience, race, culture—all the barriers that, in male or mixed society, seem so difficult to cross." She no longer felt strange by herself or with a group of women in public. "I feel just fine. I am continually moved to discover I have sisters."[43]

By 1973, a wide network of feminist organizations and institutions had emerged: women's clinics, credit unions, rape crisis centers, bookstores, newspapers, book publishers, and athletic leagues. Activists had established few of these institutions with cultural feminist objectives. They had just formed spontaneously, out of the immediate needs of the women's movement. Few, if any, self-consciously sought to serve a specifically female culture or to construct an explicitly feminist set of separate, alternative institutions.

But by the mid-1970s, the sheer weight and influence of women's institutions had prompted a rethinking of their origins and missions. In 1970, there were no battered women's shelters in the United States, no rape crisis centers, no services for displaced homemakers. By the mid-1980s, literally thousands of institutions dedicated to women's needs dotted the landscape. In 1970, American universities offered fewer than twenty courses about women; two decades later, there were more than 30,000 on the undergraduate level alone.[44]

This explosion of feminist scholarship and female institutions reflected not just an expansion of the women's movement but a reorientation of it. Early Seventies radical feminist publications had titles like "It Ain't Me Babe," "Tooth 'n Nail," "off our backs," "No More Fun and Games." Late Seventies cultural feminist publications revealed a new emphasis with names like *Amazon Quarterly, Womanspirit,* and *Chrysalis: A Magazine of Women's Culture.*[45]

Cultural feminism accepted gender difference, but without a sense of hierarchy or inferiority. "Women have been socialized to be passive," one publication explained. "But they also learned to be nurturing, affiliative, cooperative, in short endowed with more truly human qualities than men are currently socialized with." Cultural feminism pointed not toward mere equality but toward a feminist reconstruction of American society based on gender differences.[46]

Instead of radical egalitarianism, such as Shulamith Firestone's insistence that women's liberation required the abolition of pregnancy and motherhood, feminists increasingly stressed the positive virtues of female biology and women's culture. Women's health advocates campaigned for breastfeeding and natural childbirth; they redefined pregnancy as a gift rather than a burden. The findings of psychologists Nancy Chodorow and Carol Gilligan proved particularly influential in this reassertion of difference. According to Chodorow, girls and boys followed vastly different paths of individuation and identity formation. Sons early learned to separate from their mothers; they became competitive, focused on rules and rights. But daughters discovered themselves through their relationships with their mothers. They thus became empathic, relationship oriented, interested in consensus.[47]

In a series of results published beginning in 1971 and eventually collected in the 1982 book *In a Different Voice,* Gilligan extended and popularized Chodorow's ideas about female development. Gilligan's most famous conclusions derived from her analysis of the Heinz dilemma, a standard test of children's moral development. Heinz's wife lay dying, psychologists told children, but he could not afford to buy the medicine that would save her. Should he steal the drug? Boys answered clearly, usually invoking abstract principles of laws and rights: No, Heinz should not steal the drug and violate the law; yes, he should because the right to life supersedes the prohibition on robbery. Girls responded differently; often they refused to answer at all. They would reject the terms of the question, attempt to inject new information, seek a negotiated solution. And psychologists would dutifully conclude that girls suffered from arrested moral development.[48]

Gilligan reinterpreted those results. Women were not underdeveloped, she maintained, but other-developed. Girls saw a world of connection and relationship, a world that cohered through human connection rather than through a system of laws. They insisted on solutions to the Heinz dilemma that recognized this set of relationships. Psychologists, Gilligan concluded, have tried to fashion women out of masculine cloth by implicitly adopting the male as the norm. "It all goes back to Adam and Eve," Gilligan wryly added, "a story which shows, among other things, that if you make a woman out of a man, you are bound to get into trouble."[49]

Celebrations of women's differences gained greater currency in the late 1970s.[50] Theologian Mary Daly, author of such books as *Beyond God the Father* and *GynEcology,* argued that feminism had awakened a "new and post-patriarchal spiritual consciousness"—that women possessed a different relationship to the earth and to the divine. In 1979, Barnard College assembled leading figures in academia, politics, and the media for a major women's studies conference, "The Future of Difference."[51]

But the drive toward cultural feminism derived as much from practical experience as from theory. Women's groups founded new businesses—Diana Press, Olivia Records, Women in Distribution, Feminist Credit Unions. "It's useless to advocate more and more 'political action,'" a founder of Olivia Records argued, "if some of it doesn't result in the permanent material improvement of the lives of women." Feminist writers or musicians would not have to please male editors or executives. Women would not have to submit to sexist doctors or bankers. And feminist businesses could provide opportunity and self-sufficiency for activists—economic space truly free of the patriarchy.[52]

Even the Battle of the Sexes reflected the ascendance of cultural feminism. During the late 1960s, the major events in the tennis world finally opened to professionals, ending the phony amateurism and under-the-table payments that had long corrupted the system. But when tournaments openly awarded prize money, women players suffered from a vast disparity in the size of purses. Billie Jean King won the Italian Open in 1970 and earned only one-sixth of what the men's champion earned.[53]

In response, King and six other top players joined with publisher Gladys

Heldman and the Philip Morris Tobacco Company to create the Virginia Slims tennis circuit in the fall of 1970. The idea of the Slims tour was to build an autonomous, alternative institution, controlled by women for the benefit of women. The tour—and the players' aggressive promotion of it—allowed the circuit to grow despite constant disruption and opposition from the old-line tennis federations. The Slims tour gradually added tournaments and prize money. Billie Jean King had consecutive seasons winning purses over $100,000, the first woman athlete to accomplish that feat.[54]

The women's health movement was perhaps the most substantial achievement of the 1970s push toward separate but different. Feminists opened abortion clinics, natural birth control centers, and more than one hundred freestanding birth centers. Staffed by female midwives, these centers offered alternatives to the anonymous, sterile, technological procedures of most hospital maternity wards, where obstetricians treated pregnancy as a disease and dismissed the concerns of laboring mothers.[55]

This increased attention to women's bodies and their needs also pointed toward more complex shifts in social behavior, especially with regard to female sexuality. The Seventies witnessed the so-called sexual revolution—a problematic term, but still a meaningful one. It referred to a wide spectrum of experimentation, from more permissive attitudes about obscene materials to almost comic accounts of swinging suburbanites and spouse-swapping parties. The sexual revolution involved at least equal parts exploitation and liberation, and feminists remained ever on uneasy terms with it.[56]

Erica Jong's sensational bestseller *Fear of Flying* crystallized the feminist debate over sexuality when it topped the bestseller charts in 1973–1974. Jong's roman-à-clef told the story of Isadora, a married woman who flees her husband for a lover and ultimately discovers she must find freedom and fulfillment on her own. The novel featured frank female sexuality and explicit language. Isadora openly rated the physical characteristics and sexual skills of her lovers, talked freely about limp pricks, "silky penises," and her "unappeasable hunger for men's bodies," and idealized the "Zipless Fuck"—perfect, meaningless sex between strangers. Reviewers (mostly male) read the book as an erotic novel. John Updike praised it as the "most uninhibited, delicious erotic novel a woman ever wrote," and *Newsweek* called it a "funny, horny first novel that would scare any male who believes women 'don't think like that.'" Some feminists dismissed the book, finding Isadora naive and weak. NOW's president charged Jong with "confusing libidinal bluntness with liberation." Still, many readers recognized *Fear of Flying* as a feminist odyssey of consciousness raising rather than a brief for sexual license. Jong had sketched a portrait of an authentic woman, one who wanted freedom, autonomy, and the right to express herself in many different ways.[57]

Whatever its doubts about the sexual revolution, feminism greatly influenced the new, freer forms of sexuality. Premarital sexuality or sexual assertion of any kind no longer made a woman a social pariah, ostracized as easy or immoral. In fact, the women's movement revolutionized the understanding and the experience of female sexuality. In the Seventies, Americans discovered the clitoral orgasm (and simultaneously uncovered the "myth" of the vaginal orgasm). This "discovery," of course, did not imply that no one had previously experienced clitoral stimulation. Masters and Johnson's landmark 1966 study, *Human Sexual Response,* had established that women could experience multiple orgasms in sexual encounters and that female orgasms were anatomically centered in the clitoris. But there had been no such term in the lexicon, no such concept, no understanding of women's sexual pleasure that was not morally suspect.[58]

Feminism popularized a new language and a new ideology of sex. In a famous 1970 essay, Ann Koedt described the vaginal orgasm as a male deception, a tool of domination. Men fear lesbianism, Koedt asserted; they worry "that they will become sexually expendable if the clitoris is substituted for the vagina as the center of pleasure for women." The myth of the vaginal orgasm also made women invisible and insignificant. It defined women—or, in this case, women's sexuality—only in terms of their benefits to men. "Sexually," Koedt concluded, "a woman was not seen as an individual wanting to share equally in the sexual act, any more than she was seen as a person with individual desires when she did anything else in society."[59]

The debate over female sexuality penetrated popular culture in 1975 with the release of Donna Summer's disco hit "Love to Love You Baby." The record featured sixteen minutes of "persuasive moaning" and inspired rumors that Summer had recorded the song *in flagrante delicto.* "Love to Love You Baby" inspired intense controversy. Clearly an expression of female sexual assertion, even sympathetic critics wondered whether the song, like much of the sexual revolution, treated women as liberated individuals or dehumanized sex objects. But as one defender of the song concluded, "If a woman felt it, don't discount it." Sex was different after the early 1970s, with all the possibilities and dangers that presented to American women.[60]

More than anything else, however, it was the vexed question of lesbianism that linked assertions of a distinctive feminine sexuality to broader conceptions of an autonomous women's culture. Throughout the 1970s, opponents of women's liberation equated feminism with lesbianism and denounced women's libbers as hairy-legged, unfeminine man haters. Mainstream feminist organizations like NOW repeatedly refuted these charges, often taking great pains to distance themselves from the aims of lesbian activists. This cold-shoulder treatment so upset some women that a group of lesbian feminists, led by the writer Rita Mae Brown, resigned from NOW.[61]

Nonetheless, self-identified lesbians played a critical role in the evolution of the women's movement, supplying much of its theoretical edge and rhetorical thunder and laying the foundations for many women's institutions and organizations. During the 1970s, lesbians identified much more often, and more prominently, with feminism than with the gay rights movement. They defined lesbianism not as a form of sexuality or a community based on sexual orientation, but as an expression of feminine identity—a purer distillation of female culture. Soon after departing from NOW, Radicalesbians circulated "The Woman-Identified Woman." What is a lesbian? the broadside asked. "A lesbian is the rage of all women condensed to the point of explosion." The manifesto laid out the argument for cultural feminism, stressing "the primacy of women relating to women, of women creating a new consciousness of and with each other, which is at the heart of women's liberation, and the basis for the cultural revolution."[62]

By the late 1970s, that woman-centered version of feminism would dominate the movement, among lesbians and heterosexuals, younger radicals and older liberals.[63] Although this attitude never entirely displaced the more mainstream legal and political agenda of egalitarian feminism, it became a characteristic way of seeing the world—one that resonated with the broader cultural and religious developments of the decade. In their growing distrust of government and politics and their embrace of a distinctive subculture, feminists echoed the tenor of the times. By the early 1980s, they relied more and more on their own organizations and communities, touting the virtues of local institutions, entrepreneurship, and shared identity. Ironically, feminists shared far more with their new-right enemies than either side recognized.

From "The Duke" to Alan Alda: Men and Masculinity

As feminism spread, it inevitably affected men as well as women, fracturing the once-dominant male archetype just as it had the female. Men had to face new social conditions: renegotiating family roles at home and confronting women in the workplace, the political arena, the club, and the classroom. By challenging ideas about femininity and women's nature, feminist thinkers also made it clear that conceptions of masculinity were up for grabs. Americans' most basic notions of manhood needed to be worked out; they could no longer be assumed.

A few snapshots framed this shift from John Wayne to Alan Alda; from New York Yankees Iron Man Lou Gehrig to *Iron John*, the mythic hero of men's movement leader Robert Bly; from the strong, silent type to the sensitive New Age male.

For postwar Americans, the Duke—movie actor John Wayne—had long conjured the very ideal of American manhood. Wayne embodied at once the western frontiersman of yore and the great cinema heroes of the 1950s. Tough, even violent, and fiercely independent, this emblematic man knew the ways of the world. He lived by a code, even if he did not live by the law. He never revealed his feelings. Although he might be burning up inside, he never showed it. He barely even talked.

John Wayne's starring role in the classic 1948 western *Red River* offered a potent example of this postwar American machismo. Wayne's character—a gruff, tough Texas rancher named Dunson—enters into a dispute with an intrepid younger man played by Montgomery Clift. The audience knows Dunson loves his younger antagonist. Clift's Matthew Garth is the son he never had. The female lead begs Dunson to forgive Garth, but Wayne's character refuses, impassively declaring, "Woman, next time I see him, I'm gonna kill him and there's nothing you can say or do that's gonna change my mind."

Dunson is torn apart inside, but duty, violent duty, calls. The two men finally meet, but Garth refuses Dunson's challenge to a gunfight. Calling him yellow, Dunson throws away his six-shooter and socks Garth in the face. A fist-fight ensues until Joanne Dru, the female star, picks up the discarded revolver and stops the fight. In a barrage of words, an unstoppable flow of verbiage these laconic men can never even contemplate, Dru says what they cannot. She had been scared for days, but everyone could see that Garth and Dunson loved each other, that they would never hurt each other. The men look on in silent amazement. These guys can express themselves only through violence; they need women to say for them in words, in emotions, what they feel but cannot or will not say.

During the 1970s, new representations of maleness appeared. Actor Alan Alda became, in the words of *Redbook* magazine, "America's Sweetheart." He is "something more complicated than just a nice guy," the women's magazine reported in 1976. "He is that interesting combination, a man ambitious and successful in his professional life who also is intensely concerned about his emotional and personal life." A friend of the women's movement, Alda served as the spokesman for Men for the Equal Rights Amendment. He was a member of the National Commission for the Observance of International Women's Year and a self-declared feminist. Alda embodied the new breed of sensitive man who did the dishes and made professional sacrifices for his family. "You might say," one profile concluded, "that he has the kind of personality that's recently labeled 'androgynous,' combining strengths and values traditionally associated with both masculinity and femininity."[64]

Alda found "it harmful that many people think men and women can only come together for the purposes of sex. I find pleasure in working with women," he explained, "working for women's rights, talking with women, associating with them, becoming *friends*."[65] In *Ms.*, the actor laid out the male argument for feminism. The women's movement in general and the ERA in particular, Alda claimed, would liberate men as well as women. Men, "with all their bravado, have seldom had the courage to stick a flower on their desks."[66]

A spate of serious books emerged in the Seventies to examine the problem that Alda identified—*The Male Machine, The Liberated Man, The Hazards of Being Male.* All of them diagnosed the suffering that traditional notions of masculinity imposed on men and the benefits of becoming more sensitive, more liberated. Medical science seemed to confirm pop psychology. Seventies authorities noted that men developed more ulcers and died younger than women. Men suffered higher incidences of lung, heart, and liver disease and higher death rates from cancer. They shunned nutritious diets as "rabbit food" and loaded up on unhealthy red meat and martinis. Most ominous, as two cardiologists showed in their 1974 best-seller, *Type A Behavior and Your Heart,* machismo caused heart attacks. Aggressive, competitive behavior and reserved, repressed emotions constituted the Type A personality; these characteristically male behaviors predicted increased risk of coronary heart disease and premature death.[67]

One of these 1970s excavations of masculinity, *The Season's of a Man's Life,* suggested that the pivotal life change for men came in their thirties and forties, when they must "experience the emergence and integration of the more feminine aspects of the self." These successful Seventies men possessed the traits that earlier sociological surveys had labeled stereotypically female: interest in their own appearance, aware of the feelings of others, gentle, talkative.[68]

By the end of the decade, profound confusion over men's nature and men's roles would give rise to a self-conscious men's movement. It would eventually produce the poetry and meditations of Robert Bly, the men's studies movement in academia, the drum-beating retreats and new men's journals of contemporary America.

Even during the 1950s, Americans had recognized that their cinema heroes represented a lost archetype. They were idealizations of a glorious but vanished male past. Long before Betty Friedan shattered the domestic ideal of the Fifties—with its housewives slaving away in what she called the "comfortable concentration camp" of the suburban home—other critics had condemned the domestic, suburban ideal as a prison for men. Trapped in gray flannel suits and commuter trains, inmates of the "organization," they led lives of not-so-quiet desperation and railed against their overly comfortable, overly feminized lives.[69]

Social science like William Whyte's *Organization Man*, novels like Sloane Wilson's *The Man in the Gray Flannel Suit*, and the rebellious youth culture of bearded bohemians and leather-clad rock 'n' rollers suggested that American men had become soft, dependent, feminine. They all promoted rebellion against the life of the corporation, the commute, the little league and the barbecue.

To be a man in postwar America had been defined more by its negations than by itself. More than anything else manliness meant not to be womanly—and not to be homosexual. The 1950s and 1960s witnessed particularly intense fears of and hostility toward homosexuality; in fact, Americans linked homosexuality closely to communism, that gravest menace of the cold war. It was no coincidence that John Wayne, the era's model of assertive masculinity, also served on the Hollywood Committee for the Re-Election of Joseph McCarthy.[70]

Thus, the gay rights movement of the late 1960s and 1970s would play a crucial role in transforming American ideals of masculinity. Most postwar Americans understood sexuality as a spectrum running from most manly to most womanly. They assumed that homosexual men were effeminate, lesbians masculine. For a man to prove his heterosexuality, he had to eschew any effeminate behavior or trait.

During the 1950s and early 1960s, gay rights activists had fought against this stereotype; they had argued that sexual preference was incidental, that homosexual men were regular guys, professionals, working men. But during the late 1960s, a new generation of gay rights protest emerged. Just as in the civil rights movement Stokely Carmichael and the Black Panthers challenged the orientation of older leaders like Martin Luther King, Jr., and within feminism younger radical feminists had challenged their older liberal allies, a more militant gay politics developed. Inspired by the social movements of the Sixties, the new activism also acknowledged and joined with a growing gay subculture in places like San Francisco's Castro District and New York's Christopher Street.[71]

Stonewall defined the emergence of this new activism. On June 27, 1969, police officers from Manhattan's Sixth Precinct entered the Stonewall Inn, a gay bar on Christopher Street in the heart of Greenwich Village. They expected a routine raid. The Stonewall Inn operated without a liquor license, had reputed ties with organized crime, and featured "scantily clad go-go boys as entertainment." The Stonewall catered to a young and largely nonwhite clientele, including many drag queens. But the patrons at the Stonewall reacted to the raid in anything but the routine way. According to the *Village Voice*, "The scene became explosive. Limp wrists were forgotten. Beer cans and bottles were heaved at the windows and a rain of coins descended on the cops." The *Voice* reporter "heard several cries of 'let's get some gas,' but the blaze of flame which soon appeared in the window of the Stonewall was still a shock." Reinforcements arrived on the scene, but the trouble had barely started. Rioting continued into the night, with angry protesters leading assaults on rows of uniformed police. The next evening, graffiti touting "Gay Power" had appeared along Christopher Street.[72]

Stonewall sparked a nationwide liberation struggle; it also led to more open, assertive statements of homosexuality. The *Village Voice*'s silly headline, "Limp Wrists Are Forgotten," captured a basic truth. Among gay America's many varied subcultures emerged a sexually assertive, muscle-building, leather-wearing, almost hypermacho element. During the 1970s, gay males were associated increasingly with short hair, leather boots, Levi jackets, and tight jeans.[73] In 1978, record producer Jacques Morali playfully exploited the new gay machismo when he dressed struggling musical stage actors as a cowboy, a construction worker, a military man, an Indian chief, a leather-clad biker, and a "hot cop" to form the "Village People." The disco combo would score platinum hits with ironic invocations of machismo like "Macho Man" and "In the Navy."

The gay rights movement transformed Americans' understanding of homosexuality, and of masculinity in general. Straight men could "soften" themselves without fearing they might be labeled effeminate or latent homosexuals. They could become less aggressive and competitive, more sensitive, more concerned about their appearance, their feelings, and their relationships. "It is now in straight discos," one observer wrote in the Seventies, "that we see soft-looking men."[74]

Feminism also contributed to this rethinking of John-Wayne-ish masculinity. In 1974, Warren Farrell published *The Liberated Man,* which denounced the insidious effects of the masculine value system, for women and for men. "If John Wayne—the Moses of masculinity—were to hand down the 'The Ten Commandments of Masculinity,'" Farrell explained, "they would forbid crying or exposed emotions, shows of vulnerability, empathy, or doubt." Men must cultivate ego, bring home the bacon, devote their lives to work, and "have an answer to all problems at all times." And "above all: Thou shalt not read *The Liberated Man* or commit other forms of introspection."[75]

The book identified "twenty-one specific areas in which a man could benefit from what is now called women's liberation." They included freedom from the responsibilities of being sole breadwinner, so a husband could take risks on the job or pursue more fulfilling work, even if it paid poorly. Liberated women also promised freer, more open sexuality and relief from nagging. "If a woman has her own life and destiny to control," *The Liberated Man* promised, "she will not be as likely to feel the need to control her husband."[76]

If a relationship soured, Farrell concluded, it would be easier to break up with a liberated woman without "guilt feelings of leaving her with nothing when she has given up the best years of her life to him." Farrell and other "liberated men" recognized that many feminist achievements—like liberalized divorce laws and weakening taboos against sexual expression outside marriage—benefited men. In the 1970s, men initiated most divorces under the new no-fault laws, and more American men chose to live as bachelors. The number of men living by themselves doubled over the course of the decade.[77]

In *The Male Machine,* Marc Fasteau described traditional notions of masculinity as a "Male Mystique." A male machine lurked in the background of every man, Fasteau warned, "a special kind of being, different from women, children, and men who don't measure up." This stereotype harnessed men, restricted them, cut them off from their true, authentic selves. "He has armor plating," Fasteau wrote, "which is virtually impregnable. His circuits are never overrun by irrelevant personal signals."[78]

Conforming to these stereotypes forced men to repress fears, to stifle the compassion and sensitivity that women were encouraged to feel. In the wake of feminism, Fasteau imagined a future of more natural, androgynous gender roles: "In such a society girls will be allowed to play baseball, and boys will be allowed to play with dolls; girls will call boys for dates, and boys won't always pay for the movie."[79]

Gloria Steinem hailed Fasteau's conclusions. "Yes," she affirmed, "this book is about the destructiveness of the sexual caste system" and "supports most feminist criticisms of current injustice." But Fasteau and his fellow sensitive men did not merely voice a condescending sympathy for women's liberation, "the usual 'let me help you' liberalism that demands gratitude, and probably continued inferiority, in return." Fasteau and his fellow sufferers applied the insights of feminism to themselves, raised their own consciousness, and changed their own lives.[80]

Masculinity, all the 1970s explorations of the man problem agreed, caused endless suffering.[81] And Seventies men paid heed. At decade's end, an *Esquire* magazine survey of "today's young men" discovered widespread uncertainty over gender roles. Young men valued success and professional achievement every bit as much as their stuffy elders; they also wanted families. But these twentysomething males insisted on freedom and independence. They feared responsibility and worried about stress. They did not want the heart attacks, the ulcers, the nervous breakdowns of their own Organization Man fathers.[82]

These confused young men tended to put off life decisions; *Esquire* called them "the Postponing Generation." According to pop sociologist Gail Sheehy, "Young men aren't the same anymore." A new dream had "seeped out of the social upheaval of the Sixties and has been progressively softening the edges of the old success mold." American men in their twenties "don't want to work hard. They demand more time for 'personal growth.' They are obsessed by what they call 'trade-offs' in life." Responding to an *Esquire* magazine survey, these men ranked "being loving" highest on the list of personal qualities they deemed important. "Being ambitious" and "Being able to lead effectively" fell to the bottom of the list.[83] "I don't think I would consider myself overindulgent," one young man reported. "My father would. But my generation, even those of us who are big achievers, has respect for people who manage to create meaningful lives for themselves doing something other than work. My contemporaries see being laid-back as a virtue."[84]

These sensitive, self-exploring, unafraid-to-cry men became the subject of some fun. A decade later, folksinger Christine Lavin would lampoon them in song as "Sensitive New Age Guys." These men "like to talk about their feelings." They cry at weddings and "are hard to tell from women." But although "their consciousness is always raising," their "tax-free income is amazing." They are even "concerned about your orgasm, even though they think it's more important that they have 'em."[85]

By the time of Lavin's parody, the 1970s conflicts over masculinity had received the attention of a vast, self-conscious men's movement. It began formally in 1970 with the founding of the first men's center at Berkeley, over the next two decades, it would spread across the nation. Men's forums and consciousness-raising groups appeared, along with weekend retreats in the woods, men's studies sections in bookstores, even a political mobilization based on assumptions about men's special identity and aggrieved status.

During the Seventies, the men's movement appeared in three distinct manifestations. First, there emerged a tiny political movement organized around so-called men's issues like reforming the child custody laws, which usually awarded children to mothers. This movement originated with small groups like Boston's Fathers for Equal Justice and eventually found its institutional home in the National Organization for Men. Founded in 1983, the organization modeled itself on the women's movement and consciously sought to promote men's rights.[86]

Second, a men's studies movement developed in academia. It spawned numerous books and journals and eventually received much attention from the national press. Unlike the National Organization for Men, men's studies arose as an outgrowth of women's studies scholarship and remained sympathetic to feminism.

The third, and by far the biggest and most important, element was the mythopoetic men's movement—the motley assemblage of drum-beating retreats, New Age–style group therapy, men's health magazines and cosmetics, poetry readings, and celebrations of primal masculinity. Led by poet Robert Bly, this phenomenon burst into the national imagination after Bly's appearance on a 1990 Bill Moyers TV special and the simultaneous publication of his book *Iron John*. But Bly and others had originated the movement during the mid-1970s, in the midst of their own wrestling with new ideas about manhood. By 1974, more than 300 men's groups had organized and one journalist heard "the first, faltering footsteps of a men's liberation movement."[87]

Like so many of his contemporaries, Bly denounced the narrowness and limitations of inherited notions of masculinity. "We who are now alive," the early

Bly concluded, "represent the tail end of a long development of masculine consciousness," a flight away "from the mother goddess. . . . American humanity has
gone as far as it's going to go in the direction of masculine consciousness." Bly
discovered he could no longer write poems relying only on his masculine side;
he turned to the mother goddess within as a "matter of desperation."[88]

But the "Deep Masculine" soon reemerged. In 1975, Bly organized a "Great
Mother" conference for writers, artists, and intellectuals. On the men's beach,
from which women were banned, male conferees constructed a *temenos,* a
giant penis. They chanted, sang, and talked, engaging in ceremonies that somehow merged premodern initiation rites with New Age encounter sessions. Out
of this strange event, Bly and like-minded men built a vast movement.

The mythopoetic men's movement repudiated both the macho and sensitive models of masculinity. Bly himself rejected "the savage within men," which
he blamed for much violence, environmental degradation, and other evils, but
he also wanted to "dethrone the Great Mother" that had turned men into
wimps. In the aftermath of feminism, Bly and his allies attempted to forge a
new American man.

Bly agreed with Alan Alda and Marc Fasteau that "the images of the right
man, the tough man, the true man which he received in High School do not
work in life." But Bly pointed American men in a different direction, toward
ancient texts and oral traditions. "It is in the old myths," Bly explained, "that we
hear of Zeus energy, that positive leadership energy in men, that popular culture declares does not exist; from King Arthur we learn the value of the male
mentor in the lives of young men." Men should not reject the troubling, domi-
neering, aggressive sides of their nature, but accept it, nurture it, channel it.[89]

The Seventies had witnessed a flurry of new identities and associations;
Americans found new affiliations, alternatives to the public sphere and the
national community. Even feminism split into numerous factions that disagreed as often as they united. The rise of self-conscious masculinity organized—and divided—men over questions that many had never previously
realized existed. If John Wayne represented one pole, the Hegelian thesis, and
Alan Alda the other, the Hegelian antithesis, *Esquire,* Robert Bly, and the
National Organization for Men formed the synthesis. The men's movement
often sparked ridicule, but what it was trying to accomplish was no joke. For
example, the revised model of masculinity it forged stimulated new interest in
fatherhood.[90]

The Seventies witnessed a redefinition of fatherhood. No longer would
Americans accept and even applaud disconnected, distant, disciplinarian dads.

Fathers wanted, and their families expected, much more paternal involvement in child rearing. *Esquire*'s 1979 survey reported that raising children gave young men more life satisfaction than any other experience.[91]

In 1979, Robert Benton directed a film investigating these new family dynamics. *Kramer vs. Kramer* starred Meryl Streep as a wife and mother who splits, leaving her young son with his father (played by Dustin Hoffman), a distant parent who hardly knows his son and has no idea how to run the household. Over the course of the film, that all changes, and Hoffman's Kramer becomes a devoted father, even losing his high-powered job in the process. Kramer cooks meals, arranges play dates, reads bedtime stories. Ultimately he fights—and wins—a custody battle against his ex-wife. At the film's end, Kramer is a lesser advertising executive but a greater man.

Many real men expressed similar sentiments. In "Conflicting Interests," one of the first columns to run in the *New York Times*'s "About Men" feature, Harvard professor Donald H. Bell noted the confusion and resentment men of his generation had experienced. "There is a sense that somehow we have been deprived of the chance to become the sort of men we expected to be as we grew up—men who, like those of earlier generations, possess a sure-footed sense of what is expected and of how to meet those expectations." But in the end, for Bell, the career sacrifices his new familial duties compelled proved more satisfying than conventional achievements. After spending a workday at home with his sick toddler, Bell "found that I had learned something further about what it means to be a man, something that goes beyond simply bringing home a paycheck."[92]

Still, despite these metamorphoses in fatherhood, much of the old style endured, and confusion prevailed where there had once been consensus. When surveyed by pollsters, men affirmed the priority of spending time with children and helping out with the housework. But fathers and husbands only slowly increased their actual time commitment to family activities, even when their wives were working full time. "More couples wanted to share and imagined they did," one study of family dynamics in the late 1970s concluded. But "behavior changed little."[93]

The Battle over Family Values

Such dramatic changes in male and female roles were bound to induce anxiety and conflict in family life. A 1980 Gallup poll reported that 45 percent of Americans felt that family life had gotten worse over the past decade; only 37 percent thought it had improved.[94] This uncertainty came to a head in two major events of the late 1970s: the Houston conference to celebrate International Women's Year in 1977 and the White House Conference on the Family in 1980.

In many ways, the November 1977 National Women's Conference in Houston marked the crest of the women's movement. Feminists gathered to consolidate their achievements, legitimate their influence, and introduce an ambitious agenda for further action. "Houston," Gloria Steinem asserted, represented a "Constitutional Convention for American women. They ratified the existing Constitution by demanding full inclusion in it, and then outlined the legislative changes that must take place if female citizens are to fully enjoy those rights for the first time."[95]

The conference report, *What Women Want*, laid out an impressive list of demands. It called for feminist education in the schools, including books and curricula that would "restore to women their history and their achievements and give them knowledge and methods to reinterpret their life experiences." It warned about glass ceilings in industry, politics, and academe and recommended steps to promote women to the highest levels of American institutions. The conference also resolved that the federal government "should assume a major role in directing and providing comprehensive, voluntary, flexible-hour, bias-free, non-sexist quality child care."[96]

The four-day conference marked the culmination of months of preparation and years of political action. It assembled more than 20,000 women (only 2,000 of whom served as official delegates) and attracted many of the most famous women in America. Bella Abzug chaired the proceedings, and participants included first ladies Rosalynn Carter, Lady Bird Johnson, and Betty Ford, tennis champion Billie Jean King, actress Jean Stapleton, and anthropologist Margaret Mead. Many activists saluted the "spirit of Houston." "If you say 'Houston' to people, that connects you, just like that," one woman told an interviewer. "It gives you entrée, like the 'old boys network.'"[97] Reporting back to its English readers, the *Evening Standard* declared, "The women's movement is now a truly national, unified engine of change which could conceivably become the cutting edge of the most important issues America faces in the next decade."[98]

But the spirit of Houston proved too intoxicating for sober assessment. Already in 1977, the policy-oriented reforms the conference championed struck many Americans, including many committed feminists, as hopelessly ineffective and bureaucratic. The conclave's central demand—immediate ratification of the ERA—would prove unattainable. Clear-eyed observers could tell the amendment would wither in the harsh, dry soil of the Sunbelt, where the tenacity of antiabortion and antifeminist counterprotests stunned the conferees.

In Missouri, antifeminists led by Phyllis Schlafly actually took over the delegate nominating process for the Houston conference. Arriving in chartered buses on voting day, a horde of New-Right women registered at the door and overwhelmed the feminists who had assembled for a three-day regional planning session. After electing a conservative delegation, this "new suffragist" faction departed in their buses without attending any of the workshops or entering into dialogue with the rest of the participants. Similar guerrilla actions took place in other states, so that antifeminist women controlled about one-fifth of the seats in Houston.[99]

While the National Women's Conference convened, Schlafly organized a counterconference across the city. The "Pro-Family rally" drew large crowds and considerable media attention. "Houston will finish off the women's movement," Schlafly crowed. "It will show them off for the radical, anti-family, pro-lesbian people they are."[100] The Sweetheart of the Silent Majority did not fire far off-target. Indeed, the New-Right opposition, not the woman's movement, would emerge as the "national, unified engine of change," the real cutting edge of the next decade.

This momentum shift became evident during the 1980 White House Conference on the Family. During his 1976 presidential campaign, Jimmy Carter had proposed a national conference on family life, wanting "to see what we can do, not simply as a government, but as a nation to strengthen the family." After winning the election, the administration repeatedly delayed the conference. More than most other Democrats, Carter and his top aides understood the growing power of evangelical Christians and Sunbelt conservatives. The Houston conference had prominently featured radical feminists and lesbian activists, and the president realized that association with such militants would not help his campaign for reelection. The administration moved slowly and laboriously to redeem Carter's campaign pledge, attempting to install moderate elements like the Red Cross, church groups, and Planned Parenthood in leadership positions.

But the administration could not control the planning or delegate selection processes. Conservative, profamily activists assailed the dominance of profeminist, pro-ERA, prochoice forces. In some states, like Virginia and Oklahoma, the New Right took over the state meetings. In New York, an influential state legislator threatened to hold up funding for the state's delegation if the governor did not include more "pro-family, pro-life" members. In Alabama, Governor Forrest H. James announced that his state would not participate in the conference. "Terminology used in White House guidelines," the governor's wife complained, did not "establish traditional Judeo-Christian values." Governor and Mrs. James found the conference's directive to choose delegates without regard to sexual orientation and to respect differences in lifestyle and family structure "offensive" and believed that they in no way reflected "the basic concepts of most Alabamians."[101]

The White House Conference on the Family convened not in Washington, but in three regional conclaves during the summer of 1980. President Carter attended the Baltimore meeting in June and tried to balance contending interests. "Where Government involvement is helpful, let it be strengthened," he declared in his opening remarks. "Where it is harmful, let it be changed." But the president's plea for cooperation fell on deaf ears. Antifeminist groups stormed out of the Baltimore meeting, allowing healthy majorities to endorse abortion rights and the ERA. "The Baltimore Conference," conservative columnist James J. Kilpatrick complained, "had been stacked, packed, and rigged to produce these prepared affirmations. Fiasco No. 2 and Fiasco No. 3 will follow identical scripts."[102]

In Minneapolis, the profamily delegates stayed, and the rival factions remained more balanced. After heated debate, 6,000 southern and midwestern delegates endorsed the ERA and rejected a ban on abortion, but the conclave nonetheless approved a definition of families that excluded homosexual relationships. The Minneapolis meeting also denounced the domination of public institutions by "secular humanism."[103]

In the end, the White House conference reached broad agreement on such noncontroversial measures as encouraging employers to adopt flex-time, efforts to stem drug and alcohol abuse, and home assistance for the disabled.[104] But the conflicts over ERA, abortion, and government social spending pointed to a tidal wave of discontent that had been gathering throughout the Seventies. Americans distrusted the political institutions in Washington and resented the cultural authority of New York and Hollywood. They relied more and more on their own initiative, on constructing alternative institutions, nurturing alternative private cultures.

In the early 1970s, these rumblings of dissent had cloaked themselves most often in reformist garb—feminists and racial minorities, New Age gurus, independent films, and angry punks had effected the most change. But by decade's end, the storm approached from a different direction. With northerners squabbling over petty differences, the southerners, who had long bridled at the arrogance of the eastern establishment, came closer to defining the nation's familial values. Evangelical Christians defended their own underground culture; ordinary citizens preferred building their own amenities to spending their tax dollars on public services. In the background, amid the wasted days and disco nights of the 1970s, rumbled a new, furious political movement. Thunder was gathering on the right.

PART III

"HIP TO BE SQUARE"

1978–1984

8

"THE MINUTEMEN ARE TURNING
IN THEIR GRAVES"
The New Right and the Tax Revolt

SEVENTIES AMERICA REMAINED AMBIVALENT ABOUT conservatism. The American right seemingly belonged on the lunatic fringe.[1] Most establishment experts had simply not heard the thunder on the right— the rise of conservatism in the years before 1980 into a potent ideological and political force in American life. In an unusually astute remark, a New Right financier and organizer, Richard Viguerie, declared that the election of 1980 marked the first modern conservative landslide, but not the first modern antiliberal landslide. That had been 1968, when liberal poster boy Hubert Humphrey pulled a paltry 40 percent share of the vote against Richard Nixon and George C. Wallace.

In the late 1960s and early 1970s, there had been plenty of discontent with and antagonism toward liberalism: hard hats outraged by hippies and antiwar protesters; parents, mainly northern white ethnics, hostile to forced busing; born-again Christians disturbed about sex on television and sex education in the schools; antifeminists frightened by the ERA; blue-collar workers fed up with seemingly profligate welfare spending; right-to-lifers fighting against legal abortions; business interests resisting excessive regulation. "Things are going mighty wrong when respect for law is gone and it seems that everyone hates the uniform," country singer Ernest Tubb crooned, capturing this revulsion against the left. "It's America: Love It or Leave It."[2]

As "a member of the silent majority," one North Carolinian had written President Nixon at the beginning of the decade, "I have never asked what anyone in government or this country could do for me; but rather have kept my mouth shut, paid my taxes and basically asked to be left alone." It "is time the law abiding, tax paying white middle class started looking to the federal government for something besides oppression."[3]

Yet before Ronald Reagan's stunning victory in 1980, this broad antiliberal phalanx had never coalesced into anything like a coherent conservative coalition or movement. Liberals and liberalism had angered many Americans, but most voters had been unwilling to identify themselves with conservatism. As late as the mid-1970s, the Republican right still carried the taint of Goldwaterite extremism. It evoked fears of race baiting, hard-line anticommunism, and the destruction of social security and other beloved government programs. Working Americans associated conservatism with an assault on unions, deregulation of business, and the weakening of environmental protections.

But by 1980, a vague antiliberalism had transformed into avowed conservatism. Americans were voting for Reagan. The metamorphosis, however, did not occur overnight. The first step involved organization: forging conservatism into a powerful movement through the construction of a New Right that could raise money, support candidates, create issues, and mobilize millions of voters, including millions of previously disorganized and largely nonpolitical evangelical Christians.

Second, movement leaders had to tame conservatism, to soften and domesticate it. Conservatives needed to sell their philosophy to Michigan hard hats, South Boston housewives, Florida retirees and California aerospace workers—Americans who found its basic tenets attractive but remained wary of its hard edges.

Finally, the right needed a match—something to ignite a grass-roots chain reaction. Conservatism would find it with the tax revolt of the late 1970s, and the economic turmoil of the era would provide its tinder. Where previously no flame had been able to burn, the disaffection of the Seventies would provide pure oxygen. Out of the fire something entirely new would emerge: a love-it-or-hate-it political force that would indelibly reshape the political landscape and elect as president its once absurdly extremist leader, Ronald Reagan, who would go on to make the once orphaned movement he embodied more popular still.

The New Right Network

The decades before the Seventies had not been kind to American conservatism. From the 1930s through the 1960s, conservatives attracted no mass constituency, as the vast majority of Americans embraced the liberal New Deal coalition. The old right also lacked coherence. Bitterly divided among themselves, conservatives could not agree on a program or unite into powerful organizations.

Nor did conservatives possess a real home. Before the mid-1960s, a moderate eastern establishment dominated the Republican party. It represented what their leader, President Dwight D. Eisenhower, called "Modern Republicanism," a gentle corrective to New Deal liberalism that nonetheless accepted the necessity of the welfare state and the existence of the labor movement. Modern Republicans would not rule out negotiations with the Soviet Union and tacitly accepted the division of the world into rival blocs. At the very least, they would not contemplate a war to roll back communism in Eastern Europe. These eastern Republicans—men like President Eisenhower and New York senator Kenneth Keating in the 1950s and New York governor Nelson Rockefeller and Pennsylvania governor William Scranton in the 1960s—also affected a moderate style and manner. Overt displays of religious piety or patriotic enthusiasm made them uncomfortable.

In those days, committed conservatives toiled in the wilderness—in fringe organizations, second-rate colleges, unread publications. In the 1950s and 1960s, according to Nixon aide Richard Whalen, the conservative movement was long on "egotists, dogmatists, hucksters and eccentrics, all engaged in a childish sandbox politics and being very noisy about it." They formed not so much the radical right that opponents charged, Whalen reflected, but an "irrelevant Right."[4]

Still, the fledgling conservative movement found some important voices in the wilderness, voices that would, in Richard Viguerie's terms, form the foundations of the modern New Right. The first was William F. Buckley, Jr. Buckley managed to unite disparate factions of conservatives—to pull together traditionalist, religious conservatives worried about moral decay, libertarian free-marketeers concerned about government interference with the economy, and hard-line anticommunists primarily interested in the twilight struggle against the Soviets. Buckley created a forum for all conservatives in the pages of his magazine, the *National Review*, and in 1960 helped found the principal conservative youth group, Young Americans for Freedom.[5]

Senator Barry Goldwater became the second pillar of modern conservatism. Unlike earlier Republican leaders, Goldwater was an authentic conservative. Against the prevailing consensus, he promised "a choice not an echo." And indeed, Goldwater advocated positions none of his Republican rivals would even have contemplated: rapid escalation of the war in Vietnam, including possible use of tactical nuclear weapons; elimination of popular government programs; opposition to the Civil Rights Act. "In your heart, you know he's right,"

Goldwater's loyal admirers declared. "Yeah, far right" responded his opponents. Most Americans, the overwhelming majority, rejected Goldwater in 1964, deciding, as the opposing slogan charged, "In your guts, you know he's nuts."

Still, the Goldwater campaign proved crucial to the development of modern conservatism. It energized a generation of conservative activists, veterans of Young Americans for Freedom like Patrick Buchanan, Howard Phillips, Richard Viguerie, Robert Bauman, and Tom Huston. They would serve in the Nixon and Reagan administrations and found New Right organizations. It also marked the emergence of Ronald Reagan, who first entered national politics to campaign on Goldwater's behalf. Most important, the Goldwater campaign culminated a long grass-roots effort by young conservatives to take over the Republican party and transform it into a truly conservative organization. They did not succeed immediately, but they quickly built conservatism into the dominant force within the national Republican party.[6]

Building on the foundations laid by Goldwater, Buckley, and their supporters, a revived conservative movement emerged after 1970. By the middle of the decade, American conservatism had become "an institutionalized, disciplined, well-organized and well-financed movement of loosely knit affiliates."[7] This New Right, as it was called, included large umbrella groups like the American Conservative Union and the Conservative Caucus, youth organizations like Young Americans for Freedom, think tanks like the Heritage Foundation, publications like *Conservative Digest,* lobbying organizations, and political action committees.

New Right leader Richard Viguerie summarized the various elements of the emerging conservative movement as "the Four Keys to Our Success." First, Viguerie identified single-issue groups. Consciously mirroring liberal activists like NOW, the NAACP, the Sierra Club, and Planned Parenthood, the emerging conservative alliance tapped into a number of existing and newly formed single-issue groups like the National Rifle Association, Stop-ERA, and a number of right-to-life organizations. These groups could mobilize millions of people around hot-button issues like gun control and abortion, people who might not share a broader conservative agenda or agree on other issues.[8]

Multi-issue, broad-spectrum conservative organizations formed the second component of the New Right network—groups like the Conservative Caucus, the Committee for the Survival of a Free Congress, the Heritage Foundation, and the National Conservative Political Action Committee (NCPAC). Although they lacked the mass support of the NRA or the pro-life movement, these groups could map out a broad-based conservative agenda and organize the pressure groups into an effective movement, teaching the techniques of lobbying, fund raising, and grass-roots organizing. They schooled local and single-issue constituencies in guerrilla theater and protest tactics, helped them qualify ballot initiatives, and printed their newsletters.

These broad-spectrum organizations also generated a leadership cadre for the movement, nurturing the careers of men like Paul Weyrich, Howard Phillips, and Terry Dolan. Dolan, for example, headed NCPAC and proved instrumental in the unseating of liberal senators in 1980. He identified opposing candidates, coordinated efforts of many local and single-issue groups, and raised the money. In short, he masterminded the operation.

Viguerie termed the third key feature of the New Right coalition politics; others called it the New Right network or the New Right interlocking directorate. Although no "vast right wing conspiracy" ever emerged, the New Right constructed a well-disciplined national network, linking together many local groups that organized from time to time in response to specific concerns. Many movement leaders, including conservative organizers like Dolan and Viguerie, activists like Schlafly, religious figures such as the Reverend Jerry Falwell, and journalists like Pat Buchanan met regularly in Washington with conservative congressmen and senators to plan strategies and establish objectives. During the late 1970s, they helped defeat a common situs picketing law championed by organized labor, the creation of a new consumer protection agency, and federal financing of congressional elections.[9]

This network assembled for the first time in August 1974, when President Gerald Ford announced his selection of Nelson Rockefeller as vice president—the same liberal Republican who had opposed Goldwater for the GOP presidential nomination in 1964. Outraged, a group of fourteen young conservatives met in Richard Viguerie's home. They immediately recognized their impotence in the face of this insult; at that time, conservatives lacked the strength to block Rockefeller's confirmation on Capitol Hill.

Disappointment clarified the need for extensive consultation and more rigorous organization. Larger, more successful conservative planning sessions became routine. Often at these meetings, leaders of local struggles involving school textbooks or gay rights or abortion would participate. So although they never built a single, hierarchical organization, the various New Right groups formed a well-disciplined, interlocking network. "Organization is our bag," Paul Weyrich declared. "We preach and teach nothing but organization."[10]

Fourth and finally, the New Right pioneered and perfected a new mode of political communication. "Like all successful political movements," Viguerie declared, "we must have a method of communicating with each other," and for conservatives in the 1970s, that method was direct mail. "Frankly," the New Right guru admitted in 1981, "the conservative movement is where it is today because of direct mail. Without direct mail, there would be no effective counterforce to liberalism."[11]

Viguerie and his fellow conservatives believed they had no choice but to operate outside standard channels of communication, to make an end run around the traditional media, which they insisted were controlled by liberals. Ironically, direct mail organization and solicitation owed its success to the post-Watergate reforms in campaign finance laws. The new regulations placed strict curbs on individual donations to political candidates, ending officeholders' reliance on a few rich fat cats. Limiting individual contributions to $1,000, campaign finance reforms put a premium on being able to reach and bundle together large numbers of small donors.[12]

Direct mail made that possible. From his vast computer facility in Falls Church, Virginia, Richard Viguerie's operation alone collected the names of 15 million conservatives, potential donors to New Right candidates and causes. Opponents so feared the power of Viguerie's IBM mainframes and magnetic tape units that the head of the United Auto Workers Community Action Project believed that Viguerie had the capacity to generate as much money for a campaign as the entire American labor movement.[13]

Direct mail soon became a tool not merely for fund raising but for communication and organization. "The purpose of direct mail," Viguerie explained in 1978, "isn't just to raise funds. We are building a movement. Direct mail is a way to get people involved, to educate them, to turn out the vote. Direct mail is a form of advertising and conservatives have found a way to communicate with people and pay for the communication."[14]

A well-placed mailing could generate thousands of letters and telephone calls to congressmen. In one famous "panic letter," a mailing from the Conservative Caucus included two flags—the red, white, and blue of Old Glory and the white flag of surrender. After attacking the proposed Strategic Arms Limitation Treaty (SALT II) with the Soviet Union, the mailing warned, "You and I must choose—and the Senate must decide—whether we will personally accept the White Flag of Surrender as America's banner." Another notoriously effective solicitation from Americans for LIFE asked recipients to "take a second look at the outrageous pro-abortion political propaganda I've enclosed and then help me STOP THE BABY KILLERS by signing and mailing the enclosed anti-abortion postcards to your U.S. Senators (You'll find a list of all U.S. Senators on the back of that sickening baby killer propaganda)."15

By the late 1970s, conservatives had organized. Through the New Right network, they had formed a movement. But organization would have meant little without issues around which to organize, and for the first time since the 1930s, conservatives felt they had them. Basically, the New Right agenda revolved around three main areas of concern. The first was national defense. Movement conservatives deeply resented and passionately resisted the nation's seeming loss of international dominance after Vietnam. In particular, they rejected the stabilization and thawing of the cold war that Nixon, Ford, and Kissinger had launched and that Jimmy Carter continued. The New Right distrusted the Chinese and opposed all negotiations with the Soviets. They especially opposed arms control and favored a major buildup of American military might. A country western hit, by a singer calling himself Stonewall Jackson, captured this sentiment in the mid-1970s. "The minutemen are turning in their graves," Jackson warned. "Washington and Jefferson are crying tears of shame. To see these men who'd rather live as slaves, the minutemen are turning in their graves."

Politicians "have lied to the American people about the Soviet threat," one New Right leader told an *Atlantic Monthly* reporter in 1978. "They indicate that we can work things out with the Russians instead of spelling out that this is the enemy, the same as Nazi Germany. When have you heard a leader of the free world say that freedom is the way of the future and someday will prevail over slavery? . . . It's hardly a fair fight if one side believes it is a fight to the death and the other side doesn't think it's a fight at all."16

Late in 1977, the New Right mobilized a massive campaign against the Panama Canal treaty. Nine million cards and letters flooded the postal system, asking people to express opposition to the canal giveaway. Although almost all establishment voices—in business, academia, and government—supported the treaty, movement conservatives waged a spirited battle. Surprising nearly everyone, they fell just two votes short of defeating the treaty in the Senate.

Defeat on Capitol Hill turned into victory at the polls and turned out new legions of conservative voters. In 1978 and 1980, twenty supporters of the canal treaty lost their seats, while only one opponent met defeat. In the New Hampshire U.S. Senate race, an unknown thirty-seven-year-old former airline pilot named Gordon Humphrey made the election a referendum on the canal and unseated Democratic incumbent Tom McIntyre. The canal fight also built a close relationship between the New Right network and the treaty's most famous opponent, Ronald Reagan. "The canal is ours," Reagan famously declared. "We built it, we paid for it. And we intend to keep it."[17]

The rising tide of nationalist sentiment about the canal, the Soviet Union, and the military budget surprised and pleased conservatives. In 1980, the Charlie Daniels Band acknowledged it appreciatively in their hit song "In America." The band confessed that "a lot of people are saying that America's fixin' to fall." But the decline had been reversed: Lady Liberty had regained her footing and the Russians had sure as hell watch out. Americans, the song concluded, were "walking real proud and talking real loud again."[18]

In the skepticism that conservatives showed diplomats and policy experts, the canal fight also pointed up a second crucial aspect of the emerging New Right agenda: antielitism. This passionate class resentment represented a profound shift for American conservatism. In his 1962 book *Conservatism in America,* historian Clinton Rossiter had identified the classic political style of American conservatives. Conservatives, Rossiter explained, were suspicious of grass-roots activism and drew support principally from people "who have a sizable stake in the established order." The left, on the contrary, "is made up of those who demanded wider popular participation in public life and draw particular support from the disinherited and disgruntled."[19]

Just ten years later, that traditional distinction no longer applied. New Right strategists like Kevin Phillips and Patrick Buchanan realized that conservatives need not fit the image of country club Republicanism. They could reverse all that, linking liberals with a snooty, snobbish, out-of-town establishment and allying themselves with ordinary folks.[20]

This antielitism manifested itself in resentment against bureaucrats and "pointy-headed intellectuals," the alleged architects of busing and affirmative action, the haughty elite who sneered at Mom, apple pie, and the flag. This conservative version of class warfare emerged in challenges to schoolteachers and administrators over which textbooks to assign, curricula to follow, and library books to retain. It expressed itself as attacks on universities and their faculty and against the national news media.

Spiro T. Agnew, the attack-dog vice president under Richard Nixon, perfected this political style. With help (and some fancy vocabulary) from speechwriter William Safire, Agnew assailed the liberal bias in the media and lambasted the press as "nattering nabobs of negativism." The vice president repeatedly rallied the "hardhats," "the forgotten Americans," and the "Middle Americans" against an enemy he called elitist, radical chic, limousine liberals.

At a Republican party dinner in Houston, Texas, Agnew attacked college students and their professors. Education, he charged, "is being redefined at the demand of the uneducated to suit the ideas of the uneducated." Students attend college to "proclaim rather than to learn," encouraged by an "effete corps of impudent snobs that characterize themselves as intellectuals."[21]

The New Right also charged the liberal establishment with immorality. Liberal elites in the universities, the press, and the government, conservatives declared, had undercut traditional notions of decency and undermined established sources of authority. In the New Right's terms, the nation's ruling class displayed contempt for "family values." Thus, efforts to protect and restore family values formed the third major component of the emerging New Right agenda.[22]

The family values coalition included the antifeminism personified by Phyllis Schlafly; the right-to-life movement, which fought to place new restrictions on abortion after the Supreme Court legalized the procedure in *Roe v. Wade;* and textbook protests, a series of local efforts to remove supposedly immoral textbooks or library books and to purify the curriculum in public schools. The issue first received national attention during the 1974 West Virginia textbook battle. Alice Moore, a young mother of four school-aged children in Charleston, West Virginia, emerged as the leader of protests against what her children were being taught in the schools. She first assailed the school's sex education program and won election to the school board based on her opposition to it. Led by Moore, the new board decided to reform the curriculum, removing such authors as black militant Eldridge Cleaver and Beat poet Lawrence Ferlinghetti from the school's assigned readings.[23]

Moore proved so successful and her local struggle gained such national attention because of their connections to the burgeoning conservative network. The Heritage Foundation sent a lawyer to represent Moore and other conservative parents. Texas activists, skilled in battles in the Lone Star State, came to West Virginia to help organize. In the aftermath of the West Virginia fight, the Heritage Foundation founded and bankrolled the National Congress for Educational Excellence, which united some 200 parents' groups seeking curriculum changes around the country.[24]

Homosexuality, especially civil rights protections for homosexuals in general and gay teachers in particular, constituted another major front in the battle over family values. In 1977, former beauty queen Anita Bryant, best known as the spokesperson for the Florida citrus industry, led a successful referendum campaign to repeal a Miami gay rights ordinance. The national New Right network heavily financed the Miami campaign and helped build Bryant's organization, Save Our Children. Bryant and her allies mounted similar efforts across the nation, scoring successes in Oregon, Minnesota, and Kansas in the late Seventies.[25]

Finally, the profamily coalition drew considerable strength from the Christian schools movement and the broader Christian right that developed around it. During the late 1960s and early 1970s, Christian schools had burgeoned in response to court-ordered racial integration and the banning of prayer in school. As religious-oriented nonprofits, these fundamentalist academies paid no federal taxes, and a number of civil rights groups, viewing these lily-white academies as nothing but an attempt to resist racial integration, pressed the government to revoke their tax exemptions.[26]

In 1978, Jimmy Carter's new IRS commissioner, Jerome Kurtz, issued new regulations and moved to withdraw the exemptions. Provoked, conservative Christians launched a battle against the IRS and the federal government. For generations, the fundamentalist right had remained politically quiescent. As a rule, evangelical Christians had avoided partisan politics and even sat out most elections. Focused on matters of individual salvation, they had paid little attention to national politics and had been content to withdraw from the corrupt secular world and build their own shelters from the storm.[27]

The IRS fight threatened one of these havens and energized the Christian right. "It kicked the sleeping dog," Richard Viguerie remembered. "It galvanized the religious right. It was the spark that ignited the religious right's involvement in real politics."[28] The proposed regulations produced more than 125,000 letters of protest. As IRS chief, Kurtz was accustomed to hate mail, but the anonymous threats surrounding the Christian academies proved so alarming that the commissioner requested Secret Service protection for his family.[29]

The furor over tax exemptions for Christian academies also linked religious conservatives to the broader tax revolt of the 1970s, uniting religious and secular conservatives against a common enemy. In 1979, the Reverend Jerry Falwell, an ambitious minister and shrewd organizer from Lynchburg, Virginia, formed the Moral Majority, drawing much of its staff and resources from the school debate. The organization would play a key role in Ronald Reagan's race for the Republican presidential nomination. A year later, the Republican party included a plank in its party platform opposing the "regulatory vendetta launched by Mr. Carter's IRS Commissioner against independent schools."[30]

This potent coalition—and the ambitious agenda around which it was shaped—were formidable achievements. But if conservatives hoped to succeed in American politics, they would have to reach out more broadly. A Jewish teacher in New York, discouraged by black nationalism in the schools and crime in the neighborhood, might be ripe for conservative pickings but would worry about a movement led by evangelical Protestants committed to creating a Christian republic. A Polish Catholic steelworker in Chicago might like to see America stand tall against the commies, but would not want anyone to mess with his union. An Oregon lumberjack might resent tree-hugging environmentalists and their restrictions on logging, but not want to remove sex education from the schools or *Playboy* and *Penthouse* from the local convenience stores. A small businessman in Dubuque wants the IRS off her back but cannot embrace a foreign policy she thinks might start another world war.

So even if the country was moving in the direction the New Right was leading it, there remained a residual scariness about the conservative movement. Conservatives seemed too ready, in pop parodist Randy Newman's words, to "drop the big one and pulverize them." Asia's "crowded and Europe's too old, Africa's far too hot, and Canada's too cold," crooned Newman, satirizing the tone of a New Right patriot. "South America stole our name. Let's drop the big one and there'll be no one left to blame."[31]

But during the early 1970s, as the movement organized, a new strain of conservative thought emerged that would help smooth the edges of conservatism and sell its worldview. Contemporaneous with the rise of the New Right, but mainly outside of it, a more practical and politically palatable conservative philosophy was developing in the work of the so-called neoconservatives.

Refugees from the campus struggles and leftist politics of the 1960s, the neoconservatives had defected from the liberal camp and included even some ex-socialists among their ranks. Highly educated and urban, they were largely Jewish and Roman Catholic—strangers in the suburban Protestant Sunbelt communities that nourished the New Right. They had grown up in the old left (against which the 1960s new left had rebelled) and found themselves sickened by the excesses of radical youth, especially their embrace of Chairman Mao and Ho Chi Minh and their attacks on the university.

The neoconservative high command included influential magazine editors, such as Norman Podhoretz of *Commentary,* Martin Peretz of the *New*

Republic, and Irving Kristol of the *Public Interest.* It drew on the brain power of prominent scholars like Daniel Bell, Nathan Glazer, Gertrude Himmelfarb, and James Q. Wilson. And it claimed a number of political figures, most prominently future U.N. ambassador Jeanne Kirkpatrick and New York senator Daniel Patrick Moynihan.

Neoconservatives, in Irving Kristol's famous definition, were "liberals who've been mugged by reality." They were former leftists who came to share conclusions with conservatives, but whose rightward tilt seemed more practical, less motivated by crusading principle, closer to the mainstream of American political debate. On foreign policy, for instance, neoconservatives remained rigorously hawkish; they largely supported the war in Vietnam, the overthrow of Chilean leftist Salvador Allende, and the Nicaraguan contras in their guerrilla war against the Marxist Sandinista government. But they lacked the religious zeal that motivated most movement conservatives. Instead they grounded their passionate anticommunism in realpolitik, a cool-headed calculus of national interest.

As a matter of basic philosophy, neoconservatives shied away from the crusading ideologies of other American conservatives. They believed, as did the champions of family values, that the left had forsaken moral values, but they had no desire to establish a Christian republic or a traditional hierarchical society. Like the libertarian, free-market conservatives, neoconservatives asserted that liberal big government interfered too much with the market, but they did not oppose all economic regulation on principle. They opposed inefficient, counterproductive, wrongheaded programs without threatening to eliminate social security or shut off Medicare payments to the elderly.[32]

Neoconservatism always remained a primarily intellectual movement. Adherents never developed any neoconservative party or organization. Nevertheless, they exerted influence well beyond their small numbers, reshaping policy debate and political strategy in the late 1970s. Most important, they domesticated American conservatism; they redefined it in terms that made it a responsible alternative to liberalism. They offered Ronald Reagan intellectual and political legitimacy, echoing Reagan's odyssey from New Deal liberal to disaffected scourge of the left.[33]

Neoconservatives helped to turn the growing conservative political movement into a powerful mainstream force, but building a winning conservative coalition required more than an appealing ideology and a well-organized, energized cadre of activists. It required popular leadership and effective communication (which Ronald Reagan would provide). And it needed an issue to unite its various factions, cement its disparate, multifaceted agenda, enliven a mass constituency, and empower a movement that had been gestating for a decade. That political birth came in the tax revolt of the late 1970s.

From Tax Shifts to Tax Cuts: Origins of the Tax Revolt

The tax revolt began in California. After the passage of Proposition 13 in 1978, tax-cutting and service-slashing popular initiatives swept the nation. More than twenty states, from Maine to Alaska, rapidly followed California's lead. The tax revolt overran high-tax states like Massachusetts, which enacted property tax caps in its Proposition 2 1/2 and even low-tax states like Idaho, which barely had any taxation to rebel against.

In California, protests against property taxation had erupted regularly since World War II. The state's phenomenal growth and soaring property values stung homeowners with huge increases in their tax bills even though prevailing tax rates hardly changed. In 1957, homeowners in the San Gabriel Valley, a mushrooming community on the suburban frontier east of downtown Los Angeles, opened their mailboxes to find 30 to 50 percent jumps in their property tax assessments and a new levy to fund school construction. The steep hikes ignited months of resistance, including a mass meeting at the Los Angeles Coliseum that drew more than 6,000 angry homeowners.[34]

The San Gabriel flare-up, like most such tax protests, fizzled quickly. The indignation remained local, usually manifesting itself in immediate, unorganized responses to the arrival of tax bills in the mail. Most protesters, even the leaders of the hastily assembled neighborhood groups, possessed little political experience. The very names of these groups advertised their amateur status: cutesy acronyms like OUCH (Organization of United California Homeowners) and TUFF (Taxpayers United For Freedom).[35]

The property tax only became a major state-wide issue in 1965 when the *San Francisco Chronicle* published a series of exposés on unsavory practices by California tax assessors. California's constitution required that property be assessed at "full cash value" and that all property be taxed at the same rate. In practice, assessments never reached more than a third of actual value, and in some cities, like San Francisco, the assessor valued residential property at less than 10 percent of its market price.

Tax assessors, who were elected officials in California, depended on the votes of the constituents they assessed, and many collected "campaign contributions" or received laundered kickbacks in exchange for making low assessments on business properties. After the story broke, the assessors for San Francisco and Alameda County served jail sentences. San Diego's assessor committed suicide. The Los Angeles assessor, Philip Watson, was indicted but found not guilty.[36]

The state legislature quickly moved to reform the property tax system. The 1966 Petris-Knox Act required uniform assessment of all property at 25 percent of actual value, mandated systematic reassessment every three years, and sharply limited the discretion of county assessors. The state attorney general estimated that the new law would recover more than $200 million in taxes from business properties. The League of California Cities expected a windfall of nearly $500 million.

But the experts had not understood the true nature of old system's depravity. Sure, a few large businesses and political insiders paid bribes in return for favorable valuations, but most business properties faced substantially higher assessments than homeowners did. Corrupt assessors had been overtaxing businesses so they could keep homeowners' taxes artificially low and ensure their popularity with the voters on Election Day. Then they lined their pockets by offering a few businesses discounts. When the reforms came into effect, most businesses received steep cuts in their tax bills, but the new law socked homeowners with an entirely unexpected increase. In San Francisco, where assessor Russell Wolden had held residential assessments at an absurdly low 9 percent of market value, angry residents even trotted out a new bumper sticker: "Bring Back the Crooked Assessor."[37]

The uproar over assessment reform inspired a new, sustained wave of property tax rebellion across California. In 1966, the Los Angeles–based United Organizations of Taxpayers (UOT), a confederation of neighborhood homeowners' groups, called for a county-wide property tax strike. A year later the UOT attempted to abolish property taxes altogether. UOT canvassers tried to qualify a state ballot initiative, but collected only 100,000 signatures, barely a fifth of the total needed to place the measure on the state ballot.[38]

Protests fell off in the late 1960s and early 1970s, as the initial shock of the assessments wore off and the state legislature cushioned the blow with a series of adjustments that eased the bite. But the tax rebels kept at it. Led by Howard Jarvis, a retired businessman and cigar-smoking Mormon from Utah, the UOT repeatedly introduced tax-cutting ballot measures. While Jarvis's radical proposals fell short, establishment figures joined the battle against the property tax. Hiring paid signature gatherers, Los AngelesCounty assessor Philip Watson qualified a measure for the 1968 ballot. Proposition 9 would have restricted the use of property tax revenues to "property-oriented services" such as police and fire protection. The measure failed, and Watson tried again in 1972. In both cases, the state legislature defused support for the initiatives by offering a bundle of tax relief measures. By 1972, California devoted 11 percent of the state budget to property tax relief for local government.[39]

Even Governor Ronald Reagan joined in. Despite his limited-government rhetoric, Governor Reagan had actually raised sales and income taxes by more than 50 percent during his eight years in Sacramento. In 1973, the governor sponsored a referendum to control state spending. Proposition 1 proposed a spending cap that would steadily tighten over a ten-year period. The 5,700-word proposal struck voters as absurdly complicated; Reagan himself confessed to not understanding it. But Proposition 1 fared better than any of Jarvis's or Watson's proposals, losing by 54 to 46 percent.

This embryonic agitation, in California and elsewhere, sent out ambiguous signals. First, these early tax rebellions did not ally closely with conservative politicians or policies. Indeed, they displayed a genuine populist, progressive streak. They aimed not so much against high taxes as at the inequitable distribution of the tax burden. During the 1960s and early 1970s, tax rebels sought to shift the burden to the wealthy and business, not to shrink government and cut taxes altogether. In California, for example, the Statewide Homeowners Association, a Los Angeles–based property tax group, championed homeowners and "working businessmen" against the "non-creators, the non-builders, those who sit back fat and lazy." The Statewide Homeowners did not advocate cuts in government; in fact, a 1964 broadside suggested that the property tax could raise millions more for the public schools if land speculators and "slumlords" were assessed fairly.[40]

In Massachusetts, the tax revolt actually began as a movement of the political left. Led by a former SDS organizer, Massachusetts Fair Share formed in Chelsea, Massachusetts, in 1973. Five years later, the organization claimed more than 12,000 dues-paying members scattered throughout the Bay State. In the mid-1970s, as assessments on modest homes in blue-collar neighborhoods spiraled upward, Fair Share led battles against sweetheart tax deals for downtown developers and to collect back taxes from delinquent big businesses like Eastern Airlines and New England Life Insurance. Fair Share also proposed a progressive "taxbraker" plan, one that would cut property taxes up to 20 percent and replace the lost revenue with new taxes on professional transactions used mainly by the affluent—legal fees, accounting services, stock transfers. Equity, as much as demands for tax cuts, sparked the opening salvoes of the tax revolt.

Even Howard Jarvis's UOT, which contained many conservative, small-government fanatics, felt it had to make concessions to the liberal sentiments of the late 1960s. Jarvis himself claimed that his organization represented the little guy against big business. "We've got teachers who belong to this organization, and labor people," Jarvis told the *Los Angeles Times* in 1970. "We've got a great number of Negroes." We "don't have any oil company money and no title insurance money. No bank money and no land speculators."[41] Although Jarvis despised unions and activist government and had even supported formation of an independent Conservative party, he still needed to clothe the tax revolt in progressive, populist terms.[42]

The early tax revolt possessed no clear conservative pedigree and few close links to the emerging New Right. It also achieved little success. On four separate occasions, Jarvis and the UOT failed even to qualify tax-cutting initiatives for the ballot. California voters rejected the Watson and Reagan propositions. Across the country, Massachusetts Fair Share made limited headway. In 1976, referenda to limit taxes and government spending appeared on five state ballots. Every single one failed.[43]

By the late 1970s, runaway inflation had changed the economic landscape, and the political climate had altered. A new generation of tax protesters had emerged, demanding steep tax cuts, not tax equity. They focused their anger on the crushing burdens they faced and the public officials who imposed them—the governing class, not the upper class. Demands to soak the rich or remove special breaks for business disappeared from the debate.

In California's San Fernando Valley, even former radical Howard Farmer allied his United Voters League with antigovernment tax rebels. A one time Communist party member and longtime union activist, Farmer had long championed big government as the people's instrument in the struggle for social and economic justice. But in 1976, as skyrocketing taxes threatened to drive working people from their homes, Farmer denounced public servants as "those leeches who must have more and more taxes." His group spearheaded a campaign to deprive the city council of a pay raise.[44]

In 1977 Howard Jarvis ran for mayor of Los Angeles and, in one historian's words, campaigned as "a different Jarvis—an out of the closet libertarian." He denounced government as "evil" and questioned such basic public services as garbage collection, parks, and libraries.[45] In "Tax Relief, Shift, Or Shaft?" the *Taxpayer's Watchdog,* a southern California newsletter, warned that shifting tax burdens onto the privileged would offer only a temporary fix for ordinary citizens. "Without cutting down the size and variety of government," the *Watchdog* asserted, "there is little that can be offered in terms of tax relief since the money has to come from somewhere."[46]

Tax rebels boiled over with rage at public employees, venting discontent at their supposed inefficiency, their corruption, their cruel indifference to human suffering. "Here's why I voted for Proposition 13," one California woman wrote Governor Edmund "Jerry" Brown in 1978. "I'm tired of paying for politicians' dinners and lunches when my family can't afford to go out to dinner even once a month. . . . I'm tired of doing without so that you all can have everything."[47] Angry voters targeted prevailing wage laws, which guaranteed high union wages to municipal workers. They opposed pay raises for public officials and complained about phony sick leaves and extravagant perquisites.[48] They called not just for tax relief but for spending limits that would tie the hands of bureaucrats and politicians. Howard Jarvis tirelessly retold the story of a dear friend hounded to death by insensitive tax collectors. She suffered a fatal heart attack in the county offices, "in the very act of pleading about the prohibitive level of property taxes on her home."[49]

The emerging tax revolt thus offered conservatives an opening, the chance for rewriting the rules of American politics that Richard Nixon had first envisioned as he strolled the beach at San Clemente. As Nixon had recognized, Americans hated government in the abstract but supported and appreciated most existing programs. Poll after poll confirmed that Americans rejected steep reductions in public services just as adamantly as they opposed taxes and resented bureaucracy. Attacks on waste and corruption resonated so deeply because they promised something for nothing—a way to cut government without slashing essential services.

Conservatives needed to exploit the visceral feelings about taxes and government without spawning fears of Goldwater-like cuts in cherished programs. Even at the height of the tax revolt, Americans never embraced the views of libertarian extremists. Across the nation, taxpayers selected carefully among spending cap and tax cut proposals, often rejecting measures they found irresponsible or extreme. Voters balanced their demands for tax relief against their desire for good schools, smooth roads, and reliable amenities. But during the late 1970s, the scales tipped. The era's peculiar economic and political conditions intensified resentments against taxes and government, eroding Americans' resistance to cuts in public services.[50]

Rising prices were the biggest culprit. Runaway inflation meant that property values soared and incomes crept up into higher tax brackets, while people's standard of living hardly changed. Families suddenly had to pay twice or three times the property taxes for the same modest home. As the 1970s proceeded, astronomical increases in assessments led many homeowners to fear the loss of their houses. "There is no way I can come up with the expected taxes," one woman wrote Governor Jerry Brown. "I had hoped that by age 65 the house would be paid for and I would have a place to live. But I now see that all the planning is in vain because our government will not allow this to happen." Adding insult to injury, inflation swelled the coffers of state and local governments even as it squeezed taxpayers. California and many other states ran huge budget surpluses in the late 1970s.[51]

The stagflation of the 1970s meant, among other things, that Uncle Sam took ever larger bites out of the average American's wallet. Between 1964 and 1980, the social security payroll tax rose eightfold, lightening workers' pay envelopes.[52] As inflation mounted, the cost-of-living increases in people's paychecks, the raises that barely kept pace with the latest outrages at the gas pump and the butcher's counter, bumped them into steeper tax brackets. Ordinary people paid more in taxes even though their real incomes had remained level or even declined.[53]

In 1976–1977, new property assessments sparked intense protests in California. Groups like Taxpayers United for Freedom and the Sherman Oaks Homeowners Association mounted massive letter writing campaigns. Burying the governor's office under more than 200,000 letters, angry homeowners petitioned Jerry Brown to convene a special session of the state legislature to offer relief before the new higher tax bills kicked in. When Brown refused and the legislature again failed to compromise on tax relief, a new generation of protesters joined the UOT's fifth petition drive. Aided by northern California activist Paul Gann, a retired Sacramento car dealer, they collected 1.25 million signatures, far more than the required number to place a major cut in property taxes, Proposition 13, on the state ballot in June 1978.[54]

The campaign was heated. Opponents filled the airwaves with tales of doom. Schools would close in midyear, thousands of public employees would lose their jobs, affirmative action would grind to a halt. The measure, some claimed, threatened losses of local revenue severe enough to force major cutbacks in police and fire protection.[55]

These dark prophecies might have swayed the electorate, except that the massive state budget surplus strained their credibility. As Election Day neared and the estimated surplus swelled to nearly $6 billion, predictions of fiscal catastrophe seemed laughable. Moreover, early projections had so underestimated the surplus that many Californians believed their politicians had been hiding something. Only Proposition 13, they concluded, could discipline the rogues in Sacramento.

Still, the likely vote remained close until the state's most populous county dropped a bombshell only a few weeks before the election. The Los Angeles County assessor revealed that new property assessments, to take effect shortly after the balloting, would skyrocket by an average of 125 percent. On L.A.'s prosperous West Side, values would double, even triple in many cases. The new assessments provoked such uproar that the county canceled the increases and restored the old valuations. Governor Brown ordered other counties to freeze assessments.

That episode erased any lingering doubts about Proposition 13. Approved on June 6, 1978, by a two-to-one margin, the measure immediately slashed property taxes by 57 percent and rolled back tax rates to 1 percent of market value based on the 1975 assessment. It ensured that values could rise no more than 2 percent a year—unless a property was sold, in which case it was reassessed at market value. The initiative also amended the state constitution, requiring a two-thirds vote of the legislature to increase state taxes and requiring that voters approve any new local levies by a two-thirds vote.[56]

The scope of the victory stunned nearly every observer. Proposition 13 won broad support across the ideological spectrum and among all economic strata.[57] Only African Americans and public employees outright opposed the measure. The crusade drew most heavily on middle-class homeowners, especially modest householders who could not pay their tax bills. According to historian David Koistenen, three-quarters of the San Fernando Valley protesters he sampled lived in homes smaller than 2,000 square feet. A third owned very small houses, under 1,250 square feet. Elderly people, whose incomes remained fixed while their taxes soared, residents of older subdivisions, and owners of small businesses figured heavily in the campaign for Proposition 13.[58]

The effects were immense. The measure immediately reduced property tax revenues by more than $7 billion. When Prop 13 passed, Californians were facing one of the stiffest tax burdens in the United States; the average property tax bill reached 50 percent above the national average. Tax bills plummeted overnight. A year later, Californians paid 35 percent below the nationwide standard. At the same time, the dreaded declines in services did not materialize. The huge state surplus muted the tax cut's initial impact; for the first three years after Prop 13, the state cushioned the blow with massive bailout payments to cities, counties, and towns.[59] Tax rebels declared Proposition 13 a total victory.

A "Modern Boston Tea Party"

Outside California, pollsters and pundits immediately interpreted Proposition 13 as the opening salvo in a national tax revolt. A Harris Poll, released just after the California vote, reported that Americans favored similar measures for their own communities by more than two to one. The *New York Times* surveyed the nation and discovered a "modern Boston Tea Party." Conservative guru Milton Friedman brimmed with glee. "The sweeping victory of Proposition 13," he predicted, "will be heard throughout the land. The 'brewing' tax revolt is no longer brewing. It is boiling over."[60]

These predictions quickly bore fruit. In Tennessee, three months before Proposition 13, voters had approved the Copeland amendment—revisions in the state constitution that capped the growth of government spending.[61] Over the next four years, from 1978 to 1981, Delaware, Hawaii, Idaho, Louisiana, Michigan, Missouri, Nevada, South Carolina, Texas, Utah, and Washington approved similar spending limits, while Californians continued their revolution. In November 1979, by an overwhelming majority, California voters approved Proposition 4, a state constitutional amendment proposed by Paul Gann. Called the "Spirit of 13" initiative, it capped state and local spending, allowing growth only on par with inflation and population. It also mandated immediate return of budget surpluses to the taxpayers.[62]

Antitax fever so frightened the governing class that most state legislatures cut taxes voluntarily, hoping to avoid the fiscal straitjacket that California voters had wrapped around their government. In the immediate aftermath of Proposition 13, thirty-seven states reduced property taxes, and twenty-eight cut their state income tax. Early in 1978, according to *Newsweek,* state and local governments enjoyed an aggregate surplus of nearly $8 billion. By the end of 1979, after two years of aggressive tax cuts, they showed deficits of $6 billion.[63]

After Proposition 13, no skirmish in the tax revolt proved more important than the enactment of Proposition 2 1/2 in Massachusetts. Like California, the Bay State imposed high property taxes, and new assessment standards had transferred a heavier burden onto residential property owners.[64] The Massachusetts state legislature had also failed to take remedial action to cut off tax rebels at the pass. That failure proved particularly decisive because Massachusetts voters never expressed the same antipathy toward government that appeared in Far West. The legislature's inaction seemed to leave desperate Bay State taxpayers with no choice.[65]

Citizens for Limited Taxation (CLT) spearheaded the Massachusetts campaign. The organization had formed in the 1970s, mainly representing small businesses and cranky conservatives. CLT had fought its first battles against the graduated tax, an unsuccessful effort by Massachusetts Fair Share to enact a progressive, graduated income tax.[66]

Prop 13 emboldened conservative tax rebels in Massachusetts. "We couldn't have done it if Proposition 13 hadn't passed in California," CLT director Barbara Anderson reflected. "Certainly, the big argument we used was, 'California did it, and they didn't fall into the ocean."[67] Anderson's predecessor and colleague, Don Feder, agreed: "We were watching proposition 13 very carefully through the Spring of 1978. We were thinking that if this goes over well in California—which is a fairly liberal state—perhaps we should try it in Massachusetts."[68] After Prop 13, Feder, Anderson, and CLT advanced a much more aggressive antigovernment line. Testifying before the Massachusetts legislature's Joint Committee on Taxation, Feder dismissed most government services as unnecessary. He opposed plans to build swimming pools for high schools, municipal tennis courts, and a new city hall for Boston. He also denounced what he described as lavish pensions for public employees.[69]

CLT carefully cultivated a reputation as the champion of ordinary taxpayers. During the struggle over Proposition 2 1/2, the organization elevated Barbara Anderson to the directorship. The former swimming instructor boasted that the only credentials she brought to the post were "a degree in water safety instructorship from the Red Cross." But the Massachusetts rebellion never was the people's crusade that Anderson made it out to be. The state's growing high-technology industry proved crucial to the success of Proposition 2 1/2. In fact, a consortium of firms, the Massachusetts High Tech Council, underwrote almost the entire cost of the campaign.[70]

In November 1980, Massachusetts approved Proposition 2 1/2, the same year that notorious bastion of liberalism cast a narrow majority for Ronald Reagan. The measure, as its awkward name suggested, capped local property taxes at 2.5 percent of the full and fair cash value of the local tax base. It also limited future tax hikes to 2 1/2 percent per year, with no exceptions for inflation or population growth.[71]

If California ignited the tax revolt, Massachusetts legitimated it. The success of Proposition 2 1/2 indicated that tax cut fever could spread anywhere; no state or region possessed immunity. The tax revolt no longer belonged to Sunbelt extremists—reckless cowboys, single-issue Goldwaterites, and antigovernment crazies. The Sunbelt tax rebels had won the battle; they had even gained the support of established interests. Tax relief had become a national issue.

Washington clearly heard the echoes from the statehouses and ballot boxes. Days after the passage of Prop 13, Kansas senator Bob Dole introduced a series of tax cut measures in the U.S. Senate, including a constitutional amendment requiring a balanced federal budget.[72] Acting "in the spirit of Proposition 13," Wisconsin Democrat William Proxmire urged an immediate 5 percent cutback in the appropriations for the Department of Housing and Urban Development.[73] Meanwhile, Representative Philip Crane (R, Illinois), a leading New Right politico, proposed a constitutional amendment limiting federal spending.[74]

But beyond the boost it supplied to the burgeoning conservative movement, what were the immediate, practical effects of these cuts? Prophecies of doom—of massive unemployment and crippled public services—did not pan out. In California, the surplus alleviated most of the pain, although the state imposed a salary freeze on state employees and made some difficult cutbacks, especially in the politically unprotected areas of libraries, mental health services, facilities for the disabled, and recreational activities. Many public schools eliminated entire programs—sports, art, extracurricular activities—and dropped support staff like teachers' aides. Still, in the short run, overall spending on education and public employment remained steady and even grew slowly.[75]

Other places faced greater struggles. Although state aid offset most of the first year's hardships, Massachusetts cities faced painful economies. Despite a $40 million injection of new state aid, Boston had to make sharp cuts in police and fire protection. Brookline, a prosperous suburb, imposed charges for trash collection; working-class Somerville closed many of its firehouses. Proposition 2 1/2 especially hammered public schools, which relied heavily on local property taxes to finance their programs. Many towns eliminated music, art, intramural sports, and teacher sabbaticals. Cambridge dismissed one in four teachers; Quincy laid off one in three. But the Bay State never looked back. Massachusetts voters continued to appreciate Proposition 2 1/2 and adjusted to its strict limits on public services.[76]

Eventually the tax revolt in the provinces lost momentum. There would be few more renewals of the Boston Tea Party. By 1981, when Ronald Reagan signed national tax cut legislation, new initiatives had failed in Arizona, Nevada, Oregon, South Dakota, and Utah. Even in California, Proposition 9, a Howard Jarvis–backed measure to halve income taxes, failed to win majority support. But the tax revolt did not so much fizzle as complete its work. Spending limits, lower tax receipts, and scared politicians made further rebellion unnecessary and unproductive. Americans applauded smaller government and accepted diminished services. Increasingly over the course of the 1980s, consumers, taxpayers, and their elected representatives would turn to the private sector to provide the amenities, the services, the essentials of community that the public had once provided for itself.

The Triumph of "Reagan Country"

The tax revolt need not have fueled the rise of the right or the triumph of conservative ideology, but it did. Desperate taxpayers readily accepted the New Right critique of big government and the conservative promise of low taxes and broad prosperity. "The property-owning class," which "by now includes most members of what used to be referred to as the working class," *Fortune* magazine asserted in the summer of 1978, was "voting for capitalism." They were reaching the conclusion that if "the load of government could be lightened, if young and old were allowed not only to get capital but to keep it, the private economy could propel the country into a new era of expansion."[77]

Americans wanted a change, and the New Right offered the only authentic alternative. "The real issue," Barbara Anderson told a *Washington Post* reporter, "wasn't money, it was control and attitude. People were fed up with the attitude of government toward them." Public opinion surveys confirmed that sentiment. The message of Proposition 13, according to *Newsweek* columnist Meg Greenfield, "could most aptly be headlined: CALIFORNIA TO LIBERAL GOVERNMENT: DROP DEAD."[78]

The rebellion against taxes and the governments that imposed them fused together many different aspects of the conservative message. It highlighted the use of tax money for supposedly immoral purposes, like sex education, abortion, and permissive curricula in schools. It dramatized an overweening big government, with briefcase-toting bureaucrats imposing crippling regulations on businesses and telling ordinary working Americans how to live. High taxes confirmed the New Right portrait of a government out of touch—one that favored the lazy over the hard working, welfare over national defense, opera and museum exhibitions for the elite over relief for struggling citizens.

The tax revolt also provided a more acceptable outlet for some brands of racial hostility. In the racially polarized United States of the 1970s, it allowed conservatives to tap into the fears and resentments of some white voters. Without even mentioning race, Republican candidates and New Right demagogues could exploit the pervasive feeling that the liberal welfare state unfairly benefited blacks and racial minorities—the sense that OUR tax money was being spent on THEM. Welfare, public housing, and urban services became the most frequently stigmatized examples of waste and the preferred targets for cuts.

Ronald Reagan whipped these ingredients into a winning coalition, into a new force in American public life. After the tax revolt swept his native California, candidate Reagan began stressing tax cuts in his preliminary campaigning and speaking. He even endorsed the Kemp-Roth tax bill, the 30 percent income tax cut proposed by Congressman Jack Kemp (R, New York) and Senator William Roth (R, Delaware). During the 1980 campaign, Reagan embraced supply-side economics. He insisted that steep tax cuts, even without corresponding reductions in spending, would so feverishly stimulate the economy as to balance the budget by his second year in office and produce a large surplus by the end of his first term.[79]

Ronald Reagan simultaneously reached out to conservative evangelical Christians, appealing to their new-awakened antipathy to the IRS and the Department of Education, the ERA and legalized abortion. The Reagan campaign hired Moral Majority executive director Robert Billings as liaison to the Christian right and openly appealed for the votes of evangelicals. Reagan was the only major presidential candidate to appear at the Religious Roundtable's National Affairs Briefing, a two-day "revival meeting cum political rally" that attracted 15,000 activist evangelicals to Dallas. "I know you can't endorse me," Reagan told the pious horde. But "I want you to know that I endorse you."[80]

Reagan also tapped into the New Right network and the neoconservative brain trust. Unlike Richard Nixon or George Bush, Reagan's political organization did not have to rely on Republican party regulars for intellectual firepower, organizational talent, and fund-raising ability.[81] It could draw on the brain power of the neoconservatives, the organizational vigor of the New Right, the direct mail and fund-raising skills of Richard Viguerie and his allies.

In a prescient 1967 essay, Harvard professor James Q. Wilson had interpreted the appearance of Ronald Reagan for his colleagues in the eastern establishment. In "A Guide to Reagan Country," Wilson warned the readers of *Commentary* not to underestimate Reagan or to dismiss "Reaganism" as an oddity, a product of southern California's bizarre sun-baked culture. Reaganite conservatism, Wilson predicted, "will be with us for a long time under one guise or another. We will not take it seriously by trying to explain it away as if it were something sold at one of those orange juice stands."[82]

Anticipating the emerging New Right, Wilson understood that Sunbelt conservatism represented a new and potent force, not some bitter, nostalgic remnant from an outmoded, idealized past. Reagan's followers voiced discontent, but it was "not with their lot that they are discontent, it is with the lot of the nation. *The very virtues they have and practice are, in their eyes, conspicuously absent from society as a whole.*" They were determined to restore them, and they were developing the will and the means to do so.[83]

Still, Wilson expected Reaganism to remain a minority sentiment. The "political culture of Southern California," he concluded, "will never be the political culture of our society."[84] Only there did Wilson guess wrong. Reaganism would become America's prevailing political culture. Ronald Reagan, that bone-chilling extremist, would become a venerated national father figure—the grinning, impossible-not-to-love undertaker burying the casket of liberal reform and 1960s public purpose. His ready smile and preternatural optimism would mock the malaise, the irony, and the foreboding that soaked through Seventies America. The times they were a-changin'.

9

THE REAGAN CULMINATION

TWO YEARS AFTER HE TOOK OFFICE, AS PRESIDENT REAGAN prepared to deliver the annual State of the Union Address, it seemed that not even he could save America. His approval rating had plummeted to 35 percent, the lowest midterm assessment in forty years. A grim recession stalked the land; assembly lines stalled, stores closed, the national economy shriveled. Yes, inflation, that bane of the Carter years, had subsided, but only because the Federal Reserve had strangled the money supply with punishing interest rates. The prime rate soared to a usurious 15 percent. Major corporations, icons of American industry like Chrysler and International Harvester, teetered on the edge of bankruptcy. Unemployment skyrocketed to its highest level since the Great Depression, and Reagan's cutbacks in social programs seemed to flood the nation's streets with the homeless, the mentally ill, the victims of drug and alcohol abuse.[1]

Time magazine warned of "Gloom and Doom for Workers." *Newsweek* featured "Jobs That Vanish Forever." *Washington Post* cartoonist Herblock captured the national mood in a pointed editorial cartoon. Gathered in a dingy alley, a group of homeless men warmed their hands over a garbage can fire. A copy of the president's State of the Union Address supplied the only fuel. The devastating caption: "very warming."[2]

So thoroughly did the bad news clog the airwaves and darken the national mood that President Reagan blamed the national media for blocking economic recovery. "In a time of recession like this," the president asserted in March 1982, "there's a great element of psychology in economics." The "constant downbeat" in the national news contributed "psychologically to slowing down a new recovery that is in the offing." Is it news, Reagan whined, "that some fellow out in South Succotash someplace has just been laid off?"[3]

The president's economic program seemed headed for oblivion.[4] The Congress, initially cowed by Reagan's victory margin and his rapport with the voters, showed increasing contempt for the president's policies. With large numbers of Republicans joining the majority, Congress easily overrode Reagan's veto of a series of recession relief measures in August 1982. House Speaker Tip O'Neill mocked the president: "One would have to have a glib tongue, an effervescent personality, and a stone heart to oppose this bill."[5]

The president's closest advisers wondered whether he would seek reelection. William Clark, Reagan's national security adviser and horseback riding companion, even counseled him to step down after one term in the White House. The president was, in one of his aide's words, a "warmly ruthless man." But neither Reagan's firm resolve nor his benevolent smile could lift the nation from despair, from feelings of decline. The malaise of the Seventies lingered.[6]

It would not be until 1984 that everything would change. As Reagan recited the oath of office for the second time, he celebrated one of the greatest electoral victories in American history. Nearly 60 percent of the electorate— every state but Minnesota and the District of the Columbia—had endorsed four more years of Reaganism in November 1984. The brutal recession had finally tamed galloping inflation, wringing the wicked wage-price spiral out of American life. Economic growth returned with a vengeance, employment exploded in a blizzard of new jobs, the real estate and stock markets boomed. A new youth culture of brash entrepreneurs and extravagant consumers appeared, toasting Reaganomics with rivers of chardonnay and mountains of French brie. With their designer clothes and imported cars, these young professionals so much defined the age that *Newsweek* magazine declared 1984 the "Year of the Yuppie."[7]

Meanwhile, Reagan had flexed the military's muscles and restored the nation's wounded pride around the globe. The president had installed intermediate nuclear force (INF) missiles in Europe, cleared the Cubans off the Caribbean island of Grenada, and confounded the Kremlin with his scheme to build a nuclear shield in outer space. Reagan had massively rearmed, convincing the Soviet leadership that they could not keep up in the arms race. In one admirer's words, the "ship of state was realigned, empowered, larger, prouder." The president's reelection slogan captured the national mood; it was morning again in America.[8]

Reagan's America had witnessed a profound transformation—a sea change in its public policy, national mood, and social and cultural profile. White House aide Martin Anderson proudly declared it a revolution. "What was happening in America," Anderson asserted, "was a revolution, not a violent, physical revolution driven by guns, but a revolution of political thought, a revolution of ideas." Reagan had unleashed an "earthquake that would shake the political establishment of the United States—and the world—for some time to come."9

At the end of his presidency, Reagan defined his achievement in similar, if slightly more modest, terms. "They called it the Reagan Revolution," he conceded in his Farewell Address, "and I'll accept that, but for me it always seemed more like The Great Rediscovery: a rediscovery of our values and our common sense." The president pointed to "two great triumphs": the "economic recovery" and the "recovery of our morale."10

In that same time, Reagan's own image had been transformed. The heartless, warmongering extremist of the early 1980s had become a revered national father figure—a little doddering perhaps, but well loved. "Some pundits said our programs would result in catastrophe," Reagan remembered. But "what they called 'radical' was really 'right'; what they called 'dangerous' was just 'desperately needed.'"11

The president and his admirers only barely exaggerated. Reagan had transformed American life. The first four years of his presidency reshaped politics and public policy in the United States, restructured the economy, and reshuffled the global balance of power. But they also profoundly altered the way ordinary Americans experienced daily life—the communities where they lived, the jobs they worked, the products they consumed, the families they loved.

The nation and the world looked very different in 1984 than they had in 1980. Certainly Americans looked at them very differently. But the early 1980s did not so much repudiate the political and cultural legacies of the Seventies as complete and consolidate them. Ronald Reagan enjoyed the fruits of the regional power shift that Richard Nixon had first attempted to exploit. Reagan epitomized a buoyant Sunbelt conservatism—contemptuous of the Nanny state, unabashed in its red-blooded American patriotism, brimming with a cattle rustler's love for the hurly-burly of the marketplace. The early 1980s also represented the culmination of a decade-long ideological shift—a change in attitudes that sprang from but extended even further than the changes in latitudes. Reagan embodied a deep suspicion of the public sphere, finding the public purpose of old-style Rustbelt liberals both corrupt and counterproductive. At the same time, he possessed an exuberant faith in both the efficiency and the morality of the market. During his first term, Ronald Wilson Reagan would wrestle with the demons of the Seventies, and no one—not the president, his opponents, or his constituents—would emerge from the ring the same.12

Standing Tall Again

In foreign policy, Reagan promised that the United States would stand tall again; the nation would reclaim its stature as the dominant power on the globe and win the fight against communism. The president made an unwavering commitment to military spending, expanding and intensifying the rearmament that Jimmy Carter had begun after the Soviet invasion of Afghanistan in 1979. The Pentagon enjoyed lavish rations; defense spending soared from $134 billion in 1980 to $253 billion by the end of Reagan's first term.[13] The president ordered a buildup of conventional forces with an emphasis on readiness around the world—more battleships, warplanes, aircraft carriers. He also upgraded the nuclear arsenal, moving forward with high-tech weapons such as the Stealth bomber, the MX missile, and the new-generation Trident submarine. Cost was no object. When budget director David Stockman asked the president to shrink the looming deficit by trimming the Pentagon budget, Reagan famously refused. "Defense is not a budget item," the president asserted. "You spend what you need."[14]

But Reagan's foreign policy involved far more than throwing money at the Pentagon. It aimed to reverse the decade-long drift of American diplomacy in the post-Vietnam era. The administration launched an aggressive, interventionist program around the globe, redeeming the president's pledge not merely to stand tall in the world but to stand tall *again*.

After the defeat in Southeast Asia, conceptions of the U.S. role in the world had changed. Foreign policy debate revolved around the slogan "No More Vietnams"—around bitterly contested understandings of the failed war in Indochina. For many Americans, "No More Vietnams" embodied a dovish, neoisolationist lesson. Never again should the United States interfere in the internal affairs of another nation, impose its imperial will on tiny, backward countries, or send its young people to die in a distant and ignoble cause. But the Vietnam syndrome also produced a hawkish interpretation. Never again should the United States fight with one hand tied behind its back, without the commitment and resources necessary for total victory. Former President Richard Nixon endorsed such a view in a book he entitled *No More Vietnams*.[15]

The Reagan administration agreed. According to Secretary of State Alexander Haig, America had gone to hell in a handbasket since the surrender in Southeast Asia. The United States in 1981, Haig believed, faced "a worldwide climate of uncertainty . . . dangerous in the extreme." The Soviet Union "had been seduced by the weakness of the American will and extended itself far beyond the natural limits of its own apparent interests and influence." The Chinese leaders "were wondering," Haig maintained, about the value of their relationship with a United States "enfeebled by its malaise." Propaganda against NATO was circling in Europe, and "the fires of insurrection spread unchecked in Latin America."16

The United States had to demonstrate its will. And President Reagan quickly obliged, flexing military muscles most dramatically in the tiny Caribbean nation of Grenada. In 1983, a Cuban-backed military junta toppled the island's civilian government and executed President Maurice Bishop. The junta imposed a twenty-four-hour curfew, essentially placing the entire island, including six hundred American medical students, under house arrest. Reagan quickly diverted a detachment of marines bound for the Middle East and, after six Caribbean governments formally requested assistance, ordered the troops ashore. The heavily armed U.S. invasion force overthrew the newly installed Marxist government and cleared Cuban soldiers off the island.

Grenada marked the most dramatic display of a new assertiveness around the globe. The Reagan administration sent military advisers to El Salvador to assist in the government's struggle against leftist guerrillas. U.S. forces mined the harbors of Nicaragua and applied military and economic pressure against the Marxist Sandinista regime. The Pentagon drew up invasion plans for Cuba, supplied aid to the UNITA rebels fighting against the Cuban-backed government of Angola, and struck at Libyan dictator Mu'ammar al-Gadhafi, a widely acknowledged mastermind of international terrorism.17

In Grenada, El Salvador, and Angola, it appeared that Reagan and the United States had reclaimed world leadership, rejecting the legacy of Vietnam. This renewed confidence permeated American life. It certainly revealed itself in the evolution of Sylvester Stallone's popular First Blood action-adventure movies. The original film, *First Blood* (1982), introduced John Rambo, a traumatized Vietnam veteran wandering across the American West. Haunted by memories of Vietnam, Rambo suffers flashbacks to his torture in a North Vietnamese prison camp. In the Oregon backcountry, Rambo faces off against a sadistic, redneck sheriff in a film of nonstop action and violence.18

First Blood conveyed a mixed political message. John Rambo certainly embodied an antiestablishment, antigovernment ideology. But he fought a conservative, racist western sheriff. Rambo also struggled with the grim pain of Vietnam, his personal suffering mirroring that of a nation that also could not forget. *First Blood* was no Reaganite film. It was more an action-adventure version of *Easy Rider*, the 1969 counterculture classic that pitted a pair of dope-smoking, motorcycle-riding drifters against a similar redneck sheriff.[19]

But then, in 1985, at the height of the Reaganite "Morning in America," Stallone starred in *Rambo: First Blood, Part II*. The film opened with the captured Rambo breaking rocks in an Oregon labor camp. An old army mate, played by Richard Crenna, finds Rambo and offers him a way out if he agrees to a dangerous, covert mission back in Vietnam. Rambo agrees but asks a pointed, sarcastic question: "Do we get to win this time?"[20]

At first it seems the answer might be no. Rambo retrieves an American prisoner of war from a North Vietnamese prison camp and proceeds to the rendezvous point. But when the operation's commander learns that Rambo has found an American prisoner, he calls off the rescue helicopter. The brass had wanted Rambo to discover an empty camp; finding American prisoners threatened the bureaucrats' plans for a diplomatic opening to the Vietnamese. While the Richard Crenna character fumes, Rambo is hung out to dry, once again captured by ruthless communists in the remote jungles of Southeast Asia. But no one—not the Vietnamese, their Russian advisers, or the Pentagon bureaucrats in Washington—had figured on John Rambo. He escapes and single-handedly destroys an entire army, blowing up a convoy of armored vehicles and trapping an entire detachment of commies with his bow and incendiary arrows. Rambo refights the Vietnam War and wins.

Rambo captured the spirit of Reagan's diplomacy, its assertive nationalism. Not accidentally did a popular poster of the mid-1980s place Reagan's smiling face on Stallone's buff body over the title "Ronbo." It seemed that Reagan wished to reverse the post-Vietnam tide. Critics lamented the seeming return to brash interventionist diplomacy, but few observers disputed that Reagan had transformed the nation's approach to international affairs.

Still, Reagan's foreign policy ran up against real limits. The United States lacked the wherewithal—the unchallenged economic hegemony that had underwritten the ambitious interventionism of the early cold war. After 1945, the war-revved U.S. economy so outperformed its exhausted allies and defeated enemies that Americans could afford economic sacrifices for political or strategic objectives. The United States rebuilt Japan and Western Europe, revived the German steel industry, and enforced trade restrictions against the communist bloc. But the stagflation of the 1970s and the return of genuine international competition eliminated such luxuries.[21]

Most important, Reagan confronted domestic political constraints. Endless Rambo films and constant Ronbo rhetoric could not erase the legacy of Vietnam. The defeat in Southeast Asia still mattered. It may not have tempered policymakers' zeal to project American power, but it radically changed popular attitudes about sending Americans into foreign foxholes. When the president summoned a joint session of Congress to warn about Soviet infiltration in Central America and make the case for aid to the contras in Nicaragua, his audience remained skeptical. Only the declaration that he would not consider sending American troops won him a standing ovation, from both sides of the aisle.[22]

Reagan's 1983 foray into Lebanon vividly demonstrated the forces handcuffing even the most aggressive American policymakers. Israel had invaded neighboring Lebanon to clear away Palestinian guerrillas and Syrian-backed militias from its northern border. As the fighting reached Beirut, Lebanon's capital city, U.S. forces intervened to stabilize the military situation and to broker a peace settlement. American troops withstood several attacks; eventually an Arab suicide bomber crashed into a U.S barracks, killing more than 200 marines. President Reagan immediately withdrew the troops and abandoned the intervention.

Soon after the Lebanon debacle, Secretary of Defense Caspar Weinberger enunciated new guidelines for committing U.S. forces overseas. The Reagan administration would send soldiers and sailors into combat, Weinberger explained, only if the operation had a clear objective, if the circumstances permitted the United States to marshal sufficient firepower to finish the job quickly, and if the intervention received overwhelming public support. The Grenada invasion satisfied these conditions; Lebanon had not.

The administration understood that it could not always flex America's muscles in the international arena; it could not entirely exorcise the ghosts of Vietnam and Tehran. Instead the White House developed the so-called Reagan Doctrine. America would not send its own troops into the world's hot spots, would not replay Vietnam or Korea. Instead the United States would support "freedom fighters"—indigenous anticommunist guerrillas—in their armed struggles against Marxism. Reagan would send money, advisers, and materiel, but leave the troops (and the body bags) at home. Reagan continued aid to the Afghan rebels who were resisting Soviet invaders in Afghanistan, supplied Jonas Savimbi's UNITA rebels fighting against the Cuban-backed government of Angola, and backed the contras in Nicaragua.

But Reagan also resolved the contradiction between saber-rattling rhetoric and straitjacketed diplomacy by backing off, accepting the limits, and living within the constraints. After the Soviets shot down Korean Air flight 007, a passenger plane that had strayed over Soviet airspace with 269 passengers aboard, the president denounced the attack in the harshest possible language. He called it "an act of barbarism born of a society which wantonly disregards individual rights, the value of human life and seeks constantly to expand and dominate other nations." Yet he ignored calls for reprisals, even among the Republican leadership and his own staff, and announced only a few mild responses, such as extending the ban on Soviet airline flights to the United States. After the incident, Richard Viguerie rightly labeled Reagan "a reverse Teddy Roosevelt"—a leader who spoke loudly and carried a small stick.[23]

A similar pattern reappeared in the Middle East, in Latin America, around the world. As Weinberger's analysis of the Lebanon fiasco revealed, the Reagan administration strove mightily to avoid unpopular foreign adventures. Maintaining public approval often took precedence over standing tall. Indeed, that concern largely explained the most controversial and least successful diplomatic initiative of Reagan's presidency—the failed arms-for-hostages deals that mushroomed into a national scandal.[24]

Reagan had to take such extraordinary, even illegal, measures because of real limits on his ability to project American power abroad. In international affairs, Reagan adopted a new posture, he established a mood. Unlike his predecessors—Nixon, Ford, and Carter—he refused to accept that the United States had entered an age of limits. But his diplomacy recognized those constraints even as his rhetoric denied them. Reagan could not, would not, banish entirely the legacy of the Seventies.[25]

Defeating the Evil Empire

This mixture of stridency and strategy also played itself out in the most crucial of international arenas: the twilight struggle against Soviet communism. When Reagan entered office, he determined to reverse the direction of superpower relations in the 1970s. For over a decade, American foreign policy had drifted toward détente—peaceful coexistence and constructive engagement with the Soviet Union. Henry Kissinger had been the architect of détente, and Presidents Nixon, Ford, and Carter had pursued it. Détente featured trade and travel between the rival nations, cultural exchanges, and arms control agreements.

Reagan hated détente. He believed it immoral to negotiate with the Soviets and thought that trade agreements only propped up the communist regime. Rather than promote peace, he asserted, arms control left the United States vulnerable to attack and emboldened the Soviets to expand around the globe.[26] Reagan decided to replace détente with confrontation. First and foremost, he authorized a massive military buildup. In five years, from 1981 to 1986, the Pentagon budget more than doubled. The administration revived major weapons systems that Carter had iced and lavished resources on conventional forces, such as the building of 150 new naval ships.

Reagan poured money into the military to erase what he saw as vulnerabilities. But he also, in one aide's words, wanted to apply "the full-court press"—to use the arms race to strain and bankrupt the Soviet economy. "The Russians know they can't match us industrially or technologically," Reagan had declared even before becoming president. He believed a new arms race would break the Soviets. At its high point, the Pentagon spent some $34 million per hour. The Kremlin could not hope to match that largesse.[27]

At the same time, Reagan rejected arms control. The United States took off the table every offer except the so-called zero option. Under that proposal, the United States would not deploy its new INF missiles if the Soviets pulled out all their existing missiles trained on Europe. That is, the Reagan administration asked the Soviets to withdraw existing weapons in return for missiles yet to be installed. U.S. negotiators knew that the Soviets would find the proposal unacceptable.[28]

President Reagan also mounted an unprecedented rhetorical attack on the Soviet Union. In spring 1983, appearing before the National Association of Evangelicals, Reagan labeled the Soviets an evil empire. They are, he declared, "the focus of evil in the world." The cold war was not "a giant misunderstanding," but a "struggle between right and wrong, good and evil."[29]

Reagan had expressed similar sentiments in the Seventies. But now he was president, and Americans were shocked to hear such harsh, uncompromising words from their chief executive.[30] In response to this confrontational rhetoric and Reagan's buildup, a genuine international peace movement emerged. In the United States, it took shape as the nuclear freeze—a massive social movement encompassing a wide spectrum of social activists across America. In June 1982, more than half a million people thronged New York City's Central Park in what was then the largest political rally in U.S. history. At another mass rally against the arms race, in the Hollywood Bowl, Reagan's own daughter spoke out against his policies. The U.S. Council of Roman Catholic Bishops issued a pastoral letter, calling for a freeze on the testing and deployment of all U.S.

nuclear weapons. On Capitol Hill, Senators Ted Kennedy (D, Massachusetts) and Mark Hatfield (R, Oregon) introduced just such a freeze plan.

The peace movement displayed even greater strength across the Atlantic. Protesters in England and Germany demanded a nuclear-free Europe and opposed the installation of INF missiles in Western Europe. Some NATO leaders even suggested delays in the deployment. But the pressure did not move Reagan; in the fall of 1983, he went ahead with the installation of new missiles in Britain, Italy, and Germany. The Soviets immediately broke off arms control negotiations.

Finally, in March 1983, Reagan committed the United States to "Star Wars"—the Strategic Defense Initiative. The president announced a five-year $26 billion program to research and deploy a nationwide defense system against Soviet missiles. This shield, as Reagan envisioned it, would involve both ground- and space-based weapons—lasers, honing rockets, particle beams—that would knock out Soviet missiles before they could land. "What if free people could live secure in the knowledge that their security did not rest upon the threat of instant U.S. retaliation to deter a Soviet attack?" the president asked a national television audience. What if "we could intercept and destroy strategic ballistic missiles before they reached our soil or that of our allies?"[31]

SDI alarmed the Soviets more than any of Reagan's confrontational policies and pronouncements. The Kremlin did not so much fear the Star Wars shield; Soviet leaders knew that such a plan, if it would ever work, could not be completed for decades. Rather, they realized that the first step in building SDI would be the development of ground-based missile defenses—weapons designed to protect U.S missiles from attack. The defenses would violate the 1972 Anti-Ballistic Missile Treaty and upset the longstanding deterrence policy of mutually assured destruction. SDI thus threatened the surety that nuclear war meant the end of the world; it destabilized the fragile balance that had governed the globe throughout the atomic age and upped the ante in the cold war.

Reagan absolutely refused to compromise on SDI. Skeptics, even some within his own administration, accused the president of sacrificing meaningful arms control for a pipe dream. During his second term, Reagan would famously walk away from a deal to eliminate most nuclear weapons because he refused to limit SDI research to the laboratory. But Reagan understood the real significance of SDI: Star Wars convinced the Soviets that they could no longer afford the nuclear arms race.

President Reagan's many-pronged strategy of confrontation backfired in

August 1984. Speaking into a microphone that he did not know was recording, the president joked, "My fellow Americans, I'm pleased to tell you today that I've signed legislation that will outlaw Russia forever. We begin bombing in 5 minutes."[32]

That unfortunate joke marked the crescendo of the confrontational approach. During the 1984 campaign, Reagan moved toward a new, much more flexible approach in U.S. relations with the Soviets. The shift certainly expressed an election year desire to moderate his position, but it also reflected substantial changes in the international situation and in the president's own strategy. In part, Reagan's softer line revealed the influence of Nancy Reagan. The first lady did not like her Ronnie being portrayed as a warmonger and later claimed that she whispered "peace" in his ear every night. (Reagan biographer Edmund Morris joked that she must have spoken into his deaf right ear since the president never dropped his hatred and suspicion of the Russians.) Others believed the new approach bespoke the mounting influence of George Shultz, who had replaced the hard-line Alexander Haig as secretary of state and lobbied Reagan to negotiate with the Soviets.[33]

The turn toward flexibility and negotiation also attested to Reagan's growing sensitivity to Soviet fears. When CIA reports informed the president that U.S. military exercises simulating the release of nuclear weapons had frightened the Soviets, Reagan was amazed. He confessed that he was surprised to learn that the Soviets genuinely feared an American attack.[34]

Last but not least, the thaw in Soviet-American relations accelerated in 1985 when Konstantin Chernenko died. The decrepit Communist party general secretary had been the third Soviet leader to expire since Reagan took office. This time the Politburo installed in the premiership fifty-four-year-old Mikhail Gorbachev—a healthy, energetic reformer. A former agriculture minister, Gorbachev understood the crippling weaknesses of the Soviet economy and the nation's pervasive social crises: rampant alcoholism, worker absenteeism, high infant mortality. The new general secretary moved immediately to scale down Soviet aid to revolutionary regimes in Third World, pull out of the quagmire of Afghanistan, and slow the arms race.

Gorbachev convinced many hard-line conservatives to take up the olive branches he proffered. Even that most hard-nosed of conservative leaders, the Iron Lady, British prime minister Margaret Thatcher, declared that "we can do business together with this man." Reagan initially resisted Gorbachev's blandishments, but finally agreed to a summit meeting and eventually met with the Soviet leader several times.

By the end of his presidency, the seemingly impossible had occurred. Ronald Reagan visited Moscow, embraced the Soviet leader in front of Lenin's tomb, and declared that the Soviets had changed. No longer were they the focus of evil in the modern world. The cold war was coming to an end. But ultimately, Reagan's rhetoric—his political commitments—redefined the cold war more decisively than his summit conferences or arms reductions. The Seventies vision of the Soviet Union—and of world politics—had changed so much that Americans could barely remember them.[35]

"Government Is the Problem"

At home as well as abroad, Reagan wrestled with the legacies of the Seventies. For the president who succeeded Jimmy Carter, no other mission—not even the somber struggle with Soviet Union—mattered so much as nursing the United States itself back to health. But Reagan would pursue an unprecedented path to this objective, involving a direct assault on American government and public life, a culmination of Richard Nixon's fantasies that even he would have looked on with incredulity.

When Reagan took office, the nation appeared to be careening down a precipice, with the economy in recession, the prime interest rate above 20 percent, the federal budget deficit more than $50 billion, and the national debt about to top a mind-boggling $1 trillion. For Reagan, according to one White House insider, economic policy was "the first and overriding concern." The president believed that unless he "restored the nation's economic health, he could not tackle any of the other problems, especially national defense."[36]

The Carter administration, Reagan declared during the campaign, had cooked up "a new and altogether indigestible economic stew, one part inflation, one part high unemployment, one part recession, one part runaway taxes, one part deficit spending seasoned with an energy crisis. It's an economic stew that has turned the national stomach." Reagan prescribed an altogether new, and far more abstemious, diet. The heart of the president's program—the centerpiece of the Reagan Revolution—was an attack on big government—the greedy, arrogant establishment that Reagan claimed taxed too much, spent too much, regulated too much, and meddled too much. In memorable words in his inaugural address, Reagan laid out his position: "In the present crisis, government is not the solution to our problem; government is the problem."[37]

The new president conceded that the nation's maladies would not disappear quickly but reassured the nation that they would go away. While his predecessor had introduced Americans to an age of limits, Reagan laid the blame for the nation's woes squarely on Washington. He attacked Carter for both crippling the economy and imposing "the further indignity of being told by the Government that it is all their fault."[38]

In his first months in office, Reagan laid out his agenda. His administration sought nothing less than a "fundamental reorientation of the role of the Federal Government in our economy—a reorientation that will mean more jobs, more opportunity, and more freedom for all Americans." National policy should no longer micromanage the economy or redistribute existing income; instead it must encourage the "development of private institutions conducive to individual responsibility and initiative."[39]

In practice, that "Second American Revolution" involved three great changes. First, Reagan demanded a dramatic reduction in taxes. The president proposed to reduce individual tax rates by 25 percent over three years. At the same time, he sharply cut the rates for the wealthiest taxpayers and indexed taxes to inflation, ending the bracket creep that had eroded Americans' few salary increases and made their tax burdens seem so heavy in the 1970s. Second, Reagan moved drastically to redefine the relationships—to shift the balance of power—among business, labor, and government. He accelerated deregulation, weakening the power of federal agencies to supervise industry's health, safety, and environmental performance. He struck hard at organized labor, removing the public backing that had armed unions in their struggle against business. And he devolved responsibility to the private sector, freeing entrepreneurs and giving business much more responsibility not just for economic but for social and cultural life as well.

Third, Reagan declared war on the federal government itself. He promised not only to end its interference in economic life, but to starve it of funds and shrink its bureaucracy. He targeted waste and inefficiency, but also attacked the welfare state he thought intrusive and counterproductive. He pledged to eliminate two cabinet departments.

He also vowed to eliminate deficit spending. During the campaign, he had blasted Jimmy Carter as "the head of a Government which has utterly refused to live within its means." Candidate Reagan published a plan to balance the federal budget by the end of his second year in the White House and to generate a sizable surplus one year after that. "You and I, as individuals, can by borrowing, live beyond our means, but only for a limited period of time, "the president sermonized on inauguration day. "Why, then, should we think that collectively, as a nation, we're not bound by that same limitation?"[40]

Reagan embraced no coherent economic philosophy; indeed, he borrowed elements from many rival conservative strategies.[41] Still, his basic thrust was to set loose the market—to fix the economy by shrinking government. During the transition, President-elect Reagan willingly tossed aside some of the economic policy tools his predecessors Nixon, Ford, and Carter had relied upon. He eschewed wage and price controls to fight inflation and Keynesian demand management—massive jobs and public works spending—to ease the recession.[42]

In February 1981, Reagan appeared before a joint session of Congress to introduce his new economic program. The plan, immodestly titled "America's New Beginning," marked the real start of Reagan's presidency. His appearance in the House chamber, the president remarked in his diary, had been thrilling. It had made him feel like a president.[43]

Reagan's program endorsed the Kemp-Roth tax cut (30 percent over three years), cut more than $40 billion in spending from Carter's final budget, and promised to eliminate social programs and business regulations.[44] The proposals seemed so ambitious, so radical, that even his own party's leadership on Capitol Hill declared the proposals dead on arrival and suggested the president seek much more modest tax and budget cuts.[45] House Speaker Tip O'Neill (D, Massachusetts), the leading congressional Democrat, warned the former governor that Sacramento lay 3,000 miles behind him. He was in the big leagues now and would find the U.S. Congress far more resistant to his charms than the California legislature had been.[46]

O'Neill underestimated his man. Only a few months later, on July 29, the Congress passed the Economic Recovery Tax Act of 1981. More than sixty House Democrats deserted the party leadership and voted for the tax cut plan, which slashed income tax rates by 25 percent (slightly less than the 30 percent cuts Reagan had requested). The act also rewarded the nation's wealthiest citizens, cutting the taxes on capital gains, gifts, and inheritances.[47]

Meanwhile, Reagan moved rapidly to free business from federal supervision. During the late 1970s, the Carter administration had begun easing the regulatory burden on American industry. In particular, Carter had dismantled the anticompetitive practices that had maintained artificially high prices in trucking, air travel, and telecommunications. Reagan accelerated and expanded the process of deregulation. The administration relaxed Depression-era controls on banks, brokerages, and savings and loan institutions. It decontrolled energy prices and permitted wider oil and gas exploration on federal land. It dropped restraints on offshore oil drilling, logging restrictions in national forests, and requirements for air bags and stronger automobile bumpers.[48]

Reagan handed over the reins of the major oversight agencies to business leaders and opponents of federal regulation. As director of the Occupational Health and Safety Administration (OSHA), the president appointed a businessman who had once been cited for OSHA violations. The Antitrust Division of the Department of Justice announced a new policy of friendliness toward mergers, stimulating an unprecedented wave of corporate buyouts. The Consumer Product Safety Commission, the Federal Trade Commission, and the Federal Communications Commission also relaxed regulations in their bailiwicks. Surveying the flattened regulatory landscape in 1984, Texas oil baron T. Boone Pickens credited these policies for restoring free enterprise and offering American businessmen unparalleled freedom and opportunity.[49]

At the same time, Secretary of the Interior James Watt and EPA director Anne Gorsuch led a counterrevolution against environmental protection. The controversial Watt criticized even the most cherished achievements of the conservation movement. He openly organized a counteroffensive, uniting landholders, businessmen, off-road-vehicle enthusiasts, and hunting groups in opposition to environmental regulations. As interior secretary, Watt authorized expanded surface mining and oil drilling in the West, stepped up timber harvests on public lands, slowed the creation of new parks and wilderness areas, and attempted to privatize many of the functions of the national parks. The secretary was also something of a loose cannon; he ensured his own downfall when he cavalierly announced that one of his department's advisory boards consisted of a black, a woman, "two Jews and a cripple." Over at the EPA, Anne Gorsuch pursued a less flamboyant, more effective strategy, quietly relaxing enforcement of the nation's principal pollution control laws.[50]

In many cases, Reagan loosened the reins on business without repealing regulations or eliminating programs. The administration simply cut the agencies' budgets, leaving them too short-staffed and underequipped to investigate claims or enforce existing rules. The Enforcement Division of the Department of Energy, the office responsible for policing the natural gas and oil industries, saw its staff cut by two-thirds in the first two years of Reagan's presidency. Meanwhile, the administration's budget for fiscal year 1984 requested less funding for water quality, air quality, hazardous waste, and pesticide reduction programs in fiscal year 1984 than Jimmy Carter had appropriated in fiscal year 1981.[51]

The Reagan administration also pleased business interests with its open hostility toward organized labor. In August 1981, nearly 12,000 members of the Professional Air Traffic Controllers Organization (PATCO) violated a no-strike clause in their contract and walked out of the nation's airport control towers. The controllers expected support from the public and the administration; they had raised many legitimate safety concerns about outmoded equipment, long shifts, and understaffed air traffic control centers. Moreover, PATCO had flouted the majority of the American labor movement and supported Ronald Reagan in the 1980 election. They relied on a sympathetic hearing from the former union leader, a one-time president of the Screen Actors Guild who had proudly led his colleagues out on strike.[52]

But the president wasted no time in crushing the illegal strike. He ordered the controllers to return to work or face dismissal. The controllers, Reagan announced, "are in violation of the law, and if they do not report for work within forty-eight hours, they have forfeited their jobs and will be terminated." Congressional and airline industry leaders urged the president to relent. A delegation of Republican former secretaries of labor offered to mediate the strike. But the president remained unmoved. When his deadline passed, Reagan fired the controllers, decertified their union, and ordered military personnel into the control towers. The nation's air traffic control system limped along for months and did not return to full strength until 1988.[53]

Still, Reagan won a major victory. The public applauded his principled stance, admired his toughness, and blamed the controllers for the ensuing delays at the airports. Business leaders realized that management had a staunch ally in the White House and turned up the pressure on organized labor. Even the Soviets sat up and took notice when the Reagan administration hauled the PATCO leadership off to jail. Tip O'Neill visited Moscow soon after the strike and learned how much Reagan's steel will had impressed the Soviets.[54]

The PATCO strike left organized labor in disarray. Most unions had not supported the air traffic controllers—out of unwillingness to support an illegal strike by federal employees, a lack of sympathy for the highly paid controllers who had never supported union causes, or fear of the popular president. When Jerry Wurf, president of the American Federation of State, County, and Municipal Employees, attempted to show support for the strikers at Chicago's O'Hare International Airport, he could not even find their picket line. Wurf, leader of the nation's largest public employee organization, believed the PATCO debacle a "watershed moment" for the American labor movement. It was a "terribly important strike," Wurf told *the New York Times*. "There is a message being sent that the Administration in power is hostile to the ambitions of trade unions and it's going to bang labor in the head whenever it can."[55]

Unions and management heard the message loud and clear. An intimidated labor movement lost influence, tamed its militance, and moderated its demands. Reagan scoured the corporate community to staff the National Labor Relations Board, eschewing the more sympathetic university professors, congressional staffers, and union officials that his predecessors had called on to supervise labor-management relations. Labor secretary Raymond Donovan, a former building contractor, worked to erode preferences for union labor in government contracts and tried to ease regulations on industrial home work.[56] The Reagan recovery did little for working people. Real earnings of production workers actually fell between 1980 and 1987.[57]

Unions fell back in disorganized retreat. The meatpacking industry shied away from heavily unionized slaughterhouse districts in Chicago and Omaha, opening new low-wage, nonunion facilities in the outlying towns of Iowa, Illinois, and Nebraska. In Austin, Minnesota, Hormel packinghouse workers organized the entire community in a struggle against wage concessions and other "givebacks" to management. Despite its herculean efforts, Austin Local P-9 could not win a battle against a company armed with hungry strikebreakers from nearby farming communities, national guard troops sent in by the governor, and even the national leadership of their own union.[58]

To be sure, the union's share of the nation's nonfarm workforce had fallen steadily since the late 1950s. But Reagan's first term proved a catastrophe for organized labor. Unions experienced their first absolute drop in membership since World War II; organized labor's share of the workforce plummeted from 23.6 percent in 1980 to 19.4 percent in 1984.[59]

But for Ronald Reagan, not even unions posed the biggest obstacle to prosperity and personal freedom. The federal government itself—huge, stolid, insensitive, intrusive—was the main problem. After only a year in office, Reagan had already succeeded in cutting taxes and empowering business. But the most crucial component of his antigovernment agenda—cutting spending and shrinking the federal establishment—proved more difficult. The budget certainly offered little wiggle room. In 1982, defense constituted a quarter of federal spending, and Reagan had committed to a vast arms buildup. Debt service remained an inviolable 10 percent of outlays, and the entitlement programs—popular universal benefit programs like social security and Medicare—occupied nearly half.[60]

At the beginning of his presidency, just as he announced his tax proposals, Reagan presented plans to slash the budget. He asked Congress to knock $41 billion off his predecessor's proposals for the coming year. Defense spending would increase—its share of the budget rising from 24 to 32 percent of spending. Nearly every other program and agency faced cuts, although the president promised to preserve the "safety net" in social programs. In practice, he saved the politically sensitive middle-class entitlements—Social Security, Medicare, veterans' benefits—while shredding the actual safety net, the means-tested programs for the poor. Reagan called for dramatic cuts in food stamps, student loans, public service jobs, training programs, welfare, school lunches, and urban mass transit.[61] The plan dropped almost half a million households from Aid to Families with Dependent Children (AFDC), the major federal welfare program. Another 350,000 lost support when the administration closed down CETA, the national job training program.[62]

Writing in the *Nation*, liberal critics Derek Shearer and Martin Carnoy called Reagan's program "the most significant income redistribution since the 1930s." Reaganomics, the liberal academics asserted, "does not really mean getting the government off people's backs; it means repealing the hard-won social gains of the last fifty years and using the government to transfer money to large corporations, high-income earners and military contractors."[63]

Reagan certainly made no secret of his disdain for the welfare state. The president truly lacked sympathy for the downtrodden, accepting the canard that the poor deserved and even desired their own misery. Asked if he could have done more for the homeless, Reagan told his authorized biographer that his opponents had exaggerated the scope of the problem. There were few homeless people, he asserted, "and a lot of those are the type of people that have made that choice."[64]

In purely budgetary terms, Reagan's assault on the social safety net remained modest; total welfare expenditures still grew during the 1980s.[65] But the administration consciously reduced the share of national resources dedicated to the neediest. It tightened eligibility requirements and eliminated services for the impoverished, making public assistance much less accessible. The 1981 Omnibus Budget Reconciliation Act allowed states to impose fees on Medicaid patients for each doctor or hospital visit and reduced outlays for food stamps and AFDC by 14 percent each. The administration also phased out social security benefits for college-aged children of deceased adults, eliminated the public service employment program, and raised the rent contribution expected from recipients of housing assistance.[66]

While total welfare spending continued to mount, the administration slowed its rate of growth. Social welfare spending (even including the social security program) occupied a smaller share of federal outlays in 1985 than in 1981. Social spending also fell as a share of gross domestic product (GDP).[67]

Moreover, Reagan reduced the federal government's role in the welfare state. Wherever possible, the administration contracted out social services to private firms, especially with regard to nursing homes and federally supported child care. The president also replaced direct spending on social programs with tax incentives and shifted welfare burdens to state and local government.[68] In these ways, the Reagan Revolution displayed signature features that distinguished the American experience from other revolts against the liberal welfare state that swept simultaneously across the industrialized world.[69]

Finally, Reagan shifted the terms of the welfare debate. For a generation, ever since President Lyndon B. Johnson had asked Americans to join in building what he called the Great Society, American social policy had aimed to eliminate poverty and redress the most blatant extremes of inequality. Johnson's successors lacked his commitment to total victory over poverty, but their welfare policies followed his lead. From Nixon's guaranteed income proposal to Carter's PBJI, policymakers regarded poverty and inequality as economic and social defects and the welfare state as the medic.

Reagan turned the tables; welfare now became the problem, not the solution. Drawing on the work of conservative thinkers Charles Murray and George Gilder, Reagan's first economic report rejected "paternalism" in welfare policies, suggesting that antipoverty programs only aggravated the problems of the poor and trapped them in a cycle of poverty and dependence. Indeed, Reagan went so far as to argue that Great Society programs had actually harmed the impoverished—encouraging illegitimacy, welfare dependence, and hopelessness. "With the coming of the Great Society," President Reagan insisted in 1982, "government began eating away at the underpinnings of the private enterprise system. The big taxers and big spenders in the Congress had started a binge that would slowly change the nature of our society and, even worse, it threatened the character of our people. . . . By the time the full weight of Great Society programs was felt, economic progress for America's poor had come to a tragic halt." With such sweeping assertions, Reagan succeeded in refocusing debate from poverty to dependency.[70]

But pulling the reins on big government proved far more difficult. During the 1980 campaign, Reagan pledged to eliminate two cabinet portfolios, junking the recently created Departments of Education and Energy. The president wanted not only to strip the Education Department of its cabinet rank, but also to cut federal education programs to the bone. Terrel Bell was thus mystified when Reagan offered him the position of secretary of education. Bell possessed strong educational credentials and supported federal aid to education; he told Reagan he would go along with downgrading the department to a lower-level agency but would not dismantle its programs. The president still appointed Bell, and, of course, Reagan never abolished the Education Department. Ignored by the White House, the secretary formed a commission to investigate the baleful state of American public schools. The report, *A Nation at Risk: The Imperative for Educational Reform,* became a national cause célèbre after its release in April 1983. By 1984, the Reagan administration had adopted education reform as a campaign issue, the Republican party platform pledged support for the Department of Education, and federal education spending reached record levels. After William Bennett replaced Bell as secretary, the Department of Education became one of the most high-profile departments in the administration.[71]

Most dramatically, Reagan ignored his own homilies against excess spending and racked up tremendous budget deficits. From the start, administration officials recognized that their budgetary math did not square; they could not fulfill Reagan's promises of tax cuts, rearmament, and a balanced budget, at least not without massive cuts in public services. David Stockman certainly understood. He believed that Reaganomics necessarily implied a "blueprint for radical governance." The administration's commitments to tax relief and the Pentagon, the budget director believed, required deep cuts in spending. Just to balance the ledgers, Reagan would have to shred the federal establishment— canceling whole programs, eliminating entire agencies, returning to an almost nineteenth-century conception of small government. Two weeks before inauguration day, Stockman spent two hours with the president-elect, informing him of the "dire shape" of the federal budget. Immediately, the new administration would have to trim $40 billion from Carter's last budget. "Do you have any idea what $40 billion means," Stockman gleefully teased *Atlantic Monthly* writer William Greider. "It means I've got to cut the highway program. It means I've got to cut milk price supports. And Social Security student benefits. And education and student loans. And manpower training and housing. It means I've got to shut down the synfuels program and a lot of other programs."[72]

But Reagan had drafted no such radical blueprint. Stockman quickly discovered the president's distaste for drastic cuts in popular programs when his second round of proposed economies languished unattended on the president's desk. Reagan simply did not share his budget director's zeal to shrink government, even when it offended the interests of big business. Stockman's "Chapter II"—a plan to axe corporate welfare like the oil depletion allowance and remove tax breaks for mansions and tax exempt industrial bonds—merited no more than a disinterested sniff from the president.[73]

Despite his folksy denunciations of charge-card government and his rhetorical support for a constitutional amendment requiring a balanced federal budget, Reagan hesitated little about racking up ever larger deficits. During Reagan's presidency, one distinguished economist noted, the U.S. government spent $1,413 billion more than it received in revenues. "The borrowing that the treasury did to cover this shortfall approximately tripled its outstanding interest-bearing debt, or about doubled it after allowance for inflation." Pundits complained of the deficit's adverse effects on economic performance, savings, interest rates, and investment. "It is not clear whether President Reagan actually meant to throw this party or whether things simply got out of hand," chastised the *New Republic*. Another critic lambasted Reagan as "the king of the deficit-makers and undisputed master of the national debt mountain." American society, he warned, was devouring its seed corn instead of planting it.[74]

But the deficit never bothered the president; he never noticed the egg on his face. In part, the administration understood that the deficits were not as large or as damaging as they appeared to be. Compared to the size of the economy and the crushing shortfalls that many Western European nations faced, the problem was manageable. Moreover, in the federal system, state and local governments also collect and expend revenues; the general government deficit, the total for all levels of government, remained far more modest.[75]

The president's calm also reflected his famous optimism. In discussing the deficit, many of Reagan's economic advisers recalled, he frequently repeated his favorite anecdote about the boy who looked at a pile of manure and assumed he must have received a new pony. One aide recalled the president's views on the deficit "going through three stages: one, they won't occur; two, they'll be temporary; three, when they stick they serve a good purpose—they keep the liberals from new spending programs. Oh, sure, that was Reagan." On that last point, Reagan was right. The unpaid bills choked off future spending and prevented even the most committed liberal activists from proposing new programs. Reagan's budgets ensured that Reaganomics would continue long after the president had departed the White House.[76]

But the paradox of antigovernment ideology and massive federal spending remained. On Reagan's watch, the federal government grew larger and larger; it cost more dollars, employed more bureaucrats, sustained more agencies, departments, and programs. Reagan's reputation, and real achievements, as the scourge of big government owed more to acts of omission than actual cutbacks. The administration slowed the growth rate of the federal establishment; it simply crossed many new programs off congressional wish lists before they could be proposed. Reagan's success reminded conservative columnist James J. Kilpatrick of "a Sherlock Holmes story where the key fact was that the dog did not bark." Many of Reagan's triumphs involved "political things that were not done and in many cases were not even attempted." In the final session of the Carter administration, congressional leaders had championed national health insurance, a stronger National Labor Relations Board, and the creation of a new consumer protection agency. "All of those dropped out of sight after Reagan's election."[77]

Surveying the American landscape in the early 1970s, Richard Nixon had envisioned a new American majority, a conservative revolution that would transform national politics and topple the balance of power within American culture. Nixon's strategy rested on the burgeoning influence and freewheeling conservatism of the rising Sunbelt. He had imagined an antiestablishment coalition, drawing together northern workers and Sunbelt entrepreneurs in common disgust with a decadent, liberal Ivy League elite. Nixon had dreamed of a nation where the dog—the manicured poodle of the eastern establishment—no longer barked. Without the pessimism and menace of Tricky Dick, Reagan realized that objective.

But if Reagan dulled the sharper edges of American conservatism, it surely never seemed that way to most Americans. In his public statements and his displays of presidential pomp and power, Reagan never backed down. That air of command and commitment proved to be the most potent and enduring feature of his presidency. More than any policy achievement or failure, that feeling—the seismic shifts in national mood and political debate—constituted the real Reagan Revolution.

Reagan delegitimized government. By the end of his first term, leaders across the American political spectrum embraced Reagan's conviction that government had grown too large, too intrusive, too unwieldy. The democratic system "has never failed us, but for a time we failed the system," Reagan preached in his Second Inaugural Address. "We asked things of government that government was not equipped to give."[78]

He also wrote taxation out of the policy options book. In 1984, former

Vice President Walter Mondale launched his campaign for the White House by confessing the obvious need for a tax increase. Facing a record budget short-fall, the Democratic nominee insisted that the next president would have to raise taxes. Unlike Reagan, he would be honest enough (and have enough on the ball) to admit it. But Mondale's gambit proved a miserable failure. It immediately identified him as a prophet of malaise, a relic of outmoded tax-and-spend liberalism.[79]

Taxation had always been unpopular, of course, but it had long remained a weapon of class warfare—a way ordinary Americans could limit the power and influence of the nation's wealthiest citizens. After all, it was not Ronald Reagan, but Franklin D. Roosevelt's adviser Harry Hopkins who coined the term tax-and-spend Democrat. But for Hopkins, that had been a recipe for success: "tax and spend and elect, tax and spend and elect." Reagan trans-formed taxation; it ceased to be an issue of equity, and it became a matter of tyranny or freedom. Instead of dividing rich and poor, business and labor, the tax issue united them against big government and elitist bureaucrats. Reagan did not begin the tax revolt, but he guided it to victory.

Instead of government activism and political participation, Reagan turned to the market and the nation turned with him. Usually remembered for their patriotic exuberance and the ubiquitous chant "USA, USA!" the 1984 Los Ange-les Olympics signaled the triumph of privatization in American life. In the words of one major newsweekly, they were the "Summer Olympics, Capitalist Style." "Ordinarily," *U.S. News* reflected, "the host country funds the games. But the good burghers of Los Angeles," the minutemen of the tax revolt, "declined to donate their tax dollars and even amended the city charter to prevent any federal subsidy."[80] So the corporate cavalry rode to the rescue; major corpora-tions paid hundreds of millions to finance the games, banking on "prestige, publicity, and profits" in return. "Never before," noted *Business Week,* have the games been tied so tightly to the coattails of big business." One way or another, corporate America paid nearly all of the event's half-a-billion-dollar cost.[81]

Southland Corporation sold Olympic flashlights, mugs, and bicycle horns at its 8,000 7-Eleven stores. Levi Strauss stamped the Olympic rings on visors, caps, and luggage. Converse Athletic Shoes, Murray Ohio Bicycles, Stuart Hall school supplies, and Longines-Wittenauer Watch all jumped on the bandwagon and produced licensed products. Buick, the official car of the Olympics, introduced a special Century Olympia model—"a white sedan emblazoned with Olympic emblems, gold stripes, and headrests sporting embroidered Olympic rings."[82]

In the spirit of privatization, Peter Ueberroth, president of the Los Angeles Olympic Organizing Committee (LAOOC), took pride in the total absence of public support for the games. "We are not using," Ueberroth boasted, the "primary sources of funding used by all other Olympics."[83] Instead of the vast army of employees previous organizing committees had hired to manage the event, Ueberroth relied on volunteers and sponsors to staff many activities. (The LAOOC employed just half the people used by the Soviets in 1980 and Montreal in 1976.)[84] Ueberroth's successful stewardship of the games won him so exalted a reputation that Republican circles began touting him as a possible candidate for the California governorship, and he eventually won the plum position of commissioner of Major League Baseball.

Ueberroth's fortunes rose with the unfolding recovery, but more than economic revival underlay the new confidence. The boom, after all, hardly restored the nation's faith in established institutions. Americans distrusted them all: Wall Street and Washington, universities and the press. Rather, the exuberance of the times reflected confidence in entrepreneurship—not in social movements but in personal networks. The Olympic Games foreshadowed not only the triumph of Reaganism in November and the impending victory over the communist bloc in the cold war. They suggested the ascendance of a new ideology and a new cultural style. In 1970, everyone understood the initials "VC." They meant Vietcong—the intransigent communist guerrillas who pinned down American troops in Vietnam. The Vietcong had been implacable enemies, exposing to many Americans weaknesses in national power and national will. For others, the VC had become heroes. The initials evoked an entire culture of political protest, even dreams of revolution. By 1984, "VC" had become an acronym for *venture capital*. The years of the market—and the yuppie—had begun.

"Arise Ye Yuppies": Economy and Culture in the 1980s

On December 31, 1984, *Newsweek* magazine devoted its year-end issue to "The Year of the Yuppie." The young urban professionals have arrived," the newsweekly declared, "they're making lots of money, spending it conspicuously and switching political candidates like they test cuisines." In that same year, a satirical how-to guide, *The Yuppie Handbook*, climbed the best-seller lists, and all the major news outlets focused on the yuppie phenomenon—charting its effects on American consumption patterns, popular culture, religion, politics, and economic life.[85]

The very term *yuppie* remains shrouded in mystery and controversy. Most chablis-swilling sociologists believe the word first saw print in March 1983, when syndicated columnist Bob Greene dropped it offhandedly into a piece on ex-Sixties radical (and ex–Seventies New Ager) Jerry Rubin and his reemergence as an investment banker. Still, San Francisco Bay–area humorist Alice Kahn probably deserves the credit (or the blame) for defining and delineating this new social class—developing *yuppie* as a modified acronym for young urban professional.

Kahn's June 1983 article in the *East Bay Express* created the familiar profile of the typical yuppie that the national press would soon adopt. Kahn wrote about how well-off young professionals—who worked long hours at basically unfulfilling jobs, but earned loads of money—formed their identities through luxurious leisure activities and consumption of big-name purchased goods. She noticed yuppies driving out community shops with their preferences for upscale boutiques.[86]

A few months later, Americans began discovering yuppies everywhere. Carmakers, demographers, academics, film and television producers, record company executives, journalists, and politicians began to see yuppiedom as the new, influential wave in American life. Corporate America developed new marketing strategies for the yuppie market: "Detroit's New Goal—Putting Yuppies in the Driver's Seat," reported *Business Week* in 1984.[87] "Saab Hitches Its Star to the Yuppie Market." Advertisers, a *U.S. News and World Report* survey concluded, "say yuppies are disproportionately important in the marketplace."[88]

Young urban professionals also flexed their muscles in the political and cultural arenas. Colorado senator Gary Hart's upstart 1984 campaign for the Democratic presidential nomination credited his hip appeal to yuppie voters. "Now that the Gary Hart campaign is more or less over," *New Republic* columnist Michael Kinsley joked in the summer of 1984, the "specter of a federal quiche stamps program has passed. There will be no transatlantic Perrier pipeline, no National Tennis Elbow Institute, no Department of Life Style."[89] *U.S. News* ran a story on "How Churches Try to Woo the Yuppies." A strange new illness—chronic fatigue syndrome—was renamed "yuppie flu."[90]

The term *yuppie* proved so contagious because it evoked the yippies—the most outrageous, anarchic cultural radicals of the 1960s. Many observers fastened onto Jerry Rubin's odyssey from yippie to yuppie. Rubin had helped to mastermind the disturbances at the 1968 Democratic National Convention in Chicago. In 1968, he and Abbie Hoffman had thrown dollar bills onto the floor of the New York Stock Exchange, laughing as the brokers scurried madly for the cash and the television cameras rolled. Now, fifteen years later, Rubin himself scurried for cash. It struck many as a fitting emblem of failed idealism.[91]

Yuppie also implied an alternative to, even a rejection of, *hippie*. Young professionals rejected the values of the counterculture, or at least they had thoroughly tamed and domesticated them. The yuppie lifestyle drained from the hippie ideal the spirit of rebellion, the need to create alternative institutions, families, and selves. As journalist and former Carter speechwriter Hendrik Hertzberg put it, "Yuppiedom carried over from hippiedom an appreciation for things deemed 'natural,' an emphasis on personal freedom, and the self-absorption of that part of the counterculture known as the human-potential movement." But, Hertzberg jibed, "Hippies thought property was theft; yuppies think it's an investment. Hippies were interested in karma; yuppies prefer cars."[92]

At the same time, *yuppie* echoed the term *preppie*. It evoked a sense of entitlement—a privileged way of life and its exclusive accoutrements. Still, yuppiedom diverged from preppiedom in one crucial respect: birth, family, and upbringing made a preppie, but anyone with money could enter the terrain of the yuppies. Just don't forget your American Express Gold Card.[93]

Fleeting as it was, the yuppie phenomenon represented the ascendance of a new cultural style. In many ways, the boisterous, consumerist spirit of the mid-1980s signaled the triumph of Reaganism. After all, the president had long wished to restore the imagined nation of his youth, his image of America as a place where anyone could get rich. The *Wall Street Journal* aptly referred to the elderly president as the nation's most aged yuppie.[94]

Still, yuppie values never implied respect for tradition or nostalgia for the small-town values Reagan liked to evoke in his signature anecdotes. Yuppies challenged the ossified structures of corporate America, the sacred rituals of academia, the bloated bureaucracies of government. According to *Newsweek*, they were three times as likely as other Americans to carry American Express cards, travel overseas, and work out in health clubs. Their primary loyalties lay not with family, corporation, or country but with their networks—"informal associations of mutual friendship that cut across corporate lines to unite people of similar ages, professional levels and interests, principally money and sex."[95]

What formed the key tenets of yuppie ideology, if they even deserved such a grandiose designation? What ideas percolated along with the gourmet coffee? First, raw accumulation of wealth for its own sake was not tawdry or immoral but worthy. Personal empowerment depended on having money; finding yourself costs!

In the 1987 film *Wall Street*, Oliver Stone's attempt to critique yuppie values, the evil character played by Michael Douglas, a ruthless capitalist named Gordon Gecko, stole the show and the audience with a now-legendary disquisition. Criticized for being greedy, Gecko does not deny but instead celebrates his avarice. "Greed is good," Gecko lectures a shareholders' meeting of an underperforming corporation. "Greed, in all its forms, greed for life, greed for love, greed for knowledge—has marked the upsurgence of man since the beginning of time.... Greed, gentlemen, can not only save this company, but it can save that other malfunctioning institution known as the United States of America." Real young professionals agreed that economic accumulation represented a good in and of itself.[96]

But that zest for wealth did not foreclose the possibility of social reform. On the contrary, the second key tenet of yuppie ideology held that money-making was not antithetical to meaningful social change, but absolutely essential for it. For yuppies, the entrepreneur had replaced the reformer or radical. One could change the world by providing it with natural, caring, environmentally safe, politically sensitive goods and services.

Geoffrey Lewis, a self-identified yuppie, explained this in a *Newsweek* feature. By 1984, the former antiwar radical had become an immensely successful New York City attorney, living in a $200,000 co-op on Manhattan's tony Upper East Side. Once tear-gassed at 1971 May Day demonstrations in Washington, Lewis remained engaged in politics, although his causes and his tactics had matured. "I will always be a community-minded person," he soberly reflected. "It's just that the shape of my concerns may change as I grow older." While Lewis and his fellow yuppies did not "want money to rule your life. You have to realize what money can bring you. In our case, I would like to think it can bring us more than just a VCR."[97]

Lewis's new sobriety reflected a third crucial tenet of yuppie ideology: a rejection of hippies, a repudiation of the cultural and political critique of the Sixties counterculture. Yuppies dismissed the antimaterialism of the counterculture as naive; they replaced the hippie quest for freedom from the aerosol and vinyl institutions of American capitalism with an equally passionate search for the best that consumer culture could offer. "The name of the game," *The Yuppie Handbook* affirmed, "is the *best*—buying it, owning it, using it, eating it, wearing it, growing it, cooking it, driving it, doing whatever with it."[98]

Yuppie-era popular culture mocked the idea of altered consciousness and decried the Sixties counterculture for its supposed naiveté.[99] Compare, as many 1980s film critics did, the 1967 classic *The Graduate* to the 1983 blockbuster *Risky Business*. Both films focused on graduating seniors with dim prospects—Benjamin Braddock, the eponymous college graduate with no hopes or plans played by Dustin Hoffman, and Joel Goodsen, a high school senior struggling to gain admission to an elite college despite his low SAT scores. Both protagonists journeyed toward personal fulfillment—literally traveling in sports cars and on public transportation. Both also receive sexual initiation by an experienced older woman. But in one reviewer's words, "Benjamin Braddock moves out of his house; Joel stays and turns it into an enterprise. Benjamin rejects further education; Joel pimps his way into Princeton. When barging into a frat house, Benjamin looks like an illegal alien; Joel probably cannot wait for rush."[100]

Benjamin Braddock's 1967 graduate ultimately rejected the materialism around him. Terminating his affair with Mrs. Robinson and her corrupt society, Benjamin escapes on a bus with the woman he loves and becomes something of a countercultural hero. But Joel finds love and success with the seductive, fallen older woman. "It was great the way her mind worked," Joel enthused. "No doubts, no fears, just the shameless pursuit of immediate material gratification. What a capitalist!" Benjamin's discomfort with wealth and luxury reflected the values of the counterculture; however dumbed down, *Risky Business* reflected a growing sentiment that capitalism offered liberation and empowerment.[101]

In the mid-1980s, during the high tide of Reaganism, Americans celebrated yuppiedom in films, television, recordings, magazine articles, marketing surveys, and sociological analyses. The nation trumpeted unabashedly the influence of yuppies; even if the media exaggerated their actual numbers, they remained the trendsetters, the opinion makers. And yuppie values seemed the perfect complement to the age of Reagan. Yuppies ruled!

The yuppie phenomenon would be short-lived. By the time Reagan left the White House, *yuppie* would become a curse word—a derogatory term that corporations, journalists, and young professionals themselves strived to avoid. Even yuppies hated yuppies. No one willingly answered to the name. BMW, the automobile that had become synonymous with yuppies on the make, launched a $30 million advertising campaign to shed itself of just that image.[102] But by then, while brand names might become clichéd, the core beliefs of yuppiedom had become so well entrenched that no one even noticed them any more. A broad consensus had emerged: Americans affirmed the superiority of the private sphere to the public sector; entrepreneurship, not political activism, marked the path to personal liberation and social transformation.

The Gospel of Privatization

Ronald Reagan preached the essential values of the yuppie creed, even if he cloaked them in anecdotes most young professionals found a bit corny. Like a good yuppie, Reagan proposed to set business free from regulation, inviting it to take over many traditional functions of government. The private sector, Reagan maintained, simply worked better than the public; it offered "creative, less expensive, and more efficient alternatives to solving our social problems."[103] Private organizations such as the Boy Scouts could provide public services far more effectively than hated government agencies. As "an efficient, nongovernmental activity, scouting costs a total of only 187 million dollars a year," Reagan announced in 1982. But if it were government run, it would cost thirty times as much, $5.5 billion.[104]

Reagan's numbers were nonsense, but Americans took seriously his pledge to turn the business of government over to business and return the tasks of public life to the private sector. Reagan may not have actually cut big government in Washington—his Presidential Task Force on Private Sector Initiatives quickly bogged down in charges of cronyism—but he did build the case for privatization on the state and local levels.

Reagan did not so much change the nation's mind as his views expressed an ongoing trend in Seventies America: a privatization of everyday life. Americans deserted parks for private health clubs, abandoned town squares for shopping malls, enrolled their children in private schools, and moved into gated communities governed by neighborhood associations and policed by private security patrols. "Do we really need to waste money on luxuries like parks, schools, and libraries," one antitax activist in California's San Fernando Valley demanded in 1977. Over the ensuing decade, many Americans answered no.

Few public amenities escaped the cycle of cutback and privatization during the early 1980s. After Proposition 2 1/2, many Massachusetts communities required citizens to pay for their own snow removal and garbage collection. Five commonwealth communities turned off their street lights.[105] In southern California, authorities consciously reduced the number of public toilets to make certain areas less attractive to "undesirables." Los Angeles's community redevelopment agency adopted a policy of relying on "quasi-public restrooms" in public spaces—toilets in restaurants, museums, hotels, and office buildings, which, according to one critic, "can be made available to tourists and white-collar workers while being denied to vagrants and other unsuitables." Even if they never formally adopted such a policy, most other cities closed public restrooms, assuming that private businesses would take up the slack.[106]

Not surprisingly, as the public sector did less, businesses and the well-to-do began to take some of government's basic functions into their own hands. In policing, for example, suburban communities and downtown business districts began relying more and more heavily on the burgeoning private security industry. The nation, the *New York Times* reported, "is putting less emphasis on controlling crime for everyone—the job of publicly employed police officers—and more emphasis on private police officers who carve out secure zones for those who pay for such protection." As one security expert concluded at the end of the decade, "We are securing more and more private space and putting less effort into securing public space."[107]

A legion of "faux police" (privately hired neighborhood patrols) developed across the nation. In Sun City, Arizona, outside Phoenix, public safety became the responsibility of the 183-man Sun City Posse. The uniformed "posse," outfitted with handcuffs, mace, and specially equipped cars with flashing lights and stars painted on the door, closely resembled a real police force. Recognizing that the posse possessed superior manpower and better equipment, Maricopa County authorities happily allowed these private guards to arrogate much of the police work in the area. These security forces aggrandized police power without public control or democratic accountability.[108]

Across the country, municipalities looked to private businesses to take over the basic functions of government. Poughkeepsie, New York, contracted out the operation of its water treatment plant. Minneapolis handed over half of its solid waste collection to a private firm. Scottsdale, Arizona, turned to a for-profit business to supply fire protection. Eight California counties hired private firms to run their county hospitals.[109]

As communities turned even the provision of such basic services as sanitation and policing over to private hands, the very institutions of democratic self-government metamorphosed. In the place of open, public spaces and communities, private shadow governments emerged, most prominently in "packaged communities"—the gated utopias that arose on the fringes of metropolitan areas and in retirement communities during the 1970s and 1980s. Private guards manned the entrances around the clock, electronic monitors ensured that dogs never strayed onto a neighbor's lawn, and by-laws dictated house colors and shrubbery heights. They could prevent a Boy Scout troop or a church from organizing, and ban sales of Girl Scout cookies or Fuller brushes. The streets were private. The sewers were private. The subdivision arranged for itself "everything that local government used to do. But in place of municipal rules are a set of regulations so restrictive that many could be found unconstitutional should a city government enact them."110

The most common and most powerful form such private governments assumed was the residential community association—homeowners' organizations that residents joined automatically when they purchased property. In 1970, 4,000 community associations were scattered sparsely across the entire United States. By the late 1980s, the Community Associations Institute counted more than 60,000 associations governing about 28 million Americans, from Bear Creek, Washington, to Kingstowne, Virginia, from Canyon Lake, California, to Sun City, Florida. These associations collected mandatory dues and promulgated rules for all homeowners in the community.111

Neighborhood associations had originated as a Seventies developer's gimmick. Builders, especially in Sunbelt locations catering to senior citizens, began packaging new homes with common spaces and shared recreation facilities. After they had sold the last parcel in the subdivision, developers did not want to maintain the pools, clubhouses, and tennis courts, so they invented neighborhood associations to assume these responsibilities. This first wave of community associations, then, concerned themselves only with amenities that government did not normally provide. Local governments still provided police, garbage collection, and road maintenance. Eventually strapped municipal governments called on the associations for assistance, using them as a vehicle for shedding such costly responsibilities as snow plowing, parks maintenance, and trash removal. As their authority and resources mounted, associations began to govern their communities more aggressively. New communities formed homeowners' associations with elaborate formal structures and far-reaching powers.112

Like regular governments, these associations possessed the power to tax, legislate, and coerce obedience (by repossessing the homes of scofflaws). But association managers rarely found themselves accountable to their constituents in a general election.113

Nevertheless, private communities became the fastest-growing residential neighborhoods in the United States. Millions of middle-class families of non-retirement age, even in largely white, racially homogeneous areas of the country, opted for private government, schools, and police. Shadow governments also appeared within the borders of the nation's great cities. Emulating the burgeoning homeowners' associations, merchants' and bankers' guilds created so-called business industrial districts (BIDs) and urban special service districts to wrest political and economic power away from city governments. In the two decades after 1970, business groups established more than one thousand BIDs across the country. BIDs rebuilt sidewalks and rekindled broken streetlights; they hired guards to move vagrants away from storefronts and ATM machines. These self-taxing private entities cleaned, policed, and refurbished their neighborhoods, supplanting municipal government in the process.[114]

Ronald Reagan cheered and supported such developments, nudging along a well-established trend. The slow march of privatization had pervaded the entire Seventies. It complemented all of the decade's changes in attitude: impatience with taxes and centralized authority, experimentation with new forms of community, Sunbelt self-reliance, and the fiscal crises that deepened municipalities' reliance on private funds. But before Reagan, the nation lacked not only the fiscal and political will to rebuild the public sector but the ideological conviction to attempt the job. The Seventies witnessed a quiet renaissance of free-market ideas, a shared sense that markets operated more fairly and efficiently than government, that the excesses of capitalism were to be chuckled about rather than checked.

Once the province of a few economists and libertarians, doctrinaire free market beliefs gained wide currency in the early 1980s. Americans not only accepted that markets performed more efficiently, but embraced the previously outlandish idea that they operated more justly and protected freedom more effectively than government. The entrepreneur became a national hero, and suspicion of business, a mistrust of unregulated corporations that had anchored American politics since the 1890s, all but vanished from American political discourse.

Ronald Reagan crystallized and popularized the new consensus. The president boasted about teaching a new command—Heel!—to the "bureaucratic monster that would slay private enterprise." He repeatedly identified abuses and failures in government programs and lauded private sector initiatives as "invariably more efficient than government in running social programs." Reagan unequivocally endorsed the operations of the market and celebrated material acquisition. "What I want to see above all," the president declared in 1983, "is that this remains a country where someone can always get rich."

Reagan's White House embodied the chief's unambiguous embrace of aggressive acquisition and conspicuous consumption. The populist cardigans and informal visits to ordinary folk of the Carter years gave way to a regal whirlwind of limousines, helicopters, exotic furs, and fine china.[115]

But Reagan and his allies did not merely exploit the vague discontent with government that the Seventies had intensified. They transformed negative impressions into enthusiastic affirmation, drawing on the ideas of a cohort of conservative economists and political analysts. Jude Wanniski, guru of supply-side economics at the editorial page of the *Wall Street Journal,* laid out the case for deregulation, low taxes, and unchecked business activity, while Charles Murray asserted the futility of the welfare state. Management guru Peter Drucker contrasted the rigidity of government with the versatility and flexibility of business; George Gilder and Michael Novak demonstrated the moral as well as economic benefits of unfettered capitalism.[116]

The dean of these conservative intellectuals, the principal ideological inspiration for the deification of the market, was Milton Friedman. A Nobel Prize–winning economist at the University of Chicago, Friedman had been the father of monetarism and the leading critic of the Keynesian orthodoxy in postwar economic policy. For decades Friedman had asserted the superiority of the market, the futility of government intervention, and the links between free markets and political freedom. But Friedman's influence had been confined largely to the technical world of academic economists, policy wonks, and fringe libertarian thinkers until the 1970s. Then his ideas began winning wide exposure and acclaim. In 1979, Friedman and his wife, Rose, published *Free to Choose,* a popular distillation of his earlier works and the accompaniment for a ten-part PBS series that aired in 1980.[117]

Friedman took no prisoners in his assault on the fortress of modern liberalism. Ending government intervention in the economy, Friedman maintained, would not only restore freedom but also promote equality. If everyone had the chance to get rich, lots of people would. Small government also empowered families and churches to restore morality—to escape secularism and amorality as well as bureaucratic red tape.[118]

The Democratic opposition never even attempted to beat these conservative challenges; they immediately joined them. Although public opinion polls documented continuing popular suspicion of big business, Democratic leaders did not allow antagonism toward business to demarcate them from the GOP. Instead they avoided attacks on corporations and the privileged and shifted hard to the right. In the wake of Reagan's election, business-oriented Democrats moved to remold their party. The Democratic National Committee elected California banker and attorney Charles Manatt as its chairman. Manatt strengthened the party's ties to corporate interests and secured large donations from business groups to stabilize the party's troubled finances. In June 1981, the Democratic National Committee appointed a commission chaired by North Carolina governor Jim Hunt, which rolled back many McGovern-era reforms, increased the power of party leaders and elected officials in the nominating process, weakened the influence of grass-roots organizations, and deepened potential candidates' reliance on fat cat donors. At the same time, California congressman Tony Coelho took over the leadership of the Democratic Congressional Campaign Committee and began playing hardball with probusiness lobbyists. "I just want you to know we are going to be in the majority of the House for many years," Coelho warned corporate political action committees that had overwhelmingly supported GOP candidates in 1980. "And I don't think it makes good business sense for you to try to destroy us and support the Republicans. We are going to keep records." Those who anted up could expect Democratic support on "capital formation and other business issues." The shakedown succeeded. Business interests cut their contributions to Republican challengers, poured money into the coffers of Democratic incumbents, and saw their influence expand.[119]

The drift to starboard continued through the 1980s. Despite his strong ties to organized labor, the party's 1984 standard-bearer, Walter Mondale, relied heavily on business Democrats for funds and policy advice. With his acceptance speech promise to raise taxes, Mondale made fiscal rectitude the centerpiece of his campaign—a program that reassured the Democratic Business Council and disappointed labor supporters who hoped Mondale would campaign for an ambitious jobs program. Mondale's principal Democratic opponent in 1984, Colorado senator Gary Hart, exalted entrepreneurship and the free market even more forcefully. Hart's brand of yuppie "neoliberalism" trumpeted tax relief for business, spurs to investment, and support for high-tech industry.[120]

Over the 1980s, the party apparatus and Democratic politicians adopted the prevailing views that markets work better than government, that the public sector should free business to "grow the economy" rather than protect the market's victims from unregulated free enterprise. Since the 1930s the Democratic party had recognized that markets frequently produced bad outcomes—that the state should regulate business and redress the worst abuses of capitalism. The party abrogated that historic commitment during the mid-1980s. Democratic support for regulation, social programs, progressive taxation, and labor organization abated. The domestic agenda of Richard Nixon, even the "Modern Republicanism" of Dwight D. Eisenhower, would have made those men too liberal for the Democrats by the late 1980s.

Even important elements of the radical 1960s left embraced untrammeled free enterprise as a sure path to personal liberation and social uplift. Many ex-radicals saw starting their own businesses and inventing their own products as a way both to free themselves from the cookie-cutter conformity of corporate life and to advance their political objectives. Jane Fonda produced best-selling workout videos and fitness guides. Jerry Rubin touted the stock market as a way to destroy ossified corporate bureaucracies and create opportunities for meaningful work. Radical feminists and black power advocates stressed community-owned businesses as vehicles for cultural survival and political empowerment. While marketing NutraSweet, one former antiwar protester and poverty warrior received letters from diabetic children who had never before enjoyed Kool-Aid or Jell-O. He decided that new products and new technologies not only produced wealth; they gave him "a chance to make a difference in the world."[121]

Countercultural capitalism flourished across the country; newspapers reported on businessmen who "wear ties with their jeans and women seen in everything from art school black to billowing 1940s pleats." Free enterprise became stylish, even avant-garde.[122] "A lot of people are going into business who in the 1970s would have gone into public service," Yale professor Rosabeth Kanter told *Newsweek* in 1984. "The whole thing has been turned around. Business is the place for people who want to make a difference."[123]

By the end of Reagan's first term, serious criticism of business and skepticism about the beneficence of markets had all but vanished from the American political mainstream. In 1978, Milton Friedman had complained that "the market has no press agents who will trumpet its successes and gloss over its failures; the bureaucracy does."[124] By 1984 the private sphere could find dedicated publicists among progressive entrepreneurs and conservative ideologues, mall walkers, local governments, and health club members. The president decorated Milton Friedman with the nation's highest civilian honors, and no one championed those feckless and detested bureaucrats. The Seventies had ended, gone forever. And the Seventies had triumphed, reinventing America for a generation to come.[125]

conclusion

End of the Seventies, End of the Century

IN 1980, THE RAMONES, THE SEMINAL 1970S PUNK ROCK BAND, released their first album of the new decade. *End of the Century* marked a major departure for the band, a collaboration with legendary Sixties record producer Phil Spector. Lionized by Tom Wolfe as the "First Tycoon of Teen," Spector had scored sixty hits in the 1960s with girl groups like the Ronettes and the Crystals, crooners like the Righteous Brothers and Gene Pitney, and soul singers like Ben E. King and Sonny Charles. For Spector, artists and songwriters were interchangeable, almost inconsequential. What mattered was the "Philles" signature, the distinctive "wall of sound" Spector constructed with multilayered tracks and subtle studio effects.[1]

Spector and the Ramones seemed an awfully odd couple. After all, the New York punkers had perfected the stripped-down, raw aesthetic of the Seventies. Their fast, loud, simple music sounded as if it came from the Queens garage where the band had formed. It rejected the artifice that record producers mastered; it resisted the kind of authority that Spector unabashedly wielded. Yes, both Spector and the Ramones famously constructed towering walls of sound, but the band built theirs simply by turning up the amp on Johnny Ramone's guitar.[2]

Critics could not decide what to make of *End of the Century.* Some dismissed the record as a sellout—a betrayal of the antiestablishment message and rock purity of the Seventies, a harbinger of the crass commercialism and shameless fakery of the Reagan era. In the late Seventies, the Ramones had "aimed their rude sonic blatz directly at the dark heart of all that was bloated, decrepit, and boring in big-time rock." Filled with Spector's famous overdubs, their new record sounded made up and manicured. One critic even worried about an "overly familiar cartoon jingoism" that had "an ugly ring in the current political atmosphere."[3]

Others viewed the album as a triumph—not a repudiation of the Ramones' earlier work but an inspiring extension of it. *End of the Century,* trumpeted Kurt Loder in *Rolling Stone,* was "the most commercially credible album the Ramones have ever made. And they did it without compromising their very real artistic premises." The album vindicated Spector as well. The producer "created a setting that's rich and vibrant and surging with power, but it's the Ramones who are spotlighted, not their producer." Spector "managed to conceal his considerable art and thus reaffirm it."[4]

The record itself offered a simple, rueful message. Its songs paid homage to a lost musical past—"Do You Remember Rock 'n' Roll Radio?" one asked—but made it clear that the time had come for something new. "It's the end, the end of the Seventies," the Ramones sang. "It's the end, the end of the century." Of course, the ultimate garage band hardly meant to weight that chorus with philosophical pretensions. They were just looking for a line that sounded good.

But the Ramones were on to something bigger than they realized. In an odd way, the band's first foray into the Eighties, and the rival assessments it provoked, limned the problem of the Seventies. *End of the Century* seemed to ask if the decade's struggles and achievements had been mere aberrations, an evanescent interlude quickly and happily forgotten, or whether the Seventies exerted lasting influence on national life. Did Americans, like their most outrageous musicians, forsake the lessons and innovations of the Seventies? Or did the nation, like the Ramones, incorporate the assumptions and achievements of the Seventies into a wholly new way of seeing the world? Did, as *U.S. News* put it, the "Stormy Seventies Reshape U.S. Future?"

Certainly 1984 marked a turning point, the end of the long 1970s. The economy had recovered, taming the ruinous inflation that had cast such a pall over American life. Malaise and Jimmy Carter had vanished; they became subjects of mockery, symbols of the bad old days forgotten in the boosterism and patriotic exuberance of Reagan's America.[5]

By 1984, disco and punk had disappeared, director's cinema had retreated into a small, insignificant corner of the film industry, and the most ambitious experiments in communal life and spiritual renewal had disbanded or become conventional. Rap, with its militant lyrics and contempt for racial integration, competed with country, the most conspicuous component of a southernized national culture, for control of the airwaves. The blockbuster dominated Hollywood, ending the great silver age of dark, paranoid, antiauthoritarian film that had gripped Seventies moviegoers. The Ramones' *End of the Century,* like so much of American life after 1984, bade good-bye and good riddance to the spirit of the Seventies.

Still, the Eighties, and American life ever since, have not really been a repudiation of the Seventies but a culmination of them. Indeed, observers of contemporary popular culture might be forgiven for concluding that the decade never ended. *Saturday Night Fever* reappeared as a Broadway musical, while Hollywood produced film versions of *Charlie's Angels* and the *Brady Bunch* and sequels to *Shaft* and *Star Wars*. At the turn of the century, *The Eagles Greatest Hits, 1971–1975,* became the biggest selling album in American recording history. Even Jimmy Carter today commands a national stage as itinerant statesman and chief spokesman for Habitat for Humanity.[6]

But the influence of the stormy Seventies goes beyond nostalgia for its sometimes edgy, sometimes cheesy popular culture. During the Seventies, national power shifted south and west. Throughout his Senate career, Lyndon Johnson had assumed that a southerner could never become president. The North, he believed, wielded all the economic might and political muscle in American life; Yankees would never countenance a southerner in the White House. Even after LBJ won the presidency in his own right and imposed racial integration on a reluctant Dixie, Johnson felt the scorn and condescension of a still-dominant northern cultural elite. But during the Seventies, the tides of American politics turned. Drawing strength from its burgeoning population and booming economy, the South and Southwest wrested control of national politics. Since the late Sixties, Sunbelt candidates have won every presidential election, sending to the White House residents of Georgia, California, Texas, and Arkansas. In fact, since Gerald Ford's close race against Jimmy Carter in 1976, no northerner has seriously contended for the nation's highest office.

Sunbelt power has extended far beyond the White House. For most of the Clinton years, the president and vice president, House Speaker and Senate majority leader hailed from states of the Old Confederacy. The South's historic policy prescriptions—low taxes and scant public services, military preparedness and a preference for state and local government over federal supremacy—came to define the national agenda during the Seventies and have remained the motive forces in American public policy ever since. In the Seventies, the torch passed from politicians like Connecticut senator Prescott Bush in the 1950s, an avatar of New England moderate Republicanism and WASP noblesse oblige, to men like his son, the preppie reborn as a Texas oil man, an advocate of state's rights, free enterprise, and voluntarism. It has since passed on to the generation of George W. Bush, a man truly at home among the good ol' boys and the faux Bubbas, comfortable with the wide-open style and deeply religious sensibilities of the Sunbelt.

Indeed, the United States experienced more than a regional power shift in the 1970s; it witnessed a thoroughgoing southernization of American life. Religion, especially the frank expression of personal spirituality, assumed a public and powerful role in American life. Public figures—politicians, actors, and artists—openly avow their religious feelings. The widespread skepticism about religion and scorn for "Bible thumping," so prevalent in the Sixties, has all but disappeared from American public life. While a formal, bloodless, dispassionate WASP Christianity held sway—the kind of elite northeastern Protestantism in which God figured little and Jesus hardly at all—a knowing, condescending attitude toward religion remained respectable. But the evangelical revival of the Seventies, the vitality of southern old-time religion, discredited that sensibility. Even Americans who loathe the religious right today share a respect for the transcendent—for the experience of personal spiritual rebirth—that attests to the cultural power of the Sunbelt.

Beyond religion, country music and stock car racing developed huge national followings, as popular in Boston and Denver as in Daytona and Nashville. Garth Brooks has sold more albums than any other solo performer, and musicians from all over the world have recorded in Nashville. More important, a kind of wide-open, libertarian boosterism, once distinctively southern, has come to permeate American life.

This "southernization" complemented and reinforced a second enduring legacy of the Seventies. Over the past two decades, entrepreneurship has replaced social and political activism as the source of dynamic cultural and political change in the United States. The political realm emptied out; in the era from Nixon to Reagan, Americans relied less on the instruments of democratic governments, almost forgetting what it is that politics does, what only the public sphere can accomplish.

More and more young Americans view starting their own businesses as the way to liberate themselves and improve the world. While big money certainly exerts a strong appeal, today's twenty-somethings neither reject the countercultural values of the Sixties nor reassert the Reaganite conservatism of the Eighties. They certainly have no desire to manage large, bureaucratic companies or climb the corporate ladder. Instead they pursue a revised but potent version of the sensibility of the Seventies, a politics of liberation focused on the marketplace rather than the streets as the engine of social transformation.

During the 1970s and early 1980s, Americans concluded that capitalist accumulation was not the enemy of doing good but the vehicle for it. The digital revolution only reinforced the conviction that technology and entrepreneurship empowered ordinary people and inspired cultural and political innovation. Contemporary opponents of globalization appear retrograde, nostalgic for an imaginary past rather than promoting progressive social change. Microsoft chairman Bill Gates even suggested that the Internet economy would promote political reform; companies like Microsoft would "take the government to the people," empowering citizens to act for themselves rather than relying on an impersonal bureaucracy.[7]

Today many commentators dismiss these entrepreneurial sentiments as mere rationalizations for greed and self-absorption. A dismissive yippie-to-yuppie myth retains a potent influence on the national imagination. Many Americans express contempt for "bleeding ponytails." They share the prevailing sense that the baby boomers of the 1970s traded in their radical politics for a selfish, corporate culture, exchanging marijuana and VW minibuses for martinis and SUVs.

The usual suspects spring to mind immediately. Yippie Jerry Rubin, who disrupted the New York Stock Exchange in the 1960s and became a yuppie stockbroker two decades later. Jane Fonda, the radical who traveled to Hanoi and married new left hero Tom Hayden, hawked fitness videos, and hitched herself to activist-entrepreneur Ted Turner in the 1990s. Ben and Jerry's, the inventors of Cherry Garcia and the "Joy Gang," literally sold out to a faceless multinational corporation.

But the "sellout" label misses the point. These icons, and their twenty-first-century children, have preserved a Seventies emphasis on authenticity and freedom, on political transformation through personal liberation. But the market—in particular, starting new businesses—became the favored means for personal liberation and cultural revolution.

To be sure, something has been lost in this metamorphosis. But the legacies of the Seventies, the changes in latitude and changes in attitudes, remain potent. The long, gaudy, depressing Seventies reinvented America. We live in their shadows.

notes

preface

1. William E. Leuchtenburg, *The Perils of Prosperity* (Chicago: University of Chicago Press, 1958), and *Franklin D. Roosevelt and the New Deal* (New York: Harper & Row, 1963).

2. William E. Leuchtenburg, *In the Shadow of FDR* (Ithaca, N.Y.: Cornell University Press, 1993); Alonzo Hamby, *Liberalism and Its Challengers: FDR to Bush* (New York: Oxford University Press, 1993). For example, Lyndon B. Johnson paid regular homage to FDR and set Roosevelt as the standard for presidential achievement. See *Public Papers of the Presidents of the United States: Lyndon B. Johnson, 1963–64* (Washington, D.C.: GPO, 1964). 1:250. Consult also Doris Kearns, *Lyndon Johnson and the American Dream* (New York: Signet Books, 1976), p. 226, and Bruce J. Schulman, *Lyndon B. Johnson and American Liberalism* (Boston: Bedford Books of St. Martin's Press, 1995), pp. 81–84.

3. Howard Junker, "Who Erased the Seventies," *Esquire* 88 (December 1977): 154. Charlie Haas, "Goodbye to the '70s," *New West*, January 29, 1979, p. 29.

4. Christopher Booker, *The Seventies* (New York: Stein and Day, 1980), p. 3.

5. Schulman, *Lyndon B. Johnson and American Liberalism.*

6. Blanche McCrary Boyd, *The Redneck Way of Knowledge* (New York: Penguin Books, 1982), p. 7.

7. "Atlanta Is Warm to Nixon on Visit," *New York Times*, October 13, 1972; "Hundreds of Thousands Acclaim Nixon in Atlanta," *Washington Post*, October 13, 1972.

8. John Egerton, *The Americanization of Dixie, the Southernization of America* (New York: Harper's Magazine Books, 1974), p. 203.

9. H. Louis Patrick, quoted in ibid., p. 198.

10. Peter Drucker and Edward K. Hamilton, "Can the Businessman Meet Our Social Needs?" *Saturday Review*, March 17, 1973, p. 41.

11. Robert Reinhold, "Changes Wrought by 60's Youth Linger in American Life," *New York Times*, August 12, 1979.

12. Peter Carroll, *It Seemed Like Nothing Happened*, rev. ed. (New Brunswick, N.J.: Rutgers University Press, 1990), pp. 235–243.

13. Peter Clecak, *America's Quest for the Ideal Self* (New York: Oxford University Press, 1983), p. 9.

14. In 1969, the British intellectual C. P. Snow delivered the Green Foundation Lectures at Westminster College in Fulton, Missouri. Standing at the same lectern where Winston Churchill had first identified the Iron Curtain, Snow prophesied that "enclave-making" would become "one of the characteristic symptoms of our unease." People, Snow feared, were ready "to draw the curtains," to seek an "enclave, a refuge, a place to shut out the noise. A group of one's own." C.P. Snow, *The State of Siege* (N.Y.: Scribners' 1969), pp. 9–10.

introduction

1. Christopher Booker, *The Seventies* (New York: Stein and Day, 1980), p. 3.

2. Georges Pompidou, quoted in Jules Witcover, *The Year the Dream Died* (New York: Warner Books, 1997), p. 215.

3. Tom Hayden, "Two, Three Many Columbias," *Ramparts* 6, June 15, 1968, p. 40.

4. Witcover, *The Year the Dreamed Died*, p. xiv. The Sixties, recalled a British correspondent, "were certainly a time when it was still possible for most people to look forward in hope to an as yet unrealized future." See Booker, *The Seventies*, p. 9.

5. Stokely Carmichael, quoted in Witcover, *The Year the Dream Died*, p. 156.

6. Ray Jenkins, "George Wallace Figures to Win Even If He Loses," *New York Times Magazine*, April 7, 1968, pp. 27, 66–68. See also Marshall Frady, *Wallace* (New York: Meridian, 1970); and Dan T. Carter, *The Politics of Rage* (Baton Rouge: Louisiana State University Press, 1995).

7. Robert F. Kennedy, address at Indianapolis, Indiana, April 5, 1968, *Great Speeches of the Twentieth Century* (Santa Monica Calif.: Rhino Records, 1991), vol. 1.

8. Witcover, *The Year the Dream Died*, p. 399.

9. The United States had so thoroughly bested its rivals and its allies after World War II that it could effortlessly make economic sacrifices for strategic objectives. Americans could finance the Marshall Plan, rebuild the steel industry in Germany, and rearm former rivals without fear of burdensome expense or ruinous competition.

10. U.S. Bureau of the Census, *Statistical Abstract of the United States: 1992* (Washington D.C.: GPO, 1992), p. 456.

11. The fight against international communism formed a central tenet of this postwar liberal creed, another defining feature of the postwar era. Liberals mocked extreme, conspiratorial forms of anti-communism like that of Senator Joseph McCarthy—the kind that found communist spies under every rock, infiltrating the highest reaches of the government and even the U.S. army. But liberal anti-communists never questioned the idea that free peoples everywhere needed assistance in the battle against communist subversion. Nor did they doubt that the United States should provide political, moral, economic, and military assistance in that struggle. Along with that commitment came support for all the accouterments of a vast national security state—the nuclear arms race, the military-industrial complex, government-supported science, the CIA, and other intelligence gathering agencies.

12. Bruce J. Schulman, *Lyndon B. Johnson and American Liberalism* (Boston: Bedford Books of St. Martin's Press, 1995), pp. 143–152.

13. Ibid.

14. Allen J. Matusow, *The Unraveling of America* (New York: Harper & Row, 1984), p. 396.

15. Thomas Sugrue, *The Origins of the Urban Crisis* (Princeton: Princeton University Press, 1996). Michael Flamm, "'Law and Order': Street Crime, Civil Disorder, and the Crisis of Liberalism" (Ph.D. dissertation, Columbia University, 1998). John T. McGreevy, *Parish Boundaries* (Chicago: University of Chicago Press, 1996). Arnold Hirsch, *Making the Second Ghetto* (New York: Cambridge University Press, 1983).

16. On conservatism in the Sixties, see Chapter 8 below.

17. Grayson Kirk, quoted in Witcover, *The Year the Dream Died*, p. 188.

18. Mark Rudd, quoted in Terry Anderson, *The Movement and the Sixties* (New York.: Oxford, 1995), p. 195.

19. On the Columbia uprisings, see Matusow, *Unraveling of America*, pp. 331–335; Nicholas Von Hoffman, "How Columbia Pulled Down Its Pillars," *Washington Post,* June 16, 1968; and Anderson, *The Movement and the Sixties,* pp. 194–200.

20. Hayden, "Two, Three Many Columbias," p. 40.

21. Von Hoffman, "How Columbia Pulled Down Its Pillars."

22. Kenneth Cmiel, "The Politics of Civility," in David Farber, ed., *The Sixties* (Chapel Hill: University of North Carolina Press, 1994), pp. 263–290.

23. Beth Bailey, "Sexual Revolution(s)," in Farber, ed., *The Sixties,* pp. 235–262. Quotations from 1970 University of Kansas "Co-Ed Survey," on pp. 253–254.

24. "No More Miss America!" in Robin Morgan, ed., *Sisterhood Is Powerful* (New York: Random House, 1972), p. 522. Alice Echols, *Daring to Be Bad* (Minneapolis: University of Minnesota Press, 1989), pp. 93–96.

25. David Farber, *Chicago '68* (Chicago: University of Chicago Press, 1988), pp. 149, 169–170. Anderson, *The Movement and the Sixties,* pp. 216–217.

26. Eugene McCarthy, quoted in Albert Eisele, *Almost to the Presidency* (Blue Earth, Minn.: Piper, 1972), p. 357.

27. Patrick Buchanan, C-Span interview, 1993, quoted in Witcover, *The Year the Dream Died,* p. 336.

28. Student organizations splintered into rival factions, losing focus, membership, and resources. Some descended into decadence and violence or went underground. Others, infiltrated by undercover FBI agents, fell apart.

29. Anderson, *The Movement and the Sixties,* p. 246.

30. Richard Goldstein, interview with Country Joe McDonald, quoted in Anderson, *The Movement and the Sixties,* p. 239.

31. Ibid.

32. *Woodstock* (film directed by Peter Wadleigh, 1970).

33. Peter Berger and Brigitte Berger, "The Blueing of America," *New Republic,* April 3, 1971, p. 20.

34. Ray Mungo, *Famous Long Ago* (Boston: Beacon Press, 1970), p. 3. James Kunen, *The Strawberry Statement* (New York: Avon Books, 1969), p. 94.

35. Anderson, *The Movement and the Sixties,* p. 251.

36. Barry Melton, quoted in *Berkeley in the Sixties* (film by Mark Kitchell, First Run Features, 1990). Country Joe McDonald, quoted in Anderson, *The Movement and the Sixties,* p. 247.

37. Anderson, *The Movement and the Sixties,* p. 244.

38. *Woodstock* (film directed by Peter Wadleigh, 1970).

39. Jonathan Vogels, "'Outrageous Acts of Faith': The Films of Albert and David Maysles," (Ph.D. dissertation, Boston University, 2000). *Gimme Shelter* (film directed by Albert and David Maysles, 1970). Matusow, *Unraveling of America,* pp. 303–305.

40. "Rock Festivals: Groovy, But No Gravy," *Business Week,* August 8, 1970, pp. 20–21.

41. Dennis Hopper, quoted in Dan Wakefield, "The War at Home," *Atlantic Monthly* (October 1969): 123.

42. *Easy Rider* (film directed by Dennis Hopper, 1969).

43. Hunter S. Thompson, *Fear and Loathing in Las Vegas* (New York: Popular Library, 1971), p. 68.

1. "Down to the Nut-Cutting"

1. William Safire, *Before the Fall* (Garden City, N.Y.: Doubleday, 1975), pp. 82–83.

2. Richard Nixon, quoted in *New York Times,* November 6, 1968, p. 1. See also Safire, *Before the Fall,* pp. 92–94.

3. Safire, *Before the Fall,* pp. 92–93.

4. For repeated and vivid examples, see H. R. Haldeman, *The Haldeman Diaries: Inside the Nixon White House* (New York: Putnam, 1994), and Stanley I. Kutler, ed., *Abuse of Power: The New Nixon Tapes* (New York: Free Press, 1997).

5. Nixon's early career has been the subject of sustained scholarly inquiry. See Herbert Parmet, *Richard Nixon and His America* (Boston: Little, Brown, 1990); Stephen E. Ambrose, *Nixon: The Education of a Politician, 1913–62* (New York: Simon & Schuster, 1987); Jonathan Aitken, *Nixon: A Life* (Lanham, Md.: Regnery, 1994); Roger Morris, *Richard Milhous Nixon: The Rise of an American Politician* (New York: Henry Holt, 1990). For an incisive analysis, consult Theodore Draper, "Nixon Redivivus," *New York Review of Books,* July 14, 1994, pp. 26–30.

6. Haldeman, *Diaries,* p. 326.

7. *New York Times,* January 7, 1971, p. 19. "A Boost for Growth, A Slap at Prices," *Business Week,* January 16, 1971, pp. 22–23. For a detailed examination of Nixon's economic policies, see Allen J. Matusow, *Nixon's Economy* (Lawrence: University Press of Kansas, 1998).

8. Patrick Buchanan to Richard Nixon, memorandum, January 6, 1971, Nixon Presidential Materials Project, National Archives, quoted in Stephen E. Ambrose, *Nixon: The Triumph of a Politician, 1962–72,* (New York: Simon & Schuster, 1989), p. 405. The "last of the liberals" argument is best developed in Joan Hoff, *Nixon Reconsidered* (New York: Basic Books, 1994). Among its adherents is conservative columnist George F. Will. See George F. Will, "In Nixon's Ups and Downs, a Constant Griminess," *Boston Globe,* April 25, 1994.

9. Rod MacLeish, "The Legacy of Richard Nixon," *CBS Evening News,* August 9, 1974.

10. *Public Papers of the Presidents: Richard Nixon, 1973* (Washington, D.C.: GPO, 1974), p. 14. The most thorough statement of the first of the conservatives argument is Matusow, *Nixon's Economy.*

11. Clare Crawford, "The Square Elephant at Work and Play," *Washingtonian* (October 1969). "A New Way of Life at the White House," *U.S. News and World Report,* February 24, 1969.

12. Crawford, "The Square Elephant."

13. Ibid.; "A New Way of Life at the White House."

14. Memo on NEA Budget, October 31, 1974, WHCF:SF: Federal Aid, FA (Arts), Nixon Presidential Materials, National Archives, Box 2. For a detailed discussion of Nixon's arts policies, see Donna Binkiewicz, "Painting, Politics, and Cold War Culture: United States Arts Policy and the

National Endowment for the Arts, 1960–1975" (Ph.D. dissertation, UCLA, 1997). I thank Donna Binkiewicz for making this material available.

15. Binkiewicz, "Painting, Politics, and Cold War Culture."

16. Ibid.

17. For example, federal outlays for housing programs nearly quintupled during Nixon's presidency, from $426 million in 1969 to more than $2 billion in 1974. See U.S. Census Bureau, *Statistical Abstract of the United States, 1977* (Washington, D.C.: GPO, 1978), p. 317.

18. *The Report of the President's Commission on Housing* (Washington, D.C.: GPO, 1982), pp. xxiii–xxiv, 17–18. U.S. Department of Housing and Urban Development, *Block Grants for Community Development* (Washington, D.C.: GPO, 1977), pp. 3–5, 16–60. In 1972, HUD launched a new program; rent subsidies, which had previously accounted for a negligible share of housing expenditures, rose to almost a third of total housing assistance. See *Statistical Abstract, 1975*, p. 284. *Statistical Abstract 1977*, p. 322. I thank Alice O'Connor for this insight.

19. John C. Whitaker, *Striking a Balance: Environment and Natural Resources Policy in the Nixon-Ford Years* (Washington, D.C.: AEI, 1976), p. 27. Hoff, *Nixon Reconsidered*, pp. 21–23.

20. Whitaker, *Striking a Balance*, pp. 39–41, 93. U.S. Environmental Protection Agency, "Environmental Protection: A Historical Review of Legislation and Programs of the Environmental Protection Agency," Report No. 83–34 ENR, March 1, 1983, pp. 1–2, 14. Richard Nixon, Special Message to the Congress on Environmental Quality, February 10, 1970, in *Public Papers, Nixon, 1970*, bk.1, p. 95.

21. Nixon Tapes, White House conversation with Henry Ford II and Lee Iacocca, April 27, 1971, quoted in Tom Wicker, *One of Us* (New York: Random House, 1991), p. 515.

22. Hoff, *Nixon Reconsidered*, p. 23.

23. Whitaker, *Striking a Balance*, pp. 4–7. The Alaska oil pipeline project was anathema to environmentalists. For a discussion of Earth Day and the environmental movement, see Chapter 3.

24. Environmental Protection Agency, "Environmental Protection: A Historical Review," p. 2. Whitaker, *Striking a Balance*, pp. 73–79. See also John Brooks Flippen, "The Nixon Administration, Timber, and the Call of the Wild," *Environmental History Review* 19 (Summer 1995): 37–54, Samuel Hays, *Beauty, Health, and Permanence* (New York: Cambridge University Press, 1987), pp. 365–66; and Hoff, *Nixon Reconsidered*, p. 23. Nixon largely fulfilled the requirements of the 1964 Wilderness Act, designating substantial portions of National Park Service and Fish and Wildlife Service lands as protected wilderness. But he steadfastly refused to alienate timber interests by removing lands from national forests. He voiced support for pesticide reform but kept the EPA "on a short leash" to placate farming interests. See Flippen, "Nixon Administration," and "Pests, Pollution, and Politics," *Agricultural History* 71 (Fall 1997): 442–456.

25. Nixon, veto of the Federal Pollution Control Act Amendments of 1972, October 17, 1972, in *Public Papers, Nixon, 1972*, bk. 2, pp. 991–992. "Environmental Protection: A Historical Review," p. 34.

26. Whitaker, *Striking a Balance*, p. 111.

27. Nixon, Annual Message to the Congress on the State of the Union, January 22, 1970, in *Public Papers, Nixon, 1970*, p. 13.

28. Whitaker, *Striking a Balance*, pp. 185–190.

29. *Public Papers of the Presidents: Richard Nixon, 1969* (Washington, D.C.: GPO, 1970), pp. 637–645. Parmet, *Nixon and His America,* pp. 553–554.

30. *Public Papers, Nixon, 1969,* pp. 637–645.

31. Alice O'Connor, "The False Dawn of Welfare Reform: Nixon, Carter and the Quest for a Guaranteed Income," *Journal of Policy History* 10 (Spring 1998): 99–129.

32. Ibid. Consult also Gilbert Steiner, "Reform Follows Reality: The Growth of Welfare," *Public Interest* (Winter 1974): 47–65.

33. Daniel Patrick Moynihan, *The Politics of a Guaranteed Income* (New York: Random House, 1973). Hoff, *Nixon Reconsidered,* pp. 120, 132.

34. O'Connor, "The False Dawn of Welfare Reform." NWRO sought thoroughgoing reform of the welfare system: an end to snooping and supervision by social workers, to endless paperwork and red tape, to the overly complex system of overlapping grants from different agencies for different purposes. NWRO pursued a deliberately subversive strategy, hoping to force the collapse of the existing system by overwhelming the welfare rolls. In 1968–1969 in New York City, the NWRO succeeded. Caseloads swelled so rapidly that overworked and overwhelmed social workers refused to work; they joined in protests against the system. The New York State legislature had no choice but to replace New York's system of special categorical grants with flat payments. But the grant was so meager that NWRO rebelled, staging major protests that soon spread across the United States. See Guida West, *The National Welfare Rights Movement* (New York: Praeger, 1981).

35. For an overview of Friedman's views, consult Eammon Butler, *Milton Friedman: A Guide to His Thought* (New York: Universe, 1985), pp. 22, 222–223. See also Milton Friedman, *Tax Limitation, Inflation, and the Role of Government* (Dallas: Fisher Institute, 1978); Friedman, *Free to Choose* (New York: Harcourt Brace Jovanovich, 1980); and Friedman, *From Galbraith to Economic Freedom* (London: Institute of Economic Affairs, 1977).

36. Since 1961, the AFDC program had allowed families with unemployed fathers present to receive aid, but fewer than half of the states had adopted the option by the late 1960s. See West, *National Welfare Rights Movement,* p. 17n.

37. *Public Papers, Nixon, 1969,* pp. 637–645.

38. The program's solicitude for the working poor would also allow Nixon to neutralize his political opponents—to relieve the welfare crisis while appealing to working-class whites suspicious of handouts and resentful of government assistance to inner-city blacks.

39. Some critics insist he never wanted to see the costly FAP enacted, but Daniel Patrick Moynihan, the author of the FAP, regarded Nixon as genuinely dedicated to seeing that FAP was enacted. Indeed, long after Watergate and Nixon's resignation, Moynihan told Nixon biographer Stephen Ambrose that he still "regarded Nixon as good and honest and decent." Ambrose himself, however, concluded that Nixon dramatically announced FAP "while simultaneously making certain that it would never be adopted." See Ambrose, *Nixon: The Triumph of a Politician,* pp. 292, 367, 402–403; and Parmet, *Nixon and His America,* p. 560.

40. When Nixon proposed FAP in 1969, he set the income floor at $1,600; when the plan was finally resubmitted in 1971, the proposal set it at $2,500.

41. West, *National Welfare Rights Movement,* pp. 312–313. A number of conservative organizations joined the fight against FAP, including the U.S. Chamber of Commerce and the American Conservative Union.

42. Parmet, *Nixon and His America,* p. 559.

43. The best account of Nixon's southern strategy and the politics of the metropolitan South in the 1960s and 1970s is Matthew Lassiter, "The Rise of the Suburban South" (Ph.D. Dissertation, University of Virginia, 1999). See also Harry Dent, *The Prodigal South Returns to Power* (New York: Wiley, 1978); Dan T. Carter, *The Politics of Rage* (New York: Simon & Schuster, 1995); and Reg Murphy and Hal Gulliver, *The Southern Strategy* (New York: Charles Scribner's Sons, 1971). Strom Thurmond had run for president in 1948 as the candidate of the States Rights Democratic Party, best known as the Dixiecrats.

44. Richard Nixon, *RN* (New York: Simon & Schuster, 1978), pp. 316–317. Lassiter, "The Rise of the Suburban South." Dewey Grantham, *The South in Modern America* (New York: Harper Collins, 1994), pp. 281–310. Numan V. Bartley and Hugh Graham, *Southern Politics and the Second Reconstruction* (Baltimore: John Hopkins Univ. Press, 1975), pp. 126–135. Joseph A. Aistrup, *The Southern Strategy Revisited* (Lexington: University Press of Kentucky, 1996).

45. Lassiter, "Rise of the Suburban South." Aistrup, *Southern Strategy Revisited.*

46. Lassiter, "Rise of the Suburban South."

47. Timing also proved critical. In 1968, Nixon voters in the South did not share Wallace's desire to roll back the *Brown* decision and the Civil Rights Act. They believed their neighborhoods were already in compliance with federal court decrees. "Freedom of choice" plans and token school integration had taken place, residential segregation seemed secure, and two-way busing orders lay beyond the worst dreams of most southerners. See ibid.

48. Kevin P. Phillips, *The Emerging Republican Majority* (New York: Anchor Books, 1970), p. 437.

49. Ibid., p. 443. Although much of his postelection southern strategy faltered, especially his attempt to reach out to Wallace voters in the 1970 midterm elections and his nomination of two conservative southerners to the Supreme Court, Nixon understood that American cultural geography had shifted. See Lassiter, "Rise of the Suburban South."

50. Richard M. Scammon and Ben J. Wattenberg, *The Real Majority* (New York: Coward-McCann, 1970). Nixon quoted the cited passage in his own memoirs. See Richard Nixon, *RN: The Memoirs of Richard Nixon* (New York: Grosset and Dunlap, 1978), p. 491.

51. Haldeman, *Diaries,* p. 191. Nixon, *RN,* p. 491. On Nixon's political strategy, see Ambrose, *Nixon: The Triumph of a Politician,* p. 374, and Matusow, *Nixon's Economy,* pp. 79–80.

52. Nixon, *RN,* p. 491.

53. Ibid., p. 539.

54. Matusow, *Nixon's Economy,* pp. 159–161. On the hard hat parade, consult *New York Times,* May 9, 1970, p. 1. On Nixon's reaction to it, see Safire, *Before the Fall,* pp. 585, passim. The president also made frequent overtures to AFL-CIO president George Meany. At a lavish Labor Day banquet at the White House, Nixon praised Meany as "a pillar in the storm—strong, full of character, devoted to his church, devoted to his family." Nixon, Labor Day speech, quoted in Matusow, *Nixon's Economy,* pp. 80–81.

55. Henry Kissinger, *Years of Upheaval* (Boston: Little, Brown, 1982), p. 386.

56. Haldeman, *Diaries,* pp. 444–445.

57. *The Haldeman Diaries: Inside the Nixon White House: The Complete Multimedia Edition* (Santa Monica: Sony Imagesoft, 1994), September 20, 1972.

58. Herbert Klein, quoted in *New York Times*, July 26, 1970.

59. Haldeman, *Diaries*, pp. 506–507. The president felt, Haldeman recorded in his diary, that "the huge colossus of government is a mess. The people running it are incompetent and won't change, and the American people don't want to support it."

60. Kandy Stroud, "Atty. Gen's Mouth: Bigger than Martha's?" *Women's Wear Daily*, September 18, 1970, pp. 1, 32. Ambrose, *Nixon: The Triumph of a Politician*, p. 375.

61. Nixon, *RN*, p. 761.

62. *Public Papers, Nixon, 1973*, p. 14.

63. *Haldeman Diaries: Complete Multimedia Edition*, January 24, 1973.

64. On congressional opposition to the fiscal year 1974 budget, see *New York Times*, February 4, 1973, IV:1.

65. *Public Papers, Nixon, 1973*, pp. 32–48. *National Journal*, February 3, 1973. In April 1973, Nixon showed a stunned Congress he meant business by vetoing a popular appropriation for vocational rehabilitation. Matusow, *Nixon's Economy*, p. 218.

66. *Public Papers, Nixon, 1973*, p. 14.

67. Kissinger, *Years of Upheaval*, p. 386.

68. Michael Schudson, *Watergate in American Memory* (New York: Basic Books, 1992), pp. 150–152.

69. By graft, I refer to the ordinary sort of money-making, influence-peddling scandals like the subsequent Wedtech, Abscam, and Whitewater affairs. Constitutional crises, like Iran-contra, are those in which high officials contravened laws to pursue policies in direct contradiction of an act of Congress.

70. Nixon's taste for covert activities reached even the most trivial matters. When an obscure magazine, *Scanlan's Monthly*, published a report linking Vice President Spiro Agnew to an alleged scheme to cancel the 1972 elections and repeal the Bill of Rights, Nixon demanded a lawsuit. Apprised that there was no basis to file a suit, Nixon ignored his counsel's advice to forget the matter and ordered Haldeman to have the IRS conduct a field investigation on *Scanlan's Monthly*. See Ambrose, *Nixon: Triumph of a Politician*, p. 374.

71. The President, Haldeman, Ehrlichman, and Kissinger, Oval Office conversation, June 17, 1971, in Kutler, ed., *Abuse of Power*, p. 3.

72. The President and Haldeman, Oval Office conversation, June 23, 1971, in Kutler, ed., *Abuse of Power*, p. 4.

73. The President, Haldeman, and Ehrlichman, Oval Office conversation, August 3, 1972, in Kutler, ed., *Abuse of Power*, pp. 112–113.

74. Mary McCarthy, *The Mask of State* (New York: Harcourt Brace Jovanovich, 1974), p. 3.

75. G. B. Trudeau, *Guilty, Guilty, Guilty!* (New York: Bantam, 1974), p. 87.

76. *Public Papers, Nixon, 1974*, pp. 626–630.

77. Ibid., p. 633.

78. Sam J. Ervin, remarks on Watergate, 1974, in Robert Griffith, ed., *Major Problems in American History Since 1945* (Lexington, Mass.: Heath, 1992), pp. 564–568. Schudson, *Watergate in American Memory*. John J. Sirica was the presiding judge in the Watergate court cases.

79. Thomas Cronin, "The Swelling of the Presidency," *Saturday Review* (February 1973): 30ff. Arthur M. Schlesinger, Jr., *The Imperial Presidency* (Boston: Houghton Mifflin, 1973).

80. Andrew Hacker, *The End of the American Era* (New York: Atheneum, 1970), p. 6. *Newsweek* quotation from jacket blurb, 1972 edition of *The End of the American Era.*

81. "American Pie" (words and music by Don McLean, United Artists, 1971).

82. "Montage of Loss," *Time*, January 3, 1972, p. 55.

83. Gordon Sinclair, "Americans (A Canadian's Opinion)," broadcast over CFRB Radio, June 5, 1973, Toronto, Canada.

84. "'Let's Hear It!' for U.S.," *U.S. News and World Report*, November 19, 1973, p. 120. "In Praise of America," *Washington Post*, December 13, 1973, p. A18. "A Canadian Stands Up for the U.S.," *Chicago Tribune*, January 6, 1974, sec. 2, p. 9. *Billboard*, January 12, 1974, p. 36. Joel Whitburn, *The Billboard Book of Top 40 Hits, 1955 to Present* (New York: Billboard Publications, 1983), p. 175. Bill Williams, "Nashville Scene," *Billboard*, January 5, 1974.

85. Schudson, *Watergate in American Memory*, pp. 11–12.

86. On the Republican side, the sitting president, Gerald Ford, barely held off conservative champion Ronald Reagan in the fight for the 1976 GOP presidential nomination.

2. E Pluribus Plures

1. Louie Robinson, "The Jeffersons: A Look at Life on Black America's New 'Striver's Row,'" *Ebony* 31 (January 1976): 112–115. John J. O'Connor, "TV: Lear's Jeffersons," *New York Times*, January 17, 1995, p. 67. Gary Deeb, "Now the Jeffersons Battle the Nielsons, Not the Bunkers," *Chicago Tribune*, June 17, 1975, sec. 3, p. 13. Advertisement, *Washington Post*, January 18, 1975, p. B5. Vincent Terrace, *Television Characters and Story Facts* (Jefferson, N.C.: McFarland, 1993), p. 235. Tim Brooks and Earle Marsh, *The Complete Directory to Prime Time Network TV Shows, 1946–Present*, rev. ed. (New York: Ballantine Books, 1981), p. 376.

2. Joel Dreyfuss, "All in the (Black) Family," *Washington Post*, January 18, 1975, sec. B, pp. 1, 5.

3. Richard Kluger, *Simple Justice* (New York: Vintage Books, 1974), p. 774. Thomas Byrne Edsall with Mary D. Edsall, *Chain Reaction* (New York: Norton, 1992), pp. 116–117. Access to higher education peaked in the late 1970s. See National Research Council, *A Common Destiny: Blacks and American Society* (Washington, D.C.: National Academy Press, 1989).

4. National Research Council, *A Common Destiny*, pp. 69, 233–238. John Herbers, *The Lost Priority* (New York: Funk and Wagnalls, 1970), pp. 222–223. In 1973, Coleman Young won the mayoralty in Detroit, and thirty-five-year-old Maynard Jackson grasped the reins of power in Atlanta. In tiny Fayette, Mississippi, Mayor Charles Evers erected a memorial to his brother, slain civil rights champion Medgar Evers, alongside the statue of a Confederate soldier in the town's courthouse square. On black advances in politics generally, see Steven F. Lawson, *Running for Freedom* (New York: McGraw-Hill, 1991).

5. National Research Council, *A Common Destiny*, passim. Lawson, *Running for Freedom*, p. 167. Edsall, *Chain Reaction*, p. 117. William L. Taylor, "Affirmative Action: The Questions to Be Asked," *Poverty and Race* 4 (May–June 1995): 2.

6. Andrew Hacker, "Black Crime, White Racism," *New York Review of Books*, March 3, 1988, pp. 36–41. William Van Deburg, *New Day in Babylon* (Chicago: University of Chicago Press, 1992), p. 249. Black faces, almost entirely missing from the nation's airwaves and movie screens in the early 1960s, suddenly appeared widely in television series and feature films. "The enor-

mity of the achievement of the last forty years in American race relations cannot be overstated," Harvard sociologist Orlando Patterson has concluded. "A mere 13 percent of the population," blacks dominated the nation's cultural life: "its music, its dance, its talk, its sports, its youths' fashions. . . . So powerful and unavoidable is the black popular influence that it is now not uncommon to find persons who, while remaining racists in personal relations and attitudes, nonetheless have surrendered their tastes, and their viewing and listening habits, to black entertainers, talk-show hosts and sit-com stars." Even America's most potent racial taboo slowly eroded. In the two decades after *Guess Who's Coming to Dinner* appeared in the nation's movie houses and the Supreme Court struck down antimiscegenation laws, the number of interracial marriages more than tripled. See Orlando Patterson, "The Paradox of Integration," *New Republic,* November 6, 1995, pp. 24–25; and Sylvester Monroe, "Love in Black and White," *Los Angeles Times Magazine,* December 9, 1990, pp. 14–62.

7. Patterson, "Paradox of Integration," p. 25. Sam Fulwood III, "Blacks Find Bias Amid Affluence," *Los Angeles Times,* November 20, 1991, pp. A1, A16. Eugene L. Meyer, "Curious Prince George's," *Washington Post,* July 18, 1993, p. C5.

8. National Research Council, *A Common Destiny,* pp. 9, 16, 169, passim. Andrew Hacker, "The Myths of Racial Division," *New Republic,* March 23, 1992, pp. 21–25. Andrew Hacker, *Two Nations* (New York: Scribner's, 1992). Frank Gilliam, "Black America: Divided by Class?" *Public Opinion* (February–March 1986): 53–57.

9. Martin Luther King, Jr., "A Testament of Hope," *Playboy* (January 1969): 175–194, reprinted in Clayborne Carson et al., eds., *Eyes on the Prize: A Reader and Guide* (New York: Penguin, 1991), pp. 234–235. Douglas Massey and Nancy Denton, *American Apartheid* (Cambridge: Harvard University Press, 1993). For commentaries on persistent residential segregation in contemporary America, see Nathan Glazer, "A Tale of Two Cities," *New Republic,* August 2, 1993, pp. 39–41; and Andrew Hacker, "'Diversity' and Its Dangers," *New York Review of Books,* October 7, 1993, pp. 21–25. *Psychology Today* magazine's "Black and White," a bookshelf board game, wryly captured this uncertain legacy of the civil rights movement when it hit the market in 1970. Originally designed by faculty at the University of California at Davis to sensitize white students, the "Role Identity and Neighborhood Action game" forbade blacks from buying property in the suburbs until one black player received permission from a special opportunity card. Once a black family had moved in, the zone converted, and blacks were free to control it. In the game's mixed neighborhoods, "riot rumors" regularly depressed property values and scared white residents to the suburbs. See "Blacks and Whites: A Psychology Today Game," Communications Research Machines, 1970.

10. National Research Council, *A Common Destiny,* p. 62. Edsall, *Chain Reaction,* p. 227. On the ability of Sunbelt cities to avoid white flight, see David Rusk, *Cities Without Suburbs* (Washington, D.C.: Woodrow Wilson Center Press, 1993). The quotation is from Jonathan Rieder, *Canarsie* (Cambridge: Harvard University Press, 1985), p. 90.

11. The literature on racial desegregation is voluminous. For able summaries, see Richard Kluger, *Simple Justice* (New York: Vintage, 1977); Raymond Wolters, *The Burden of Brown* (Knoxville: University of Tennessee Press, 1984); and J. Harvie Wilkinson III, *From Brown to Bakke* (New York: Oxford University Press, 1979).

12. J. Anthony Lukas, *Common Ground* (New York: Knopf, 1985). Ronald Formisano, *Boston Against Busing* (Chapel Hill: University of North Carolina Press, 1991). Thomas F. Mulvoy, Jr., "Buses and Bitterness," *Boston Globe Magazine,* March 2, 1997, p. 43.

13. Herbers, *Lost Priority,* p. 202. National Research Council, *A Common Destiny,* pp. 131–134.

14. Bruce J. Schulman, *Lyndon B. Johnson and American Liberalism* (Boston: Bedford Books of St. Martin's Press, 1995), pp. 78–79, passim.

15. To be sure, a strong nationalist strain had pervaded black life for two centuries, ever competing with the integrationist strain. Under Jim Crow, black southerners had constructed a vibrant all-black world of colleges, churches, fraternal organizations, and hospitals. The Montgomery bus boycott had demanded the hiring of black drivers as well as an end to segregation. But in this period, the nationalist strain remained in eclipse; integration formed the principal objective and liberal universalism the principal mode of thought.

16. This literature is ably summarized in Van Deburg, *New Day in Babylon*, pp. 55–56. See also Alice O'Connor, *Poverty Knowledge* (Princeton, New Jersey: Princeton University Press, forthcoming).

17. Gerald Early, "One Nation Under a Groove," *New Republic*, July 15 and 22, 1991, pp. 30–41.

18. Greil Marcus, *Mystery Train* (New York: Dutton, 1975), pp. 79–82.

19. Ibid.

20. Sylvester Stewart, "Everybody Is a Star" (Epic Records, 1970).

21. This rejection of assimilation bound together conflicting notions of black power in the late 1960s, from the most radical separatists to moderate champions of racial pluralism. Even opponents of black nationalism, like the African American cultural critic Albert Murray, carefully staked out a defense of a distinctive black culture and an indictment against assimilation. Albert Murray, *The Omni-Americans* (New York: Avon Books, 1970). For an able summary of the rejection of integration as assimilation, see Van Deburg, *New Day in Babylon*, pp. 27, 44, passim.

22. Harold Cruse, *The Crisis of the Negro Intellectual* (New York: Morrow, 1967), pp. 8–9.

23. "The Black Mood: More Militant, More Hopeful, More Determined," *Time*, April 6, 1970, p. 28. Van Deburg, *New Day in Babylon*, pp. 17–18.

24. Harold Cruse, *Plural But Equal* (New York: Quill, 1987), p. 346. Catholic intellectual Michael Novak, for example, denounced the liberal imagination as "astonishingly universalist and relentlessly missionary." The entire Enlightenment project, Novak complained, "sundered people from their roots, their histories, their communities in the cause of a colorless, deracinated, soulless religion of individual rights and universal citizenship." See Novak, *The Rise of the Unmeltable Ethnics* (New York: Macmillan, 1971), p. 58. The most important academic critiques of liberal universalism emerged in the late 1970s and early 1980s and can be found in Michael Sandel, *Liberalism and the Limits of Justice* (New York: Cambridge University Press, 1982), Alaisdair MacIntyre, *After Virtue* (Notre Dame: University of Notre Dame Press, 1981), Michael Walzer, *Spheres of Justice* (New York: Basic Books, 1983), and Richard Rorty, *Contingency, Irony, and Solidarity* (New York: Cambridge University Press, 1989). For stimulating meditations on the eclipse of philosophical liberalism and the emergence of republican and "ethnocentric" alternatives, see Laura Kalman, *The Strange Career of Legal Liberalism* (New Haven: Yale University Press, 1996); and David Hollinger, *Post-Ethnic America* (New York: Basic Books, 1995).

25. George Clinton, "Chocolate City" (1975). For the recording history of "Chocolate City," see *Billboard*, May 3, 1975, p. 30 and May 24, 1975, p. 52.

26. Marcus, *Mystery Train*, pp. 82–91.

27. During the 1970s, according to one important study of race relations, the word *segregation* all but "disappeared from the American vocabulary." Integration, barely tried though it was, appeared a conspicuous failure, undesirable even as an objective. See Massey and Denton, *American Apartheid*.

28. Malcolm X was one of the first to embrace the term *black* as a badge of honor and to turn *Negro* into a contemptuous epithet. Malcolm X eventually broke with the Nation of Islam and was gunned down in February 1965, but his influence remains. According to one historian, "he became a Black power paradigm—the archetype, reference point, and spiritual adviser in absentia" for a rising generation of activists. Van Deburg, *New Day in Babylon*, p. 2.

29. Calvin C. Hernton, "Dynamite Growing Out of Their Skulls," in LeRoi Jones and Larry Neal, eds., *Black Fire* (New York: Morrow, 1968), pp. 89–90.

30. For radicals like H. Rap Brown, Carmichael's successor as SNCC chairman, it threatened guerrilla warfare. "Get you some guns," Brown warned black audiences. "I mean, don't be trying to love that honky to death. Shoot him to death." Others used it to signify less violent actions: local control of ghetto businesses, electing African American public officials, forming a black political party. From the beginning, black power evoked cultural as well as political aspirations. Before his death, Malcolm X had envisioned a "cultural revolution to unbrainwash an entire people." Malcolm X, "The Statement of Basic Aims and Objectives of the Organization of Afro-American Unity" (June 1964), in George Breitman, ed., *By Any Means Necessary* (New York: Pathfinder, 1970), pp. 53–56.

31. James Boggs, "Black Power—A Scientific Concept Whose Time Has Come," *Liberator* (1967), reprinted in LeRoi Jones and Larry Neal, eds., *Black Fire* (New York: Morrow, 1968), p. 115 (italics and capitalization in original). Lawson, *Running for Freedom*, pp. 129–130. Without the guns, less revolutionary versions of black power retained the focus on accumulating and maintaining power. Growing out of the formation of the Congressional Black Caucus in 1969, mainstream but militant black leaders launched an effort to form an independent black political party and subvert the traditional two-party system. Although their efforts never bore fruit, they organized three black political conventions in the early 1970s. On the Black Panthers in general, see G. Louis Heath, ed., *Off the Pigs! The History and Literature of the Black Panther Party* (Metuchen, N.J.: Scarecrow, 1976); Earl Anthony, *Picking Up the Gun* (New York: Dial, 1970), Reginald Major, *A Panther Is a Black Cat* (New York: Morrow, 1971); Bobby Seale, *Seize the Time* (New York: Random House, 1970); and Gene Marine, *The Black Panthers* (New York: New American Library, 1969). On the independent black party, consult Lawson, *Running for Freedom*, and Cruse, *Plural But Equal*.

32. LeRoi Jones (Amiri Baraka), "Black Art," in Jones and Neal, *Black Fire*, p. 302.

33. Van Deburg, *New Day in Babylon*, p. 171.

34. Black studies programs, one of the principal loci of developing cultural nationalism were hastily constructed to satisfy the demands of campus protesters, and they experienced this same shift in emphasis. Efforts in the late Sixties focused on political organization and racial uplift. "Black today is revolutionary and nationalistic," the director of one program intoned. "A black studies program which is not revolutionary and nationalistic is, accordingly, quite profoundly irrelevant." Early demands focused on creating programs with entirely black staff and student bodies and on training black students to "organize the urban ghettoes and the black-belt South." Academic credentials and cultural history struck early black studies activists as irrelevant: "Lectures on such esoteric topics as 'the social dynamics of a fifteenth century West African agricultural village' or 'Camille Thierry, free Negro poet in Paris' may indeed warm the cockles of the scholastic heart, but they seem rather pointless to those whose daily lives have been endless struggles against ghetto rodents or 'white only' restrooms." At Merritt College in Oakland, California, black instructors blocked enrollment of white students in black studies courses. Summarily barring white students from its Afro-American Studies Institute, Antioch College's program operated a gas station and a bookstore to offer job opportunities in nearby black neighborhoods. By the early 1970s, most black studies programs mainly offered courses along the lines that early activists had decried. The shift reflected not just a dilution of militant protests

and an affirmation of traditional standards by black academics running the programs, but a renewed emphasis on African and African American history and culture. Consult Roger A. Fischer, "Ghetto and Gown: The Birth of Black Studies," *Current History* 57 (November 1969), reprinted in John W. Blassingame, ed., *New Perspectives on Black Studies* (Urbana: University of Illinois Press, 1971), pp. 16–27; and Julie A. Reuben, "Reforming the University: Student Protests and the Demand for a 'Relevant' Curriculum," in Gerald J. DeGroot, ed., *Student Protest Since 1960* (Essex: Addison Wesley Longman, 1998). The cultural turn alarmed some civil rights voices. What really concerns black Americans, Albert Murray insisted, "is not too little identity or beauty or pride but too much exclusion from the power mechanisms and resources of the nation." But Murray was shouting in the dark. Consult Murray, *The Omni-Americans*, p. 293.

35. The Black Panther party even tempered its hard-edged Marxist-Leninist version of black nationalism by adopting a new commitment to "intercommunalism," a vision of postrevolutionary multiculturalism. Cultural autonomy had replaced political power as the principal objective of black militants.

36. Armando B. Rendon, *Chicano Manifesto* (New York: Macmillan, 1971), pp. 4, 14, 322.

37. Rodolfo Acuna, *Occupied America* (San Francisco: Canfield Press, 1972), pp. 22, passim. The cry of "Goodbye America" also represented an assertion of political power for Chicanos, akin to the cry of "black power." In East Los Angeles, activists formed Young Citizens for Community. Eventually known as the Brown Berets for the military headgear they sported, these young militants rejected the defensive, assimilationist posture of previous generations of Mexican American leaders and adopted a paramilitary stance reminiscent of the Black Panthers. They also eventually came to deal with the needs of the barrio, opening a free clinic and providing food and housing for the needy. In South Texas, Mexican Americans formed their own political party, La Raza Unida. The party strove to achieve political power, influence policy, and elect Mexican American candidates, but from the outset it also affirmed "the greatness of our heritage, our history, our language, our traditions, our contributions to humanity and our culture." See "Plan De La Raza Unida," October 28, 1967, reprinted in Rendon, *Chicano Manifesto*, p. 331. On Chicano nationalism, consult Matt S. Meier and Feliciano Ribera, *The Chicanos* (New York: Hill and Wang, 1972); Mario T. Garcia, *Mexican Americans: Leadership, Ideology, and Identity, 1930–1960* (New Haven: Yale University Press, 1989); Peter Skerry, *Mexican Americans: The Ambivalent Minority* (New York: Free Press, 1993); and Gilberto Lopez y Rivas, *The Chicanos* (New York: Monthly Review Press, 1974).

38. Before the 1960s, Chicano voices had been little heeded in American public life. This reflected the peculiar features of Mexican immigration to the Southwest, particularly the very low naturalization rates for Mexican immigrants. A number of factors, including the active efforts of the Mexican government, discouraged most Mexican immigrants from applying for U.S. citizenship. The rising militance of the 1960s marked the coming of age of a second generation—children of immigrants born north of the border who were native-born citizens of the United States. Thus, most Chicano organizations before 1970 had occurred outside the formal political system—in church groups, student groups, and fraternal organizations and preeminently in a tradition of labor activism, especially in the fields, canneries, and factories of the Southwest. On the rise of the second generation and Chicano politics, see George J. Sanchez, *Becoming Mexican American* (New York: Oxford University Press, 1993); and Garcia, *Mexican Americans*.

39. See, for example, Richard Rodriguez, *Hunger of Memory* (New York: Bantam, 1983); Harlan Lebo, "Resolving Weighty Issues," *UCLA Magazine* (Summer 1993): 8–10, and Gregory Rodriguez, "Rethinking Latino Identity," *Los Angeles Times*, October 13, 1996, pp. M1–M6. Even Chicano organizations laboring through conventional legal and political channels, like the Mexican American Legal Defense and Education Fund, committed themselves to

community control and cultural preservation. Peter Skerry sees a tension between a nationalist Chicano leadership, largely based in California, and a more assimilationist one centered in Texas. See Skerry, *Mexican Americans*.

40. James J. Rawls, *Chief Red Fox Is Dead* (Fort Worth, Tex.: Harcourt Brace, 1996); Hazel W. Hertzberg, *The Search for an American Indian Identity* (Syracuse, N.Y.: Syracuse University Press, 1971); James S. Olson and Raymond Wilson, *Native Americans in the Twentieth Century* (Provo, Utah: BYU Press, 1984); Alvin M. Josephy, Jr., *Red Power* (New York: McGraw-Hill, 1971); and Kenneth S. Stern, *Loud Hawk* (Norman: University of Oklahoma Press, 1994). A compelling example of the odyssey from "red power" to renewed tribalism and Indian cultural nationalism is Vine Deloria, Jr., *We Talk, You Listen* (New York: Dell, 1970).

41. Nancy Lo, quoted in John Powers, "The Myth of the Model Minority," *Boston Globe Magazine,* January 9, 1994, p. 8. See also Sucheng Chan, *Asian Americans* (Boston: Twayne, 1991); and Ronald Takaki, *Strangers from a Different Shore* (Boston: Little, Brown, 1989). Early cultural nationalist efforts focused on attention to the cultural diversity of Asian immigrant communities, to combating discrimination in college and graduate school admissions, and to rebuffing outbreaks of anti-Asian racism.

42. Details of the Vincent Chin case can be found in the *New York Times:* April 26, 30, May 10, August 5, November 3, 1983, September 19, 1984.

43. Alice Yang Murray, "'Silence, No More': The Japanese American Redress Movement, 1942–1992" (Ph.D. dissertation, Stanford University, 1994).

44. Nobu Miyoshi, "The Identity Crisis of the Sansei and the American Concentration Camps," *Pacific Citizen,* December 19–26, 1980, pp. 41–55. U.S. Commission on Wartime Relocation and Internment of Civilians, *Personal Justice Denied* (Washington, D.C.: GPO, 1982). "The Commission on Wartime Relocation and Internment of Civilians: Selected Testimonies from the Los Angeles and San Francisco Hearings," *Amerasia Journal* 8 (1981): 55–105. Don Nakanishi, "Seeking Convergence in Race Relations Research: Japanese-Americans and the Resurrection of the Internment," in Phyllis Katz and Dalmas Palmer, eds., *Eliminating Racism* (New York: Plenum, 1988), pp. 159–180. See also Chan, *Asian Americans;* and Takaki, *Strangers from a Different Shore.*

45. On the new immigration, see David Reimers, *Still the Golden Door,* 2nd ed. (New York: Columbia University Press, 1992). Even Boston, which the busing controversy had turned into a symbol of Irish intransigence, wore a different, more cosmopolitan face. In 1974, when the buses started rolling, more than 80 percent of Bostonians were white, most of them ethnic Catholics. Two decades later Asians, Hispanics, and blacks numbered nearly half of the city's population, and the Hub boasted enclaves of new arrivals from Brazil, Haiti, Ethiopia, Russia, Cambodia, Colombia, Vietnam, and the Cape Verde Islands.

46. U.S. Advisory Commission on Intergovernmental Relations, *Regulatory Federalism* (Washington, D.C., ACIR, 1984). Hugh Davis Graham, "Civil Rights Policy in the Carter Presidency," in Graham and Gary Fink, eds., *The Carter Presidency: Policy Choices in the Post–New Deal Era* (Lawrence: University Press of Kansas, 1998), pp. 202–223.

47. Timothy J. O'Neill, *Bakke and the Politics of Equality* (Middletown, Conn.: Wesleyan University Press, 1985), pp. 20–26.

48. In August 1977, the U.S. Department of Justice prepared an amicus curiae brief supporting Bakke's claims, harshly criticizing separate admissions standards like those in the University of California at Davis task force program. In the White House, President Jimmy Carter's senior staff argued about the brief and about the position the administration should take on the issue. Some, like chief of staff Hamilton Jordan, worried that the pro-Bakke brief would alienate impor-

tant constituencies. "Because the Bakke case has taken on tremendous symbolic significance to the minorities of this country," Jordan warned, "we should realize that they are going to pay little attention to our eloquent language and focus almost exclusively on which side we support." The fact that black officials had authored the Justice Department brief would not make the administration's support of Bakke more palatable but would only discredit those officials in their own community. Memo, Hamilton Jordan to the President, n.d., Chief of Staff Files, Jordan, Bakke Case 1977 Folder, Box 33, Jimmy Carter Library. Others, like Carter's White House counsel, Robert Lipshutz, and his domestic policy adviser, Stu Eizenstat, believed that the brief failed to articulate the administration's essential position: vigorous support of affirmative action coupled with opposition to "rigid quotas." At his aides' urging, Carter ordered the Justice Department to redraft the brief along those lines. The final version, which featured a strong defense of affirmative action, did not call on the Court to rule in Bakke's favor, instead recommending that the case be returned to California to decide several questions of fact. Although the White House considered the brief an improvement over the initial draft, it still worried that the administration had not gone on record against quotas. Carter's top advisers, then, resisted the shift from integration to diversity. They criticized efforts to ensure proportional representation of groups on a fixed, permanent basis. In the end, they drafted a new brief that offered no opinion on Bakke's fate. They endorsed temporary affirmative action programs, aimed at hastening "the day when they are no longer needed—when the vestiges of discrimination have been eliminated and men and women can compete freely and fairly in an atmosphere where no one is concerned with race or sex." The Court soon rendered that integrationist argument obsolete. See Memo, Stuart Eizenstat and Bob Lipshutz to the President, September 6, 1977, Chief of Staff Files, Jordan, Bakke Case 1977 Folder, Box 33, Jimmy Carter Library. For additional Bakke materials, see Staff Files, DPS-Eizenstat, Boxes 148–149; Jimmy Carter Library. Burton I. Kaufman, *The Presidency of Jimmy Carter* (Lawrence: University Press of Kansas, 1993), pp. 70–71; and John Dumbrell, *The Carter Presidency* (Manchester: Manchester University Press, 1993), pp. 93–94.

49. *Regents of the University of California v. Bakke,* 438 U.S. 265 (1978). Bruce Ackerman, quoted in O'Neill, *Bakke and the Politics of Equality,* p. 277.

50. Kelly Wachowicz, "A History of Affirmative Action in Undergraduate Programming and Admissions at UCLA, 1960–1991" (senior honors essay, UCLA, 1991).

51. Office of Civil Rights, U.S. Department of Health, Education and Welfare, "Task Force Findings Specifying Remedies Avaliable for Eliminating Past Educational Practices Ruled Unlawful Under *Lau v. Nichols*," summer 1975, quoted in Graham, "Civil Rights Policy in the Carter Presidency."

52. Graham, "Civil Rights Policy in the Carter Presidency." "Ending the Bi-Lingual Double-Talk," *New York Times,* August 8, 1980.

53. Jacob Heilbrunn, "Speech Therapy," *New Republic,* Jan 20, 1997, pp. 17–19.

54. Jesse Jackson, address at the Democratic National Convention, San Francisco, July 17, 1988, in *Great Speeches of the Twentieth Century* (Santa Monica: Rhino Records, 1991).

55. Cruse, *Plural but Equal,* p. 249. For analyses of contemporary ideas about diversity and multiculturalism, see Orlando Patterson, "Black Like All of Us: Celebrating Multiculturalism Diminishes Blacks' Role in American Culture," *Washington Post,* February 7, 1993, p. C2; and Hacker, "Diversity and Its Dangers."

56. Heather MacDonald, "The Diversity Industry," *New Republic,* July 5, 1993, pp. 22–25.

57. A murkiness remained. Patrons of bilingual education could invoke both building English proficiency and preserving cultural distinctiveness; African American leaders could canonize both Malcolm X and Martin Luther King. A handful of wary civil rights champions kept

"ethnic diversity" at arm's length. They remained committed to the beloved community, seeing integration as more desirable and more authentically radical than cultural nationalism. At the same time, a few black intellectuals resisted the swelling multicultural tide in American letters. The new emphasis on the integrity and diversity of ethnic subcultures, these scholars maintained, neglected the exceptional history of black Americans and undervalued the extraordinary contributions of African Americans to the common national culture. For a trenchant discussion of African American objections to multiculturalism, see Orlando Patterson, "Black Like All of Us," *Washington Post,* February 7, 1993, p. C2. More recently, die-hard integrationists like former SNCC chairman and current Georgia congressman John Lewis and retired Duke University historian John Hope Franklin have reflected on the difficulties they experienced during the immediate post–civil rights era. See Peter Applebome, "John Hope Franklin," *New York Times Magazine,* April 23, 1995, pp. 34–37; and Sean Wilentz, "The Last Integrationist," *New Republic,* July 1, 1996, pp. 19–26.

58. Michael Novak, *The Rise of the Unmeltable Ethnics* (New York: Macmillan, 1971), pp. 270, passim.

59. Ed Ward, Geoffrey Stokes, and Ken Tucker, *Rock of Ages: The Rolling Stone History of Rock and Roll* (New York: Rolling Stone Press, 1986), p. 524.

60. Ibid.

61. Jefferson Morley, "The Myth and Meaning of Disco," *New Times,* March 1–7, 1989, pp. 15–20. Morley, "Twentysomething," *City Paper* (Washington, D.C.), February 19, 1988, pp. 18–20.

62. Morley, "Myth and Meaning of Disco." Ward et al., *Rock of Ages,* pp. 525–30. Mikal Gilmore, "Donna Summer: Is There Life After Disco?" *Rolling Stone,* March 23, 1978, p. 15.

63. "Colossally Outrageous and Black," *New York Times,* June 23, 1995, p. C12. Van Deburg, *New Day in Babylon.*

64. Influenced by "Jamaicans who brought the West Indian tradition of toasting to New York, Harlem and South Bronx disc jockeys sustained a seamless dance groove, hopping from one catchy instrumental break to another as they segued from record to record and excited the crowd by shouting out the names of people in the audience over a microphone. Eventually teams emerged, with the disc jockeys mastering the turntables, often scratching across the grooves of the record to produce their own sound, and the masters of ceremony (MCs or rappers) spinning elaborate tales in rhyme." David Samuels, "The Rap on Rap," *New Republic,* November 11, 1991, p. 25. Jefferson Morley, "Rap Music as American History," in Lawrence Stanley, ed. *Rap: The Lyrics* (New York: Penguin, 1992), pp. xv–xvi. For the Sugar Hill Gang, the all-star team of New York rappers assembled by producers Joe and Sylvia Robinson, consult Sugar Hill Gang, "Rapper's Delight," in Stanley, ed., *Rap: The Lyrics,* pp. 318–327. See also *Billboard,* October 13, 1979, p. 50. *Billboard,* November 10, 1979, p. 82.

65. White disco performers appeared as latter-day Elvis Presleys, domesticating a black musical form for mainstream white consumption. See Nelson George, *The Death of Rhythm and Blues* (New York: Dutton, 1988).

66. On the crossover trajectory of rap, see Samuels, "The Rap on Rap." Rap spawned its own would-be Elvises, but followed a very different path to commercial success. On the political content of rap records, rap, as the anthology *Rap: The Lyrics* put it, captured "the sound of black urban youth creating a musical alternative to urban contemporary radio and a sociocultural alternative to the integrationist policies of the 1960s and the white backlash that accompanied them." Rap records offered unstinting, unsentimental portraits of the starker realities of ghetto life. But in the age of diversity, they emphasized a mostly cultural rather than political form of

black nationalism, promoting Afrocentric attitudes, black speech, and the preservation of the African American heritage. See Morley, "Rap Music as American History," pp. xxi, xxviii.

67. Meg Greenfield, "Ethnic and Son," *Newsweek*, September 29, 1975, p. 96.

68. Remarks of Hubert H. Humphrey, December 11, 1972, quoted in Timothy N. Thurber, "Liberalism and the Economic Crisis in Black America" (paper delivered at the conference on "The Carter Presidency, Policy Choices in the Post–New Deal Era," Jimmy Carter Presidential Library, Atlanta, Georgia, February 21, 1997).

3. "Plugging In"

1. Richard Bach, *Jonathan Livingston Seagull* (New York: Macmillan, 1970), p. 14.

2. Ibid., p. 35.

3. Doug Rossinow, *The Politics of Authenticity* (New York: Columbia University Press, 1998), pp. 4, 19, 340. Benjamin Zablocki, *Alienation and Charisma* (New York: Free Press, 1980), p. 56.

4. "'Seagull' Reprint Soars to $1.11-Million," *New York Times*, August 23, 1972, p. 31. *Publisher's Weekly*, August 3, 1970, p. 60. "Book Sales Soar for Fable of a Seagull," *New York Times*, Janary 18, 1972, p. 22.

5. "It's a Bird! It's a Dream! It's Supergull!" *Time*, November 13, 1972, p. 60. The novelist Ray Bradbury, a friend of Richard Bach, described *Seagull* as a "great Rorschach test. You read your own mystical principles into it." Bach himself explained that "Jonathan is that brilliant little fire that burns within us all, that lives only for those moments when we reach perfection."

6. Tom Wolfe, "The Me Decade and the Third Great Awakening," in Tom Wolfe, *The Purple Decades* (New York: Berkley Books, 1983), pp. 265–296.

7. Ibid., p. 290.

8. Frances FitzGerald, *Cities on a Hill* (New York: Simon & Schuster, 1981), p. 16. The classic portrait of an American society rapidly losing ethnic, religious, and cultural variation is Will Herberg, *Protestant, Catholic, Jew* (Garden City, N.Y.: Doubleday, 1955).

9. "He was our man," Schrag wrote of this model of the assimilated American. "The all-purpose, real-life, bigger-than-life, wide-screen, three-dimensional, stereophonic, amalgamated, now-and-forever certified American. Our man. Who built the country and held it together, who was what every immigrant was supposed to be and every boy to idolize, who spoke plain, fought fair, worked hard, and feared God." This American ideal had been "part Leatherstocking, part John Wayne, with a little Ben Franklin thrown in for good measure—frontiersman, cowboy, soldier, entrepreneur—plus a lot of other things besides, a real-life nephew of you-know-who, red white and blue, free white and twenty-one, who didn't fire till he saw the whites of their eyes . . . couldn't tell a lie, and regretted that he had but one life to give to his country." Peter Schrag, *The Decline of the WASP* (New York: Simon & Schuster, 1970), p. 13.

10. Ibid., p. 14.

11. Ibid. Richard Gambino, *Blood of My Blood* (Garden City, N.Y.: Anchor Books, 1975). Michael Novak, *The Rise of the Unmeltable Ethnics* (New York: Macmillan, 1971). Andrew M. Greeley, *That Most Distressful Nation* (Chicago: Quadrangle Books, 1972). W. H. Auden, "America Is NOT a Melting Pot," *New York Times Magazine*, March 18, 1972. For a searing critique of the literature of the ethnic revival and the revival of white ethnicity itself, see Stephen Steinberg, *The Ethnic Myth* (Boston: Beacon Press, 1981).

12. *New York Times*, June 29, 1971, pp. 1, 20. At the rally, the league honored Colombo for "restoring dignity, pride, and recognition to every Italian," but as he mounted the Unity Day platform, a black assailant, probably working for a rival crime family, assassinated him. Concluding the now somber rally in front of a statue of Christopher Columbus, Natale Marcone, the league's president, admonished the crowd, "Go home but never forget, be proud to be Italian all the time!"

13. Barbara Mikulski, "Who Speaks for Ethnic America," *New York Times*, September 29, 1970. "Angry Ethnic Voices Decry a 'Racist and Dullard' Image," *New York Times*, June 17, 1970.

14. On the 1970 Freedom Bus for Soviet Jewry, consult Manuscript Collection 202, "Freedom Bus, 1970," Box 63, American Jewish Archives, Cincinnati, Ohio. Thanks to Marc Dollinger for making this material available. See also Marc Dollinger, "American Jews and the Politics of Cultural Nationalism" (paper presented to the Annual Meeting of the American Historical Association, Atlanta, Georgia, January 7, 1996.

15. Ibid.

16. Ibid.

17. Safam, "Just Another Foreigner" (words by Joel Sussman and Robbie Solomon, music by Joel Sussman, 1983). Samuel C. Heilman, *Portrait of American Jews: The Last Half of the Twentieth Century* (Seattle: University of Washington Press, 1995), pp. 101, passim.

18. Andrew M. Greeley, *That Most Distressful Nation* (Chicago: Quadrangle Books, 1972).

19. They could manifest themselves in earnest commitments, such as aid to Soviet Jewry or the efforts of the Italian American League. Or they could appear in less serious form, as vast numbers of so-called Saturday ethnics—successful, assimilated professionals—made weekly pilgrimages from their suburban homes to the old neighborhood, to eat, shop, breathe the pungent air. In one commentator's words, many Italians "return, after all, not only for the bread, tiny bitter onions, bushels of snails and dried cod, but also to enjoy a weekend heritage that their education, bland wines, and the English language have begun to deny them. . . . It is only with a trunk filled with Italian market produce that a Saturday Italian can face six days in the suburbs." For Saturday Italians, Slavs, Poles, and Germans, ethnic identity granted solace; it seemed a form of "revolt against the smooth edges of suburban life." See Novak, *Rise of the Unmeltable Ethnics*, p. 33.

20. Ibid., pp. 3, 270.

21. Interview with Francis Ford Coppola, Commemorative Video Edition of *The Godfather* (1997).

22. *The Godfather* (directed by Francis Ford Coppola, written by Mario Puzo and Francis Ford Coppola, 1972).

23. Ibid. A few years later, in a smaller, less celebrated movie, a young Jewish American director, Joan Micklin Silver, also painted a bleak picture of the costs of assimilation. Silver, whose later films like *Crossing Delancy* would examine Jewish life in contemporary America, set *Hester Street*, her 1975 examination of ethnicity, in turn-of-the-century New York and filmed it in black and white. Like *The Godfather*, *Hester Street* chronicled a family, featuring Yankel, the thoroughly assimilated father-husband who calls himself "Jake" and has been conducting an affair with a "modern," Americanized woman; his wife, Gitl, who follows her husband to America years later; their son and heir Yossele (Joey); and Mr. Bernstein, the learned man who boards with the family. Played by Carol Kane, Gitl is the focus of *Hester Street*. Hers is a tale of courage to be sure, a proto-feminist assertion of female autonomy, but it is mainly a tale of woe. "A pox on Columbus"—that is, on the discovery of America—becomes, in a mixture of Yiddish and English, the refrain of Gitl and her ally, Mr. Bernstein. Gitl finds American customs destructive and corro-

sive. The old ways remain the rock of her life, her only solace. Even as her marriage breaks up, Gitl resists assimilation. The costs of resistance prove nearly unbearable, but she never surrenders.

24. Mikulski, "Who Speaks for Ethnic America." "Angry Ethnic Voices Decry a 'Racist and Dullard' Image," *New York Times,* June 17, 1970. For an analysis of the grievances of white ethnics in the early 1970s, see Harold Cruse, *Plural But Equal* (New York: Morrow, 1987), pp. 279–288.

25. U.S. Senate, *Developments in Aging: 1980,* A Report of the Special Committee on Aging, 97th Cong., 1st sess., 1981, pp. vii, xiii, xxxii–xxxiii. National Council on the Aging, *Fact Book on Aging: A Profile of America's Older Population* (Washington, D.C.: National Council on the Aging, 1978).

26. U.S. Senate, *Developments in Aging: 1980,* pp. vii, xvi–xvii, 29ff. According to the Senate Special Committee on Aging, 60 percent of the aged would have sunk below the poverty line were it not for social security and other federal transfer programs.

27. Maggie Kuhn, "New Life for the Elderly: Liberation from 'Ageism,'" reprinted in Ronald Gross, ed., *The New Old* (Garden City, N.Y.: Anchor Books, 1978), p. 296.

28. Hope Bagger, "Mandatory Retirement Is Death to Personality," in Gross et al., eds., *The New Old,* pp. 339–341. Harriet L. Perretz, ed., *The Gray Panther Manual* (Philadelphia: Gray Panthers, 1977). Tish Sommers, "A Free-Lance Agitator Confronts the Establishment," in Gross et al., *The New Old,* pp. 231–240. "Catering to Older Age Groups," *New York Times,* March 24, 1984, p. D1. For contemporary accounts of elderly activism, see Fred Harris, "Old People Power," *New Republic,* March 23, 1974, pp. 10–11; and Barbara Isenberg, "Senior Power: Aging in America," *Nation,* May 14, 1973, pp. 626–628.

29. Kuhn, "New Life for the Elderly," pp. 299–300.

30. Charles R. Morris, *The AARP* (New York: Times Books, 1996), p. xi. Older Americans emerged as a force in American public life. Robert Butler, author of the Pulitzer Prize–winning book *Why Survive: Being Old in America,* became the founding director of the National Institute on Aging and laid out a national policy agenda on aging issues. Robert N. Butler, "Toward a National Policy on Aging," in Gross et al., *The New Old,* pp. 250–256.

31. Membership statistics provided by the AARP Research Information Center, 601 E Street N.W., Washington, D.C. 20049. See also Morris, *The AARP,* pp. 9–13.

32. "Catering to Older Age Groups," *New York Times,* March 24, 1984, p. D1.

33. National Council on the Aging, *Fact Book on Aging: A Profile of America's Older Population* (Washington, D.C.: National Council on the Aging, 1978), pp. 184–185. FitzGerald, *Cities on a Hill,* p. 209. William A. V. Clark and Suzanne Davies, "Elderly Mobility and Mobility Outcomes: Households in the Later Stages of the Life Course," *Research on Aging* 12 (1990): 430–462.

34. National Council on the Aging, *Fact Book on Aging,* pp. 183–185. FitzGerald, *Cities on a Hill,* p. 210.

35. There's a "Leisure City in Clearwater Florida," Kuhn told an interviewer in 1977. Called "Top of the World," it "is a prime example of age segregation. The residents have several golf courses and tennis courts. To meet ethnic needs, they have Mediterranean, Spanish, Contemporary, American types of architecture so people can live in the style of house they want. It's right in the middle of Clearwater, but it's a secluded community, self-contained with its own buses and its own guard." See Dieter Hessel, ed., *Maggie Kuhn on Aging* (Philadelphia: Westminster Press, 1977), pp. 41–43.

36. Martin Gotwalt and Jim Sheely, quoted in Michael D'Antonio, "The New Generation Gap," *Los Angeles Times Magazine,* March 14, 1993, p. 16. FitzGerald, *Cities on a Hill,* pp. 226–235.

37. Kuhn, "New Life for the Elderly."

38. Wolfe, "The Me Decade and the Third Great Awakening," pp. 274–275. The English writer C. P. Snow diagnosed the same phenomenon. "Great strata of the young," Snow warned, "have turned inwards: into their own customs, and often their own private language: often into a private fairyland where what some of them call 'structures' do not exist." C. P. Snow, *The State of Siege* (New York: Scribner's, 1969), pp. 9–10.

39. William Hedgepath, "The Alternative" (1970), reprinted in Alexander Bloom and Wini Breines, eds., *"Takin' It to the Streets"* (New York: Oxford University Press, 1995), pp. 329–334. For rival accounts of the communes, consult Hugh Gardner, *The Children of Prosperity* (New York: St. Martin's Press, 1978), pp. 8–9. On the commune phenomenon generally, see John Rothchild and Susan Berns Wolf, *The Children of the Counterculture* (Garden City, N.J.: Doubleday, 1976); Ron E. Roberts, *The New Communes* (Englewood Cliffs, N.J.: Prentice Hall, 1971); Benjamin Zablocki, *Alienation and Charisma* (New York: Free Press, 1980); Zablocki, "Communes, Encounter Groups, and the Search for Community," in Kurt W. Back, ed., *In Search for Community (Boulder:* Westview Press, 1978), pp. 97–142; Rosabeth Moss Kanter, *Communes* (New York: Harper & Row, 1973); Ross V. Speck et al., *The New Families* (New York: Basic Books, 1972); and Laurence Veysey, *The Communal Experience* (Chicago: University of Chicago Press, 1978).

40. Martin Jezer, quoted in Terry H. Anderson, *The Movement and the Sixties* (New York: Oxford University Press, 1995), p. 270.

41. Anderson, *The Movement and the Sixties,* pp. 270–271. Rothchild and Wolf, *The Children of the Counterculture.* Veysey, *The Communal Experience.*

42. Mary F. Corey (Red Rocker), conversations with the author.

43. Gardner, *Children of Prosperity,* p. 19. Stewart Brand, ed., *The Last Whole Earth Catalog* (Menlo Park: Portola Institute, 1971), p. 43. Anderson, *The Movement and the Sixties,* p. 272. Warren J. Belasco, *Appetite for Change* (New York: Pantheon, 1989), pp. 26, passim.

44. Gary Snyder, quoted in Belasco, *Appetite for Change,* p. 21. See also Robert Gottlieb, *Forcing the Spring* (Washington, D.C.: Island Press, 1993), p. 102.

45. Belasco, *Appetite for Change,* p. 24. At Morning Star Ranch, communards preached "voluntary primitivism." Live lightly on the land, they insisted, and "subvert the establishment geared toward waste and wanton destruction." See Gardner, *Children of Prosperity,* p. 14.

46. Joni Mitchell, "Big Yellow Taxi" (1970). Belasco, *Appetite for Change,* p. 27.

47. Sara Davidson, "Open Land: Getting Back to the Communal Garden," *Harper's* 240 (June 1970): 91–93. Belasco, *Appetite for Change,* p. 27.

48. Gottlieb, *Forcing the Spring,* p. 100. Ecology addressed not just a set of practical problems but a spiritual crisis: modern Americans' alienation from the world around them. Like the Peace Corps volunteers of the mid-1960s, the new generation wanted not merely to do good but to be good, to experience life on the frontier, to find and redefine themselves. See Elizabeth Cobbs Hoffman, *All You Need Is Love: The Peace Corps and the Spirit of the 1960s* (Cambridge: Harvard University Press, 1998).

49. Gottlieb, *Forcing the Spring,* pp. 105–108. On Earth Day, see also Hal K. Rothman, *The*

Greening of a Nation? (Fort Worth, Tex.: Harcourt Brace, 1998), pp. 121–125; and Whitaker, *Striking a Balance*, pp. 3–7.

50. *New York Times*, April 23, 1970, pp. 1, 30. *Washington Post*, April 23, 1970, p. 20. Gaylord Nelson interview with Robert Gottlieb, quoted in Gottlieb, *Forcing the Spring*, p. 106. The nation's political and business elites enthusiastically joined in. Sun Oil, Texas Gulf Sulphur, Scott Paper, and Reynolds Metals all announced pollution abatement programs. New York City mayor John Lindsay drove an electric car to work, while Governor Nelson Rockefeller rode a bicycle for photographers in Brooklyn. Across the country, politicians announced environmental initiatives. See Whitaker, *Striking a Balance*, pp. 3–7.

51. Edgar Wayburn, "Survival Is Not Enough," *Sierra Club Bulletin* 55 (March 1970): 2. Others among the old guard proved more sympathetic; the leaders of the Wilderness Society and the Conservation Foundation, for example, envisioned a fruitful synthesis of approaches. See Gottlieb, *Forcing the Spring*, p. 108.

52. On the growth of the alternative environmental network, see Gottlieb, *Forcing the Spring*.

53. U.S. Environmental Protection Agency, "Environmental Protection: A Historical Review of Legislation and Programs of the Environmental Protection Agency," Report No. 83-34 ENR, March 1, 1983.

54. Hedgepath, "The Alternative," pp. 333–334. The vast majority of rural communes, for example, engaged in rituals like meditation, prayer, mantra chanting, and yoga. See Benjamin Zablocki, *Alienation and Charisma* (New York: Free Press, 1980), p. 287.

55. Dollinger, "American Jews and the Politics of Cultural Nationalism." Jack Wertheimer, *A People Divided: Judaism in Contemporary America* (New York: Basic Books, 1993). Jacob Rader Marcus, ed., *The Jew in the American World: A Source Book* (Detroit: Wayne State University Press, 1996), pp. 546, 563–564. Samuel C. Heilman, *Portrait of American Jews: The Last Half of the Twentieth Century* (Seattle: University of Washington Press, 1995), pp. 107–109. Jonathan Shenker, "The Havurah Movement Comes of Age," Robert Gordis, "The Seven Principles of Conservative Judaism," and "*Emet Ve-Emurah:* Conservatism's True Faith," in Marcus, ed., *The Jew in the American World*, pp. 553–559.

56. Marcus, *The Jew in the American World*, p. 563. Dollinger, "American Jews and the Politics of Cultural Nationalism." Designed to accommodate six hundred campers, Camp Swig, a Reform Jewish camp in Saratoga, California, enrolled one thousand children by the mid-1990s and had to open a second site, Camp Newman, in Santa Rosa, to satisfy demand. Still, there remained considerable disagreement about the general health of the Jewish community in the 1970s and 1980s. A strongly positive account of Jewish rebirth is Charles Silberman, *A Certain People* (New York: Summit, 1985). For a more morose assessment, emphasizing assimilation and decline, see Arthur Hertzberg, "The Triumph of the Jews," *New York Review of Books*, November 21, 1985, pp. 18–22. For an assessment of this controversy, consult Wertheimer, *A People Divided*.

57. George Gallup, Jr., and Jim Castelli, *The People's Religion* (New York: Macmillan, 1989), p. 17.

58. Ibid. Paul Boyer, *When Time Shall Be No More* (Cambridge: Harvard University Press, 1992), pp. 1–5. For a nuanced journey through the evangelical subculture, see Randall Balmer, *Mine Eyes Have Seen the Glory* (New York: Oxford University Press, 1989). On the collapse of the religious middle in American Christianity, see Phillip E. Hammond, *Religion and Personal Autonomy* (Columbia: University of South Carolina Press, 1992); and Wade C. Roof and William McKinney, *American Mainline Religion* (New Brunswick, N.J.: Rutgers University Press, 1987).

59. Edwin Diamond, "God's Television," *American Film* 5 (March 1980): 30–35.

60. Jeffrey K. Hadden and Anson Shupe, *Televangelism* (New York: Henry Holt, 1988), p. 86. Boyer, *When Time Shall be No More*, p. 2.

61. Hal Lindsey, *The Late Great Planet Earth* (Grand Rapids, Mich.: Zondervan, 1970). Boyer, *When Time Shall Be No More*, pp. 5–7. Nelina E. Backman, "Christianity And/In Modern Literary Discourse" (Ph.D. dissertation, Brown University, 1999).

62. It embraced the Pentecostal or charismatic movement, including such denominations as the Church of the Nazarene and the Assemblies of God. Pentecostals believe in a "second blessing" of the Holy Spirit (after the first, conversion, or being born again in Jesus). This second blessing transforms the believer into a "spirit-filled Christian," often accompanied by the gift of faith healing or by speaking in tongues. Most other evangelical Christians, including the vast Southern Baptist Convention, reject the idea of the second blessing. They acknowledge the existence of such spiritual gifts among the early Christians in the New Testament, but see them as confined to the founding days of the faith and not applicable to the modern church.

63. Bumper sticker quoted in Balmer, *Mine Eyes Have Seen the Glory*, p. 13.

64. Boyer, *When Time Shall Be No More*, passim.

65. William D. Romanowski, "Where's the Gospel?" *Christianity Today*, December 8, 1997, pp. 44–46. Tim Stafford, "Has Christian Rock Lost Its Soul," *Christianity Today*, November 22, 1993, pp. 14–20.

66. Steve Rabey, "Pop Goes the Gospel," *Christianity Today*, May 15, 1995, p. 55.

67. Romanowski, "Where's the Gospel?" pp. 44–46. Patrick Connolly, "Amy Grant: Charting a New Course," *Saturday Evening Post* 263 (November–December 1991): 39ff. In 1982, Grant released *Age to Age*, the first million-selling gospel record. *Age to Age* featured explicitly Christian songs like "Sing Your Praise to the Lord." As Grant pursued crossover dreams, her subsequent albums broadened her appeal beyond the clientele of religious record shops to people who sought "wholesome Adult contemporary music in general." Balancing religious songs with tracks about love and everyday life, Grant developed a huge following. While some chastised Grant for selling out the CCM movement, others embraced her as "the Yuppie Christian." See Connolly, "Amy Grant: Charting a New Course."

68. Stafford, "Has Christian Rock Lost Its Soul," pp. 14–20. "God and Cookies and Rock 'n' Roll," *Economist*, May 8, 1993, p. 94.

69. Backman, "Christianity And/In Modern Literary Discourse." See also Hanna Rosin, "Books of Virtue," *New Republic*, November 24, 1997, pp. 12–14.

70. Backman, "Christianity And/In Modern Literary Discourse."

71. *Heartsong Presents: Guidelines for Authors* (Uhrichsville, Ohio: Barbour and Company, 1996), quoted in ibid. Over the course of the 1980s, more explicit sexuality became available in Christian romances (bodices were ripped) but always in association with Christian marriage.

72. Backman, "Christianity And/In Modern Literary Discourse." For pungent examples, see Sharon Gillenwater, *Texas Tender* (Sisters, Ore.: Pallisades-Questar, 1997), p. 45; and Colleen Reece, *A Torch for Trinity* (Uhrichsville, Ohio: Barbour, 1993), p. 12.

73. Hadden and Shupe, *Televangelism*. FitzGerald, *Cities on a Hill*. Jerry Falwell, *Strength for the Journey: An Autobiography* (New York: Simon & Schuster, 1987). Sean Wilentz, "God and Man at Lynchburg," *New Republic*, April 25, 1988, pp. 30–38.

74. Wade C. Roof and William McKinney, *American Mainline Religion* (New Brunswick, N.J.: Rutgers University Press, 1987), pp. 33–40. Hammond, *Religion and Personal Autonomy*, p. 10. Indeed, one scholar of church affiliation in contemporary American society discerned a "shift in the meaning of a church from that of a collective-expressive agency to that of an individual-expressive agency." Americans calculated church involvement, he concluded, by "individually derived equations," so that churches no longer played the role of "automatic social centers for neighborhoods and small towns." See Hammond, *Religion and Personal Autonomy*, pp. 169–171.

75. Richard Kyle, *The New Age Movement in American Culture* (Lanham, Md.: University Press of America, 1995), p. 147.

76. J. Gordon Melton, Jerome Clark, and Aidan A. Kelly, eds., *New Age Encyclopedia* (Detroit: Gale Research, 1990), pp. xxii–xxxviii, passim. Robert J. L. Burrows, "Americans Get Religion in the New Age," *Christianity Today*, May 16, 1986, p. 19. Important antecedents included the founding of Esalen Institute in 1962, the formation of the Integral Yoga Institute by Swami Satchidananda in 1966, the introduction of Shiatsu by Tokijiro Namikoshi in 1969, and the establishment in 1970 of the Guild for Structural Integration by Ida P. Rolf.

77. Leonard Nimoy, *You and I* (Millbrae, Calif.: Celestial Arts, 1983). Kyle, *New Age Movement in American Culture*, p. 151.

78. Matthew Fox, *Original Blessing: A Primer in Creation Spirituality Presented in Four Paths, Twenty-Six Themes, and Two Questions* (Santa Fe, N.M.: Bear and Co., 1983); Marilyn Ferguson, *The Aquarian Conspiracy* (Los Angeles: J. P. Tarcher, 1980); and David Spangler, *Emergence: The Rebirth of the Sacred* (New York: Dell, 1984). On Fox's dispute with the Vatican, see "Discipline and Silence for a 'New Age' Priest," *New York Times*, October 21, 1988, sec. 2, p. 2.

79. "Human Potential Hits 30," *U.S. News and World Report*, June 29, 1992, pp. 69–71. Personal accounts include Walter Truett Anderson, *The Upstart Spring: Esalen and the American Awakening* (Menlo Park, Calif.: Addison-Wesley, 1983); and Stuart Miller, *Hot Springs* (New York: Viking, 1971). *The New York Times* described Esalen as "a sort of cyclotron for gestalt and encounter therapy, where anthropologists, gurus and teachers of Eastern religion and brand-new instant-enlightenment programs helped to get a generation of Americans into the all-consuming process of self-actualization." See "Divine Reinvention," *New York Times*, March 2, 1995, pp. C1, C10.

80. Leo Litwack, "Pay Attention, Turkeys!" *New York Times Magazine*, May 2, 1976, p. 44. Lisa Schwarzbaum, "est! est! est!" *Mademoiselle* 81 (May 1975): p. 74. On Esalen's relations with Erhard, see Anderson, *Upstart Spring*, pp. 272–277.

81. Robert J. L. Burrows, "Americans Get Religion in the New Age," *Christianity Today*, May 16, 1986, p. 19. Richard P. Marsh, "I Am the Cause of My World," *Psychology Today* (August 1975): 82. Paul Boyer, "Erhard, from est to Worst," *Washington Post Book World*, December 9, 1993.

82. Werner Erhard, quoted in Litwack, "Pay Attention, Turkeys!" p. 44.

83. Marsh, "I Am the Cause of My World," p. 38. Litwack, "Pay Attention, Turkeys!" p. 44. On est's later transformation into a business management program called the Forum, see J. Yutaka Amano, "The Reincarnation of est," *Christianity Today*, May 16, 1986, p. 21.

84. Matthew Fox, "Spirituality for a New Era," in Duncan S. Ferguson, ed., *New Age Spirituality: An Assessment* (Louisville: Westminster/John Knox Press, 1993), pp. 196–198. Wade C. Roof, *A Generation of Seekers: The Spiritual Journeys of the Baby Boom Generation* (New York: HarperCollins, 1993), pp. 243–245. According to Roof, boomers invoked "creation spirituality,

Eucharistic spirituality, Native American spirituality, Eastern spiritualities, Twelve-Step spiritualities . . . Goddess spirituality and men's spirituality," as well as attempting to revive the mystical elements in their inherited religious traditions.

85. Carl Raschke, "The New Age: The Movement Toward Self-Discovery," in Ferguson, ed., *New Age Spirituality*, pp. 106–120.

86. Melton, Clark, and Kelly, *New Age Encyclopedia*, pp. xiii, xiv. After the initial intense transformation, most New Agers find their *sadhana;* they move onto their spiritual path. New Agers typically entered a period of continued "'seeking' within the New Age community and the sampling of various tools," or the adoption of a disciplined spiritual lifestyle. See J. Gordon Melton, "A History of the New Age Movement," in Robert Basil, ed., *Not Necessarily the New Age* (Buffalo, N.Y.: Prometheus, 1988), pp. 46–47.

87. Boyer, "Erhard, From est to Worst."

88. Melton, "History of the New Age Movement," p. 46.

89. Melton, Clark, and Kelly, *New Age Encyclopedia*, p. xxi. David Spangler, *Emergence: The Rebirth of the Sacred* (New York: Dell, 1984). On new age politics, see the entry in Melton, Clark, and Kelly, *New Age Encyclopedia*, p. 323.

90. Dave Hunt, *The New Age Movement in Prophecy*, quoted in Boyer, *When Time Shall Be No More*, pp. 231–232.

91. Sally Cunneen, "On Being Roman Catholic in '72," *Christian Century*, March 1, 1972, pp. 239–240. Carol McLennon, quoted in Roof, *A Generation of Seekers*, p. 230. The Roman Catholic church also witnessed growing involvement of the laity in church affairs. See "Special Report: Religion," *U.S. News and World Report*, April 4, 1983, pp. 38–42.

92. Robert N. Bellah et al., *Habits of the Heart* (Berkeley: University of California Press, 1985), pp. 220–221. Wertheimer, *A People Divided*, p. 45.

4. The Rise of the Sunbelt and the "Reddening" of America

1. "The good ol' fellow," one Mississippian explained to novelist V. S. Naipaul when he asked for an explanation of poor white southern culture, "he's just going to work six or eight months a year. He's going to tell his old lady, 'I'm going to work.' And he ain't going. If it rains . . . he's going to the crummiest dump he can find, and he's going to start drinking beer and shooting pool." V. S. Naipaul, *A Turn in the South* (New York: Knopf, 1989), pp. 203–212.

2. Southern Growth Policies Board, *The Report of the 1986 Commission on the Future of the South* (Chapel Hill, N.C.: 1986), p. 7.

3. Soon after, Los Angeles–based pop parodist Warren Zevon piled dirt on the grave, mocking Skynyrd and the way of life it had celebrated in his song "Play It All Night 'Long.'" "Daddy's doing sister Sally, Grandma's dying of cancer now," Zevon crooned, extracting every drop of sarcasm from his burlesque portrait of redneck culture. "The cattle all have brucellosis, we'll get through somehow." And then, with his session guitarists mimicking Skynyrd's distinctive sound, Zevon delivered his cruelly funny chorus: "'Sweet Home Alabama,' play that dead band's song. Turn the speakers up full blast, play it all night long."

4. William Gildea, "The Great Promotion," *Washington Post*, July 10, 1974, p. B2.

5. "The Great Rip-Off," *Nation*, September 28, 1992.

6. George F. Will, "Death as a Spectator Sport," *Washington Post*, August 27, 1974, p. A19.

7. "The Gathered Tribes," *Time*, September 23, 1974, pp. 64–65.

8. Naipaul, *A Turn in the South*, p. 203.

9. "The Gathered Tribes."

10. Doug Marlette, *Faux Bubba* (New York: Times Books, 1993).

11. "The Second War Between the States," *Business Week*, May 17, 1976. *New York Times*, February 8–11, 1976. Quotation from Jon Nordheimer, "Sunbelt Region Leads Nation in Growth of Population," *New York Times*, February 8, 1976, p. 1.

12. "The Northeast Vows That It Will Rise Again," *New York Times*, January 9, 1977, sec. 3, p. 41. Hugh L. Carey, "Pulling Together," *New York Times*, February 14, 1977, p. 27.

13. Richard S. Morris, "Regional Robbery," *Village Voice*, October 11, 1976, pp. 22–25. Neal R. Peirce, "The Northeast Campaign," *Washington Post*, December 22, 1976, p. A19. Paul Delaney, "More Federal Funds Sought by 14 States," *New York Times*, October 22, 1976, p. 1. Warren Brown, "Federal Expenditures Flowing to South and West," *Washington Post*, August 22, 1976, pp. G1, G4. "In Northeast: A Challenge to the Growing Muscle of the Sunbelt," *US News and World Report*, October 18, 1975, p. 65.

14. "Transcript of President-Elect Carter's News Conference," *New York Times*, December 15, 1976, p. B12. Lloyd Bentsen, "On the Sunbelt-Snowbelt Controversy," *New York Times*, June 10, 1977, p. 27. B. Drummond Ayers, "South's Governors Fear the Region May Lose Out on Aid and Energy," *New York Times*, August 31, 1977. *Birmingham News*, editorial, reprinted as "Feelin' Gray," *New York Times*, November 30, 1976, p. 39.

15. Garry Wills, "God So Loves Spiro Agnew," *Esquire* (February 1969).

16. William S. Kowinski, *The Malling of America* (New York: Morrow, 1985), pp. 245, 259. On Houston's rise, see James P. Sterba, "Houston, as Energy Capital, Sets Pace in Sunbelt," *New York Times*, February 9, 1976, p. 1.

17. *San Diego Union*, September 13, 1981.

18. U.S. National Emergency Council, *Report on Economic Conditions of the South* (Washington, D.C.: Government Printing Office, 1938).

19. Gurney Breckenfeld, "Business Loves the Sunbelt (and Vice Versa)," *Fortune* (June 1977): 133.

20. For a discussion of southern efforts at industrial promotion, see James C. Cobb, *The Selling of the South* (Baton Rouge: Louisiana State University Press, 1982).

21. Kirkpatrick Sale, *Power Shift* (New York: Vintage, 1975).

22. For a detailed analysis of the federal government's role in southern regional development, see Bruce J. Schulman, *From Cotton Belt to Sunbelt* (New York: Oxford University Press, 1991).

23. William Faulkner, "On Fear," in James Meriwether, ed., *Essays, Speeches, and Public Letters by William Faulkner* (New York: 1965), p. 98.

24. Marshall Frady, "The Sweetest Finger This Side of Midas," *Life*, February 27, 1970, pp. 50–57. Not surprisingly, defense spending became the focus of Frostbelt grievances in the 1970s. See *Los Angeles Times*, September 27, 1977, p. 1.

25. When Kevin Phillips first laid out this model of Sunbelt-based, radical conservatism in 1969, the voices of northeastern conservatism were among those who mocked it. New

York–based *National Review,* the conservative magazine edited by William F. Buckley, Jr., entitled its critique of Phillips "To the Nashville Station," jokingly comparing Phillips's manifesto of proletarian conservatism to Lenin's vision of proletarian revolution.

26. Melton A. McLaurin, "Songs of the South," in Melton McLaurin and Richard A. Peterson, eds., *You Wrote My Life* (Philadelphia: Gordon and Breach, 1992), pp. 15–34.

27. McLaurin and Peterson, eds., *You Wrote My Life.* See also Dorothy Horstman, *Sing Your Heart Out, Country Boy* (Nashville: Country Music Foundation, 1986); and Bill C. Malone, *Country Music, U.S.A.* (Austin: 1985).

28. In 1992, *Billboard* replaced the telephone survey with a tabulation of sales receipts based on computer bar codes. Almost immediately, country performers soared up the pop charts. Garth Brooks scored a number one national hit and soon hosted his own network television special. Hollywood quickly recognized the audience for country and produced *Pure County,* a full-length feature, starring Nashville recording artist George Strait. Many experts concluded that country had long commanded such an audience; *Billboard,* with its big city biases, had simply missed it. In recent years, the country music business has boomed, its revenues almost quadrupling since the mid-1980s. Country stars like Vince Gill and Garth Brooks have become America's heart-throbs, shocking industry veterans with their wholesomeness and popularity. "They're in their thirties," one industry executive wondered. "They all have their teeth, they don't all wear pigtails, and the boys wear shoes. They all don't have a plug of tobacco in their cheek. You know, that was the impression the world had of country music. Hillbillies!" By 1996, Garth Brooks trailed only the Beatles as the all-time leader in U.S. record sales. According to *New York Times* reporter Peter Applebome, Brooks brought "a whole new level of marketing savvy and stagecraft to country music, along with an unerring instinct for the gut of a nation that has become a whole lot more like Tulsa or Oklahoma City than Boston or New York." See Applebome, *Dixie Rising* (New York: Times Books, 1996), pp. 241, 259.

29. Ben Marsh, "A Rose Colored Map," *Harper's* (July 1977). In the case of *redneck,* the country anthems of the 1970s transformed what had originally been a more positive term, indicating a person who worked out in the sun all day, and later became a synonym for an intolerant, violent bigot.

30. "I Believe the South Is Gonna Rise Again" (written by Bobby Braddock, recorded by Tanya Tucker, Sony Music Entertainment, 1974). "A brand new breeze is blowin' across the Southland," the song hopefully concluded, sounding a theme of racial concord unheard in other examples of the genre, "and I see a brand new kind of brotherhood."

31. The term "Reddening of America" was introduced by Roger Shattuck in his review of Naipaul's *Turn in the South.* See Shattuck, "The Reddening of America," *New York Review of Books,* March 30, 1989, pp. 3–6. It deliberately echoes *The Greening of America,* a 1970 book that suggested that the Sixties counterculture has ushered in a new form of conciousness. Charles A. Reich, *The Greening of America* (N.Y.: Random House, 1970).

5. Jimmy Carter and the Crisis of Confidence

1. "America's Mood: Hopeful—Sort Of," *Time,* January 24, 1976. John Updike, *Rabbit Is Rich* (New York: Knopf, 1981), p. 3. The novel is set during the 1979 oil boycott.

2. Paul Jensen to Stuart Eizenstat et al., memo, n.d., DPS-Special Projects, Stern, Declining Regions Folder, Box 2, Jimmy Carter Library (hereafter JCL). "Playboy Interview: Jimmy Carter," *Playboy* (November 1976): 66.

3. "America's Mood: Hopeful—Sort Of," p. 8.

4. Robert Scheer, "Jimmy, We Hardly Know Y'all," *Playboy* (November 1976): 91. For an analysis of Carter's religious beliefs, see John Dumbrell, *The Carter Presidency* (Manchester: Manchester University Press, 1993), pp. 19–20, and N. C. Nielsen, *The Religion of President Carter* (London: Mowbrays, 1977).

5. "Playboy Interview," pp. 63–86. Scheer, "Jimmy, We Hardly Know Y'all," p. 91.

6. Interview with Gerald Rafshoon, Miller Center interview, Carter Presidency Project, vol. 21, April 8, 1983, JCL, p. 28. Erwin C. Hargrove, *Jimmy Carter as President* (Baton Rouge: Louisiana State University Press, 1988), p. 24.

7. Ibid. See also Burton I. Kaufman, *The Presidency of James Earl Carter, Jr.* (Lawrence: University Press of Kansas, 1993), p. 31.

8. Charles Schulze, Miller Center interview, vol. 11, January 8–9, 1982, JCL, p. 3. "Playboy Interview," p. 64.

9. Schulze interview, p. 3. According to Schulze, this engineering outlook allowed Carter to master the technical complexities of policy issues that a more ideologically oriented president would not have troubled with. "If I scratch Ronald Reagan," Schulze mused soon after leaving the White House. "I know which way his knees are going to jerk. If I submit a list of a hundred questions to him, I can forecast 99 of the answers. The same thing would have been true with Hubert Humphrey." Carter often surprised him.

10. Rafshoon interview, p. 22. Gary Fink and Hugh Davis Graham, eds., *The Carter Presidency: Policy Choices in the Post–New Deal Era* (Lawrence: University Press of Kansas, 1998). See especially the chapters by Thomas Sugrue on urban policy, James Patterson on welfare reform, and John Barrow on energy. See also Hargrove, *Carter as President*, p. 11.

11. Hargrove, *Carter as President*, pp. 16, 34–43. John C. Barrow, "An Age of Limits: Jimmy Carter and the Quest for a National Energy Policy," in Fink and Graham, *Carter Presidency*, pp. 158–178. Carter was also uncomfortable with many Democratic interests like labor, the Black Caucus, and environmentalists. See Hargrove, *Carter as President*, p. 79, and Kaufman, *Presidency*, p. 111.

12. James Fallows to Jody Powell, memo, December 28, 1977, Staff Offices–Speechwriters, Chronological File, Box 12, JCL.

13. *Public Papers of the Presidents, Jimmy Carter, 1977* (Washington, D.C.: GPO, 1978), bk. 1, p. 2. On Carter as Reagan's precursor, see Bruce J. Schulman, "Slouching Toward the Supply Side: Jimmy Carter and the New American Political Economy," in Fink and Graham, *Carter Presidency*, pp. 51–71. Steven M. Gillon, biographer of Carter's vice president, Walter F. Mondale, got Carter's relationship to New Deal liberalism precisely right. Like the old-line liberal Mondale, Carter possessed a populist disdain for wealth and affection for the common man; but he defined the common man not as a struggling, blue-collar union member on the shop floor, but as a rural, Protestant, politically independent, financially secure fiscal conservative. See Gillon, *The Democrats' Dilemma* (New York: Columbia University Press, 1992), p. 171.

14. James McIntyre (including Hubert Harris, Van Ooms), Miller Center interview, vol. 5, October 28, 29, 1981, JCL, pp. 3–4. Stuart Eizenstat, exit interview, JCL, Jan. 10, 1981, pp. 20, passim.

15. Eizenstat to President (with attached message to Congress), memo, February 22, 1997, Aviation-Airline Regulatory Reform (1) Folder, DPS-Eizenstat, Box 148, JCL. Stuart Eizenstat to the President, memo, October 24, 1978, Aviation-Airline Regulatory Reform (2) Folder, DPS-

Eizenstat, Box 148, JCL. McIntyre, Miller Center interview, pp. 3–4. Eizenstat, exit interview, pp. 20, passim. Alfred Kahn, exit interview, JCL, Oct. 21 and Nov. 14, 1980, tape 1, side 1.

16. Executive Action Summary, December 8, 1976, DPS-Eizenstat, Pardon Folder, Box 252, JCL. Jimmy Carter, Message to Congress, January 31, 1977, Economic Stimulus Package—Final Message to Congress Folder [CF, 0/A 27], Box 192, JCL.

17. Cardigan speech, February 2, 1997. Barrow, "Age of Limits."

18. Thomas P. O'Neill, Jr., quoted in *Energy Policy*, 2nd ed. (Washington, D.C.: Congressional Quarterly, 1981), p. 2. For a discussion of energy policy under Nixon and Ford, see Barrow, "Age of Limits."

19. "Back on a Dangerous Binge," *Time*, August 30, 1976, pp. 65–66.

20. "Convoy" (MGM Records, 1976). Liner notes, *Super Hits of the 70s*, Vol. 15 (Rhino Records, Los Angeles, 1990).

21. Barrow, "Age of Limits." John Barrow, "Circumventing the Establishment" (paper presented at the Conference on the Carter Presidency, Jimmy Carter Library, Atlanta, Georgia, February 1997). "Energy Squeeze Coming for All Americans," *U.S. News and World Report*, April 11, 1977, p. 26.

22. Barrow, "Age of Limits" and "Circumventing the Establishment." "Energy: Where Intervention Is Inevitable," *Business Week*, April 4, 1977, pp. 80–81.

23. *Public Papers, Carter, 1977*, bk. 1, pp. 656–663. Barrow, "Age of Limits," and "Circumventing the Establishment." "Energy: Where Intervention Is Inevitable," pp. 80–81.

24. "What Price Energy?" *Newsweek*, May 2, 1977, p. 12.

25. Barrow, "Age of Limits." Eventually, later in his term, Carter would get parts of a much more modest, piecemeal energy policy, but only after consulting in advance with various constituencies and congressional leaders.

26. "Energy: Will Americans Pay the Price?" *U.S. News and World Report*, May 2, 1977, pp. 13–17. Jimmy Carter, *Keeping Faith* (New York: Bantam, 1976), pp. 93–96. Barrow, "Circumventing the Establishment."

27. Jeffrey K. Stine, "Environmental Policy During the Carter Presidency," in Fink and Graham, *Carter Presidency*, pp. 179–201. On environmental policy under Nixon, see John C. Whitaker, *Striking a Balance* (Washington, D.C.: AEI, 1976); and Russell E. Train, "The Environmental Record of the Nixon Administration," *Presidential Studies Quarterly 26* (Winter 1996): 185–196. In May 1977, Carter laid out a broad-based environmental agenda. See "The Environment: Message to Congress, May 23, 1977," in *Public Papers, Carter, 1977*, bk. 1, pp. 967–986.

28. Steven D. Jellinek to Bert Lance, February 2, 1977, NR 7-1, 1/20/77–3/15/77 folder, Box NR-14, WHCF, JCL. Stine, "Environmental Policy During the Carter Presidency."

29. More savvy members of Carter's administration approved water project reform in theory but were more circumspect about its practicability. "Many of these projects are of dubious merit and should be stopped or curtailed at this point," Interior Secretary Cecil Andrus agreed, "if political problems can be overcome." But those obstacles were intractable. "I am not arguing against eliminating some of these projects—some definitely merit action—but I want you to know that there will be political retaliation from the Congress when we do." Cecil D. Andrus to President, memo, February 14, 1977, NR 7-1, 1/20/77–3/15/77 folder, Box NR-14, WHCF, JCL. Stine, "Environmental Policy During the Carter Presidency."

30. Samuel P. Hays, *Beauty, Health, and Permanence* (New York: Cambridge University Press, 1987), p. 113. Stine, "Environmental Policy During the Carter Presidency."

31. For the Carter administration's understanding of prevailing economic conditions in the 1970s, see Stuart Eizenstat, "A Non-Economist's Look at Economic Policy for the 1980s," speech, May 10, 1980, Box 5, James McIntyre Papers, JCL.

32. Charles Schulze, "Has the Phillips Curve Shifted? Some Additional Evidence," *Brookings Papers on Economic Activity* (1971): 452–467.

33. Eizenstat, Miller Center interviews, JCL, pp. 101–102.

34. Harrison Wellford to James McIntyre, memo, March 20, 1978, Domestic Policy Staff Files—Eizenstat (hereafter DPS-Eizenstat), Box 144, JCL. Frank Moore to Les Francis, memo, March 20, 1978, DPS-Eizenstat, Box 144. David P. Calleo, *The Imperious Economy* (Cambridge: Harvard University Press, 1982), p. 143.

35. Ann Mari May, "Fiscal Policy, Monetary Policy, and the Carter Presidency," *Presidential Studies Quarterly* 23 (Fall 1993): 700. Calleo, *Imperious Economy,* p. 139.

36. Charles Schulze, testimony before the House Budget Committee, January 27, 1977, DPS-Eizenstat, Box 192, JCL. May, "Fiscal Policy," pp. 706–707. Hargrove, *Carter as President,* pp. 88–89.

37. Charles Schulze to EPG, memo, January 24, 1977, DPS-Eizenstat, Box 192. Gene Godley to Michael Blumenthal, memo, February 18, 1977, DPS-Eizenstat, Box 192. Hargrove, *Carter as President,* pp. 81–83. Kaufman, *Presidency of Carter,* pp. 28–31. McIntyre, Miller Center interview, pp. 18, passim.

38. "Summary and Outline of First-Year Domestic Accomplishments, n.a., December 17, 1977, McIntyre Papers, Box 7, JCL. James Fallows to Jimmy Carter, memo, October 31, 1977. Remarks at signing ceremony for minimum wage bill, Jimmy Carter, November 1, 1977. Both in Staff Offices Files, Speechwriters Office—Chronological File, Box 11, JCL. Signing statement draft, January 19, 1978, Staff Offices Files, Speechwriters Office—Chronological File, Box 17, JCL. McIntyre, Miller Center interview, pp. 4, 48–49.

39. Remarks of the president at ceremony honoring Senator Hubert H. Humphrey, Washington Hilton Hotel, December 2, 1977, JCL. On problems with congressional leaders, see Frank Moore to the President, memo, July 20, 1977, Jordan—Chief of Staff, Congress/President Folder, Box 34, JCL.

40. Theodore H. White, *America in Search of Itself* (New York: Harper and Row, 1982).

41. Alfred Kahn to EPG Steering Committee, memo, May 17, 1979, DPS-Eizenstat, Box 146, JCL. Joseph Nocera, *A Piece of the Action* (New York: Simon & Schuster, 1994).

42. Sidney Weintraub, "Carter's Hoover Syndrome," *New Leader,* March 24, 1980. Seymour Melman, "Jimmy Hoover?" *New York Times,* February 7, 1979.

43. For a detailed analysis of Carter's economic policy, see Bruce J. Schulman, "Slouching Toward the Supply Side: Jimmy Carter and the New American Political Economy," in Fink and Graham, *Carter Presidency,* pp. 51–71.

44. Esther Peterson to Robert Strauss, memo, June 1, 1978, DPS-Eizenstat, Box 144. Strauss to Eizenstat, memo, September 6, 1978, DPS-Eizenstat, Box 143. Briefing materials, June 1978, DPS-Eizenstat, Box 143. Ginsburg to Eizenstat, memo, July 31, 1978, DPS-Eizenstat, Box 143.

Jimmy Carter to the American Society of Newspaper Editors, address April 11, 1978, DPS-Eizenstat, Box 144. Stuart Eizenstat, exit interview, address, pp. 17–18. McIntyre, Miller Center interview, p. 6.

45. Jerry Rafshoon to the President, memo, September 1, 1978, DPS-Eizenstat, Box 145. Kaufman, *Presidency of Carter*, p. 101.

46. Nearly two months of internal debate and negotiations ensued. The administration also undertook a program of briefings and outreach on the inflation package with congressional leaders, agency heads, and key interest groups. Schulze to the President, memo, September 24, 1978. Schulze to the President, memo, October 5, 1978. Califano to the President, memo, September 18, 1978. McIntyre to the President, memo, n.d. Stern to Eizenstat, September 8, 1978. All in DPS-Eizenstat, Box 145. See also Briefing/Outreach Materials collected in Anti-Inflation 9/78 [2] Folder, DPS-Eizenstat, Box 145.

47. Fact Sheet on Anti-Inflation Program, October 24, 1978. Jimmy Carter, speech, October 24, 1978. Rafshoon, memo for distribution, October 23, 1978. All in DPS-Eizenstat, Box 145.

48. Jimmy Carter, presidential statement, November 11, 1978, DPS-Eizenstat, Box 144. Hargrove, *Carter as President*, 100. Garland A. Haas, *Jimmy Carter and the Politics of Frustration* (Jefferson, N.C.: McFarland, 1992), p. 72.

49. Kahn, exit interview, tape 1, side 1. The position of inflation czar, Kahn reflected, offered only an "unmanageable, amorphous, social, economic, political, inspirational task" with insufficient authority. But the president's request was "irresistible. "I knew," Kahn concluded with his wonderful combination of bravado and self-deprecation, "that I was taking on something that probably any God could do."

50. James Reston, "The New Aga Kahn," *New York Times*, April 13, 1979. See also Nocera, *Piece of the Action*, p. 173.

51. Warren Zevon, "Mohammed's Radio" (Zevon Music, 1976). Altered live version performed at the Roxy, Hollywood, California, released on *Stand in the Fire* (Asylum Records, 1980).

52. Frank Moore to Les Francis, memo, March 20, 1978. Harrison Wellford to James McIntyre, memo, March 20, 1978. Both in DPS-Eizenstat, Box 144, JCL. Orin Kramer to Eizenstat, memo, December 4, 1978, DPS-Eizenstat, Box 143. William D. Nordhaus to Schulze, memo, November 27, 1978. "Report on Reforming Social Regulation," n.d. Department of Treasury to EPG Steering Committee, memo, November 27, 1978. Bill Johnson to Eizenstat, memo, November 29, 1978. Don Haider to Roger Altman, memo, December 15, 1978. Curt Hessler to EPG Steering Committee, memo, November 20, 1978. Above six documents in DPS-Eizenstat, Box 191. Robert S. Greenberger, "Odd Man Out," *Wall Street Journal*, January 10, 1980, 1, 36.

53. Schulman, "Slouching Toward the Supply Side." (Al)Fred Kahn to the President, memo, April 25, 1979, DPS-Eizenstat, Box 143. Kahn to the President, memo, January 24, 1979, and Ralph Schlosstein to Eizenstat, memo, January 4, 1979, both in DPS-Eizenstat, Box 229. Minutes of June 28, 1979, Meeting of Inflation Working Group, DPS-Eizenstat, p. 191. Kahn, exit interview. Greenberger, "Odd Man Out," pp. 1, 36. Regulatory Review Grade Sheets, McIntyre Papers, Box 1.

54. On Volcker and the Federal Reserve, see below.

55. Cambridge Survey Research to DNC, memo, February 1979. Cambridge Survey Research to DNC, memo May 25, 1979, and, Patrick Caddell to Jimmy Carter, memo, June 11, 1979. All in Chief of Staff—Jordan, Box 33, JCL.

56. White, *America in Search of Itself*, pp. 137–64. Nocera, *Piece of the Action*, passim.

57. Nocera, *Piece of the Action*.

58. Nocera, *Piece of the Action*, pp. 190–191.

59. Ibid., pp. 191–192.

60. Christopher Rupkey, "The Have It All Now Generation," *New York Times*, May 13, 1979, quoted in Nocera, *Piece of the Action*, pp. 192–193.

61. Nocera, *Piece of the Action*, pp. 74–85.

62. Ibid., pp. 83–87.

63. Richard Phalon, "Ned Johnson of FMR: Watch Your Flank, Merrill Lynch," Forbes, October 26, 1981, pp. 158–162. Michael VerMeulen, "The Son Also Rises," *Institutional Investor* (February 1986): 136–144.

64. Johnson, quoted in Phalon, "Ned Johnson of FMR," p. 159. Nocera, *Piece of the Action*, p. 86.

65. VerMeulen, "The Son Also Rises." Phalon, "Ned Johnson of FMR."

66. Nocera, *Piece of the Action*, p. 87.

67. Ibid., pp. 197, 219–225.

68. On reform of the exchanges, see Chris Welles, *The Last Days of the Club* (New York: Dutton, 1975). On the rapid success of Schwab and other discount brokerages, see "Brokers No Longer Ignore Discounters," *New York Times*, March 4, 1979, sec. 3, p. 1.

69. "Once-Tiny Discount Brokerage Leaps to Top, Propelled by End of Fixed Fees," *Los Angeles Times*, November 25, 1979. On the rapid success of Schwab and other discount brokerages, see "Brokers No Longer Ignore Discounters," *New York Times*, March 4, 1979, Sec. 3, p. 1.

70. Martin Mayer, "Merrill Lynch Quacks Like a Bank," *Fortune*, October 20, 1980, pp. 135–143.

71. Mayer, "Merrill Lynch Quacks Like a Bank." See also Carol J. Loomis, "The Merrill Lynch Bull Is Loose on Wall Street," *Fortune* (May 1972): 174–178, 302–322; Lee Smith, "Merrill Lynch's Latest Bombshell for Bankers," *Fortune*, April 19, 1982, pp. 67–69; and Nocera, *Piece of the Action*, pp. 149–166.

72. Mayer, "Merrill Lynch Quacks Like a Bank"; Loomis, "The Merrill Lynch Bull Is Loose"; Smith, "Merrill Lynch's Latest Bombshell for Bankers," pp. 67–69.

73. White, *America in Search of Itself*, pp. 153–159.

74. Michael Harrington, quoted in Roberta Brandes Gratz, *The Living City* (New York: Touchstone, 1989), pp. 85–86.

75. "Next: Challenges at Home," *Time*, April 2, 1979, p. 14.

76. "Energy and National Goals: Address to the Nation, July 15, 1979," in *Public Papers of the Presidents: Jimmy Carter, 1979* (Washington, D.C.: GPO, 1980), bk. 2, pp. 1235–1241.

77. Ibid.

78. Ibid.

79. Charles D. Ravenal to Eizenstat, memo, February 26, 1980, DPS-Eizenstat, Box 143, JCL. Address on Economic Policy, Jimmy Carter, March 14, 1980, DPS-Eizenstat, Box 192. For a detailed discussion, see Schulman, "Slouching Toward the Supply Side."

80. Hargrove, *Carter as President*, pp. 104–105. May, "Fiscal Policy," 701.

81. *New York Times*, October 29, 1980, p. A29.

6. "This Ain't No Foolin' Around"

1. Mark Salzman, *Lost in Place: Growing Up Absurd in Suburbia* (New York: Random House, 1995), p. 161. For analyses of Seventies nostalgia in the contemporary United States, see "The Decade That Won't Go Away," *New York Times*, October 12, 1997, Sec. 9, pp. 1–3; "Boogeying on Back to '70s," *Los Angeles Times*, April 26, 1991, pp. E-1, E-10; "The 70's (Stayin' Alive) Won't Die," *New York Times*, November 13, 1991, pp. B1–B5. For ten years, I have conducted such informal surveys in my courses at UCLA and Boston University. Asked to identify one person who embodies each of these recent decades, contemporary college students answer JFK, Martin Luther King, or Bob Dylan for the Sixties; and Ronald Reagan, Madonna, or Michael Milken for the Eighties. But for the seventies, the same person is proffered every time: John Travolta.

2. Norman Mailer, "Mailer on the '70s—Decade of 'Image, Skin Flicks, and Porn,'" *U.S. News and World Report*, December 10, 1979, p. 57.

3. On the Us Festival, see *New York Times*, September 6, 1982, p. 11. See also ibid., September 4, 1982, p. 12.

4. James Wolcott, "A Time to Boogie," *New Yorker*, January 10, 1994, p. 74.

5. Ibid.

6. Paul Cowan, review of *Blood on the Tracks*, *The Village Voice*, February 3, 1975, quoted in Robert Shelton, *No Direction Home: The Life and Music of Bob Dylan* (New York: Ballantine, 1986), p. 514.

7. Bob Dylan, *Lyrics, 1962–1985* (New York: Knopf, 1985). For analyses of Dylan's career, see also Alan Rinzler, *Bob Dylan: The Illustrated Record* (New York: Harmony Books, 1978); Robert Shelton, *No Direction Home* (New York: Ballantine, 1986); and Bob Spitz, *Dylan: A Biography*, (New York: McGraw-Hill, 1989).

8. Dylan, *Lyrics, 1962–1985*, pp. 375–377. Rinzler, *Dylan*, p. 103.

9. Lee Keyser, *Hollywood in the Seventies* (New York: A. S. Barnes and Co., 1981), p. 1.

10. Pauline Kael, interviewed on National Public Radio/Weekend Edition, March 9, 1991. See also Diane Jacobs, *Hollywood Renaissance*, (New York: Dell, 1980), and Keyser, *Hollywood in the Seventies*.

11. Bob Dylan, quoted in Shelton, *No Direction Home*, p. 516.

12. The best sources on the blockbuster phenomenon are Keyser, *Hollywood in the Seventies*: Ronald L. Davis, *Celluloid Mirrors* (Fort Worth, Tex.: Harcourt Brace, 1997), and Robert Sklar, *Movie-Made America* (New York: Vintage, 1994). A similar emphasis on blockbusters emerged in book publishing. For a critical commentary on the phenomenon, see Mailer, "Mailer on the '70s," p. 58.

13. Sklar, *Movie-Made America*, p. 325. In the light of *Jaws*, Sklar concluded, directors' cinema was clearly defined "as a cinema of niches—of small, defined spaces within the advertising matrix." On the film industry in the 1970s, see also David J. Londoner, "The Changing Eco-

nomics of Entertainment," in Tina Balio, ed., *The American Film Industry*, rev. ed. (Madison: University of Wisconsin Press, 1985); Keyser, *Hollywood in the Seventies;* and John Izod, *Hollywood and the Box Office, 1895–1986* (New York: Columbia University Press, 1988).

14. Sklar, *Movie-Made America*, p. 373.

15. On the recording industry in the 1970s, see David Szatmary, *Rockin' in Time* (Englewood Cliffs, N.J.: Prentice Hall, 1991), pp. 214–224; Ed Ward, Geoffrey Stokes, and Ken Tucker, *Rock of Ages*, (New York: Rolling Stone Press, 1986), pp. 468–469, passim; Nelson George, *The Death of Rhythm and Blues* (New York: Pantheon, 1979), pp. 121–146; and Greil Marcus, *Lipstick Traces*, (Cambridge: Harvard University Press, 1989), pp. 41–51.

16. Armed with a special report by the Harvard Business School, CBS moved into African American music in the 1970s. By the end of the decade, large corporations dominated the field. Black record companies either folded (like Stax Records in 1976) or made deals with the big players (like Philadelphia International Records with CBS). See George, *Death of Rhythm and Blues*, pp. 135–146. For a variety of sophisticated analyses of the music industry in the era, see Tony Bennett et al., eds., *Rock and Popular Music: Politics, Policies, Institutions* (New York: Routledge, 1993).

17. Marcus, *Lipstick Traces*, pp. 47–48. George, *Death of Rhythm and Blues*, pp. 121–146.

18. Lester Bangs, "Growing Up True Is Hard to Do," *Village Voice*, June 5, 1978, reprinted in Lester Bangs, *Psychotic Reactions and Carburetor Dung* (New York: Vintage, 1987), p. 270.

19. Both British and American punk shared roots in the late 1960s and early 1970s New York art rock scene. The Velvet Underground and the New York Dolls proved influential on both sides of the Atlantic. See Clinton Heylin, *From the Velvets to the Voidoids* (New York: Penguin, 1993); Szatmary, *Rockin' in Time;* Tricia Henry, *Break All Rules!* (Ann Arbor: UMI Research Press, 1989); and Bangs, *Psychotic Reactions and Carburetor Dung,*

20. Heylin, *From the Velvets to the Voidoids*, pp. 252–253.

21. Marcus, *Lipstick Traces*, p. 81. Bangs, "Growing Up True Is Hard to Do," p. 271.

22. Richard Hell, quoted in Szatmary, *Rockin' in Time*, pp. 228–229.

23. Ward, Stokes, and Tucker, *Rock of Ages*, p. 547.

24. Eddie "Legs" McNeil, quoted in Ira Robbins, "Strolling Down Punk-Rock Lane," *New York Times*, July 7, 1996, pp. 23–24.

25. Marcus, *Lipstick Traces*, pp. 41, 80. On the ferment and surprises of rhythm and blues in the 1950s, see Peter Guralnick, *Sweet Soul Music* (New York: Harper, 1986).

26. Chris Frantz, quoted in Heylin, *From the Velvets to the Voidoids*, p. 210.

27. John Rockwell, "Epiphanies in a Dive," *New York Times*, December 19, 1993, p. V7. Henry, *Break All Rules!* pp. 51–53. Szatmary, *Rockin' in Time*, p. 226.

28. Paul Rudnick and Kurt Andersen, "The Irony Epidemic," *Spy* (March 1989): 93–99.

29. *The Modern Lovers* (Beserkley Records, 1976). On Richman's early career and the underground reputation of the Modern Lovers, see Marcus, *Lipstick Traces*, pp. 60–63, and Parke Puterbaugh, liner notes to *The Best of Jonathan Richman and the Modern Lovers: The Beserkley Years* (Rhino Records, 1986).

30. "Monologue About Bermuda" (written and performed by Jonathan Richman, on *Havin' a Party with Jonathan Richman*, Rounder Records, 1991).

31. Ibid.

32. "Marie Provost" (written and performed by Nick Lowe, *Pure Pop for the Now People*, 1986).

33. Marcus, *Lipstick Traces*, p. 60. Jefferson Morley, "twentysomething," *City Paper* (Washington, D.C.), February 19, 1988, p. 18. Puterbaugh, liner notes to *The Best of Jonathan Richman and the Modern Lovers*.

34. Morley, "twentysomething," p. 18.

7. Battles of the Sexes

1. Bud Collins, "Billie Jean King Evens the Score," *Ms.* (July 1973): 43, 101.

2. WTBS Television Retrospective, *Idols of the Game*, Part II, 1995.

3. *Boston Globe*, September 20, 1973, pp. 1, 25.

4. Ibid., p. 1.

5. "The Tennis Battle of the Sexes," *Wide World of Sports*, ABC Television, September 20, 1973. I thank Peter Alegi for his transcripts of the broadcast.

6. Ibid.

7. *Boston Globe*, September 21, 1973, p. 11.

8. Susan J. Douglas, *Where the Girls Are* (New York: Times Books, 1994), p. 259.

9. Virginia Valian, *Why So Slow? The Advancement of Women* (Cambridge: MIT Press, 1998), pp. 210–211. U.S. Census Bureau, *Statistical Abstract of the United States, 1999* (Washington, D.C.: GPO, 1999), p. 272.

10. Ibid.

11. In 1978, the labor force participation rate for women crossed 50 percent; for women ages twenty-five to fifty-four, it rose from 50 percent in 1970 to 68 percent in 1984. See U.S. Bureau of Labor Statistics, "Trends in Labor Force Participation of Major Population Groups, 1965–92," *Monthly Labor Review* (July 1993): 11. Family size also diminished, from an average of 2.29 children per family in 1970 to 1.85 in the mid-1980s. Consult U.S. Bureau of the Census, http://www.census.gov/population/socdemo/hh-fam/htabFM-3.txt (Internet release date, December 11, 1988.

The number of female architects quadrupled, doubling their share of the total. Women leaped from 5 percent of lawyers to 14 percent, from 6 percent of judges to 17 percent. During the 1960s only 3 percent of the new lawyers admitted to the bar had been women. By the time of Reagan's reelection in 1984, women made up 36 percent of new attorneys. Hospitals, offices, and faculty lounges also opened to female professionals. Thirty thousand new women physicians began practicing during the Seventies, doubling the ranks of female doctors. In 1980, women accounted for more than 30 percent of the people the Census Bureau listed as "executives, administrative and managerial," as opposed to just 18 percent a decade earlier. See U.S. Census Bureau, *Statistical Abstract of the United States, 1985* (Washington, D.C.: U.S. GPO,), p. 400. By 1983, the changes were even more dramatic. See U.S. Census Bureau, *Statistical Abstract of the United States, 1993* (Washington, D.C.: GPO,), pp. 405–407; and Valian, *Why So Slow?* p. 199. Still, progress to real positions of authority in American business remained painfully slow. Consult Valian, *Why So Slow?* pp. 191–196.

12. Boston Women's Health Book Collective, *Our Bodies, Ourselves: A Book by and for Women* (New York: Simon & Schuster, 1971), p. 85.

13. "What's a Ms.?" *Ms.* (Spring 1972): 4.

14. Cynthia Ozick, "We Are the Crazy Lady and Other Feisty Feminist Fables," *Ms.* (Spring 1972): 40–44.

15. Pamela Allen (Member of Sudsofloppen), "Free Space," in Anne Koedt, Ellen Levine, and Anita Rapone, eds., *Radical Feminism* (New York: Quadrangle, 1973), p. 271. "Redstockings Manifesto," reprinted in Robin Morgan, ed., *Sisterhood Is Powerful* (New York: Random House, 1970), p. 535.

16. Boston Women's Health Book Collective, *Our Bodies, Ourselves*, p. 1.

17. Vivian Gornick, *Essays in Feminism* (New York: Harper & Row, 1978), p. 1.

18. Douglas, *Where the Girls Are*. Quotations from Howard K. Smith (ABC News) and Eric Sevareid (CBS News) on pp. 163–164.

19. Boston Women's Health Collective, *Our Bodies, Ourselves*, p. 6. For an analysis of the primacy of the argument against difference in the early 1970s, see Hester Eisenstein, Introduction to Hester Eisenstein and Alice Jardine, eds., *The Future of Difference* (Boston: G. K. Hall, 1980), pp. xv–xvi. Consult also Kate Millett, *Sexual Politics* (New York: Doubleday, 1970); Shulamith Firestone, *The Dialectic of Sex* (New York: Morrow, 1970); and Elizabeth Janeway, *Man's World, Woman's Place* (New York: Dell, 1971).

20. NOW Statement of Purpose, reprinted in Betty Friedan, *It Changed My Life* (New York: Random House, 1976), p. 87.

21. Ti-Grace Atkinson, quoted in "Great Moments in Herstory," *New York Daily News Magazine*, August 26, 1990, p. 16.

22. Redstockings Manifesto (1969), reprinted in Morgan, *Sisterhood Is Powerful*, pp. 598–601. Radicals found NOW as painfully earnest as it was staid and conservative; they added humor and frisson to the movement as well as militance. Radical feminists hexed Wall Street, crowned a live sheep Miss America, and occupied the offices of the *Ladies Home Journal*. Valerie Solanis opened the manifesto for SCUM, the "Society for Cutting Up Men," by declaring, "Life in this society being, at best, an utter bore and no aspect of society being at all relevant to women, there remains to civic-minded, responsible, thrill-seeking females only to overthrow the government, eliminate the money system, institute complete automation, and destroy the male sex." See Valerie Solanis, SCUM (Society for Cutting Up Men) Manifesto, reprinted in Morgan, *Sisterhood Is Powerful*, p. 514.

23. "Critique of Sexual Politics: An Interview with Betty Friedan," *Social Policy* 1 (November–December 1970): 38–40, reprinted in Friedan, *It Changed My Life*, pp. 161–164.

24. Phyllis Schlafly, *The Power of the Positive Woman* (New Rochelle, N.Y.: Arlington House, 1977), p. 20.

25. Susan Hartmann, *From Margin to Mainstream* (New York: Knopf, 1989), pp. 51–55. Winifred D. Wandersee, *On the Move: American Women in the 1970s* (Boston: Twayne, 1988), pp. 16–18. JFK showed no interest in women's politics and appointed fewer women to public office than either Harry Truman or Dwight Eisenhower before him. "For women," one commentator wrote, "the New Frontiers are the Old Frontiers." Doris Fleeson, quoted in Hartmann, *From Margin to Mainstream*, p. 50.

26. Hartmann, *From Margin to Mainstream*, pp. 72–98.

27. Patricia Schroeder, speech delivered at the National Women's Political Caucus, Houston, Texas, February 9, 1973, in Waldo W. Braden, ed., *Representative American Speeches* (New York: H. W. Wilson, 1973), vol. 45, no. 4, p. 89. "You will probably have a hard time raising money,"

Schroeder warned. "My husband often said that the money 'is controlled by male chauvinist pigs.'"

28. Wandersee, *On the Move*, pp. 23–24.

29. "Great Moments in Herstory," *New York Daily News Magazine*, August 26, 1990, pp. 13–18. Hartmann, *From Margin to Mainstream*, pp. 84–95.

30. Jane Byrne won the mayoralty in Chicago in 1979. Kathy Whitmire first won election as city comptroller in 1977. She subsequently served five terms as Houston mayor, from 1982–1992.

31. Schroeder, speech delivered at the National Women's Political Caucus, p. 87. New York City Council member Ruth Messinger agreed that a new day had dawned for political women in the Seventies. "Women are more politically ambitious than their male colleagues," Messinger declared. They are "more likely to seek an additional term in their current office, and more eager to hold other offices in the future, although they in fact advance more slowly." See Ruth Messinger, "Women in Power and Politics," in Eisenstein and Jardine, *The Future of Difference*, p. 318.

32. The Women's Educational Equity Act was recodified in 1978 as Title IX, Part C, to help agencies implement Title IX. See Wandersee, *On the Move*, p. 119.

33. Barbara Mehrhof and Pamela Kearon, "Rape: An Act of Terror" (October 1971), reprinted in Koedt, Levine, and Rapone, *Radical Feminism*, p. 230.

34. Boston Women's Health Collective, *Our Bodies, Ourselves*, pp. 92–93. Wandersee, *On the Move*, pp. 91–95. Hartmann, *From Margin to Mainstream*, pp. 121–125. Alice Echols, *Daring to Be Bad* (Minneapolis: University of Minnesota Press, 1989), pp. 280–293. On the feminist battles against rape and domestic violence, see Susan Schecter, *Women and Male Violence* (Boston: South End Press, 1982); and Susan Brownmiller, *Against Our Will* (New York: Simon & Schuster, 1975).

35. U.S. Census Bureau, "Money Income of Households, Families, and Persons in the United States: 1982," *Consumer Income*, Series P-60, No. 142 (Washington, D.C.: GPO, 1984). Jane J. Mansbridge, *Why We Lost the ERA* (Chicago: University of Chicago Press, 1986), pp. 36–44. In 1981, the U.S. Supreme Court ruled that prison matrons could sue the state of Oregon for discrimination. Although the matrons' jobs in female prisons closely resembled the work of male prison guards, the women's positions received lower pay. The Court's procedural ruling did not decide the substance of the matrons' claims, and subsequent rulings on comparable worth proved ambiguous. Still, during the late 1970s and early 1980s, a number of feminist organizations and labor unions endorsed pay equity. The movement's objective had expanded from equal pay for the same work to equal pay for work of comparable worth. See Hartmann, *From Margin to Mainstream*, p. 159.

36. Ann Scott, "The Equal Rights Amendment: What's In It for You?" (*Ms.*, July 1972), p. 82. Mansbridge, *Why We Lost the ERA*, pp. 12–19.

38. Schlafly, *Power of the Positive Woman*, p. 130.

39. Ibid., p. 68.

40. Ibid., pp. 71, 79.

41. Ibid., p. 51.

42. Mansbridge, *Why We Lost the ERA*, pp. 15–19, 213.

43. Gloria Steinem, "Sisterhood," *Ms.* (Spring 1972): 48–49. Over the course of the 1970s, numerous other women reached the same conclusion. For the twelve authors *of Our Bodies, Ourselves,* "Learning about our womanhood from the inside out" allowed them "to cross over the socially created barriers of race, color, income and class, and to feel a sense of identity in the experience of being female." Sisterhood, the theologian Mary Daly discovered, was "a revolutionary fact. It is the bonding of those who have never bonded before, for the purpose of overcoming sexism and its effects." See Boston Women's Health Book Collective, *Our Bodies, Ourselves,* p. 2; and Mary Daly, "The Spiritual Dimensions of Women's Liberation" (1971), reprinted in Koedt, Levine, and Rapone, *Radical Feminism,* pp. 265–266.

44. Catharine R. Stimpson, "The Second Wave of Feminism," *New York Daily News Magazine,* August 26, 1990, p. 13. The women's studies movement in academe both reflected and advanced this reorientation. Between 1970 and 1980, American universities formed more than 300 new programs, offering some 30,000 courses in women's history, literature, sociology, feminist theory, and feminine psychology. The scholarly journals *Women's Studies* and *Feminist Studies* began publication in 1972, and *Signs* appeared in 1975. Two years later, the National Women's Studies Association held its first annual meeting. See Florence Howe and Paul Lauter, *The Impact of Women's Studies on the Campuses and the Disciplines: A Report of the U.S. Department of Health, Education, and Welfare* (Washington, D.C.: GPO, 1980). Consult also Ellen C. DuBois et al., *Feminist Scholarship* (Champaign/Urbana: University of Illinois Press, 1985).

45. Echols, *Daring to Be Bad,* p. 284.

46. Eisenstein, Introduction, p. xviii.

47. Nancy Chodorow, "Gender, Relation, and Difference in Psychoanalytic Perspective," in Eisenstein and Jardine, *Future of Difference,* pp. 3–19. For a critique of Chodorow, see Katha Pollitt, "Are Women Morally Superior to Men?" *Nation,* December 28, 1992, pp. 800–801. Adrienne Rich's 1976 book on motherhood rebuked Firestone, suggesting that feminism would produce a new truly nurturing form of motherhood. See Eisenstein, Introduction, p. xviii.

48. Carol Gilligan, "In a Different Voice: Women's Conceptions of Self and Morality," in Eisenstein and Jardine, *Future of Difference,* pp. 274–317. Carol Gilligan, *In a Different Voice* (Cambridge: Harvard University Press, 1982), pp. 25–32, 54–105.

49. Gilligan, *In a Different Voice,* p. 6.

50. These celebrations of difference emerged, despite the warnings of some feminists that the movement not find itself "marooned on Gilligan's Island." See, for example, Pollitt, "Are Women Morally Superior to Men?," pp. 799–807. On the radical feminist critique of cultural feminism generally, see Echols, *Daring to Be Bad,* pp. 281–284.

51. Eisenstein and Jardine, *Future of Difference.* Daly, "Spiritual Dimensions of Women's Liberation."

52. Jennifer Woodul, quoted in Echols, *Daring to Be Bad,* p. 274.

53. Billie Jean King, *Billie Jean* (New York: Harper & Row, 1974), pp. 99–101.

54. Peter Alegi, "Ace! Sports, the Women's Movement, and Post-war American Society" (unpublished research paper, Boston University, May 1996). Valian, *Why So Slow?* p. 213.

55. Wandersee, *On the Move,* pp. 84–89. Lyon-Martin Women's Health Services, http://www.sfccc.org/clinics/lmwhs.htm. Boston Women's Health Book Collective, *Our Bodies, Ourselves.*

56. Many cultural feminists would denounce the sexual revolution as phony, seeing it as a male revolt against tradition that only reinforced the subjugation of women.

57. Erica Jong, *Fear of Flying* (New York: Signet, 1973), p. 89. John Updike, "Jong Love," *New Yorker*, December 17, 1973, pp. 149–153. Updike blurb on back cover of paperback edition. "Sex and the Woman Writer," *Newsweek*, May 5, 1975, pp. 70–71. Becky Gould (NOW president), quoted in "The Sexes," *Time*, February 3, 1975, p. 70.

58. Susan Lydon, "The Politics of Orgasm," in Morgan, *Sisterhood Is Powerful*, pp. 221–222.

59. Anne Koedt, "The Myth of the Vaginal Orgasm" (1970), reprinted in Koedt, Levine, and Rapone, *Radical Feminism*, pp. 198–207. Other experts reaffirmed Koedt's arguments. See Barbara Seaman, "The Liberated Orgasm," *Ms.* (August 1972): 65–69; and Lydon, "Politics of Orgasm."

60. Donna Summer, "Love to Love You Baby" (written by Pete Bellotte, Georgio Moroder, and Donna Summer, produced by Georgio Moroder, 1976). Jefferson Morley, "The Myth and Meaning of Disco," *New Times*, March 1–7, 1989, p. 18.

61. Wandersee, *On the Move*, p. 65.

62. Radicalesbians, "The Woman-Identified Woman," in Koedt, Levine, and Rapone, *Radical Feminism*, pp. 240–243.

63. Even sensitive Seventies men, like actor and ERA advocate Alan Alda, embraced the cultural feminist line. "Without ascribing to women any mystical and unattainable qualities of gentleness and wisdom," Alda asserted in *Ms.*, "I think I have observed that where men work without women there is just a little less warmth, a little less laughter, and a little less relaxation. There seem to be culturally 'feminine' qualities that have for too long been absent from our working environments" See Alan Alda, "Alan Alda on the ERA," *Ms.* (July 1976): 93.

64. Susan Edmiston, "America's Sweetheart," *Redbook* (July 1976): 88.

65. Susan Edmiston, "Alan Alda: A Man Who Really Respects Women," *McCall's* (October 1979): 74–80.

66. Alda, "Alan Alda on the ERA," pp. 49, 93. Alda heralded the arrival of a new model of American manhood. In 1976, pop singer Jackson Browne released *The Pretender*, an album that chronicled the singer's loneliness, desolation, and free-flowing tears. One song recreated a conversation between a grown man and his father—an attempt at emotional exchange and intimacy between men that the generation of *Red River* could never imagine. The album's title track laid out the crisis of the modern American male: the masks men had to wear, the damage done to men by fulfilling their traditional roles. "Say a prayer for the Pretender," the song concludes, "who started out so young and strong only to surrender."

67. Warren Farrell, *The Liberated Man* (New York: Random House, 1974). Herb Goldberg, *The Hazards of Being Male* (New York: Nash Publishing, 1976). Marc Feigen Fasteau, *The Male Machine* (New York: McGraw-Hill, 1974). Meyer Friedman and Ray H. Rosenman, *Type A Behavior and Your Heart* (New York: Knopf, 1974). The study identified a familiar behavior pattern, including status insecurity, hyperaggressiveness, free-floating hostility, and "hurry sickness," a pervasive sense of time urgency. These "Type A" behaviors proved as reliable predictors of coronary heart disease as hypertension or elevated cholesterol levels. Indeed, the authors suggested that macho behavior itself raises blood pressure and cholesterol. Although the doctors carefully noted that women could fall into Type A (and that the number of Type A women seemed on the rise), they understood that "relatively few women exhibited Type A behavior." It remained a male disease. The doctors, however, held out hope for American men; Type A behavior was treatable and reversible. American men could unclog their arteries by unblocking their

feelings and unburdening themselves of responsibilities. For a further elaboration of the argument and a history of the Type A concept, see Meyer Friedman and Diane Ulmer, *Treating Type A Behavior—and Your Heart* (New York: Knopf, 1984).

68. Daniel J. Levinson et al., *The Seasons of a Man's Life* (New York: Knopf, 1978), pp. 25, 228–239, 333–338.

69. On gender roles and masculinity in the 1950s, see Elaine May, *Homeward Bound* (New York: Basic Books, 1988); Stephanie Coontz, *The Way We Never Were* (New York: Basic Books, 1992);Andrew Jamison and Ron Eyerman, *Seeds of the Sixties* (Berkeley: University of California Press, 1994); Barbara Ehrenreich, *The Hearts of Men* (New York: Anchor, 1983); and John D'Emilio, *Sexual Politics, Sexual Communities*, 2nd ed. (Chicago: University of Chicago Press, 1998).

70. Stephen J. Whitfield, *The Culture of the Cold War* (Baltimore: Johns Hopkins University Press, 1991), p. 148.

71. Not surprisingly, the 1950s and early 1960s proved to be a difficult period for gay rights activists. The homophile movement toned down its earlier efforts pressing for civil rights and proudly emphasizing differences. Indeed, the period's favored term, *homophile*, downplayed sexuality and stressed the mildness and conservatism of the movement. Gay organizations such as the Mattachine Society stressed political gradualism rather than protest and direct action and, most important, the idea that sexual expression mattered little. Homosexual men were not fundamentally different from other men; they deserved freedom from discrimination because they were essentially the same as all other Americans. Sexual preference was incidental, not central to their identity. The Mattachine Society and other homophile groups carefully avoided flamboyant or obvious enunciations of sexuality. They frowned on even mild public displays of affection. See D'Emilio, *Sexual Politics, Sexual Communities;* Andrea Weiss and Greta Schiller, *Before Stonewall* (Tallahassee: Naiad Press, 1988); and Martin Duberman, *Stonewall* (New York: Dutton, 1993).

72. D'Emilio, *Sexual Politics, Sexual Communities* (Chicago: University of Chicago Press, 1983), pp. 231–232.

73. Ehrenreich, *The Hearts of Men,* p. 130. See also Frances FitzGerald, *Cities on a Hill* (New York: Simon & Schuster, 1986), pp. 54–57, passim.

74. Denis Altman, *The Homosexualization of America* (New York: St. Martin's Press, 1982), quoted in Ehrenreich, *Hearts of Men,* p. 130.

75. Farrell, *Liberated Man,* pp. 32, passim.

76. Ibid., pp. 175–189.

77. Ibid. See also Lenore J. Weitzman, *The Divorce Revolution* (New York: Free Press, 1985); and Ehrenreich, *Hearts of Men,* pp. 120–121.

78. Marc Feigen Fasteau, *The Male Machine* (New York: McGraw-Hill, 1974), pp. 1–2, 5.

79. Ibid., p. 198.

80. Gloria Steinem, introduction to ibid., p. xiv. Many men's groups began as reactions to feminism, prompted by guilt and fear, and made the slow, difficult transition to discussions of masculinity and men's liberation. See Michael Weiss, "Unlearning," in Joseph H. Pleck and Jack Sawyer, eds., *Men and Masculinity* (Englewood Cliffs, N.J.: Prentice-Hall, 1974), pp. 166–167.

81. The "masculine value system," Warren Farrell warned, not only oppressed women but

crippled men. It reduced them to mere breadwinners, measured only by the dollars they earned, and denied them access to tenderness, affection, "sugar and spice and everything nice." Farrell, *Liberated Man*, pp. 16–17, 32, 50. Herb Goldberg found the male condition positively hazardous. The male, Goldberg insisted in his 1976 book *The Hazards of Being Male*, "has paid a heavy price for his masculine 'privilege' and power. He is out of touch with his emotions and his body." See Goldberg, *Hazards of Being Male*, pp. 11–13. The manifesto of the Berkeley Men's Center declared: "We no longer want to strain and compete to live up to an impossible oppressive masculine image—strong, silent, cool, handsome, unemotional, successful, master of women, leader of men, wealthy, brilliant, athletic, and 'heavy.' We no longer want to feel the need to perform sexually, socially, or in any way live up to an imposed male role, from a traditional American society or a 'counterculture.'" Berkeley Men's Center Manifesto (1973), in Pleck and Sawyer, *Men and Masculinity*, p. 173.

82. Gail Sheehy, "The Postponing Generation," *Esquire* (October 1979): 26–39.

83. Ibid.

84. Ibid.

85. "Sensitive New Age Guys" (words and music by John Gorka and Christine Lavin, Flip-a-Jig tunes, 1990).

86. http://www.tnom.com. See the sections on "Background and Philosophy" and "Short and Long Term Goals." Barbara J. Katz, "Women's Lib Auxiliaries?" *National Observer*, December 29, 1973, p. 8.

87. Katz, "Women's Lib Auxiliaries?" p. 8.

88. Robert Bly, *Talking All Morning* (Ann Arbor: University of Michigan Press, 1980), pp. 207–208, 215. Robert Bly, *Sleepers Joining Hands* (New York: Harper & Row, 1973). See also Marianna Torgovnick, "Tracking the Men's Movement," *American Literary History* 6 (Spring 1994): 155–170.

89. Robert Bly, *Iron John: A Book About Men* (Reading, Mass.: Addison-Wesley, 1990), p. ix–x, 6. "Welcoming the Hairy Man is scary and risky," Bly explained in the vague, poetic language favored by the movement's poets, drummers, Indian shamans, and Viking warriors. "Contact with Iron John requires a willingness to descend into the male psyche and accept what's dark down there, including the nourishing dark."

90. One of the most influential outgrowths of the renewed soul searching about men's roles was Promise Keepers, an evangelical Christian men's movement begun in 1990 by former University of Colorado football coach Bill McCartney. From a local fellowship of 72 men, Promise Keepers has grown into a vast national movement with over 4 million men participating in organization events by December 2000.

91. Sheehy, "Postponing Generation," p. 29.

92. Donald H. Bell, "Conflicting Interests," *New York Times Magazine*, July 31, 1983, p. 32. On the significance of the "About Men" column, see Edward Klein and Don Erickson, eds., *About Men: Reflections on the Male Experience* (New York: Poseidon, 1987); Andrew Ferguson, "The About Men Men," *American Spectator* 19 (May 1986): 24–25; and Nancy Gruskin, "A Silent Bond: The Father-Son Relationship in the 'About Men' Column of the *New York Times*" (unpublished manuscript, Boston University, April 1994).

93. Arlie Hochschild, *The Second Shift* (New York: Penguin, 1989), pp. 18–20. Mary Frances Berry, *The Politics of Parenthood* (New York: Viking, 1993), pp. 20–31. Kerry J. Daly, "Spending Time with the Kids," *Family Relations* 45 (October 1996): 466–476.

94. White House Conference on Families, *Listening to America's Families: The Report* (Washington, D.C.: GPO, 1980), p. 182.

95. Gloria Steinem, "An Introductory Statement," in National Commission on the Observance of International Women's Year, *What Women Want* (New York: Simon & Schuster, 1979), p. 11.

96. National Commission, *What Women Want*, pp. 97–106.

97. Wandersee, *On the Move*, pp. 191–192.

98. Quoted in ibid., p. 176.

99. National Commission, *What Women Want*, p. 49.

100. Ibid., p. 60.

101. "White House Conference on the Family: A Schism Develops," *New York Times*, January 7, 1980, p. D8. "Family Roster Attacked by Marchi," *New York Times*, February 6, 1980. "Alabama Will Bypass the Conference on Families," *New York Times*, February 12, 1980.

102. "Carter Opening Family Conference, Calls for Creative Solutions," *New York Times*, June 6, 1980, p. B4. "2nd Day of Family Conference: Workshops and a Walkout," *New York Times*, June 7, 1980. James J. Kilpatrick, quoted in White House Conference on Families, *Listening to America's Families: The Report* (Washington, D.C.: GPO, 1980), p. 194.

103. "Second Parley on Families Opens Quietly," *New York Times*, June 20, 1980. "Family Conference Ends in Agreement on 10 Goals," *New York Times*, June 23, 1980. "Debate Shapes Up as Western Conference on Families Opens," *New York Times*, July 11, 1980, p. A14. "After Heated Debates, Family Parley Ends Quietly," *New York Times*, July 14, 1980. "Family Conference Rejects Antiabortion Amendment," *New York Times*, June 22, 1980.

104. White House Conference, *Listening to America's Families.* "A White House Report on Family Issues," *New York Times*, October 23, 1980.

8. "The Minutemen Are Turning in Their Graves"

1. Reagan's predecessor as governor of California, Edmund "Pat" Brown, captured a broader assessment of Reaganism when he reflected, "I am chilled to the bone at the thought of Ronald Reagan one day becoming President of the United States." See Edmund G. Brown, *Reagan and Reality* (New York: Praeger, 1970), p. 32.

2. Ernest Tubb, "It's America: Love It or Leave It" (written by Jimmie Helms), MCA Records, 1984.

3. James E. McDavid, Jr., letter to President Nixon, February 5, 1970, quoted in Lassiter, "The Rise of the Suburban South" (Ph.D. dissertation, University of Virginia, 1999).

4. Richard Whalen, *Taking Sides* (New York: Houghton Mifflin, 1974), p. 100. The classic account of the right in the 1950s is Daniel Bell, ed., *The New American Right* (New York: Criterion, 1955).

5. John Judis, *William F. Buckley, Jr.: Patron Saint of the Conservatives* (New York: Simon and Schuster, 1988). George H. Nash, *The Conservative Intellectual Movement in America Since 1945* (New York: Basic Books, 1976).

6. John A. Andrew, *The Other Side of the Sixties* (New Brunswick, N.J.: Rutgers University Press, 1997). Mary C. Brennan, *Turning Right in the Sixties* (Chapel Hill: University of North Carolina Press, 1995). Thomas Edsall with Mary Edsall, *Chain Reaction* (New York: Norton, 1992).

7. Alan Crawford, *Thunder on the Right* (New York: Pantheon, 1980), p. 5.

8. Richard A. Viguerie, *The New Right* (Falls Church, Va.: The Viguerie Co., 1981), pp. 78–98.

9. Nick Kotz, "King Midas of 'The New Right,'" *Atlantic Monthly* (November 1978): 60. The New Right network is so tightly knit that "any diagram of its organization looks like an octopus trying to shake hands with itself, so completely interlocked are the directorates of its various components." See L. J. Davis, "Conservatism in America," *Harper's* (October 1980): 21.

10. Paul Weyrich, quoted in Crawford, p. 3.

11. Viguerie, *The New Right.*

12. Kotz, "King Midas of 'The New Right,'" p. 53.

13. Davis, "Conservatism in America," p. 22. Kotz, "King Midas of 'The New Right,'" pp. 52–58.

14. Richard Viguerie, quoted in Kotz, "King Midas of 'The New Right,'" p. 60.

15. Donald Lukens, direct mail solicitation for Citizens for Life, and Howard Phillips, direct mail solicitation for the Conservative Caucus, reprinted in Crawford, *Thunder on the Right*, pp. 53–54.

16. Richard Viguerie, quoted in Kotz, "King Midas of 'The New Right,'" p. 57.

17. Viguerie, *The New Right*, p. 66.

18. Jim Marshall, Fred Edwards, Charlie Daniels et al., "In America," 1980.

19. Clinton Rossiter, *Conservatism in America,* (New York: Knopf 1962), p. 14.

20. Crawford, *Thunder on the Right*, pp. 165–180.

21. Spiro T. Agnew, address at Houston, Texas, May 22, 1970, in *Great Speeches of the Twentieth Century* (Santa Monica: Rhino Records, 1991), vol. 4, track 9.

22. The profamily movement, as its backers called it, identified a genuine tension in American culture. The late 1960s and early 1970s had ushered in new mores in family life, sexuality, and personal behavior. Feminism had unleashed massive changes in women's roles, the structure of the family, and Americans' understanding of femininity and masculinity. The gay rights movement had moved into the open the issues of civil rights and sexual freedom for homosexuals. The courts liberalized obscenity laws, and divorces became easier to obtain across the United States. The movie censorship system broke down, and the arts included much more explicit sexuality. Abortion became legal, the equal rights amendment was being considered for ratification, and schools were offering instruction in sex education. In short, a new code of personal behavior had emerged to challenge the older values of politeness, decency, and moral tradition. This new ethic encouraged the free expression of liberated individuals and challenged traditional notions of restraint. Civil rights now trumped civility. See Cmiel, "The Politics of Civility."

23. Crawford, *Thunder on the Right*, pp. 155–159.

24. Ibid.

25. "Anita Bryant's Crusade," *Newsweek*, April 11, 1977, pp. 39–40. "Battle over Gay Rights," *Newsweek*, June 6, 1977, pp. 16–22. "Miami Vote: Tide Turning Against Homosexuals?" *U.S. News and World Report*, June 20, 1977, p. 46. "Voting Against Gay Rights," *Time*, May 22, 1978, pp. 21–22. "Why Tide Is Turning Against Homosexuals," *U.S. News and World Report*, June 5, 1978, p. 29. *New York Times*, May 24, 1978. Doug Ireland, "Open Season on Gays," *Nation*, September 15, 1979, pp. 207–210. "Law on Homosexuals Repealed in St. Paul," *New York Times*, April 26, 1978. "Laws Aiding Homosexuals Face Opposition Around Nation," *New York Times*, April 27, 1978.

26. David Nevin and Robert E. Bills, *The Schools That Fear Built* (Washington, D.C.: Acropolis Books, 1976). Thomas Byrne Edsall and Mary D. Edsall, *Chain Reaction* (New York: Norton, 1972), pp. 131–134. Lassiter, "Rise of the Suburban South."

27. On pre-millenialism and politics, see Paul S. Boyer, *When Time Shall Be No More* (Cambridge: Harvard Unversity Press, 1992); and A. James Reichley, *Religion in American Public Life* (Washington, D.C.: Brookings, 1985).

28. Richard Viguerie, telephone interview with *Washington Post* reporter Thomas Edsall, January 17, 1990, quoted in Edsall and Edsall, *Chain Reaction*, p. 132.

29. Jerome Kurtz, telephone interview with *Washington Post* reporter Thomas Edsall, January 18, 1990, quoted in Edsall and Edsall, *Chain Reaction*, p. 132.

30. Edsall and Edsall, pp. 133–134. Frances FitzGerald, *Cities on a Hill* (New York: Touchstone, 1987), pp. 121–122.

31. "Political Science," written and performed by Randy Newman, 1972.

32. Like the hard-line anticommunists, neoconservatives understood the dangers of communism and the need to contain it. They favored a big military and an interventionist foreign policy, but they also welcomed negotiations with the Soviets and a policy of flexible response to communist aggression. On the neoconservatives, see Sidney Blumenthal, *The Rise of the Conter-Establishment* (New York: Harper & Row, 1986); Peter Steinfels, *The Neoconservatives*, (New York: Simon and Schuster, 1979); and Irving Kristol, *Reflections of a Neoconservative* (New York: Basic, 1983).

33. On Reagan as "premature" neoconservative, see Sidney Blumenthal, *The Rise of the Counter-Establishment*, pp. 249–250.

34. Clarence Y. H. Lo, *Small Property Versus Big Government* (Berkeley: University of California Press, 1990), pp. 112–115. David Koistenen, "Resentment Against Government and Taxes and the Rightward Shift in American Politics" (unpublished manuscript, 1996), pp. 5–6.

35. Koistenen, "Resentment," p. 506.

36. Robert Kuttner, *Revolt of the Haves* (New York: Simon & Schuster, 1980), pp. 31–33. Alvin Rabushka and Pauline Ryan, *The Tax Revolt* (Stanford: Hoover Institution Press, 1982), pp. 15–16.

37. Bumper sticker from 1967, quoted in Kuttner, *Revolt of the Haves*, pp. 31, 35.

38. The strike did not get far. Any participation did not amount to more than the usual level of tax delinquency. See Koistenen, "Resentment," p. 7.

39. "Why the State Budget Keeps on Growing," *California Journal* (January 1976): 32. See also Rabushka and Ryan, *Tax Revolt*, pp. 17–18, Kuttner, *Revolt of the Haves*, pp. 36–39; and Koistenen, "Resentment," p. 8.

40. *California Homeowner* (April 1964): 3, (February 1964): 4–5, quoted in Koistenen, "Resentment," p. 14.

41. "Property Tax Fighter Exerts Political Muscle," *Los Angeles Times*, June 7, 1970. On Jarvis's efforts to create an independent Conservative party, see "Jarvis—Tax Fighter Is Now Fighting for Votes," *Los Angeles Times*, March 17, 1977.

42. Even in national politics, tax reform maintained a progressive cast. See Bruce J. Schulman, "Slouching Toward the Supply Side: Jimmy Carter and the New American Political Econ-

omy," *in The Carter Presidency: Policy Choices in the Post–New Deal Era* (Lawrence: University Press of Kansas, 1998), pp. 51–71.

43. Rabushka and Ryan, *Tax Revolt*, p. 185.

44. Howard Farmer, letters to the editor, *Los Angeles Valley News*, July 20, 1976, Sec. 2, p. 2, and September 8, 1976, Sec. 2, p. 2.

45. "Jarvis—Tax Fighter Is Now Fighting for Votes," *Los Angeles Times*, March 17, 1977.

46. *Taxpayer's Watchdog* (January 1977), quoted in Koistenen, "Resentment," p. 22.

47. Pamela Fulmer, letter to Governor Brown, June 8, 1978, quoted in Koistenen, "Resentment," p. 27.

48. Alan Brinkley, "Reagan's Revenge, As Invented by Howard Jarvis," *New York Times Magazine*, June 19, 1994, pp. 36–37. Koistenen, "Resentment."

49. Brinkley, "Reagan's Revenge," p. 36. See also Howard Jarvis, *I'm Mad as Hell* (New York: Times Books, 1979).

50. Rochelle L. Stanfield, "The Taxpayers' Revolt Is Alive or Dead in the Water—Take Your Pick," *National Journal*, December 10, 1983, pp. 2568–2571. On public attitudes toward services and taxes during the late 1970s and early 1980s, see David O. Sears and Jack Citrin, *Tax Revolt: Something for Nothing in California* (Cambridge: Harvard University Press, 1983).

51. Donna Turner to Brown, August 23, 1976, Brown papers d-14-5, quoted in Koistenen, "Resentment," p. 28. See also "Anatomy of the Tax Revolution," *National Review*, July 7, 1978, p. 819; and Kaufman and Rosen, *Property Tax Revolt*, pp. 4–5, 35. To be sure, inflation not only raised property tax bills but simultaneously diminished the real cost of those tax payments, since the larger taxes were worth less in real dollars. Still, even with an inflation rate of 10 or 11 percent (and equivalent increases in nominal wages) in the late 1970s, this discount effect nowhere approached the 100 to 300 percent increases in property values. Real property tax increases were lower than the nominal tax increases, but both were significant.

52. Kuttner, *Revolt of the Haves*, pp. 22–23.

53. Jeremy Main, "The Tax Revolt Takes Hold," *Money* (February 1980): 49–54.

54. Daniel A. Smith, *Tax Crusaders and the Politics of Direct Democracy* (New York: Routledge, 1988), p. 27. "Anatomy of the Tax Revolution," *National Review*, July 7, 1978, p. 819. Koistenen, "Resentment," pp. 9–10. Smith, p. 27.

55. Rabushka and Ryan, *Tax Revolt*, p. 25.

56. Jack Citrin and Frank Levy, "From 13 to 4 and Beyond: The Political Meaning of the Ongoing Tax Revolt in California," in George G. Kaufman and Kenneth T. Rosen, eds., *The Property Tax Revolt* (Cambridge, Mass.: Ballinger, 1981), pp. 1–2. Rabushka and Ryan, *The Tax Revolt*, p. 1.

57. Citrin and Levy, "From 13 to 4 and Beyond," p. 9.

58. Lo, *Small Property Versus Big Government*. Koistenen, "Resentment," p. 12. Still, the California tax revolt hardly constituted a mass movement. Supporters of Proposition 13 hired professional signature gatherers to qualify the measure for the ballot. Business, especially real estate and small business, played a heavy role. The Los Angeles Apartment Owners Association was Jarvis's organizational and financial base. On the role of business in financing the tax revolt, see Daniel A. Smith, *Tax Crusaders and the Politics of Direct Democracy*, pp. 71–80, passim.

59. *Proposition 13: Its Impact on the Nation's Economy, Federal Revenues, and Federal Expenditures* (Washington, D.C.: Congressional Budget Office, 1978).

60. "California Tax Revolt: Lesson for Legislators," *New York Times*, June 12, 1978, p. B4. Milton Friedman, "The Message from California," *Newsweek*, June 19, 1978, p. 26.

61. Citrin and Levy, "From 13 to 4 and Beyond," p. 2. "Anatomy of the Tax Revolution," *National Review*, July 7, 1978, p. 818.

62. Citrin and Levy, "From 13 to 4 and Beyond," p. 2. Meanwhile, in what *National Review* proudly proclaimed "sons of Proposition 13," Idaho and Nevada followed California with laws limiting property taxes to 1 percent of assessed valuation. Kansas, Maryland, Indiana, Arkansas, Mississippi, and Vermont lowered income taxes. Minnesota enacted a new tax law, slashing revenues by $712 million a year. Virginia, Kentucky, and New Mexico froze the amount that could be collected through property taxes. Arkansas, Louisiana, New Jersey, Virginia, West Virginia, and Ohio offered more modest property tax relief. Arizona, Hawaii, Michigan, Texas, and Utah fixed spending limits. See also "Sons of Proposition 13," *National Review*, July 20, 1979, p. 903; and "The Tax Revolt—A Year Later," *U.S. News and World Report*, June 11, 1979, p. 24.

63. "The Tax Revolt Takes a New Turn," *Newsweek*, September 24, 1979, p. 45. Jeremy Main, "The Tax Revolt Takes Hold," *Money* (February 1980): 49–54. Rabushka and Ryan, *The Tax Revolt*, p. 189. Some states—like Minnesota, Nevada, Oregon, and Wisconsin—enacted truly massive cuts. Others indexed their tax rates to prevent inflation-induced bracket creep.

64. Massachusetts also relied overwhelmingly on the property tax to finance local government, and property tax rates in the cities, where per capita property values were lower, were astonishingly high.

65. Sherry Tvedt Davis, "A Brief Proposition of Proposition 2 1/2," in Lawrence E. Susskind, ed., *Proposition 2 1/2: Its Impact on Massachusetts* (Cambridge, Mass.: Oelgeschlager, Gunn & Hain, 1983), p. 6.

66. Smith, *Tax Crusaders and the Politics of Direct Democracy*, p. 102.

67. "Proposition 13 Paved the Way for Tax Revolts Across U.S.," *Los Angeles Times*, February 14, 1988, p. 1.

68. Don Feder, quoted in Smith, *Tax Crusaders*, p. 104, n.84.

69. Smith, *Tax Crusaders*, p. 105.

70. Ibid., pp. 90, 110–124.

71. Davis, "A Brief Proposition of Proposition 2 1/2," pp. 3–4.

72. Smith, *Tax Crusaders*, p. 28.

73. "Taxpayer Revolt: Where It's Spreading Now," *U.S. News and World Report*, June 26, 1978, p. 16.

74. Ibid., pp. 16–17.

75. California further relieved the fiscal stress of Proposition 13 with "Bailout II" in July 1979. The aid package parceled out almost $10 billion more over the next two fiscal years. The impact of the tax revolt on services and public life is assessed in Chapter 9 below. See also Rabushka and Ryan, *The Tax Revolt*; Kuttner, *Revolt of the Haves*; Kaufman and Rosen, *The Property Tax Revolt*; and Terry Schwadron, ed., *California and the American Tax Revolt* (Berkeley: University of California Press, 1984).

76. "The Legacy of a Tax Cut," *Newsweek*, January 12, 1982, p. 30. See also Chapter 9 below.

77. John A. Davenport, "Voting for Capitalism," *Fortune*, July 17, 1978, pp. 46–48. *Fortune's* cheerleading for capitalism contained much wishful thinking. Despite their aversion to government waste, Americans in the late 1970s still maintained a healthy appetite for services and a skepticism about tax reduction. But the tide had turned. Business and the wealthy were no longer the enemies, equity no longer the issue. Despite President Carter's call for an increase in the capital gains tax, a levy focused on the affluent, public sentiment instead rallied behind the proposal of Wisconsin congressman William Steiger to lower that tax.

78. Eugene L. Meyer, "California's Proposition 13 Spawned Brood of Antitax Laws," *Washington Post*, August 15, 1983. Meg Greenfield, "The People's Revenge," *Newsweek*, June 19, 1973, p. 93. A CBS/*New York Times* poll, conducted two weeks after the passage of Proposition 13 in June 1978, showed widespread concern about government spending. Americans not only expressed disgust with waste, a convenient target for discontent (belief in government waste increased steadily, from 47 percent in 1964, to 66 percent in 1972, to 78 percent in June 1978). A majority actually recommended steep cuts in social services. See *New York Times*, June 28, 1978. Harris Survey, quoted in Rabushka and Ryan, *Tax Revolt*, p. 38.

79. David A. Stockman, *The Triumph of Politics* (New York: Avon Books, 1986), pp. 10–11. Lou Cannon, *Reagan* (New York: Putnam, 1982), pp. 235–236. Cannon disputes Stockman's account of Reagan's conversion to supply-side theory by Jack Kemp and Jude Wanninski and asserts that Reagan never embraced (or even understood) the economics of supply-side theory. He fully grasped its political potential as early as 1978, Cannon maintains, and that was all that concerned him. For Reagan's economic proposals in 1980, see Martin Anderson, *Revolution* (New York: Harcourt Brace Jovanovich, 1988), pp. 135, passim. For actual budget figures during Reagan's presidency, see U.S. Census Bureau, *Statistical Abstract of the United States, 1995* (Washington, D.C.: GPO, 1995), pp. 333–338.

80. "A Tide of Born-Again Politics," *Newsweek*, September 15, 1980, p. 36.

81. On the relationship between the Reagan campaign and the New Right network, see Sidney Blumenthal, *The Rise of the Counter-Establishment*.

82. James Q. Wilson, "A Guide to Reagan Country," *Commentary* (May 1967): 37.

83. Ibid., p. 45.

84. Ibid.

9. The Reagan Culmination

1. U.S. Census Bureau, *Statistical Abstract of the United States, 1986* (Washington, D.C.: GPO, 1986), pp. 406, 477–479, 505. U.S. Council of Economic Advisors, *Economic Report of the President, 1985* (Washington, D.C.: GPO, 1985), p. 271. "The Reagan Recession," *Newsweek*, November 2, 1981, p. 75. "Inflation's Painful Slowdown," *Time*, March 29, 1982, pp. 46–49.

2. Herblock cartoon, *Washington Post*, January 23, 1983, reprinted in Herbert Block, *Herblock Through the Looking Glass: The Reagan Years in Words and Pictures* (New York: Norton, 1984), p. 129. "Gathering Gloom for Workers," *Time*, December 14, 1981, pp. 64–65. "Jobs That Vanish Forever," *Newsweek*, February 15, 1982, p. 27.

3. Ronald Reagan, interview in Oklahoma City with reporters from the *Daily Oklahoman*, March 16, 1982, in *Public Papers of the Presidents, Ronald Reagan, 1982* (Washington, D.C.: GPO, 1983), bk. 1, p. 311. See also *Los Angeles Times*, March 18, 1982, p. 7.

4. "Reaganomics is dead," opined Robert Samuelson in the *Los Angeles Times*. It was nothing but "meaningless phrasemaking, a rigid, unworkable set of ideological prejudices masquerading

as an economic philosophy." See Robert J. Samuelson, "Reaganomics Is a Phantom—A Scary One," *Los Angeles Times*, December 14, 1982, Sec. 2, p. 11.

5. Thomas P. O'Neill, quoted in Robert Dallek, *Ronald Reagan: The Politics of Symbolism*, rev. ed. (Cambridge: Harvard University, 1999), pp. 111–112. Republican congressman Silvio Conte (R, Massachusetts) voiced similar, if less articulate, discontent. "The administration does not realize that some members have been in the trenches, on the hot seat," Conte complained. "We've had our backs to the wall, and we're not going to get trampled anymore." Conte, quoted in "The Reagan Recession," *Newsweek*, November 2, 1981, p. 75. The president wore a brave face and pledged to "stay the course," but his administration's policies revealed increasing doubts about its own antigovernment creed. As the budget deficit soared, Reagan agreed to a series of new taxes, disguised as "user fees" and "revenue enhancements." When he asked openly in his State of the Union speech for a "stand-by tax" to bail out the social security system, opponents felt vindicated and conservative true believers betrayed. Reagan, Address Before a Joint Session of the Congress on the State of the Union, *Public Papers of the Presidents, Ronald Reagon, 1983* (Washington, D.C.: GPO, 1984), bk. 1, pp. 102–110. See also Edmund Morris, *Dutch* (New York: Random House, 1999), pp. 469–470, passim.

6. Martin Anderson, *Revolution* (New York: Harcourt Brace Jovanovich, 1988), p. 288. Morris, *Dutch*, p. 497.

7. Census Bureau, *Statistical Abstract of the United States, 1986* (Washington, D.C.: GPO, 1986), pp. 406–407, 477–479, 505. *Economic Report of the President, 1985*, pp. 235, 239, 271. "The Year of the Yuppie," *Newsweek*, December 31, 1984, pp. 16–29.

8. For a useful summary of Reagan's foreign policy, see Ronald E. Powaski, *The Cold War* (New York: Oxford University Press, 1998), pp. 231–62. Quotation from Morris, *Dutch*, p. 506.

9. Anderson, *Revolution*, p. 6.

10. Reagan, "Farewell Address to the American People, January 11, 1989, *Public Papers of the Presidents: Reagan 1988–89*, Vol. 2 (Washington, D.C.: GPO, 1989), pp. 1718–1724).

11. Ibid.

12. On Reagan's optimism and views on the moral benefits of the marketplace, see Paul Peterson, "Ronald Reagan and the Reformation of American Conservatism," in Eric J. Schmertz, Natalie Datlof, and Alexej Ugrinsky, eds., *Ronald Reagan's America* (Westport, Conn.: Greenwood Press, 1997), 1: 72; and William K. Muir, *The Bully Pulpit: The Presidential Leadership of Ronald Reagan* (San Francisco: Institute for Contemporary Studies Press, 1992), pp. 148–155.

13. U.S. Census Bureau, *Statistical Abstract of the United States, 1995* (Washington, D.C.: GPO, 1995), pp. 336–337. Between 1980 and 1985, defense spending rose from 22.7 percent of federal budget outlays to 26.7 percent. As a share of GDP, it increased from 5.1 percent in 1980 to 6.4 percent in 1985.

14. David Stockman, *The Triumph of Politics* (New York: Harper & Row, 1986), p. 283.

15. Richard Nixon, *No More Vietnams* (New York: Arbor House, 1985).

16. Alexander Haig, *Caveat* (New York: Macmillan, 1984), pp. 26, 30–31.

17. In March 1986, U.S. forces carried out naval exercises in the Gulf of Sidra off the coast of Libya, a show of strength against the Libyan leader Colonel Mu'ammar al-Gadhafi. Predictably, the Libyans fired on U.S. aircraft, which responded by sinking three Libyan patrol boats. Libya retaliated by directing a terrorist bomb attack on a Berlin discotheque; two people died, and many, including fifty Americans, were wounded. Nine days later, after investigators established Libya's responsibility for the disco bombing, Reagan ordered an aerial attack against Libya,

including an assault on Gadhafi's personal compound. The colonel escaped, but one of his daughters was killed in the raid.

18. *First Blood* (directed by Ted Kotcheff, 1982).

19. First Blood was released in 1982, just a year into Reagan's presidency (and produced even earlier).

20. *Rambo: First Blood, Part II* (directed by George P. Cosmatos, 1985).

21. Reagan's foreign policy also faced military constraints. Vietnam and the Soviet fiasco in Afghanistan had pointed up the dangers and difficulties of guerrilla warfare for a nuclear super-power. All the high-tech weaponry in the world could not overpower a patient, determined insurgency, willing to hole up in mountains or jungles and slowly bleed its more powerful antag-onist. Firepower could not win the hearts and minds of a people or triumph in an essentially political struggle. Even the Grenada invasion had shown that real war is never easy. Nineteen American servicemen died in Operation Urgent Fury, and state-of-the art attack helicopters proved vulnerable to obsolete World War II–vintage antiaircraft guns. See "U.S. Marines Diverted to Grenada in Event Americans Face Danger," *New York Times,* October 22, 1983, pp. 1, 5. "Grenada Radio Warns of Attack," *New York Times,* October 24, 1983, p. A4. "US Says Grenada Invasion Is Succeeding," *New York Times,* October 27, 1983, pp. 1ff. "Reagan Says Cuba Aimed to Take Grenada," *New York Times,* October 28, 1983, pp. 1ff., 5. Powaski, *The Cold War,* pp. 234–235. Morris, *Dutch,* p. 504.

22. Reagan, Address Before a Joint Session of the Congress on Central America, April 27, 1983, *Public Papers, 1983,* bk. 1, p. 605.

23. Richard Viguerie, quoted in Morris, *Dutch,* pp. 493–494.

24. The background to the story involved Reagan's efforts to train, finance, and aid the con-tras—the guerrillas plotting to overthrow the Marxist Sandinista government of Nicaragua. Members of Congress worried about the scale of secret operations in Nicaragua and tried to rein them in. In 1982, in the first of a series of legislative amendments sponsored by Representative Edward Boland (D, Massachusetts), Congress capped CIA aid to the contras. After CIA-hired American operatives mined Nicaragua's harbors, a new, tighter Boland Amendment passed, bar-ring the CIA or any other U.S. agency from aiding the contras in any way.

That decision dismayed Reagan. He called the contras "freedom fighters" and likened them to the American founding fathers. The president asked his advisers to do whatever it took to help the contras. Meanwhile, Islamic radicals in Lebanon had seized and held numerous hostages, including several Americans. Reagan desperately wanted their release for a host of reasons. The president felt genuine humanitarian concern for their safety and political pressure to secure their freedom. Moreover, the endless hostage ordeal embarrassed the president; it made him look personally weak and invited comparisons to his ineffectual predecessor, Jimmy Carter.

The president thus authorized a secret overture to Iran, the government that supported the hostage takers. Although Reagan never admitted it, his aides made arm sales to Iran, after which some hostages were released. All told, however, the deals hardly proved worth the effort. Five shipments of military hardware worth more than $30 million (and one chocolate cake) won freedom for three hostages. But in the interim, six more hostages were abducted. And of course, White House staffers illegally diverted the proceeds from the arms sales to the contras. When that news leaked during Reagan's second term, the president found himself mired in scandal, and several of his top aides would serve prison sentences.

25. Kenneth Oye, Robert J. Lieber, and Donald Rothchild, eds., *Eagle Resurgent? The Reagan Era in American Foreign Policy* (Boston: Little, Brown, 1987). See also Stephen E. Ambrose,

"Reagan's Foreign Policy: An Overview," in Schmertz, Datlof, and Ugrinsky, *President Reagan and the World*, Vol. 1, pp. 5–10.

26. On Reagan's early opposition to détente, see Anderson, *Revolution*, pp. 63–79.

27. Ronald Reagan, "Where Reagan Stands," *U.S. News and World Report*, May 31, 1976, p. 20.

28. Eventually, in November 1981, Reagan backed away from the zero option and offered what became known as the "zero-zero option"—complete elimination of INFs by both sides.

29. Reagan, Remarks at the Annual Convention of the National Association of Evangelicals in Orlando, Florida, March 8, 1983, *Public Papers, 1983*, bk 1, pp. 359–364.

30. This declaration and others like it flabbergasted the nation and the rest of the world. Reagan's harsh rhetoric shocked not because of its sentiments. Ever since the Russian Revolution, American leaders had viewed the Soviet Union as a ruthless, grasping empire and communism a totalitarian evil. But presidents had usually allowed others to vent those strident condemnations, preferring to wear a milder, diplomatic face. Reagan's denunciations seemed to allow little space for compromise or negotiation.

31. Reagan, Address to the Nation on Defense and National Security, March 23, 1983, in *Public Papers, 1983*, bk. 1, pp. 437–443. White House aide Martin Anderson dated Reagan's interest in missile defense to a 1979 visit to NORAD headquarters in Colorado. The vulnerability of U.S. missiles to Soviet attack alarmed Reagan. See Anderson, *Revolution*, pp. 82–83.

32. Quoted in Michael Schaller, *Reckoning with Reagans* (New York: Oxford University Press, 1992), p. 119.

33. Recent scholarship downplays the influence of Reagan's advisers, including Shultz and Nancy Reagan, and suggests the president was himself the architect of the transformed approach to superpower relations. See Beth A. Fischer, *The Reagan Reversal* (Columbia: University of Missouri Press, 1997). Biographer Edmund Morris similarly argued that Nancy Reagan's influence has been overstated. See Morris, *Dutch*, p. 613.

34. Ronald W. Reagan, *An American Life* (New York: Simon & Schuster, 1990) pp. 588–589.

35. "The time has come to acknowledge an astonishing development," diplomatic historian John L. Gaddi, conceded in the *Bulletin of the Atomic Scientists*. "Ronald Reagan has presided over the most dramatic improvement in U.S.-Soviet relations—and the most solid progress in arms control—since the Cold War began." John Lewis Gaddis, "Arms Control: Hanging Tough Paid Off," *Bulletin of the Atomic Scientists* 45 (January–February 1989): 11–14. Ambrose, "Reagan's Foreign Policy," p. 5.

36. Anderson, *Revolution*, p. 112. See also Morris, *Dutch*, p. 422.

37. Reagan, Acceptance Speech at the Republican National Convention, August 15, 1980, reprinted in Paul Boyer, ed., *Reagan as President* (Chicago: Ivan Dee, 1990), p. 23. Reagan, Inaugural Address, January 20, 1981, In *Public Papers of the Presidents: Ronald Reagan, 1981* (Washington, D.C.: GPO, 1982), bk. 1, p. 1.

38. Ibid.

39. U.S. Council of Economic Advisors, *Economic Report of the President, 1982* (Washington, D.C.: GPO, 1982), p. 3.

40. Reagan, Inaugural Address, p. 1. Reagan, Acceptance Speech, reprinted in Boyer, ed., *Reagan as President*, p. 23. The budgetary goals from Reagan's 1980 campaign economic plan are reprinted in Anderson, *Revolution*, p. 135.

41. Reagan's program represented a harsh critique and a dramatic reversal of the liberal Keynesian economics most Democratic administrations and some Republican ones (like Nixon's and Eisenhower's) had practiced for a generation. Yet Reaganomics embraced no single coherent economic philosophy. Rather, it combined elements from three different conservative antidotes to liberal Keynesianism: monetarism, supply-side economics, and traditional Republican fiscal conservatism. See Michael J. Boskin, *Reagan and the Economy* (San Francisco: ICS Press, 1987), pp. 1–2.

42. Hugh S. Norton, *The Quest for Economic Stability,* 2nd ed. (Columbia: University of South Carolina Press, 1991), p. 222–223.

43. Reagan, private diary, quoted in Morris, *Dutch*, p. 422.

44. Reagan, Address Before a Joint Session of the Congress on the Program for Economic Recovery, February 18, 1981, in *Public Papers, 1981*, bk. 1, pp. 108–115.

45. Morris, *Dutch*, p. 423.

46. Ibid., p. 466.

47. In his famous interview with *Atlantic Monthly* reporter William Greider, budget director David Stockman asserted that bringing down the rates for the wealthiest taxpayers had always been the principal objective of the tax cut. "The hard part of the supply-side tax cut is bringing down the top rate from 70 to 50 percent—the rest of it is a secondary matter.... Kemp-Roth was always a Trojan horse to bring down the top rate." See William Greider, "The Education of David Stockman," *Atlantic Monthly* (December 1981): 46. The top bracket fell from 70 percent in 1980 to 50 percent, and, by the end of Reagan's presidency, to 33 percent. The capital gains tax and corporate income tax also fell. Modest-income people saw only a small drop in their personal income taxes, which was more than made up for by increases in the social security tax. See M. A. Akhtar and Ethan S. Harris, "The Supply-Side Consequences of U.S. Fiscal Policy in the 1980s," *Federal Reserve Bank of New York Quarterly Review* 17 (Spring 1992): 11.

48. Schaller, *Reckoning with Reagan*, p. 50. Still, Reagan's record on deregulation was decidedly mixed. See Timothy A. Canova, "The Legacy of the Reagan Administration's Deregulation of Banking and Finance," in Schmertz, Datlof, and Ugrinsky, *Ronald Reagan's America*, vol. 1, pp. 99–113.

49. T. Boone Pickens, Jr., "My Case for Reagan," *Fortune*, October 29, 1984, p. 197. Liberal critics and conservative celebrants agreed on Reagan's regulatory agency appointments. See Mark Green, "Rating Reagan: Trendlines, Fault Lines," *Nation*, November 7, 1981, pp. 461–463; and James J. Kilpatrick, "The Reagan Presidency: A Pattern of Significant Change," *Nation's Business* (January 1983): 32–36.

50. EPA funding for air pollution control, drinking water, hazardous waste, and pesticide control fell from 1981 to 1984. See Congressional Research Service, "A Department of Environmental Protection?" CRS Report for Congress, October 25, 1989, p. 25. On Reagan's environmental counterrevolution, see Jacqueline Vaughan Switzer, *Green Backlash* (Boulder, Colo.: Lynne Rienner Publishers, 1997), pts. 2, 3. See also Samuel P. Hays, *Beauty, Health and Permanence* (New York: Cambridge University Press, 1987), pp. 491–526; and Hal S. Rothman, *The Greening of a Nation?* (Fort Worth, Tex.: Harcourt Brace, 1998), pp. 169–192. Watt quotation in *New York Times*, October 10, 1983, p. 1.

51. Green, "Rating Reagan," p. 643. Congressional Research Service, "CRS Report for Congress: A Department of Environmental Protection?" 89-587 ENR, October 25, 1989, p. CRS-25. Schaller, *Reckoning with Reagan*, p. 50.

52. Reagan, Statement and a Question-and-Answer Session with Reporters on the Air Traffic Controllers Strike, August 3, 1981.

53. Ibid. *Public Papers of Presidents: Reagan, 1981* (Washington, D.C.: GPO, 1982), pp. 687–690. For accounts of the PATCO strike and its aftermath, consult Robert Dallek, *Ronald Reagan: The Politics of Symbolism*, rev. ed. (Cambridge: Harvard University Press, 1999), pp. 91–93; Haynes Johnson, *Sleepwalking Through History* (New York: Norton, 1991), pp. 163–167; and Schaller, *Reckoning with Reagan*, p. 44.

54. Christopher Matthews, an aide to Speaker O'Neill, reported this story to Reagan biographer Edmund Morris. See Morris, *Dutch*, pp. 792–793.

55. "A Union Chief Muses on Labor and the Controllers," *New York Times*, September 1, 1981, p. 12.

56. Robert Lekachman, *Greed Is Not Enough* (New York: Pantheon Books, 1982), p. 4.

57. Benjamin Friedman, *Day of Reckoning: The Consequences of American Economic Policy Under Reagan and After* (New York: Random House, 1988), pp. 152–153.

58. Roy Rosenzweig et al., *Who Built America?* vol. 2, chap. 13 (New York: Worth Publishers,forthcoming).

59. Glenn Perusek and Kent Worcester, eds., *Trade Union Politics* (Atlantic Highlands, N.J.: Humanities Press, 1995), Tables 1.1, 1.2. Walter Galenson, *Trade Union Growth and Decline* (Westport, Conn.: Praeger, 1994), p. 2.

60. Akhtar and Harris, "The Supply-Side Consequences of U.S. Fiscal Policy in the 1980s," 6. Schaller, *Reckoning with Reagan*, p. 45.

61. Bruce J. Schulman, "The Reagan Revolution and American Exceptionalism: Conservative Attacks on the Welfare State in Europe and the United States," paper presented at the Meeting of the Organization of American Historians, Chicago, March 1996. John O'Connor, "US Social Welfare Policy: The Reagan Record and Legacy," *Journal of Social policy* 27 (January 1998): 37–61. John A. Ferejohn, "Changes in Welfare Policy the 1980s," in Alberto Alesina and Geoffrey Carliner, eds., *Politics and Economics in the Eighties* (Chicago: University of Chicago Press, 1991). pp. 123–142. Robert Lekachman, *Greed Is Not Enough* (New York: Pantheon, 1982). Ronald Reagan, Address Before a Joint Session of Congress on the Program for Economic Revovery, *Public Papers of the Presidents: Reagan, 198* (Washington: GPO, 1982), pp. 108–111. US Census Bureau, *Statistical Abstract of the United States*, 1995 (Washington: GPO, 1995), pp. 335–338.

62. Frances Fox Piven and Richard Cloward, "Keeping Labor Lean and Hungry," *Nation*, November 7, 1981, pp. 466–467.

63. Martin Carnoy and Derek Shearer, "Reaganomics: The Supply Side of the Street," *Nation*, November 7, 1981, pp. 463–464.

64. Reagan, quoted in Morris, *Dutch*, p. 645.

65. The brunt of the actual cutbacks occurred during the president's first two years in the White House. Under the guidance of budget director David Stockman, the administration employed the obscure budget reconciliation process to force the Democratic leadership in the House of Representatives to accept a straight up-or-down vote on its total package. These maneuvers limited amendments and allowed a coalition of Republicans and boll weevil Democrats to approve the administration's omnibus budget bill with substantial cuts in social programs. See O'Connor, "US Social Welfare Policy," 37–61 and Ferejohn, "Changes in Welfare Policy in the 1980s," pp. 124–26.

66. Means-tested programs like AFDC, Medicaid, SSI, and food stamps suffered cuts through new eligibility requirements and controls on benefit levels, while grants programs like CETA, the Job Corps, and Head Start suffered severe cuts or elimination. See O'Connor, "US Social Welfare Policy," pp. 40–41; and Ferejohn, "Changes in Welfare Policy in the 1980s," pp. 126, 135.

67. O'Connor, "US Social Welfare Policy," pp. 48–50.

68. Ibid., pp. 52–55.

69. "Everywhere we look in the world, the cult of the state is dying," Reagan told British prime minister Margaret Thatcher during the first important summit conference of his presidency. Their joint appearance and joint backing of free enterprise and small government heralded that Reagan's America participated in a larger revolt against liberalism. On the face of it, the Reagan Revolution certainly fit a broader pattern across the industrialized world. Reagan's election in 1980 and his program of retrenchment echoed the victories of conservative parties in Britain (1979), Germany (1982), Canada (1984), and Sweden (1976 and 1979). Even nations that reversed decades of rightist rule and elected socialist presidents in the early 1980s embraced fiscal conservatism and tightened the belt on social spending. In France, the outraged world markets quickly forced François Mitterand to abandon his efforts to nationalize industry, shorten the work week, and improve social benefits. By 1984, Mitterand's government announced a program of "modernization" and "efficiency" and rolled back most of its social democratic agenda. But the Reagan Revolution differed from the Western European norm in key ways. I am preparing for publication a detailed comparative study of the politics of retrenchment in the United States and five other industrial democracies. See also Bruce J. Schulman, "The Reagan Revolution and American Exceptionalism: Conservative Attacks on the Welfare State in Europe and the United States," paper presented at the meeting of the Organization of American Historians, Chicago, March 1996.

70. Ronald Reagan, Remarks Before the National Black Republican Council, September 14, 1982, *Weekly Compilation of Presidential Documents*, vol. 18 (Washington: GPO, 1982), p. 1154. See also O'Connor, "US Social Welfare Policy," pp. 55–57; and, Michael B. Katz, ed., The *"Underclass" Debate*, (Princeton: Princeton University Press, 1993).

71. Frances FitzGerald, "Memoirs of the Reagan Era," *New Yorker*, January, 16, 1989, pp. 72–73, 76. The president did not eliminate the Energy Department either. Indeed, he created a new cabinet office: the Department of Veterans Affairs. Reagan administration officials waltzed back and forth through the Capitol's infamous revolving door, trading positions of influence in the government for lucrative jobs in the industries they had once regulated. Often they returned to government in more senior capacities and then retired again to the private sector. Conservatives also constructed their own counterestablishment in the District of Columbia, a network of Reaganite think tanks, foundations, publications, and caucuses that soon rivaled the hated liberal establishment. In "Curse of the Giant Muffins," *New Republic* editor Michael Kinsley parodied the Reagan administration official who traded in a prestigious government job for higher pay in the private sector, because his family had had to make do with supermarket brand muffins instead of Thomas's. "Their government connections, reputations, and experience is what makes them valuable," Kinsley noted. When "these people talk of returning to the 'private sector,' they do not mean they are moving to Des Moines to manufacture widgets. They are remaining in Washington to leech, in some way, off the government, usually by peddling influence." Michael Kinsley, "Curse of the Giant Muffins," *New Republic*, January 28, 1985. See also Michael Kinsley, "Welcome to the Power House," *New Republic*, December 31, 1983.

72. William Greider, "The Education of David Stockman," *Atlantic Monthly* (December 1981), p. 32.

73. Ibid., pp. 32–46. See also Stockman, *Triumph of Politics*. On the balking over deficits in

Congress by late 1981, see "The Reagan Recession," *Newsweek*, November 2, 1981, p. 75. Reagan's unwillingness to face up to (or face down) the looming deficit became clear in the summer of 1981, when the administration first tackled social security. Tip O'Neill had famously labeled the retirement program "the third rail of American politics: you touch it and you die." But the administration understood that food stamps and public service employment had been small change. Reagan could not tame the deficit without going after the big-ticket items. But he planned to boost defense spending and had no choice but to pay interest on the national debt. That left social security as the only target.

Flush with his early victories on taxes and social program cuts, Reagan considered pulling the reins on social security. In the summer of 1981, the White House released Stockman's typically draconian plan. The budget director wanted to slash pension benefits, especially for Americans who retired before age sixty-five. But the proposal aroused vociferous opposition on Capitol Hill and from the elderly across the nation. Even the Republican-controlled Senate passed a unanimous resolution criticizing the plan. In September, the president disowned the Office of Management and Budget proposal in a televised chat. Instead Reagan appointed a bipartisan commission to stabilize funding for the retirement system. Eventually, as Congress began to panic over the record shortfall in revenues for the coming year, Reagan accepted a major payroll tax increase. For ordinary citizens, the new tax offset much of the relief they would have received from the Kemp-Roth tax cut. A famous Herblock cartoon lampooned the president's seeming inconsistency. It depicted Reagan in a nightshirt and slippers opening the door of a no-tell motel. Behind him struts a buxom harlot, her lingerie bearing the inscription "Record Deficits." Meanwhile, the president palms off "proposed constitutional amendment candies" on his distraught, dissatisfied lady. She wears a modest dress marked "balanced budget" and the caption reads, "I'm always true to you, darling, in my fashion." Herblock cartoon, *Washington Post*, July 25, 1982, reprinted in Block, *Herblock Through the Looking Glass*, p. 24.

74. Benjamin M. Friedman, "Learning from the Reagan Deficits," *American Economic Review* 82 (May 1992): 299. Uwe Reinhardt, "Reaganomics, R.I.P.," *New Republic*, April 20, 1987, pp. 24–27. Sidney Weintraub, "The Budget: Guns Up, People Down," *New Leader*, February 22, 1982, pp. 3–5. Akhtar and Harris, "Supply-Side Consequences of U.S. Fiscal Policy in the 1980s," p. 6. Friedman, *Day of Reckoning*, p. 7. Scholarly appraisals of Reaganomics proved no less severe. Since 1980, according to one prominent economist, the United States pursued an economic policy "that amounts to living not just in, but for, the present. We are living well by running up our debt and selling off our assets. America has thrown itself a party and billed the tab to the future. The costs, which are only beginning to come due, will include a lower standard of living for individual Americans and reduced American influence and importance in world affairs." Reagan, it seemed, had replaced the tax-and-spend policies of his liberal opponents with a reckless spend-and-borrow regime. He cut taxes—they fell from 20 percent of national income in 1981 to 18 percent by end of his presidency, but he would not cut spending. Just like the reckless families he denounced in countless speeches, Reagan's treasury borrowed more and more and more. See Friedman, *Day of Reckoning*, pp. 4, 109–133.

75. Peter Brimelow and Lisa Scheer, "Is the Reagan Prosperity for Real?" *Forbes*, October 31, 1988, pp. 85–90. See also Alan S. Blinder, "Reaganomics and Growth: The Message in the Models," in Charles R. Hulten and Isabel V. Sawhill, eds., *The Legacy of Reaganomics* (Washington, D.C.: Urban Institute, 1984); M. Stephen Weatherford and Lorriane M. McDonnell, "Ideology and Economic Policy," in Larry Berman, ed., *Looking Back on the Reagan Presidency* (Baltimore: Johns Hopkins University Press, 1990); and Hugh Heclo and Rudolph G. Penner, "Fiscal and Political Strategy in the Reagan Administration," in Fred I. Greenstein, ed., *The Reagan Presidency* (Baltimore: Johns Hopkins University Press, 1983).

76. Sidney Blumenthal, "The Sorcerer's Apprentices," *New Yorker*, July 19, 1993, pp. 30–31. William A. Niskanen, *Reaganomics: An Insider's Account of the Policies and the People* (New York:

Oxford University Press, 1988), p. 286. See also Greider, "Education of David Stockman," p. 51. The deficit may have even foiled Reagan's anointed successor. By forcing President Bush to renege on his no-taxes pledge, the deficit may well have cost Bush reelection. But in the mid-1980s, Reagan still had no doubt he would find the pony in the back of the barn.

77. Kilpatrick, "The Reagan Presidency: A Pattern of Significant Change," *Nation's Business,* January 1983, p. 33.

78. Reagan, Inaugural Address, January 21, 1985, in *Public Papers of the Presidents, Ronald Ragan, 1985* (Washington, D.C.: GPO, 1986), bk. 1, p. 55.

79. Steven Gillon, *The Democrat's Dilemma* (New York: Columbia University Press, 1992), pp. 360–363. Reagan discredited not only taxation but many other standard tools of economic policy. See Teresa L. Amott, "Discussion of 'Economists Assess the Presidency,'" in Schmertz, Datlof, and Ugrinsky, *Ronald Reagan's America,* 1: 779.

80. "'84 Summer Olympics, Capitalist Style," *U.S. News and World Report,* May 9, 1983, p. 123.

81. "How Big Business Is Carrying Olympic Torch," *Business Week,* September 26, 1983, p. 92. '84 Summer Olympics, Capitalist Style," p. 123. "In Olympics, Business Also Goes for the Gold," *U.S. News and World Report,* June 25, 1984, pp. 73–74. On the patriotic exuberance of the games, consult "Olympic Fever," *U.S. News and World Report,* August 13, 1984, pp. 20–21, and Kenny Moore, "Hey Russia, It's a Heck of a Party," *Sports Illustrated,* August 6, 1984, pp. 26–28. One fan told a reporter that "it seems like people have not had this kind of feeling for America since World War II." UCLA sociologist William Roy concurred: "The timing of the games could not be better. People are ready, coming out of Vietnam and Watergate and the Carter era when nothing seemed to work."

82. "How Big Business Is Carrying Olympic Torch," p. 92. "'84 Summer Olympics, Capitalist Style," p. 123.

83. "A Sports Fan's Guide to the 1984 Olympics: Interview with Peter V. Ueberroth, President, Los Angeles Olympic Organizing Committee," *U.S. News and World Report,* May 9, 1983, p. 124.

84. "How Big Business Is Carrying Olympic Torch," p. 96.

85. "The Year of the Yuppie," *Newsweek,* December 31, 1984, pp. 14–31. Marissa Piesman and Marilee Hartley, *The Yuppie Handbook* (New York: Long Shadow Books, 1984). "Here Come the Yuppies," *Time,* January 9, 1984, p. 66. "Where Have All the Yuppies Gone?" *U.S. News and World Report,* September 16, 1985, p. 61. Paul Lyons, "Yuppie: A Contemporary American Keyword," *Socialist Review* 19 (January–March 1989): 112.

86. Alice Kahn, "Yuppie!" *East Bay Express,* June 10, 1983.

87. "Detroit's New Goal—Putting Yuppies in the Driver's Seat," *Business Week,* September 3, 1984. "Saab Hitches Its Star to Yuppie Market," *Business Week,* November 19, 1984.

88. "Yumpies, YAP's, Yuppies: Who They Are," *U.S. News and World Report,* April 16, 1984, p. 39.

89. Michael Kinsley, "Arise, Ye Yuppies!" *New Republic,* July 9, 1984. On the Hart campaign and the yuppie vote, see "A New Voting Bloc," *Newsweek,* December 31, 1984, pp. 30–31, and Lyons, "Yuppie: A Contemporary American Keyword."

90. "How Churches Try to Woo the Yuppies," *U.S. News and World Report,* October 26, 1985. In this same period, the term *yuppie* won out as the appropriate emblem for this new social class. The *Oxford English Dictionary* even included *yuppie, yuppiedom,* and *yuppification* in its 1989

second edition. *Yuppie* caught on, laying to rest such competitors as *yumpie* (for young upwardly mobile professional) and *YAP* (for young aspiring professional). See *Oxford English Dictionary,* 2nd ed. (Oxford: Oxford University Press, 1989), p. 786; and, "Yumpies, YAP's, Yuppies: Who They Are. For an analysis of the cultural ascendancy of *yuppie* as a term (and a concept), see Lyons, "Yuppie: A Contemporary American Keyword"; and Hendrik Hertzberg, "The Short Happy Life of the American Yuppie," *Esquire* (February 1988): 100–109.

91. David Farber, *Chicago '68* (Chicago: University of Chicago Press, 1988). Hertzberg, "The Short Happy Life of the American Yuppie," pp. 103–104.

92. Hertzberg, "The Short Happy Life of the American Yuppie," p. 103.

93. Ibid.

94. Ibid., p. 101.

95. "The Year of the Yuppie," p. 17.

96. *Wall Street* (written and directed by Oliver Stone, 1987). In 1984, Yale management professor Rosabeth Moss Kanter distinguished yuppies "not so much by their willingness to work hard for the corporation, but for their devotion to accumulating power and getting rich." Dismissing the confusion over rival terms like *yumpie* and *YAP, U.S. News* concluded that Americans would soon just be calling yuppies "boss." See "The Year of the Yuppie," p. 17; and "Yumpies, YAP's, Yuppies, Who They Are," p. 39.

97. "Year of the Yuppie," p. 24.

98. Piesman and Hartley, *The Yuppie Handbook,* quoted in "Yumpies, YAP's, Yuppies: Who They Are," p. 39.

99. Yuppies distanced themselves from their generation's hippie antecedents by mocking the very idea of altered consciousness. "We tried drugs and sex and all those things," San Francisco comedian Will Durst mused on the streets of Haight-Ashbury. "Now we're becoming the children our parents wanted us to be." One Denver lawyer told reporters that "they don't want their minds altered by introducing a substance that might lead them to question what they are doing." "I want a new drug," yuppie heartthrobs Huey Lewis and the News sang. "One that won't make me spill, one that don't cost too much or come in a pill." Another Huey Lewis hit proclaimed that "it's hip to be square." Cool "is the rule," the band conceded, "but sometimes bad is bad." See "Year of the Yuppie," pp. 19, 26–27.

100. Marc Mancini, "Risky Business," in Frank N. Magill, ed., *Magill's Cinema Annual 1984* (Englewood Cliffs, N.J: Salem Press, 1984), pp. 349–353.

101. Ibid.

102. "BMW Puts $30 Million to Drive Away Yuppie Image," *Advertising Age,* June 24, 1991. Alice Kahn, "Where Have All the Yuppies Gone?" *Washington Post,* September 6, 1995. "Where Have All the Yuppies Gone?" *U.S. News and World Report,* September 16, 1985, p. 61. Cheryl Russell, "Question: What Do You Call a Yuppie Stockbroker?" *American Demographics* (January 1988): 2.

103. Ronald W. Reagan, Remarks at the Annual Meeting of the Alliance of American Business, October 5, 1981, in *Public Papers of the Presidents of the United States: Ronald Reagan, 1981* (Washington, D.C.: GPO, 1982), p. 882.

104. Reagan, Remarks on Private Sector Initiatives, *Public Papers,* April 27, 1982, p. 522.

105. Lawrence E. Susskind, *Proposition 2 1/2: Its Impact on Massachusetts* (Cambridge: Oelgeschlager, Gunn & Hain, 1983), pp. 435–450.

106. Mike Davis, "Fortress Los Angeles," in Michael Sorkin, ed., *Variations on a Theme Park* (New York: Hill and Wang, 1992), pp. 161–163.

107. Louis Uchitelle, "Sharp Rise of Private Guard Jobs," *New York Times*, October 14, 1989. See also U.S. Census Bureau, *Statistical Abstract of the United States, 1991* (Washington, D.C.: GPO, 1991), p. 397.

108. Joel Garreau, *Edge City* (New York: Anchor Books, 1991), pp. 50–51. The privatization of policing became particularly apparent in the world of commerce. As businesses moved from Main Street to shopping malls, the store security guard or mall patrol replaced the cop on the beat. As the security chief at one New Jersey mall complex explained to *Washington Post* reporter Joel Garreau, "It's pretty hard to walk on my property without seeing some kind of highly visible security." His uniformed guards, dressed like U.S. Marines, patrolled the entire area. "We're not police and we'll never usurp the police power," the security chief explained, but he intentionally blurred the lines between his guards and actual police officers and cooperated closely with the regular police, who maintained a substation at the mall. William Jackson, quoted in Garreau, *Edge City*, pp. 48–50.

109. Marc Bendick, Jr., "Privatization of Public Services: Recent Experiences," in Harvey Brooks et al., eds., *Public-Private Partnership* (Cambridge, Mass.: Ballinger Publishing, 1984), pp. 155–156.

110. William J. Mallett, "Private Government Formation in the DC Metropolitan Area," *Growth and Change* 24 (Summer 1993): 385–415. "Many Seek Security in Private Communities," *New York Times*, September 3, 1995, pp. 1, 22.

111. "Many Seek Security in Private Communities," pp. 1, 22. U.S Advisory Commission on Intergovernmental Relations, *Residential Community Associations: Private Governments in the Intergovernmental System* (Washington, D.C.: Advisory Commission on Intergovernmental Relations, 1989). Garreau, *Edge City*, p. 187. Mallett, "Private Government Formation." About 12 percent of the nation's households in 1989 fit into such categories. In booming suburban areas, such as Fairfax County, Virginia, around Washington's Dulles Airport, southern Florida, and Maricopa County, Arizona, in the greater Phoenix area, practically every home is part of such an association.

112. Mallett, "Private Government Formation."

113. Ibid. Garreau, *Edge City*, pp. 184–187. Even neighborhood organizations that voted regularly often apportioned ballots according to the value of investment (one dollar, one vote) rather than the principle of one person, one vote. Constitutional limitations on governmental authority did not apply in these private bodies, nor did many constitutional protections for individual residents.

114. "Many Seek Security in Private Communities," p. 1. Thomas J. Lueck, "Business Districts Grow at Price of Accountability," *New York Times*, November 20, 1994, pp. 1, 46. Mallett, "Private Government Formation." Michael Sorkin, Introduction to Sorkin, *Variations*, p. xiv. Champions of redevelopment in both government and the business community, BIDs could spark an urban renaissance. One big city lauded the districts for "filling in for government" when city hall could no longer afford to keep the streets clean and safe. On the other hand, many small businesses and modest property owners worried that steep mandatory dues payments would force them out of their neighborhoods and create a new level of government not accountable to elective officials. In Virginia, for example, the creation of a special business district around Dulles Airport fast-tracked approval for new construction and stripped local citizens and their duly elected governments of the power to control development. In Fairfax County, an antigrowth candidate won election as chairman of the board of supervisors and attempted to downzone property along the Route 28 corridor near Dulles Airport and slow

development. But the developers received relief in the law establishing the special district that freed them from such regulation.

115. Ronald Reagan, Remarks to Reagan Administration Executive Forum, January 20, 1983, in *Public Papers, 1983*, p. 81. Reagan, Address Before a Joint Session of Congress Reporting on the State of the Union, January 26, 1982, in *Public Papers, 1982*, pp. 76–77. Edsall with Edsall, *Chain Reaction*, p. 195.

116. Jude Wanniski, *The Way the World Works* (New York: Basic Books, 1978). Peter Drucker, "Doing Good to Do Well," in Brooks et al., eds., *Public-Private Partnership*, pp. 285–302. George Gilder, *Wealth and Poverty* (New York: Basic Books, 1981). Charles Murray, *Losing Ground* (New York: Basic Books, 1984). Michael Novak, *The Spirit of Democratic Capitalism* (New York: Simon & Schuster, 1982). William Simon, A *Time for Truth* (New York: McGraw-Hill, 1978).

117. Milton Friedman and Rose Friedman, *Free to Choose* (New York: Harcourt Brace Jovanovich, 1979).

118. Ibid., pp. x, 39. On Friedman's influence on the Reagan administration, see Sprinkel, "Discussion of 'Economists Assess the Presidency,'" 1: 792. In this way, Reaganite thinkers resolved an apparent contradiction in conservative politics—the obvious tension between free marketeers and social conservatives who lamented (however consciously) the corrosive influence of capitalism on America's moral fabric. Or at least they decried the profit motive that produced lurid movies, violent television programs, pornographic magazines, condom shops, and gay bookstores. Conservative moralists and yuppie entrepreneurs could share a common faith in the superiority of the private sphere, whether private solutions to public problems involved a market component (such as enterprise zones for decaying inner cities) or stressed relief from a predatory culture that market forces had helped create (such as home schooling).

119. Thomas Ferguson and Joel Rogers, *Right Turn* (New York: Hill and Wang, 1986), pp. 3–4, 13–14, 143–144, 157. William C. Berman, *America's Right Turn* (Baltimore: John Hopkins University Press, 1994), pp. 116–117. Tony Coelho, interview with Thomas Edsall, November 22, 1986, quoted in Edsall and Edsall, *Chain Reaction*, p. 170.

120. Four years later presidential nominee Michael Dukakis took up these same themes. Proud author of the Massachusetts high-tech "Miracle," Dukakis repudiated the party's New Deal heritage, embracing business and the market. In 1992, Bill Clinton followed suit. The Arkansas governor positioned himself as a "New Democrat," kept his distance from labor and minority constituencies, and worked closely with business. One contemporary journalist hardly exaggerated when he assailed the "stars and operators at Democrat Central who have turned what was once the party of the common man into the party of the corporate manikins." See "The Party's New Soul," *Time*, July 25, 1988, p. 19. Thomas Ferguson and Joel Rogers, "Neo-Liberals and Democrats," *Nation*, June 26, 1982, pp. 784–785. Ronnie Dugger, "Race, Class, and Democrats," *Boston Review* (Summer 1995): 34.

121. Robert B. Shapiro, quoted in Michael Specter, "The Pharmageddon Riddle," *The New Yorker*, April 10, 2000, p. 64.

122. Johnson, "Flatiron Flair."

123. "The Year of the Yuppie," p. 18.

124. Milton Friedman, Preface to William Simon, A *Time for Truth* (New York: Reader's Digest Press, 1978), p. xii.

125. President Reagan hailed the economist as a national treasure. Friedman visited the White House and received both the National Medal of Science and the Presidential Medal of Freedom during the 1980s.

Conclusion

1. Tom Wolfe, "The First Tycoon of Teen," in *The Kandy-Kolored Tangerine-Flake Streamline Baby* (New York: Farrar, Straus & Giroux, 1965).

2. Kurt Loder, "Review of *End of the Century*," *Rolling Stone*, March 20, 1980, pp. 54–55.

3. Ibid.

4. Ibid.

5. The Los Angeles Olympics had displayed a resurgent American patriotism, a nation once again comfortable in its global leadership, its cocky conviction that the United States remained the greatest country on the earth. Later in 1984, Ronald Reagan won a stunning electoral victory. The Gipper successfully converted the broad discontent that had elected him in 1980—the widespread disgust with Jimmy Carter and Seventies malaise—into an affirmative majority for his brand of conservatism. In fact, the president's ideological victory proved even more decisive than his landslide at the polls. The Democratic standard-bearer in 1984 distinguished himself from the popular president chiefly in his willingness to raise taxes to close the deficit. Walter Mondale, once the heir to Hubert Humphrey and the aggressive big government tradition of Minnesota's farmer-labor coalition, sold himself as a more orthodox fiscal conservative than Ronald Reagan. The New Deal order had crumbled.

6. Mark Feeney, "Stayin' Alive," *Boston Globe*, March 19, 2000, pp. N1, N14.

7. Bill Gates, *Business @ the Speed of Thought* (New York: Warner Books, 1999), pp. 356–358.

acknowledgements

IT ALL BEGAN WITH A PARTY, OF COURSE. FOR YEARS, THROUGHOUT the Seventies, the characters in *Doonesbury* had gathered for revivals of the Sixties. So, in January 1980, with the old decade just barely expired, I staged one of the first Seventies revival parties. The celebration rounded up all of the usual suspects—a half dozen refugees from *Saturday Night Fever* with gold chains and shirts unbuttoned to the navel, Don Corleone from *The Godfather,* a yellow smiley face, an OPEC oil sheik, even Senator Thomas Eagleton with electrodes sticking out of his skull.

Then came the conversations: with Rich Riehl and Jeremy Greshin on the shores of Lake Ronkonkoma, trying to make sense of our lives and our times; with Jeff Morley, who coined the term "Seventies sensibility" and whose ruminations on disco, rap, and Evel Knievel inspired much of this book; with Julie Reuben and Jill Lepore, who carefully read the chapters and kept the author on track; with Jim Campbell, who reviewed the manuscript with frighteningly acute understanding of my purposes and my rhetorical tricks and subterfuges.

Along the way, I piled up numerous debts. At just the right moment, a grant from the Marjorie Kovler Fund materially aided the completion of the manuscript. A year at the Charles Warren Center for Studies in American History at Harvard University helped me launch the writing. I thank my Warren Center hosts—Ernest May, William Gienapp, and Susan Hunt—for making my fellowship year so pleasant and productive. I especially thank my Warren Center colleagues—David Blight, Kathleen Dalton, Kristin Hoganson, Jill Lepore, and Nina Silber—for making that year so productive and rewarding.

The book also benefited from the counsel, criticism, and support of many colleagues. Lisa Cobbs Hoffman, Laura Kalman, Robert Dallek, Marc Dollinger, Dave Blakely, Stephen Davis, and Regina Morantz-Sanchez read all or part of the manuscript. They offered insightful readings and much useful advice. Heather World, Tim Johnson, Matthew Nix, Gini Laffey, Paul Schmitz, and other students at UCLA and BU helped develop the ideas that metamorphosed into this book. Kate Cannon and Mary Corey supplied much of the inspiration, and the courage, to tackle a project so close to my sense of self. For nearly two decades, David Kennedy has encouraged my work with grace and warmth, and has set an exacting standard I strive to emulate but could never hope to match. At an early stage, he steered me away from harsh polemic and steered me toward the richer, fuller appreciation of the era I chronicled.

A group of crackerjack research assistants—Petula Iu, David Russo, Charles Romney, and Sarah Phillips—did much of the leg work and dug up important sources and leads. Samantha Khosla, the American Studies administrator at Boston University, helped enormously with the rights, photographs, and final preparation of the manuscript.

At The Free Press, Dan "the Butcher" Freedberg helped me sharpen the arguments and reduce the manuscript to fighting trim. The copyediting staff, led by Carol de Onís, smoothed the rough edges and saved me from numerous small errors. Joyce Seltzer signed the project and convinced me that this book could and should appear. My gifted editor, the wise, wry Bruce Nichols, helped me find my message and my voice. It has been a great pleasure to work with them all.

I completed this book despite the Herculean efforts of Jeffrey Schulman and William Schulman, albeit as an older, grayer, sillier, and wiser person than I ever imagined being. Their obstructions failed largely because of Alice Killian, who struggled mightily so that I might finish this project and, as ever, supplied laughter and love, encouragement and companionship.

Finally there are my friends, many of whom are mentioned above. Their affection and loyalty, wit and love, make up the most important inheritance I carried out of the Seventies, one I still cherish every day. To them all, with thanks, this book is humbly dedicated.

index